Computer and Communications Security

Strategies for the 1990s

Computer and Communications Security

Strategies for the 1990s

James Arlin Cooper

Distinguished Member of Technical Staff
Sandia National Laboratories
Adjunct Professor
University of New Mexico
and Webster University

Intertext Publications
McGraw-Hill Book Company

New York St. Louis San Francisco Auckland Bogotá
Hamburg London Madrid Mexico Milan Montreal
New Delhi Panama Paris São Paulo
Singapore Sidney Tokyo Toronto

Library of Congress Catalog Card Number 89-83762

10 9 8 7 6 5 4 3 2 1

ISBN 0-07-012926-6

Intertext Publications/Multiscience Press, Inc.
One Lincoln Plaza
New York, NY 10023

McGraw-Hill Book Company
1221 Avenue of the Americas
New York, NY 10020

*To Dana, David, Doug, Scott,
Brent, and Heath.*

Contents

Preface

This is an exciting time. In a few decades computing speed has increased several orders of magnitude, the physical space required by computers has been reduced several orders of magnitude, computer power consumption has decreased several orders of magnitude, reliability has improved dramatically, and computers have been interconnected nationally and internationally through satellite and terrestrial links. During this period, the cost of computing has *decreased* several orders of magnitude and the cost of interconnecting computers has decreased substantially. In no other area have we approached this kind of performance increase and cost decrease.

The first publicly acknowledged electronic computer (the ENIAC) ran at a clock speed of 100 kHz, occupied a volume of more than 10,000 cubic feet, consumed 150 kW of power, had a mean time before failure (MTBF) of less than a day, and cost $400,000 (1945 dollars) to build. Today, the much more powerful IBM Personal System/2 Model 80 runs at a clock speed of about 25 MHz, occupies a volume of less than three cubic feet, consumes a little more than 200 W of power, has an MTBF estimated at more than a year, and costs about $10,000.

One of the effects of these improvements is that computers and computer communication links are now affordable for and in the hands of more users. Most of us now use these capabilities, either knowingly or unknowingly. This proliferation has significant security implications.

A large number of individuals have personal computers, many of which can communicate through modems over ordinary telephone lines. Most businesses, small or large, depend on computers for accounting, records, and payroll functions. Minicomputers have provided small companies with the same computing capabilities once affordable only by very large organizations. Dedicated microprocessors are now used as controllers to enhance the capabilities of calculators, telephones, automobiles, microwave ovens, gasoline pump meters, sewing machines, vending machines, watches, TVs, VCRs, games, telephones, and cash registers. Financial transactions have been facilitated by computing links enabling ATM transactions, remote credit card and check authorizations, and bank transfers. Typing and editing is speeded by dedicated word processors and is available on most computers. Electronic bulletin boards and data services enhance information transfer. Recent strides in memory technology are also impressive. Cores and other bulky discrete elements are virtually obsolete. The information in a book can fit neatly on a diskette. An optical disk the size of an LP record can store the amount of information contained in a small library.

Application software such as graphics generators, spreadsheet packages, calendar management, database systems, and computer-aided design aids is easily affordable and readily available for all sizes of computers. People who never thought they would use a computer are becoming dependent on these powerful computer functions.

However, two general threats cast a sobering shadow on the excitement of these legitimate developments. One of these threats is persons who watch unscrupulously for security weaknesses on which to capitalize. Frequently, new technological developments have substantially improved opportunities for these people. The second general threat is what may appear to be a random occurrence. It is important to recognize that many things can go wrong due to human mistakes, malfunctions, accidents, and natural disasters. Many argue that this latter class of threat is the most serious current security problem we face. In any event, both classes of threat are important.

We know that the present environment has many new security problems. Some of them are obvious. The downloading and general distribution of confidential, private, and proprietary information to individual work stations makes it more difficult to assure protection of these sensitive data. The pervasiveness of communication links within buildings and around the world via phone lines, hard-wired connections, and electromagnetic transmission exposes the information to active or passive (even remote) tapping and to interference (modification, replication, deletion). EFT (electronic funds transfer) systems tempt criminals because of the large amounts of money handled and because of the potential to mount low-risk attacks.

A new vocabulary has developed in order to describe a series of new attack methods, many of which are utilized by "hackers." The techniques include "viruses," "worms," "Trojan horses," "time bombs," "logic bombs," "trapdoors," "asynchronous attacks," and the "salami" attacks. The potential sophistication of some of these (notably the virus) has led to warnings that the way in which we do computing may have to undergo significant changes during the next decade.

Information processing is changing. Information stored in modern "memory" media is packed so densely and is so transparent to the casual observer that its reading or movement becomes hard to control. For example, many libraries and businesses control unauthorized removal of books and other documents by visual observation. The amount of information in a number of books could, if written on diskettes, fit unobtrusively in a pocket.

A new problem has developed in the sale of applications software. A diskette or similar storage medium containing proprietary applications programs may represent a very small production cost. However, the information contained on it may represent a substantial program development cost. Companies marketing software are therefore faced with a formidable security problem. They would like their product to be easy to use, easy to transfer to a hard disk, and easy to copy for backup. However, illegal copying (software piracy), which can deprive software suppliers of considerable income, should be made very difficult.

Potential reliability and safety effects are also computer security concerns. It is common for computers to control manufacturing, test equipment (like centrifuges), traffic signal systems, rapid transit, air traffic control, medical treatment equipment, and even weapons and national defense systems. In these types of systems, proper performance is crucial. Threats to computer integrity include vandalism, sabotage, terrorism, hardware failures, and software bugs.

It is not surprising that the technology available in the last decade of the twentieth century should contribute to the computer and communications security threat environment. It is interesting, however, to note that the technological atmosphere that has made security more challenging has also helped contribute to better security. An impressive collection of hardware devices, software strategies, mathematical developments, and protective techniques have recently become available. Many of these are described in this book. Careful consideration of computer security tools leads one to the conclusion that the popular public image of vulnerable computers being victimized by all-powerful hackers and criminals is misleading. Certainly security breaches have occurred, many of them embarrassing to those responsible for protecting the systems. Computer and communications security will never be perfect. However, when a breach of security occurs, at least we can learn from it. This learning process may prevent similar incidents in the future and should enable us to better understand the global computer security picture of the 1990s.

Almost any level of computer security is possible with minimal user inconvenience if the financial resources are available and if the available tools are properly applied. Since finance availability is usually the biggest constraint, deriving maximum benefit from available tools is essential. I hope this book contributes to effective application of tools through describing computer and communications security problems and considering various ways to deal with those problems.

The book has three major objectives. The first is to provide an information resource on the status of computer security techniques that will be available in the 1990s. Descriptions of many of these techniques are given in sufficient detail that their general usefulness and applicability can be reasonably determined. References to more detailed information are provided for those interested in more in-depth coverage.

The second objective is to provide an analytical basis for making quantitative assessments. Analytical approaches are useful as decision-making aids, such as whether or not a particular protective feature should be implemented, what options should be incorporated for specified protection, and how well certain protective measures are performing. This analytical treatment is especially valuable because it consolidates a significant body of information not readily available in any other single source.

The third objective of the book is to survey the threats of which security practitioners should be aware. There is a concern that publicizing threat scenarios will encourage the use of those techniques by people wishing to breach security, but I believe the benefits outweigh the risks. It is likely that information on threats that are known to exist will help people implement safeguards against those threats and will also help raise their awareness about similar threats. This is one of the most important reasons for examining a variety of known scenarios. One must make sure that protective measures selected are effective against as many threats as possible.

This material has also been used in graduate-level courses in computer security, which is one of the reasons for including numerous problems. Suggested prerequisites for students in such a course are probability theory, switching theory or logic design, and linear algebra. Background in electromagnetic theory and some analytical maturity is also helpful. I believe the book is equally valuable as a text and as an information resource.

Chapters 1 and 2 serve to establish a basis from which one can begin a thorough study of computer and communications security. Chapters 3 through 8 are devoted to six particular aspects of the study: physical protection, personnel considerations, legal and regulatory aspects, hardware security, software security, and network security. In Chapter 9, a consolidated global approach is suggested, and directions for the future are considered.

I am grateful to a number of people who helped me produce this book. Duane Harder (Mantech International Corporation) provided many important technical contributions and style suggestions throughout. Gus Simmons (Sandia National Laboratories Senior Fellow) generously shared his remarkable cryptology expertise and insight. My discussions with David Snow (President of Infosec Systems) were indispensable. Merry Peterson, Russ Maxwell, Ed Graham, Ivan Waddoups, Dick Fisher, Steve Gossage, Lyndon Pierson, Ron Halbgewachs, Steve Baca, and Susan Navarro (all of Sandia National Laboratories), Ray Surface (Department of Energy), Ron DeVries (University of New Mexico), Donald Kerns (Southwest Research Institute), and Judith Sizemore contributed many useful suggestions. R. G. Cooper (retired attorney) and Roger Figge (Albuquerque Public Schools) helped with legal, government, and historical topics. Many of the ideas presented here were generated as I authored a course for Integrated Computer Systems (ICS) entitled "Computer and Communications Security," and I appreciate my association with ICS. A significant number of my students (too numerous to name, I regret) made helpful suggestions. In addition, I am indebted to my family, who understood and supported me as I once again perturbed our lives. I hope the contributors all consider the finished product worth their efforts.

— James Arlin Cooper

1

Introduction

One must resist the temptation to begin working on "improvements" until one knows the reference point from which improvements are to be made and whether or not improvements are necessary. That fundamental principle is frequently overlooked. With this principle in mind, and with some particular points to be made about how we arrived at our current situation in computer and communications security, the first chapter is devoted to establishing a reference point for the remainder of the book. The first few sections are a review of the architectural and technological developments that have changed the way we must view security. The final part of the chapter is a preview of what is usually meant by the term "computer and communications security" and how this picture provides for the organization of the book.

1.1 THE BEGINNINGS OF COMPUTING

The present computer and communications security environment evolved during two general time periods of about two decades each. The first two decades began only after a large amount of early groundwork was done in the United States (mainly by John Atanasoff, John Mauchly, J. Presper Eckert, George Stibitz, John von Neumann, and Howard Aiken), in Britain (mainly by Charles

Babbage, Alan Turing, and T. H. Flowers), and in Germany (mainly by Konrad Zuse)[*] [1–5,14,15].

The U.S. Patent Office struggled with various computer patent claims for years, and some interesting battles for credit were fought in the courts, in the press, and in the literature. Until recently, it was generally believed that the University of Pennsylvania ENIAC, operational in 1946, was the first routinely used electronic digital computer. It was not.

1.2 EARLY DEVELOPMENTS AND SECURITY

The first electronic digital computer put into service, the Colossus, became operational at Bletchley Park, England, in 1943. Even today, this fact surprises many, because the Colossus operated in one of the most secure environments ever. The time was during the darkest days of World War II, and the Colossus had the critical mission of helping to break the German communications codes. Security was so tight that a British city was allowed to be bombed without the warning that could have been provided, probably since the warning would have given evidence of the cryptanalysis successes. Winston Churchill alluded to both the success and secrecy of the Colossus project by calling it "the goose that lays golden eggs but does not quack" [14]. Security about the Colossus project was not relaxed until 1975, when its existence and history were first publicly revealed [4].

---

[*]   Charles Babbage is generally credited with the basic ideas of programmed automatic computation (approximately 1837) that were used in the first computers, although many of these ideas were apparently developed independently later. George Stibitz began working in 1937 on a program-controlled relay computer. He pioneered the concepts of binary and floating point arithmetic and remote console control. John Atanasoff won a court decision for the most basic digital computer patent in 1973, climaxing a long legal battle for recognition of his work in the mid-1930s. He was credited with the fundamental concepts of the modern electronic digital computer and built an operational model. Alan Turing proposed a mathematical model for computing based on the "automata" concept in 1937. T. H. Flowers was in charge of the Colossus development (1943). John Mauchly and J. Presper Eckert were the main developers of the decimal-oriented ENIAC (1943–1946). John von Neumann is identified with the 1944 data memory stored-program concept, although Mauchly and Eckert have also claimed the concept. Howard Aiken proposed a computer in 1937 that became the electromechanical Mark 1 in 1944. The Mark 1 led to the first IBM electronic computers and was the source of Grace Hopper's notable reference to a "bug" on finding a dead moth incapacitating a relay. Konrad Zuse began working on computing concepts in the mid-1930s and completed an operational relay computer (the Z3) in 1941.

Figure 1-1   Walter Cronkite and the UNIVAC I. (Photograph courtesy of Unisys Corporation.)

Computer security was relatively uncomplicated during and for a few years after the Colossus era. Typical of its time, the Colossus was contained in an isolated, secure room, to which only a few people had access. With no remote terminals, no time-sharing capabilities, no dialup lines, and no database systems, the computer room staff had no doubt as to who was using the computer or how it was being used.

The first general purpose computer was the UNIVAC I (see Figure 1-1), which was delivered to the United States Census Bureau in 1951 for use in compiling the 1950 census figures. It used vacuum tubes and a mercury delay line memory, technologies that are no longer used in computers.

A controversial activity began when the UNIVAC I was used (by Walter Cronkite) to predict the outcomes of the 1952 elections. The results projected Dwight Eisenhower's election over Adlai Stevenson 45 minutes after the polls closed. Future increases in computing power led to increasingly accurate forecasts prior to poll closings, a practice that was later discontinued because of the potential effect on those who had not voted.

1.2.1 Batch Processing

A result of the initial growth in computing capabilities was that ways were sought to accommodate growing numbers of users. This was first accomplished through "batch" operation of the computer systems, where several user programs could be queued and run sequentially. Programs and data were commonly entered on punched cards. Generally the user maintained control of the cards, which were under as much (or as little) protection as the user chose to provide.

1.2.2 Tape Handling

When tape capabilities were added for input and output, tape libraries were usually provided in the vicinity of the computer room. Users frequently handled their own tapes, programmed their own jobs, and deposited jobs (card decks) at a drop-off point in or near the computer room. Operators loaded and ran the jobs in batch mode, usually with the users not present. Output and the submitted program (and possibly tapes) were then picked up by the users from an output box.

1.2.3 Security Measures

It was obvious that improvements in security would be required. The output sometimes required more protection than was offered by a pickup box. The operators were often knowledgeable about the processing details and could even introduce changes if computer security procedures such as two-person control or separation of duties (see Chapter 4) were not enforced. Access to tape libraries in some cases needed to be controlled. Environmental (fire, power, air conditioning, water, lightning) protection measures were added to more traditional security concerns. The security world was changing.

1.2.4 Time Sharing

Time-sharing operating systems were developed during the 1960s in order to allow more users to be serviced per time period than for batch operation. This important technique took advantage of the inherent wasted time in-between user communications and operations and used this time to service other users, giving the appearance of dedicated computing simultaneously to a number of users. Remote computing capabilities were added so that large numbers of users, distributed over a large geographical area, had simultaneous computer access. This multiplexed access, the transparency and remoteness of the users, and the new physical entities (terminals and communication lines) challenged computer and communications security in ways we are still dealing with. Electronic data processing (EDP) auditing became a specialized science and began to depend heavily on computer auditing software.

1.2.5 Dialup Access

The proximity, and in some cases the actual use, of telephone lines made it inevitable that modems would be designed to allow computer connection over the same lines used for normal telephone connections. Low-cost modems (not much more than $100) were available in the late 1970s, making "dialup" access widely available. When this dialup access capability was added to a computer, a user could, at least theoretically, gain access to that computer from telephones located almost anywhere in the world. Dialup numbers were freely advertised and many people did not know how easily telephone lines and microwave links could be tapped, even at locations distant from the telephone. It is now well known, and the bristling collection of antennas on Russian buildings in the vicinity of U.S. microwave telephone links reminds us, that telephone transmissions are not secure.

1.2.6 Database Systems

By the late 1960s and early 1970s, database systems were being developed to deal with the large amounts of accumulating data. Database software allowed users to efficiently retrieve data by using logical descriptors. Obviously, free access could not be allowed to all data. In most databases, it became necessary to restrict the access of particular users to particular parts of the database.

1.2.7 Passwords

Passwords were nearly universally used as a solution to the problems of controlling remote access to a computer, access to a database, and to specific parts of the database. The implementation details varied widely, however. Although computer access was frequently granted uniformly to groups of people, some systems required individual passwords. Some systems having individual computer access allowed group (shared) database access. Some "mapped" the database password into the appropriate database privileges; some required other passwords for additional privileges. All of these variations arose for valid reasons, and most of the same variations exist today. Passwords are used almost universally, but as we shall see, the details of their applications warrant extensive study.

1.2.8 Observations

Some qualitative observations regarding the first couple of decades of computing are appropriate. The value of the data handled by computers and communication links steadily increased as payroll functions, financial records, corporate planning data, national security data, and private data were stored in computer memory media and transmitted across computer communication links. The value of these data (for information storage, financial representations, and scientific computations) continues to grow today. For example, complex scientific models of weather systems can be analyzed by modern scientific "supercomputers" in ways never before possible. Figure 1-2 shows a contemporary supercomputer.

A recent incident illustrates the common dependence on computers and the effect of disruption of computing services. Long lines of people at a motor vehicle department were being processed by clerks at computer terminals when a power failure occurred. A collective groan chorused from the people, because almost everyone there immediately realized that no power meant no computers and therefore no customer transactions. Even people who don't use computers are aware of their crucial role in data processing and transactions.

1.2.9 Security Strategies

During the first two decades of contemporary computer development, security strategies generally improved. Separation of duties and

Figure 1-2 The Cray-2 Supercomputer. (Photgraph courtesy of Cray Research.)

other independent functional checks were introduced, thereby helping to balance the relationship between assets to be protected and the security surrounding the assets.

Access control has continued to be a challenge. Exposure to threats worsened because of remote users and widely dispersed communication media. This was somewhat balanced by security measures such as computer access passwords, database software security features, and security software (which included auditing software and specific access control features in addition to passwords).

Physical security enhancements such as environmental controls and automated remote entry control had little chance to keep up with the challenges of widely dispersed physical assets. Pragmatically speaking, this is still one of the weakest links in security today.

1.3 RECENT CHANGES IN THE ENVIRONMENT

Although the security environment changed substantially during the first two decades of computing, these changes were overshadowed by

Figure 1-3   Photomicrograph of a microprocessor chip. (Photograph courtesy of Sandia National Laboratories.)

the changes in the last two decades. Probably the biggest problems have been created by wide-area (long haul) networks, local-area networks, and microcomputers. Basically, the problems have been caused by the increases in exposure due to communication media accessibility and computer presence in relatively unsecure locations. Some of the new technologies that encouraged and made inevitable these changes are satellite (particularly geostationary) links; fiber optic transmission media, optical transmitters and receivers; local area networks (LANS); and microprocessors (see Figure 1-3). Microprocessors and similar devices have made possible intelligent and cheap modems, powerful communications processors, and personal-size computers (see Figure 1-4). The major security problems caused by the new technologies are more difficult auditability, more locations and volume for perpetrators (including nature) to work on, and the increased number of people involved.

On the positive side, it is certainly hard in today's networked, distributed environment to lose all of one's computerized assets in one disastrous incident. More importantly, there are now powerful tools with which to address the problems.

Figure 1-4 A personal computer. (Photograph courtesy of Sandia National Laboratories.)

1.4 SOME MOTIVATION

We are frequently reminded that there are security problems. Consider some of the most highly publicized incidents that have occurred during the past several years. In 1973, a $1.2 million embezzlement was discovered in New York City [6]. A savings bank teller had been skimming money from large new accounts by making a simple computerized correction entry. His unusually large betting patterns led to a police investigation and discovery of the theft.

In 1973, an incredible insurance fraud was discovered, partly because of a tip by a disgruntled former co-conspirator [7]. The company involved sold mutual fund shares and then accepted the shares as collateral from the purchaser leveraging for loans to purchase life insurance. This legitimate practice is attractive to purchasers (and the company) as long as the shares appreciate. Unfortunately, they didn't in this case.

The company officers sought to protect themselves in various ways, all designed to project an unjustified public image of success.

An important technique involved using a computer to generate phony life insurance policies that could be sold to reinsurers. The fraud was continued for several years. About 64,000 fictitious people were created, far more than the number of real persons covered by the company. The computer was also used to create legitimate-appearing audit trails. Company assets rose on (computer) paper to nearly $150 million, spurred by about $2 billion face value in policies, and leading to apparently attractive investment prospects. Eventually, when the scam was exposed, the investors found the assets to be largely fabricated. Losses were extensive (estimated at well over $30 million).

In 1978, a computer consultant working for a Los Angeles bank saw a way to get EFT (electronic fund transfer) codes without substantial risk of detection [6,8]. He used the codes, posing as a branch manager, to call in a transfer of over $10 million to a New York bank for payment to a Swiss account. He flew to Switzerland, converted the money to diamonds, and returned to the United States, where he was eventually identified. Most of the diamonds were recovered, but overall costs to the bank were substantial.

In the 1980 time frame, an operations officer for one of the largest U.S. banks used his knowledge of limits on audit checks to continually avoid detection while covering thefts by himself and two other persons [9]. He knew the bank's computerized interbranch account settlement process whereby reconciliations were made on a 10-day cycle. Withdrawing funds from a different branch allowed him to cover the shortages within the cycle time. The rollovers went undetected for two years before a mistake was made in covering them. Losses were over $20 million.

In 1980, a group of Manhattan teenagers, using a Dalton School classroom terminal and knowledge from one of the perpetrator's brothers, dialed into a Canadian network of corporate and institutional data systems [6,8,10]. No major theft was attempted, but some valuable data files were destroyed. The press coined the name "the Dalton gang" for the group.

In 1983, another penetration of several important computers by "hackers" was discovered [11]. Following closely in time and technique the movie "WarGames," national publicity was inevitable. This incident made even more news when it was revealed that several of the penetrated computers were at a national laboratory, although none of the computers had any classified information or function. Other computers involved were at a university, several companies, a bank, and a cancer treatment center. Data at the cancer center were changed, apparently inadvertently, but no one was injured as a result. The corruption of data at a cancer treatment center and the penetration of national laboratory computers brought home an important message: The hacker threat had to be taken seriously.

In 1985, several employees of the U.S. Navy were apprehended as part of a Soviet-financed compromise involving secret communications keys [12]. The damage was retroactively traced back many years and was one of the most serious ever for the United States. One of the perpetrators received a 365-year prison sentence, the harshest U.S. penalty since the 1953 Rosenberg executions.

The purpose of outlining these highly publicized incidents is to illustrate that there is a definite threat to computers and communications. Entire books have been written on detailed descriptions of these and similar incidents [7,8].

Less exciting to the public, but equally threatening to the integrity of computing and communications, are happenstance incidents. We will illustrate many principles through description of both types of incidents as we formulate our approach to security. Motivation should be no problem!

1.5 COMPUTER AND COMMUNICATIONS SECURITY BASIC TERMINOLOGY

Complete agreement on terminology is often not achieved, even for those of us who are professionally involved in computer and communications security. Although the glossary at the back of this book is helpful as a guide to the jargon, we need to concentrate here on an understanding of some of the most fundamental terms. In this section, we will describe the terms that seem most appropriate for starting to address the subject. Not all of the descriptions are universally accepted, but they seem to be common to most practitioners and will form a basis for this book.

1.5.1 Definitions

Since our main subject is security, we might ask, "What is security?" Briefly, security is protecting "assets." The assets may be information, hardware, software, peripheral supplies, people, communication media, processing capabilities, or money (represented by information or potential for legal liability).

Computer security involves "computers," so we need a concept of the type of computing we are addressing. Certainly, general-purpose mainframe computers are an important consideration for our purposes. As we consider smaller and smaller computers, we may find less attention is warranted. There are exceptions, however. A small computer networked to a large computer may substantially increase the problems provided by the large computer itself. Some computer control functions are of interest, particularly if they involve critical or safety-related functions.

The "communications" we will be dealing with are computer communications. These are the data-flow links between computers or between computers and peripherals or terminals.

The "threats" to assets are 1) people who choose to be adversaries, and 2) happenstance due to people or nature. "Adversaries" include espionage agents, terrorists, organized crime or individual criminals, malicious people, vengeful people, disgruntled people, and people looking for low-risk challenges at the edge of what is legal or proper. "Happenstance" includes accidents or mistakes made by people, hardware failures, software errors, communication loss, and environmental problems (fire, water, power, air conditioning, structural integrity). Also included are "natural" events (lightning, earthquake, wind, tornado, flood, electrostatic discharge).

Security measures are needed where "vulnerabilities" of assets exist. Vulnerabilities are features (design, configuration, procedure) that allow threats to affect assets. For example, lack of good access control (a vulnerability) might lead to loss of information (an asset).

Incorporation of security measures to compensate for a vulnerability is not always an obvious process. Factors such as the cost and overhead of the security measure, the user inconvenience, and legal or moral constraints may be involved. It may even be appropriate to take a calculated risk. In fact "risk" is an important term to us. Quantitatively, it can be viewed as the probability (usually cited per period of time) that a given asset will be lost through a specific vulnerability due to a particular threat. Life and security are not this simple, as we shall see. However, judgment of risk (quantitatively or qualitatively) is a common and important process. Not all practitioners use the term "risk" to indicate probability of loss or compromise. Some incorporate the expected amount of loss into risk. We will not, because not all assets have quantifiable value and because the probabilistic use of the term "risk" makes it more widely applicable.

"Protective measures" are security features that are incorporated to minimize vulnerabilities and/or risk. "Responses" are security moves made after an incident. These may be in the form of corrective measures, analysis, or necessary actions (prosecution, recovery).

1.5.2 An Approach to Security

These concepts were described in a sequence that represents ordered steps in approaching security. This sequence is almost always helpful in addressing computer and communications security problems. We must first identify the assets to be protected, then identify threats to those assets. We must use the concept of a threat to an asset (or multiple threats to multiple assets) to first examine vulnerabilities and then assess risk. It will become apparent that protective measures can reduce the vulnerabilities and the risk. Responses (after-the-fact actions) can be productive. In the next chapter, we will put this approach in perspective and categorize some specific environments for our investigation of protective measures. These environments will be the basis for six of the following chapters.

PROBLEMS

1. a) Conceive of a single measure to quantify the improvement of a contemporary computer over the ENIAC described at the beginning of the preface. This measure can be a composite of the factors described or any other appropriate measure. Assume an average inflation rate of 5% per year. b) Can you think of any factors that have *not* been improvements?

2. a) Write an equation for the expected dollar value of the loss of an asset having financial value as a function of the value of the asset and the risk associated with the vulnerability of the asset to a threat. b) What is the most meaningful thing you can think of with which to compare this expected value?

3. Give an example of a computer-security asset and a computer-security threat combination for which there is no vulnerability.

4. a) What makes computer security harder today than it was 40 years ago? b) What makes computer security easier?

5. a) Would you consider the control processor in a mail delivery robot a computer (from a security standpoint)? Why? b) Would

you consider the control processor in an automobile cruise control module a computer (from a computer security standpoint)? Why?

DILEMMA DISCUSSION*

"Risk" implies the potential for loss. Dictionary definitions of risk mention "chance of loss," "degree of probability of loss," and "amount of possible loss." This reflects the variance in common usage. Some people use "risk" to mean the potential for something dangerous to happen without regard to the magnitude or the gravity of the occurrence. For example, the collision of the earth with a comparably sized body could be considered a low-risk event because the probability is thought to be remarkably low; but the potential loss could not be higher.

Others use "risk" to mean the product of the probability of loss times the potential amount of loss. The reason is that potential loss can be very different for the same probability of an event. As an example, the probability of collision damage might be the same for a new Mercedes Benz and for a 10-year-old Ford. However, the consequences would not be the same.

These are the two opposing views. What is your view?

REFERENCES

1. Metropolis, N., J. Howlett, and Gian-Carlo Rota, *A History of Computing in the Twentieth Century*, Academic Press, New York, 1980.
2. Loveday, Evelyn, "George Stibitz and the Bell Labs Relay Computers," *Datamation*, September 1977.
3. de Solla Price, Derek, "A History of Calculating Machines," *IEEE Micro*, February 1984.
4. Randell, Brian, "Colossus: Godfather of the Computer," *New Scientist*, 10 February 1977.

---

* There are a large number of significant issues in computer and communications security that we will term "dilemmas," because there is no obvious "right" or "wrong" approach. Dilemma Discussions are issues posed for assessment with the aim of demonstrating that there are grounds for opposing views. These are useful stimulants for class discussions or for personal soul searching.

5. Stern, Nancy, "In the Beginning, the ENIAC," *Datamation*, May 1979.
6. "The Spreading Danger of Computer Crime," *Business Week*, April 20, 1981.
7. Parker, Donn, *Crime by Computer*, Charles Scribner's Sons, New York, 1976.
8. Parker, Donn, *Fighting Computer Crime*, Charles Scribner's Sons, New York, 1983.
9. Bloombecker, Jay, "Lessons from Wells Fargo," *Computerworld*, July 5, 1982.
10. Kolata, Gina, "When Criminals turn to Computers, is Anything Safe?" *Smithsonian Magazine*, September 1982.
11. "Computer and Communications Security and Privacy," Hearings before the Subcommittee on Transportation, Aviation and Materials of the Committee on Science and Technology, U.S. House of Representatives, September 26; October 17, 24, 1983.
12. *Reader's Digest 1986 Almanac and Yearbook*.
13. Becker, Louise Giovane, "Get Scared," *Government Data Systems*, November/December 1983.
14. Richie, David, *The Computer Pioneers*, Simon and Schuster, New York, 1986.
15. Mackintosh, Allan R., "Dr. Atanasoff's Computer," *Scientific American*, August 1988.

2

Fundamental Approaches to Computer and Communications Security

In the first chapter, we discussed a straightforward approach to security:

1. Identify assets to protect.
2. Identify threats to those assets.
3. Identify vulnerabilities through which the assets can be affected by the threats.
4. Consider the risks (probabilities) associated with the vulnerabilities.
5. If necessary, select protective measures to reduce the risks.
6. Monitor security-related events in order to take responsive action.

This approach can be the basis of a systematic analytical treatment of computer and communications security, as will be demonstrated in this chapter.

2.1 SECURITY ENVIRONMENT CONSIDERATIONS

Preliminary considerations help put the overall approach in perspective. The suggested approach is effective, but judicious assessment of each of the steps is appropriate. For further insight, it is instructive to look more closely at some reasons for caution before proceeding toward a treatment that could otherwise be inadvertently credited with more accuracy than is appropriate.

2.1.1 Cautions Concerning the Direct Approach

Some of the factors that complicate the directness of the fundamental approach are:

1. Assets are not limited to physical entities such as computers or valuable information. Some of the less obvious assets are personnel (with their knowledge and experience), company reputation, ability to carry out business functions, ability to attract employees, ability to fight litigation, and ability to meet regulatory requirements.
2. Threats can also be subtle. The threats of customers losing confidence, customers taking business elsewhere, litigation potential, competitors gaining a competitive advantage, and regulatory agencies curtailing operations are indirect. (Note that some of these threats tend to blur into the description of assets above.)
3. Specific threats do not usually have a one-to-one correspondence to particular assets. There may be multiple threats to a single asset and multiple assets jeopardized by a single threat, for example.
4. The identification of vulnerabilities is frequently difficult. Some vulnerabilities are obvious to almost any observer; some may be found only by accident, if at all. Later, we will discuss some approaches that have been used to identify vulnerabilities more systematically.
5. Protective measures sometimes interact with each other. We will see that there is a synergistic effect in some combinations of measures; others may counteract each other.
6. Protective measures are sometimes selected for reasons other than reducing vulnerabilities. For example, encrypted communication capabilities might be implemented during network installation because the equipment is available and most easily

incorporated at the time. In this case, encryption might be installed as an opportunistic measure. In other cases, protective measures could be installed simply to be in consonance with the approach of others.

7. Not all of the values of responsive actions are obvious or easy to determine. For example, the value of prosecution may be debated in certain cases, as we will illustrate. Other advantages to responsive actions may not become apparent for some time after the action.

All of these considerations will be examined in more detail later. It is important to recognize that direct tractable approaches are necessary to make progress, but the overall problem involves a large number of considerations.

2.1.2 Partitions of the Environment

The goals of this chapter are to outline an analytical framework that is valuable in assessing security issues and to establish partitions in the overall environment within which this and other approaches to security can be examined. The analytical approach given in this chapter is generally called "risk analysis." The partitions we will suggest are two-dimensional, as indicated by the matrix shown in Figure 2-1. The rows of the matrix list the security steps we discussed in Chapter 1; the columns list the different environments within which we can look for unique situations. These environments are physical, personnel, regulatory, hardware, software, and networks. (Note that for concise nomenclature, data and records in computer memory media will be included under the heading of software in this categorization.) Within each of these environments, we will survey threats and suggest protective measures, along with analytical approaches that may be useful.

2.2 RISK ANALYSIS BASICS

Risk analysis is a technique for quantitative assessment of the relative value of protective measures. Although no panacea, risk analysis is valuable when appropriately applied and is in some cases required by regulatory agencies. First, some motivation.

Many people make decisions on the basis of intuition or a "feel" based on an accumulation of experiences. There is little argument physical personnel regulatory hardware software networks

	physical	personnel	regulatory	hardware	software	networks
assets	hardware software networks personnel	personnel	hardware software networks personnel	computers peripherals	programs data	networks
threats	personnel nature accidents	personnel nature accidents	personnel	personnel nature accidents	personnel nature accidents	personnel nature accidents
vulnerabilities	entrances environment power	weakness environment	weakness incomplete	environment design margin TEMPEST	environment access control backup lack	environment access control backup lack
risks	access damage destruction	injury corruption	fines penalties	failure damage destruction	loss alteration disclosure	failure damage destruction
protective measures	locks surveillance environment	investigation environment surveillance	laws enforcement	redundancy design margin TEMPEST equip.	access control structured encryption	access control encryption
response	recovery	prosecution	prosecution penalties	recovery repair	recovery	recovery

Figure 2-1   Security entities.

that this technique is effective, as it is used extensively in successful enterprises such as the U.S. government, Fortune 500 businesses, and sports franchises. Most of us use the same technique in making decisions about the protection of possessions such as our home and car. How much insurance is needed? How much should be spent on security systems? Although intuition and judgment are important, there is a case to be made for applying analysis in at least some situations.

2.2.1 Problems with Intuition

Consider the following classic probability problem [2]. Twenty-three people are selected at random, as they might be if guests at a party. What is the probability that at least two people at the party have the same birthday (month and day)? Perhaps bets would be made. The answer (see Problem 1) is that there is more than a 50/50 chance on the basis of the information given* (assuming equally probable

---

* Other information could be important. For example, someone who knows that his or her birthday is February 29 may bet differently than would a person who has a "typical" birthday.

birthdates distributed across 365 days). It is very hard for most people to intuitively forecast this result, although experience may lead one to accept the analysis.

The point is that analysis is frequently more valuable than intuition. It is difficult to look at a 747 aircraft loaded with fuel, people, and luggage and feel intuitively satisfied that it will not only fly, but can fly a significant fraction of the way around the world without refueling. The cumbersome-appearing Saturn rocket system defied most people's intuition by launching successful Apollo round trips for persons to the moon. The Apollo mission was initiated and construction of 747s was committed because analysis showed the plausibility of the concepts. Note that the analyses were also supported with extensive physical testing. This also should be a lesson for those of us who evaluate a security environment.

2.2.2 Risk Analysis Illustrative Examples

Having argued that analysis can be a valuable security adjunct, let's consider how it might be applied. We will start with a simple example that will serve to illustrate the basic concepts of risk analysis.

Assume that we have a computer installation valued at $100,000. Fire department statistics show that the probability of a devastating fire for a facility like ours is about once in a hundred years. (The potential for destruction could be considered a vulnerability.) We have no insurance. We can calculate an "annual loss expectancy" (ALE) based on the risk statistics and the value:

$$e = pv \qquad (2\text{-}1)$$

where e is the ALE, p is the risk in terms of probability of complete loss per year, and v is the value (of an asset).

In this example, the statistical expected loss (ALE) is $1000. Of course, no one would actually lose $1000 per year. Actual losses under the problem assumptions would be either $100,000 or zero.[*] However, the object is to quantify the effect of the risk statistically. Now assume that we could install a fire protection system for $10,000, and that the expected ALE would drop to zero. In a statisti-

---

[*]   We will return to this idea shortly with discussion of a probability model based on the "binomial distribution."

Table 2-1   Sample facility.

Facility assets and value
  computer — $100,000
  software — $10,000
  liability potential — $10,000

Threats and annual probability (risk)
  fire — 0.01
  water — 0.1
  electrical problems — 0.1
  hacker penetration — 1.0

Protective measures and cost
  Halon fire protection — $10,000
  pipe routing, drain improvement — $1000
  offsite backup — $1000
  callback modems — $1000
  power conditioning — $1000

---

cal sense, then, our $10,000 fire protection system would pay for itself in 10 years. Note again that simplified arguments were used that neglected depreciation, equipment lifetime, inflation, bank interest, maintenance, personnel considerations, etc. However, the usefulness of this approach is that we have a quantitative comparison of the effects of a risk (through a vulnerability) to an asset with the cost of reducing the risk (and vulnerability) and therefore protecting the asset.

A more instructive, but still somewhat simplified example is described in Table 2-1.

A systematic approach to risk analysis for this facility can be derived from the fundamental steps reviewed at the beginning of the chapter, with references to Table 2-1 and Figure 2-2. The approach that will be presented is one of many possible [3–7]. Some other approaches will be mentioned later. Our treatment here will be based on relatively straightforward concepts consistent with the general steps already suggested.

As a first step in the analysis, assets are identified and valued. For simplicity, we have placed a one-time value on each asset. As a second step, we have identified several threats. The third step is to

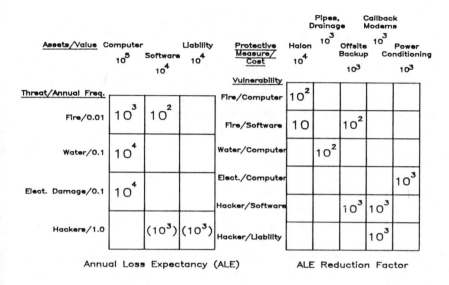

Figure 2-2   Risk analysis example.

identify vulnerabilities. Since each threat may or may not correspond to a vulnerability for a particular asset, a matrix is helpful in associating threats with assets where vulnerabilities exists. This is done in the matrix on the left side of Figure 2-2, where an entry or lack of entry signifies a vulnerability or lack of a vulnerability, respectively.

Step 4 is to determine risks, which are the probabilities associated with realization of each threat. The probabilities can be obtained from statistical compilations or can be estimated from accumulated experience. In either case, the accuracy of the input data can directly affect the resulting risk analyses.

The ALEs (annual loss expectancies) can be obtained, wherever there is a vulnerability, by multiplying the probability of a loss by the value of the associated asset (step 5). These ALEs are the entries in the left matrix in Figure 2-2. (Note that the two ALEs for losses due to hackers, indicated parenthetically, are each reduced by a factor of 10 from the amounts listed in Table 2-1. This was done on the assumption that only partial losses are likely.)

The sixth step is to identify potential protective measures and their costs. For simplicity, these are given in Table 2-1 as one-time costs.

Step 7 is to assess the potential effects of the protective measures on the vulnerabilities. This is also aided by a matrix structure, as shown in the right half of Figure 2-2. The entries in the matrix signify vulnerabilities reduced by protective measures. That is, the values of the entries are estimates of the ALE reduction factors due to the protective measures. (Note that since these ALE reduction estimates are usually based on judgment and experience, they provide another source of inaccuracy in the analysis. At this point, we are concentrating on illustrating the analysis technique, not attempting to justify the values used.)

The eighth step is to evaluate each protective measure by comparing its cost with the ALE reductions expected if it is incorporated. In our example, a Halon fire protection system ($10,000 cost) is expected to essentially eliminate the fire threat ($\approx$$1000) to the computer and to the software, thereby paying for itself in 10 years. The case is not overwhelming for or against Halon protection, but the value of the analysis is that a quantitative measure of the break-even point is at least approximately known. Assume that we decide to select this protective measure.

The pipe and drainage work is expected to save about $1000 per year at a one-time cost of $1000. Therefore the computation favors having this work done.

Offsite backup appears to save its cost ($1000) due to the hacker destruction potential and would therefore look attractive. It would also save the lesser expected loss due to fire, had we not selected a Halon fire protection system. Callback modems ($1000) also essentially remove the hacker threat to software and to liability ($1000 each) and therefore seem cost-effective. Since this is the only protective measure that we have identified for liability, its inclusion is appropriate. Having selected callback modems, the outlook for offsite backup becomes different. Offsite backup in this case would not reduce ALEs because of our other selections. For this reason, it will not be selected.

The final protective measure, power conditioning, seems cost-effective, and we will implement it. This completes the example, although there is a final step in the risk analysis process.

The last step is to respond to experiences by assessing and possibly changing the protective measures, by recovering from any degradations experienced, and by prosecuting or disciplining any persons who violate security policy or law.

The example was obviously simplified. However, the illustration is important. We must remain aware of the interrelations, inaccuracies, and role of judgment if the results of a risk analysis are to be used intelligently.

2.2.3 Risk Analysis Summary

Summarizing the steps in this form of risk analysis:

1. Identify and value assets. (What must be protected?)
2. Identify threats. (Protected against what?)
3. Identify vulnerabilities. (What are the potential ways in which threats can be realized?)
4. Estimate risks. (What is the probability of a vulnerability?)
5. Calculate ALEs for each vulnerability. (What is the statistically expected loss?)
6. Identify potential protective measures. (How can assets be protected against threats?)
7. Estimate ALE reductions for each vulnerability due to each protective measure. (What is the statistically expected amount saved?)
8. Select cost-effective protective measures. (How are assets best protected against threats?)
9. Respond to experience by modifying protective measures, by recovering from disasters, and by prosecuting transgressors. (How can feedback be used?)

2.2.4 Prevention vs. Recovery

An additional problem that must be considered is the tradeoff between 1) establishing protection to prevent unwanted incidents and 2) establishing mechanisms for efficiently recovering from unwanted incidents. Conceptually, it is preferable to act in a preventive mode. Pragmatically, it is often not economical to strictly do so. Although recovery may take time away from normal operations and may be more complex, it could be the only feasible option, or at least an option utilized. These points will be developed more fully in the next chapter.

2.2.5 Cost-Effectiveness

It is also useful to put cost-effectiveness (the basis of risk analysis) in perspective. The first goal in selecting protective measures is *not* cost-effectiveness; it is staying in business (or maintaining operations for government or other nonbusiness organizations). If this goal is not achieved, other considerations become insignificant. This is the reason that in some situations asset values are not appropriate. For example, the protection of classified information is deemed by the United States government to be crucial to the nation's survival. For this reason, no monetary value is allowed to influence the decision to protect classified information. It is also unsatisfying to put monetary value on human lives.

The actual performance of a risk analysis is an overhead cost that must also be considered as part of the expense associated with protective measures. A formal risk analysis, if not done judiciously, can be very expensive. Also, some modes of attack and the corresponding protective measures are so obvious that they should not be part of a formal risk analysis.

2.2.6 Accuracy of Data

The database on which the risk analysis is based is important. Data must be judiciously sought and recorded by organizations intending to use risk analysis. These data may be highly dependent on location. For example, lightning activity strongly varies around the world (see Chapter 6). So also do earthquakes and volcanic activity. Coastal regions of northern California, for example, have unusually high rates of earthquakes and volcanic activity and unusually low rates of lightning.

It is also obvious that the accuracy of the analysis depends directly on the accuracy of the data. This means that some idea of the accuracy of the numbers derived can be deduced from the characteristics of the data in the database. Comprehensive assessment of accuracy usually requires automated calculations (software).

Further use of risk analysis concepts is provided in the problems at the end of the chapter.

2.3 RISK ANALYSIS PERSPECTIVES

2.3.1 Background

Risk analysis concepts have been in use in many fields for centuries. The basic ideas are well known. The application of risk analysis to computer security has been more recent, but there is considerable current emphasis. U.S. government agencies and contractors are required to use risk analysis, and several guidelines are available to offer effective help. Automated risk analysis is now possible through the use of commercial software. Automated risk analysis software has a number of advantages [11]. These include savings in time spent on risk analysis and the potential for cost savings. Overall analysis is also simplified by "spreadsheet" displays, which enable outputs to be studied as a function of selected input changes. Automated risk analysis software also results in a reduction of risk analysis training needs.

A major impetus was provided for performing formal security risk analysis when the U.S. National Bureau of Standards issued Federal Information Processing Standards Publications (FIPS PUBs) No. 31 and No. 65 on risk analysis methodology.

FIPS PUB No. 31 is intended to explain and encourage use of risk analysis, along with other (physical security) guidance. The first step under the procedures suggested is to "analyze risk." Intended risk analysis benefits include giving quantitative guidance in selecting security measures, generating long-range plans, formulating contingency plans (see the next chapter), and enunciating security policy (see Chapter 4). The stated initial objectives are to identify critical aspects of the operation and to place dollar values on loss estimates. Consideration of threats is aided by numerous examples, as is calculation of ALEs. Examples of remedial measures are also given.

FIPS PUB No. 65 provides direct guidance on how to perform a risk analysis. It followed a risk analysis mandate in the Office of Management and Budget Circular A-71, Transmittal Memorandum No. 1 of July 1978. The circular required U.S. government agencies and U.S. government contractors to perform a risk analysis as part of establishing and conducting security programs for protecting unclassified but sensitive information and processing capability (sensitive applications). Sensitive applications are defined to be "those that require a degree of protection because of the risk and magnitude of harm that could occur." This is a fuzzy definition, but the intent is clearly to assure that the need for protection is not neglected for

Table 2-2   Frequency of threats.

P = 1 if once in 300 years
P = 2 if once in 30 years
P = 3 if once in 3 years (1000 days)
P = 4 if once in 100 days
P = 5 if once in 10 days
P = 6 if once per day
P = 7 if 10 times per day
P = 8 if 100 times per day

classes of data that do not fall under more formal categories, such as "Classified." The risk analysis technique offered in FIPS PUB No. 65 is based on work by Robert Courtney, then of IBM. It proposes a direct tabular approach to risk analysis that will be reviewed here.

The probability of threats is selected from a frequency table similar to Table 2-2. The purpose of the discrete values shown is to operate within the bounds of the input accuracy and to minimize computational complexity and time expended.

This table essentially uses a logarithmic conversion of the annual frequency p into the frequency indicator P:

$$P \approx 3 + \log_{10} 3p \tag{2-2}$$

A logarithmic value V is also established from the asset value v, where:

$$V \approx \log_{10} v \tag{2-3}$$

The exponential expression for the ALE (indicated as E) is calculated as:

$$E = (0.3)\,(10^{P+V-3}) \tag{2-4}$$

Table 2-3 gives solutions of Equation 2-4 for meaningful combinations of integer values for P and V.

Table 2-3   Tabular ALE solution.

P	1	2	3	4	5	6	7	8
V								
1					$300	$3k	$30k	$300k
2				$300	$3k	$30k	$300k	$3M
3			$300	$3k	$30k	$300k	$3M	$30M
4		$300	$3k	$30k	$300k	$3M	$30M	$300M
5	$300	$3k	$30k	$300k	$3M	$30M	$300M	
6	$3k	$30k	$300k	$3M	$30M	$300M		
7	$30k	$300k	$3M	$30M	$300M			
8	$300k	$3M	$30M	$300M				

Management, organization, logistics, advice on real-life effects on the inputs and use of the outputs, examples, and alternative protective measures are also discussed in FIPS PUB No. 65.

2.3.2 Statistical Considerations

Several other aspects of risk analysis merit examination.

1. The statistical probability of a loss due to several independent events is:

$$p(L) = \Sigma\, p(e_i) - \Pi\, p(e_i) \qquad (2\text{-}5)$$

where the summation is for individual event probabilities, and the products are for combinations of events.[*]

---

[*]   The exact expression for the product terms is complex. For example, for two events, the product expression is $p(e_1)p(e_2)$, for three events, the product expression is $p(e_1)p(e_2) + p(e_1)p(e_3) + p(e_2)p(e_3) - p(e_1)p(e_2)p(e_3)$, etc.

This equation indicates that overall losses are affected nearly linearly by the individual loss probabilities for very small probabilities, but that combinations of events must be considered where the product terms are too large to neglect (see Problem 10).

2. The accuracy of computations involving multiplicative variables quickly becomes poor as the number of operands increases. For example, if the two operands in Equation 2-1 are known to have accuracy $\pm a\%$ and $\pm b\%$, the accuracy of the product is approximately $\pm(a + b)\%$. This effect extends to any number of operands (see Problem 11). This means that the uncertainties in the risk analysis calculations are additive and that the accumulation of insignificant inaccuracies may yield a significant inaccuracy.

3. The accuracy of sums of variables also decreases with increasing numbers of operands. For example, given two quantities with normal (Gaussian) probability distributions having "variance" σ_1^2 and σ_2^2, the sum of these quantities has a variance of $\sigma_1^2 + \sigma_2^2$. This effect extends to any number of operands (see Problem 13) and is applicable to risk analysis computations that contain additive operations. The implications for the accuracy of multiplicative operations are similar.

4. Certain multiplicative probability calculations depend on complete independence of the variables. For the occurrence of two events of probability p and q, the probability that both events will occur is pq if the events are independent of each other. It is common for dependence to exist (see Problem 14). Depending on the type of dependence, the probability may be either more or less than that computed under the assumption of independence. Dependence effects [12] are frequently too significant to neglect.

2.3.3 Pertinence of Statistical Expectations

When an asset is repeatedly subjected to a threat, we asserted previously that statistical expectations did not directly represent reality, since for each exposure there was either complete loss or no loss. However, as the number of exposures to threats increases, the statistical expectation is gradually approached. A reasonable model for this process is the binomial probability distribution.

Consider n exposures of an asset to a threat having probability p. The probability that the threat will not occur is $1 - p$. We will term this probability q. Then the probability that the threat will affect the asset after n exposures is given by the sum of all terms except the last in the binomial expansion:

$$p^n + np^{n-1}q + (\tbinom{n}{2})p^{n-2}q^2 + \ldots + q^n = 1 \qquad (2\text{-}6)$$

The average after n exposures is therefore:

$$\bar{p} = (p^n + np^{n-1}q + \ldots + npq^{n-1})/n \qquad (2\text{-}7)$$

If p is relatively small, q approaches 1 and all but the last term of the numerator of Equation 2-7 become relatively small. This gives an approximation to the average value of $np/n = p$. This probability model is applicable to a large number of cases involving repeated exposures. It shows that in these cases the statistical value is rapidly approached, even with a small number of exposures.

With this introduction to the theory of risk analysis, we will turn to an important practical consideration: resource allocation.

2.4 RESOURCE ALLOCATION

A list of indicated expenditures and a list of the related ALE reductions result from the risk analysis we have described. Assume that the list of expenditures is $a_1, a_2, \ldots, a_n$ (n expenditures) and the list of related ALE reductions is $e_1, e_2, \ldots, e_n$. The total expenditures desired would be $A = \Sigma a_i$.

The problem is that sufficient funds may not be available to provide for A. Assume that the available budget is B, where $B < A$. This is an all-too-common situation, so it is useful to deal with the limitation.

A strategy of allocating limited resources must take the nature of the threats into consideration. If the threat is statistical, as we might view accidents and natural occurrences, a probabilistic approach is appropriate. On the other hand, the threat posed by an intelligent, thinking adversary may warrant different treatment. We will address the latter category in Chapter 4, where personnel threats are discussed. Here, partly for introductory purposes, we consider a probabilistic approach.

2.4.1   Statistically Expected Threat Distributions

The first issue we consider is the expected distribution of statistical threats against a collection of assets. The issue is whether we expect threats to cluster or be distributed in some other way as they affect various assets. The birthday problem illustrated that uniform distributions are rare; but we also might doubt that extensive clustering is likely.

The random application of threats against assets is analogous to the classic probability problem of balls distributed randomly in cells [2]. Consider m threats applied randomly against n assets. We need to know how the threats can be expected to be distributed, so we can determine the best strategy for applying protective measures.

First, note that there are a total of n^m ways in which the threats can be applied. This is the denominator in the probability calculations for the various distributions.

Consider the probability that all threats are applied against a single asset. We will call this probability p_1. This is the maximum "clustering" possible. Since there are n different assets against which the threats can be applied, the numerator of the expression for p_1 is n. Then,

$$p_1 = n/n^m \tag{2-8}$$

Now consider the probability that the threats are applied with as little clustering as possible. We will call this probability p_2. For illustration, we will choose the case where $m \leq n$. (Similar results could be obtained for the more general case, but the point we are examining is better illustrated by this example.) The minimum clustering situation with $m \leq n$ has no more than a single threat applied against any asset. This means that there are $\binom{n}{m}$ ways to select which assets are threatened and m! ways to arrange the threats. The result is:[*]

$$p_2 = m!\binom{n}{m}/n^m = n!/[\, n^m\,(n-m)!\,] \tag{2-9}$$

Comparing the maximum distribution case with the maximum clustering case can be done by calculating the ratio of p_2 to p_1. This is:

---

[*]   This is also a solution to the "birthday problem," where $n = 365$, and $m =$ the number of people considered.

$$p_2/p_1 = (n-1)! / (n-m)! \qquad (2\text{-}10)$$

This result makes it clear that the maximum cluster case is generally much less likely than the maximum distribution case. Furthermore, the maximum cluster case can be shown [2] to be at least as small as any other possible distribution. This is instructive because it illustrates that clustering cannot be expected as a high probability distribution. In general, it is more effective to distribute protective measures evenly when protecting against random occurrences.

2.4.2 Resource Allocation Strategies

Returning to the case where the available budget (B) is less than the expenditures (A), as indicated by risk analysis, we seek a strategy of allocating the budget to minimize the overall ALE. As we pointed out earlier, the available budget must be the amount left over after allowing for the cost of the risk analysis. Since we are still considering randomly generated threats, we desire a distributed allocation as indicated by the previous analysis. There are several ways to approach the allocation problem. Three methods are outlined below:

1. Proportional allotment. Proportional allotment means budgeting each protective measure expenditure proportionally to the available budget. If we let b_i indicate the amount budgeted to correspond to the a_i indicated by the risk analysis, we calculate:

$$b_i = a_i B / A \qquad (2\text{-}11)$$

Note that this strategy will force the expenditures to match the budget, where

$$B = \Sigma \, b_i \qquad (2\text{-}12)$$

A problem with this technique is that expenditures often cannot be tailored proportionally. For example, if the purchase of a Halon system is indicated by risk analysis, but resources are insufficient, say if $A = 2B$, it may not be feasible to buy half a Halon system. Like many other features of risk analysis, how-

ever, the proportional allotment gives guidance as to what can
be done within a fixed budget. As an example, proportional allotment may result in a number of mismatches between needs
and resources, but individual judgments can still be analytical-
ly aided. If the ALE associated with the fire hazard is large
enough, one would probably commit the expenditure, making
up the difference on less significant protective measures. This
leads to the next option.

2. Proportional significant allotment. As the preceding discussion
   indicates, it is not unusual for some risk analysis results to be
   more important and more significant monetarily than others.
   This situation leads to consideration of discarding insignificant-
   ly small expenditures and concentrating on major expenditures, which can then be treated proportionally in accordance
   with the resources.

3. Ordered ("squeaky wheel") allotment. On the grounds that the
   most significant problems should be treated first, this strategy
   picks the largest indicated expenditure first, then the next
   largest, etc., charging each against the available budget until it
   is gone. This strategy is to fully address the most pressing
   problems, while either neglecting or deferring the indicated
   protective measures for the others.

Other mathematical techniques (e.g., linear programming) may be
used to take into consideration the effects of interactions between
protective measures. All strategies have limitations and must be applied within reasonable bounds. Clearly the level of sophistication of
the risk analysis must match the conditions associated with the
problem. In Chapter 4, we will consider different allotment strategies
when addressing intelligent threats.

2.5 OTHER FORMS OF ANALYSIS

Risk analysis is probably the most widely used and is certainly the
most widely known form of analysis used in the process of selecting
protective measures. However, there are other techniques with which
one should be familiar, because risk analysis is not always the most
appropriate approach. In this section we will survey some alternatives.

2.5.1 Exposure Analysis

Another way to decide how to allocate expenditures for protective measures is through "exposure analysis" [3]. This means looking for assets that have the most exposure to threats. As the binomial distribution shows, repeated exposure to even a low-probability event has a good chance of eventually resulting in the realization of a vulnerability. Exposure analysis considers the degree of exposure, whether it be to people or nature or accidents. The intent is to combine degree of exposure, as measured by some numerical ranking (high numbers for high exposure), with consequences of the possible vulnerability (high numbers for serious consequences). The combination (for example, by multiplying the exposure ranking by the consequence seriousness) indicates the need for protective measures.

Examples will briefly illustrate the concept. The involvement of people can create exposure in a number of ways. People in the vicinity of an asset can cause losses through physical acts, whether through intention, inattention, or accident. The larger the number of people with such opportunities, the greater the exposure of the asset. People in operational duties can also create exposure, as can people in programming activities. Some of the critical occupations, ranked (somewhat arbitrarily) from most critical to least, are: security specialist, EDP auditor, systems programmer, operations manager, data entry clerk, computer operator, systems engineer, database administrator, tape librarian, communications engineer, applications programmer, and terminal engineer.

The reasons for the security specialist ranking in this example are that the position requires intimate knowledge of the security measures in place, their strengths and weaknesses, the security procedures followed by involved personnel, and the history of incidents. This person also is constantly on the scene, creating a high exposure to opportunities. Furthermore, the position carries with it an implied trust and a set of privileged access to physical and logical entities.

There are similar reasons for the EDP auditor ranking. The audit "triggers" are best known to this person. There is great difficulty in denying access (physical or logical) to an individual required to examine systems to any level of detail. However, the auditor generally has less exposure measured in time than a security specialist.

A systems programmer (one who develops, installs, and maintains operating system and utility software) has the next ranking in this example, because of exposure to the detailed operation of the system controls, routine exposure to memory dumps, and opportunistic access to the hardware and software controlling operations. This individual is subject to monitoring by security specialists and EDP auditors.

Similar reasoning or function/knowledge/skills/access tabulations can be cited for the remaining occupations. The operations manager has crucial access and privileges. The data entry clerk is directly involved in determining what data are stored. The computer operator has opportunity to misuse or destroy resources. The systems engineer has opportunity to modify, destroy, steal, or misuse hardware and software. The database administrator has direct access to information and can influence the modification of data. The tape librarian has custody of important data tapes. The communications engineer has access to data traffic. The applications programmer could modify or sabotage processing. The terminal engineer might have opportunity to modify, destroy, or steal terminal equipment. Each of these occupations was ranked with regard to exposure and criticality according to judgment, but the judgment was systematically applied.

Nature can also create exposure. For example, thunderstorm activity is minimal on the coast of California (exposure to lightning activity is low) but is high throughout most of Florida (exposure to lightning activity is high). Similar observations can be made for tornados, floods, volcanic activity, and earthquakes.

Since various forms of accidents can cause the loss of assets, it is important to consider exposure to construction activity, pressurized pipes (water and gas), heavy vehicle traffic, etc.

Some other examples of exposure [8] are data sharing (sequentially in applications use, simultaneously in database use), exposure due to accessibility (higher exposure for easier access), and shared systems (decentralized processing can subject data to more exposure).

In exposure analysis, the goals are to provide quantitative measures that are not tied directly to financial measures. This has the advantages of providing measures for vulnerabilities independent of any possible associations; the disadvantage is that more judgment is required, and the results may be less demonstrable to management and others.

2.5.2 Scenario Analysis

Another form of analysis is called "scenario analysis." This can take the form of attempting to conceive of and, insofar as possible, to carry out a series of potential vulnerability scenarios. In many cases, active scenario incidents are difficult to simulate and so they must be modeled on paper. In either case, the advantage consists of visualizing a range of possible vulnerabilities before actual occurrence of an event. The analysis involves the consequences and likelihood of each vulnerability, as determined by carrying out the scenario. The consequences can be measured financially, but are not limited to financial measure. The likelihood can be based on statistics or judgment.

Security consultant David Snow has suggested applying logic diagrams to scenario analysis in order to describe threat configurations, security faults that allow threats to create vulnerabilities, and "hazard" situations that cause loss of assets. The threat logic (Figure 2-3) describes combinations of threat capabilities that must be in place before a threat event can happen. The security fault logic (Figure 2-4) describes combinations of security faults that must occur in order for the threat event to cause a security failure event. The hazard logic (Figure 2-5) shows combinations of hazards that can result from the security failure event.

Scenario analysis is enhanced by a "brainstorming" atmosphere, which tends to synergistically identify vulnerabilities that might otherwise be missed. There are similarities with the "Tiger Team" operations used effectively to identify vulnerabilities in Department of Defense (DoD) computing operations. These activities will be reviewed in Chapter 7.

Judgment measures can often be enriched (i.e., determined more accurately and thus more convincingly) through "the Delphi technique" popularized by the Rand Corporation. This technique utilizes a number of qualified people, who are asked to make some form of quantified estimates. The aggregate of the estimates is computed, and the estimators are asked to consider the aggregate estimates in reevaluating their original estimates. The process tends to converge to a more realistic consensus than any one estimator could provide.

2.5.3 Questionnaire Analysis

Another form of analysis is based on questionnaires. Some forms of data required to determine protective measures can best be gathered by questioning the people most intimately involved. Questionnaires put together with the aid of human factors engineers can provide valuable insight, especially where questionnaire analysis (quantitative measure of the information provided) is skillfully done.

Situations in which questionnaires are particularly appropriate are: 1) determination of personal computer location, network connec-

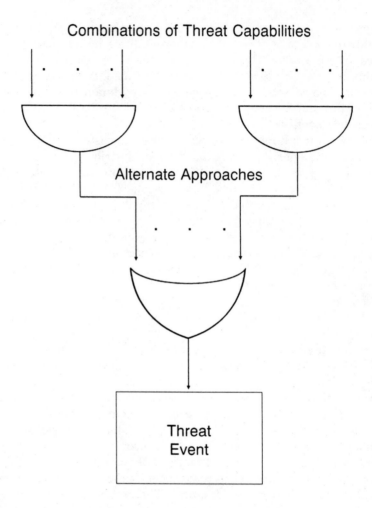

Figure 2-3   Threat logic.

tions, use, and data stored, 2) experiences (incidents) involving computer security compromises or vulnerabilities otherwise observed, and 3) gathering data to support risk analysis activities [3].

2.5.4 Check Lists

Check lists provide another aid in determining protective measures. Entire books have been written on this subject [9,10]. The value of

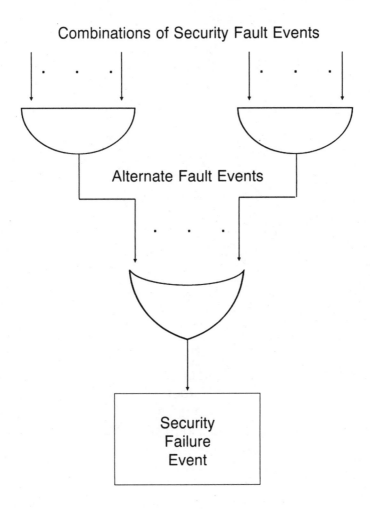

Figure 2-4 Threat logic.

the technique is that, although not strictly analytical, check lists can be derived from results of analytical approaches in order to minimize additional analysis.

Having introduced analysis in this chapter, we look ahead to the environments within which we can apply these and other forms of analysis. These environments also provide the structure within which we can examine the nature of the threats facing computer and communications security as well as the types of protective measures we can consider in meeting the threats.

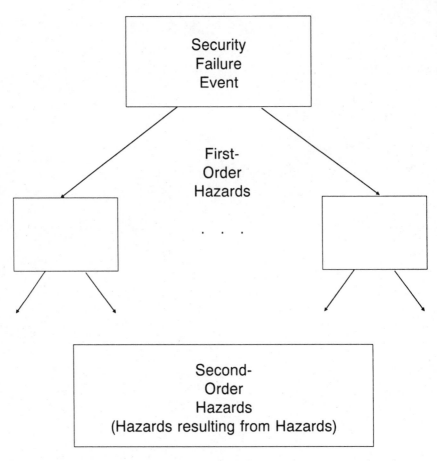

Figure 2-5   Hazard logic.

2.6 THE ENTITIES WITHIN THE ENVIRONMENTS

As Figure 2-1 suggests, there are specific entities within each environment at each step in the security approach. Note that there are six columns in the figure, each representing a different environment. These environments (physical, personnel, regulatory, hardware, software, and networks) form the basis for the organization of the next six chapters of this book.

For each environment, there are six unique areas (the six rows in Figure 2-1) of interest. These six areas correspond to the six fundamental steps we find useful in approaching security: identify assets, identify threats, determine vulnerabilities, estimate risks, select protective measures, and take responsive action. Not all 36 entities warrant equal coverage, but all should be kept in mind. The descriptive words in the matrix for each entity are brief indicators of some of the most prominent features. The descriptions that follow are also terse and meant to be illustrative. The reader should not be too concerned if these listed features appear incomplete, are not fully understood, or appear to overlap.

2.6.1 Assets

Physical assets include hardware (computers, memory devices, peripheral equipment), software (operating systems, applications programs, data), networks (transmitting, receiving equipment, and conducting media), and personnel (operators, maintenance persons, users, managers). Personnel satisfy the concept of a physical asset category because they represent an investment in terms of cost of hiring and training. People are also considered a personnel asset because they represent an intangible value that is almost universally placed on life. We feel a moral and humanitarian obligation, one that transcends any monetary investment, to protect human well-being.

Regulatory assets are those assets for which protection may be required by regulations, laws, and policy statements. The main categories are hardware, software (including, under our categorization, data), networks, and personnel.

Hardware assets specifically refers to computers and peripherals (including memory devices), because we choose to address these items under our discussion of hardware security, separating security measures from, for example, network hardware.

Software assets (programs and data, by our categorization) are viewed differently for software security assessment than are the same assets when considered from the viewpoint of other environments (e.g., physical security).

Network assets include the network components themselves (because of the threats of tapping or jamming), as well as the data that are transmitted across the networks.

2.6.2 Threats

Threats to all types of assets include people (who may intentionally damage assets), natural events (such as earthquakes, floods, and tornados), and accidents (such as fire, burst water pipes, and human mistakes). Note that the assets affected may include personnel, hardware, and software (as well as network entities such as communications media).

The physical environment encompasses all of these assets; therefore, the threats in the physical environment are listed in the previous paragraph. The regulatory environment applies only to the intentional actions of people, since this is the only control that laws, regulations, and policy can exercise.

2.6.3 Vulnerabilities

Vulnerabilities are ascertained in many ways: first-hand experience, through the experience of others, intuition, extrapolation, or through exercises (simulated or postulated attacks). One of the main objectives of this book is to point out vulnerabilities. For now, we will mention a few general vulnerabilities associated with each of the six environments.

Physical vulnerabilities include entrances to computing areas that have insufficient protection, unreliable environmental control (air conditioning, water protection), unreliable power, and weak fire protection. Environmental and fire protection can also create hardware, software, and network vulnerabilities.

Personnel environment vulnerabilities are those that can be caused by personnel (mistakes or moral and character weakness such as greed, blackmail, or bribery), and those that can happen to personnel (injury, death).

The regulatory environment vulnerabilities comprise the same personnel weaknesses mentioned above, plus those due to incomplete, contradictory, or improper regulations, laws, and policy.

Hardware vulnerabilities include environmental effects on hardware (electrical overstress, overheating, radiation), and marginal design (not allowing sufficiently for component variations, changes, or failures). Unintentional emanations (TEMPEST) are also included.

Software has some of the same vulnerabilities because of the storage media used and because of other interactions between software and hardware (electrical overstress, overheating, radiation). Software design can also create a vulnerability, for example, through unexpected performance in response to design errors (bugs). Its performance can also be affected by hardware component drift and by unexpected or improper user or operator actions. Another software vulnerability is failure to generate and update backup copies.

Network vulnerabilities include physical and hardware vulnerabilities, as well as insufficient protection against jamming, tapping, and other forms of interception. A vulnerability can also be created through lack of redundancy (alternate transmission routes).

2.6.4 Risks

We have used the term "risks" for the probabilities of the vulnerabilities, which must be individually determined, so Figure 2-1 concisely describes the effects of these failures in terms such as damage, losses, and fines.

2.6.5 Protective Measures

The identification of protective measures is another important part of this book. For now, we will briefly mention a few in each category. Physical protective measures include locks, surveillance devices (alarms, closed circuit television), and environmental protection systems (fire extinguishing, power stabilization, and backup systems).

Personnel protective measures include environmental control as a means of reducing the probability of injury or death, and measures to protect against personnel threats (background investigation, surveillance, auditing transactions, following up on tips).

The major regulatory protective measures are to formulate comprehensive, noncontradictory, and fair regulations, laws, and policies, and then to enforce them.

Hardware protective measures include redundancy and fault-tolerant design, generous design margin allowances, and designs that take advantage of particular hardware characteristics (e.g., read-only memories to which writing is essentially impossible).

Protective measures implemented in software include access control logic such as passwords, structured development methodology for correctness and transparency, and encryption.

Encryption also provides a valuable network protective measure, as do various access control schemes such as security controllers and key distribution centers.

2.6.6 Response

A response is appropriate when monitoring of events indicates a need for action. Typical responsive actions are recovery from loss or damage in the physical, hardware, software, and network environments, and prosecution in the personnel and regulatory environments.

At this point, with the overall scenario set and the fundamentals of systematic risk analysis presented, it is appropriate to address each of the six environments we have outlined. This will be done in the next six chapters.

PROBLEMS

1. a) Write a general expression for the probability that at least two people in a group of n will have the same birthdate (month and day). Assume the probability of birthdates is evenly distributed over 365 days. b) What must n be for the probability to be greater than 0.5?
2. What is the solution to Problem 1 if leap years are considered? (Assume leap years have an extra day and occur every four years. Neglect the skipped leap years at the turn of most centuries.)
3. Assume assets: computer (value $100,000), software (value $10,000), private information (liability value $10,000), and operating personnel (liability value $100,000). Assume threats: fire (risk 0.01/year), water (risk 0.01/year), earthquake (risk 0.01/year), insider snoop (risk 0.1/year). a) Determine ALEs. b) Protective measures already in place are a Halon flooding system and a backup storage site for software. Select cost-effective protective measures from: pipe rerouting ($1000 one-time cost), earthquake-resistant structure ($100,000 one-time cost), modem call back units ($1000 one-time cost), additional backup site ($1000/year cost). c) Assume your available budget is $850. How would you best allocate it?
4. Perform a risk analysis. Assume threats and annual loss probabilities: severe fire, 10^{-2} ; extensive overhead water leak, 10^{-1} ; malicious authorized user (logical vulnerability, not physical), 10^{0} . Assume assets and annualized (yearly) values: computer, 10^{4} ; commercial software, 10^{3} . a) Compute ALEs. b) Propose protective measures (at least one; no more than three).

c) Estimate costs and ALE reductions. d) Give cost-effective protective measures, if any.

5. Perform a risk analysis calculation to determine the advisability of incorporating access control protective measures for a personal computer and its data. The conditions are as follows: Software valued at $2000 is stored both on a hard disk and in an unlocked diskette repository (duplicate storage). Calculations that took one person-month to compile are stored only on the hard disk. The computer is in a business area that is either securely locked or has people present. However, there is some risk (once every five years during business hours; once every 20 years after business hours) that a person could carry away the computer. Theft of diskettes is more probable (once a year). During business hours, it is unlikely that both would be taken at once. The computer is valued at $10,000. There is some risk (once every five years) that an unauthorized person will inadvertently or intentionally destroy hard disk data while using or attempting to use the computer.

Access control measures under consideration are:

1. Secure mounting rack for the computer to prevent theft of the computer: cost $545.
2. Software access control with selectable password: cost $375.
3. Diskette case with lock: cost $15.
4. Motion alarm for computer and diskette case: cost $410 each.

6. How would you suggest determining the risk of an aircraft collision due to an air traffic control computer security failure (programming error, operator error, component failure, sabotage)?
7. a) What is the advantage of risk analysis over scenario analysis? b) What is the advantage of scenario analysis over risk analysis?
8. The last step in the risk analysis process is "monitoring." What does this mean?
9. Assume that the value of a collection of data is that it could not be recompiled if lost. For example, consider the 1990 U.S. census data. How would the value of this data collection be established for a risk analysis? Give a short discussion.
10. Equation 2-5 was given in general form. The accompanying footnote gives specific guidance for two events and for three

events. a) Give the precise form of Equation 2-5 for two events. b) Give it for three events. c) Give it for four events. d) Can you deduce a simpler form of the expression for an arbitrary number of events?

11. The probability of a particular sequence of random bits is 2^{-n}, where n is the length of the sequence. Assume that any of three particular sequences will trigger a detector at a particular time and that any or all of the possible sequences may occur simultaneously. a) What is the probability that the detector will be triggered? b) How large must n be if the answer must be determined to an accuracy of 0.1% for the product terms to be neglected?

12. Assume that five variables are each known to be bounded within a variation of ±2%. What are the bounds on the product of the variables?

13. Assume that the five variables in problem 12 are each normally distributed and have standard deviations $\sigma_1, \sigma_2, \ldots, \sigma_5$. What is the standard deviation of the sum of the five variables?

14. a) What is the probability of a particular sequence of four random bits? b) What is the probability of a particular randomly selected BCD (binary-coded decimal) digit? c) What is the probability of a particular 4-bit pattern from a random collection where the constraint is placed on the 4 bits that the fourth bit is an odd parity check on the first three? d) Explain any difference you observe in the answers to the preceding three parts to this problem.

15. a) How many ways could three threats be applied against five assets? (This is analogous to the "balls in cells" probability problem.) b) If randomly selected, what is the probability of each? c,d) Repeat parts a and b for five threats applied against three assets.

16. Give the general expression for the probability that kn (where k is an integer) threats randomly applied against n assets will result in evenly distributed threats (equal numbers applied against each asset).

DILEMMA DISCUSSION

One of the reasons for the popularity of risk analysis is that a large number of protective measure benefits can be weighed as to cost-effectiveness. In fact, some people argue that all benefits can be weighed on a cost-effectiveness basis. The contention is that the aim of a business or even government agencies must be centered on staying in operation. Since the operation depends on financial health, all protective measures must be evaluated for a cost/cost-savings balance.

Others contend that many cases cannot be assessed for cost-effectiveness. One example cited is that if you as a parent had a sick child and an expensive medicine was prescribed by a doctor, you would not perform a cost-effectiveness analysis; the medicine would be obtained. Also cited is the national policy that classified information cannot be valued for the purpose of assessing cost-effectiveness. Which view do you support?

REFERENCES

1. Cramer, H., *Mathematical Methods of Statistics*, Princeton University Press, Princeton, NJ, 1951.
2. Feller, William, *Probability Theory and Its Applications*, 2nd Edition, John Wiley and Sons, Inc., New York, 1957.
3. Parker, Donn B., *Computer Security Management*, Reston Publishing, Reston, VA, 1981.
4. Federal Information Processing Standards Publication 65, National Bureau of Standards, 1979.
5. Zimmerman, Joel S., "Is Your Computer Insecure?" *Datamation*, May 15, 1985.
6. Pate-Cornell, Elizabeth, "Risk Management," *The Stanford Engineer*, Fall/Winter, 1985.
7. Miguel, John, "A Composite Cost/Benefit/Risk Analysis Methodology," *Computer Security: A Global Challenge*, Elsevier Science Publishers, New York, 1984.
8. Perry, William E., "Developing a Computer Security and Control Strategy," Chapter 4, in *Computer Control and Security*, John Wiley and Sons, Inc., New York, 1981.
9. Wood, Charles C., et al., *Computer Security: A Comprehensive Checklist*, John Wiley and Sons, Inc., New York, 1987.
10. Browne, Peter S., *Security: Checklist for Computer Center Self-Audits*, AFIPS Press, Washington, DC, 1979.
11. Jacobson, Robert V., "Take the Guesswork Out of Security Budgets," *ABA Banking Journal*, February 1984.

12. Cooper, J. A., "Dependence Effects in Unique Signal Transmission," Sandia National Laboratories Report SAND88-0394, April 1988.

3

The Physical Security Environment

The previous chapter emphasized analysis as an important security component, because it provides a systematic way to approach computer and communications security. The next problem to be faced is that there is no single context within which to address the subject. There are distinct environments, each of which appears in a different light and must be considered with some degree of independence.

3.1 BASIC SECURITY CONCEPTS

There are two basic security concepts that are important and easily visualized. These concepts are a "building block" security support structure and a "multiple barrier" configuration of security measures.

3.1.1 Support Structure for Security

A secure overall operating environment is attained, as shown in Figure 3-1, by building a support structure based on the six environments we have outlined. We can view these environments as contain-

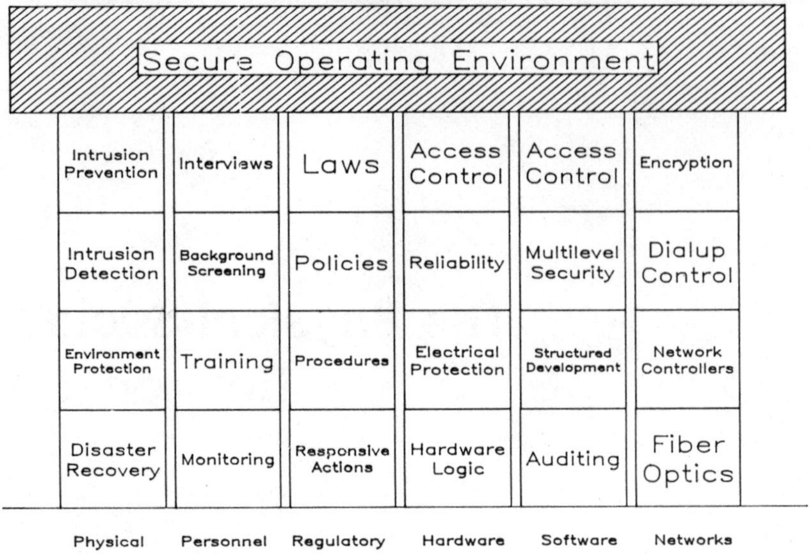

Secure Operating Environment					
Intrusion Prevention	Interviews	Laws	Access Control	Access Control	Encryption
Intrusion Detection	Background Screening	Policies	Reliability	Multilevel Security	Dialup Control
Environment Protection	Training	Procedures	Electrical Protection	Structured Development	Network Controllers
Disaster Recovery	Monitoring	Responsive Actions	Hardware Logic	Auditing	Fiber Optics
Physical	Personnel	Regulatory	Hardware	Software	Networks

Figure 3-1   Security building blocks.

ing building blocks, each of which contributes to the support structure. The arrangement of the blocks in columns illustrates the sense of independence we infer for the environments. The blocks contain a rough outline of the subjects to be addressed.

Note that an overall environment such as that portrayed can be supported to some degree without all of the building blocks. However, the more blocks used, the more solid the structure. It is appropriate to keep the analogy in mind.

Chapters 3 through 8 will be tailored to the six environments specified. For the present, we will not address these environments according to the systematic approach suggested in the first two chapters. The approach taken here will be to organize material around the features that contribute to each environment, because this appears to give a more effective presentation. For this reason, Figure 3-1 is a more suitable outline of the next six chapters than is Figure 2-1. However, it is important to keep the analytical structure in mind. In Chapter 9, we will return to the basic approach in order to consolidate and coordinate the overall subject.

3.1.2 Multiple Security Barriers Concept

Another useful visual aid is given in Figure 3-2. A protected entity, such as the data at the center of the figure, can be surrounded with any number of security barriers. The reason for considering this idea is that it is very difficult to construct completely effective security measures. It is common practice to overcome this weakness by constructing multiple barriers. A familiar example is that automated teller machine (ATM) cards are mailed separately from their associated personal identification numbers (PINs). We will find the multiple barrier idea useful but will provide some cautions about indiscriminately applying the concept.

In addition, the figure conveys the idea that physical security is frequently the first barrier with which an adversary is confronted. For this reason, we will address the physical security environment first. There are seven main aspects to physical security, each of which will be the subject of a section in this chapter. These aspects are intrusion prevention, intrusion detection, proper information destruction, power protection, fire protection, water protection, and contingency planning.

3.2 INTRUSION PREVENTION

We have all thought about intrusion prevention because we need to protect our personal property. Many of the same measures we may have considered for our own property are also appropriate in a computer and communications security environment. These include fences, guards, window barriers, lights, and locks. The differences when applying these concepts to computers and communications may be slight if the facilities involved are relatively inexpensive or have relatively relaxed security requirements. However, most facilities do not meet this description. The result is that more technical sophistication, more complexity, more expense, and more reliability are frequently appropriate.

In thinking about security for our personal possessions, most of us realize that the threat is real because of personal experience or because of the incidents reported in the news media. As reported incidents repeatedly illustrate [2], computers and communication media are subject to real threats also.

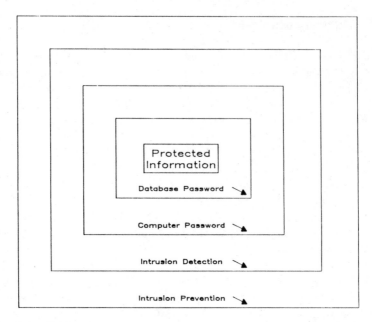

Figure 3-2   Multiple-barrier strategy.

The threats of physical penetration lead to several vulnerabilities. Among these are theft of hardware; theft of software; compromising data (copying or reading); damage to or alteration of hardware, software, or data; and misappropriation of resources (theft of computer or communication time or capabilities).

As an example, a computer and a satellite dish at Vandenburg Air Force Base in California were damaged in 1987 by a "peace activist" [19]. The attacker gained entry to the computer room by breaking a window and attacked the computer with a hammer, bolt cutters, a crowbar, and a cordless power drill. She left a poem, a pansy, a box of Mrs. Field's cookies, and a "have a nice day" note. She later turned herself in.

One of the most dramatic incidents involving physical security occurred in 1979, when $10.2 million was transferred illegally from a California bank to the thief's account. Although the case involved a complicated series of information accumulation and fortuitous (for the thief) events, a breakdown in physical security was one of the major contributors to the theft. The necessary telephone authorization code and the account number where the $10.2 million resided were discovered following unauthorized entry to the bank's wire transfer room. This was possible because the bank was carrying out extensive remodeling, and had not yet implemented all physical security measures. Intrusion protection consciousness on the part of bank personnel could probably have prevented the theft.

However, intrusion protection is almost totally a delaying measure. This means that an adversary, given enough time and resources, can penetrate any physical barrier. The effectiveness of the measure is therefore strongly dependent on the time delay an adversary will incur in overcoming the barrier. The only caveat is that some barriers are easier to couple to other security measures, such as intrusion alarms and response actions.

3.2.1 Facility Deemphasis

One of the more subtle physical security improvements of recent years is that protected facilities are physically less obvious. At one time, pride in new computer installations was responsible for public display of computer rooms and other facilities. Most people now consider this practice to be inadvisable. Computer locations may be on upper floors of multistory buildings. Contemporary computer rooms seldom have windows. This is because windows are extremely vulnerable to forced entry, and they tend to advertise the presence of computers. Where windows are used, they must be fortified with secure bars or alarmed (see next section). Eliminating windows can solve more than one problem. In one incident [1], a vandal threw five disk packs from an upper-floor computer room. Computer communications avenues are now usually made as inconspicuous as possible. These obfuscation techniques certainly provide a cost-effective contribution to security.

3.2.2 Fences

Fences of various types are commonly used as barriers. There are some important points to be made about the use of this measure. First, even protruding barbed-wire top structures are not effective deterrents against a determined adversary with minimal padding and some athletic ability. In addition, the vulnerability of wire fences to wire cutters is obvious. Where security requirements are stringent, enhancements must be considered. In the next section, we will address intrusion detection, which can be applied to fences as well as other barriers. Other forms of enhancement include multiple rings of fences, possibly with intervening guards, dogs, or intrusion detection.

3.2.3 Multiple Barriers

The common use of multiple security barriers (as mentioned at the beginning of this chapter) is an important and useful strategy, but should not be accepted without examination. One reason for using multiple barriers is that some measures have inherent weaknesses that cannot be overcome within practical expense constraints. An example is the background investigations for security clearances. Since this technique cannot assure that protected data will not be misused by "cleared" personnel, password access control is ordinarily added as a supplemental barrier.

Cost is often a reason for using multiple barriers. It might appear that since it is difficult to make any barrier completely effective, multiple barriers are more cost-effective than single barriers. This is not always true, as will be demonstrated below.

A numeric illustration of the performance of a multiple-barrier strategy can be provided by the following model. Assume that there are n possible security barriers, each having a successful protection probability of $1 - e^{-c_i}$, where c_i represents the cost spent on the ith security barrier. This model is chosen to approximate the case we intuitively expect, wherein increasing expenditures result in decreasing increments of improvement.

Now compare using one barrier to achieve a probability goal, p_g, with the strategy of using n barriers to achieve the same goal.

Using one barrier (the ith), $p_g = 1 - e^{-c_i}$. Using multiple barriers,

$$p_g = 1 - (1 - p_1)(1 - p_2) \ldots (1 - p_n)$$
$$= 1 - e^{-(c_1 + c_2 \ldots + c_n)} \tag{3-1}$$

Equating the two expressions, we find:

$$c_i = c_1 + c_2 + \ldots + c_n \tag{3-2}$$

This means (for the model we used) that one barrier at a given total expenditure can provide the same protection as multiple barriers combining to the same total expenditure.

This calculation is not intended to discredit the multiple barrier concept, but rather to reinforce the contention that intuition may mislead one as to the benefits. A model with a more precipitous decline in the security provided by additional expenses might have yielded a more favorable payoff for multiple barriers (see Problem 1).

3.2.4 Fence Vulnerabilities

The vulnerabilities of fences include the ease with which destructive devices can be thrown over, the possibility that credentials can be passed back through the barriers ("passback" attack), and their inability to protect against airborne penetration (e.g., helicopter, hang glider, parachute). As illustration that the airborne attack potential is realistic, an Arab guerilla penetrated a fortified Israeli army camp by hang glider in November 1987, and then killed six people and wounded seven. Less than a month later, a helicopter landed inside a maximum-security prison near London and picked up two prisoners for escape. There have been three prison escapes and four escape attempts using helicopters during the past three years in the U.S.

3.2.5 Walls

Another physical barrier for which the need can be easily overlooked is walls (including fire walls) that extend beyond the ceiling to the roof. One problem is that ceilings frequently comprise removable panels,[*] and space between the ceiling and the roof can be exploited by a penetrator. Fire walls are most effective against fires and penetrators if they extend all the way to the roof. This vulnerability also applies to any other walls that appear to be barriers from floor level, when they offer no barrier above ceiling level.

3.2.6 Mechanical Locks

Mechanical and electronic locks are useful for perimeter control, room control, communication media, access restriction, and direct locking of computer and peripheral equipment. Some personal computers now include locks as a fundamental security measure. Many standard mechanical locks can be readily "picked" by experienced people because of the ordinary one-dimensional tumbler construction. However, some currently available locks have unusual characteristics. For example, one company makes a "twisting tumbler" lock that requires a key with a three-dimensional key edge utilizing sloping grooves. The objective is to make picking difficult, and also to

---

[*]   Ceiling clips can be used to protect an area with removable panels against surreptitious entry.

inhibit key duplication. Standard key blanks and key duplicating equipment cannot be used to copy these keys.

3.2.7 Electronic Locks

Electronic locks (as well as mechanical push-button combination locks) are often used to control access to buildings and rooms containing computer and communications facilities. One common problem is that entry codes are frequently not difficult for an observer to read. Electronic locks now available overcome many previous lock problems. For example, locks may display on a screen touch-activated digits in locations that are randomly set for each separate user. Visibility is directionally restricted to near-perpendicular observation to hinder unauthorized viewing. Multiple incorrect tries may result in increasing time delays or alarms to authorities. User identification codes may be incorporated, along with auditable records. Card-activated and ROM-key electronic locks are also available. Obviously, electronic locks must have the same mechanical robustness as a mechanical lock in order to prevent physical bypass.

3.2.8 Guards[*]

Protective security force (guard) personnel are useful in a wide variety of ways in security programs. One obvious need is to monitor the points that control entry into fenced or otherwise secured areas. Commonly, those seeking entry must present photo badges to the guards for examination. The weaknesses of this approach are well known: Badges can be counterfeited; personnel can be disguised to match a badge photograph; and guards who are under some pressure to move people through the entry points quickly may become ineffective. Guards can also easily become bored with the routine and repetitive task of checking badges. (Personal identification will be examined in Chapter 6.)

Guards are also useful in escorting visitors and maintenance personnel, in patrolling fence or barrier areas, in checking rooms that contain equipment, and in monitoring intrusion detection and surveillance systems. Patrol frequency has an important relationship to

---

[*]   We will use the familiar term "guard," although the usual convention is now to call armed security personnel "security inspectors."

the time available to an adversary in-between guard presence. Irregular appearances at any location provide a deterrent in that an adversary has more difficulty predicting the time available for surreptitious activities.

3.2.9 Lights

Lights are a useful tool for security personnel because they improve surveillance visibility. (Surveillance will be considered under the topic of intrusion detection.) However, lights also contribute to intrusion prevention through deterrence and they can facilitate perimeter alarm assessment. It is possible to activate lights on intrusion detection, on timer control, on ambient light control, or manually.

3.2.10 Automated Entry Booths

With some kinds of automated entry booths, entry control can be exercised remotely (utilizing closed-circuit television and electrically controlled locks), which conserves personnel. An additional advantage of remotely operated entry booths is the separation of the guards from the users, thereby protecting guards from some types of attack and duress.

These entry booths also can utilize picture badges for the identification of entering personnel, and video recording for audit or investigative records. Automated entry requires (in addition to automated booths, central control, communication of video, voice, and control functions) fault-tolerance provisions and provisions for bypass (necessary, for example, if a person becomes trapped in a booth or has a handicap that prevents normal use of the devices). Emergency or standby power can be an important option. Logging capabilities are also useful. For example, investigations of incidents or peculiar behavior patterns are enhanced by such records. Two-person guard control functions are useful in many cases, because one-person control is vulnerable to an insider threat (see Chapter 4).

3.2.11 Communications

All of the above guard-related functions can be enhanced by systems for communication among the personnel involved. Secure (encrypted) communications are sometimes beneficial. In addition to eavesdropping by an adversary, the threat of deception and jamming must be considered. These threats will take on even more significance when we address networks in Chapter 8.

3.2.12 Psychological Deterrence

The use of guard forces also contributes to psychological deterrence, as do several other measures that are easily understood by the public. Awareness of guards, alarms, and response actions has a deterring psychological effect on most adversaries and a supportive psychological effect on responsible employees. This is why alarm warning stickers on homes and cars are effective. The same effects are associated with airport security checks. In all of the above cases, one must recognize that a determined adversary may not be deterred. This means that psychological deterrents almost always need to be supplemented.

3.2.13 Supplies

Another vulnerability frequently overlooked is the dependence on remotely supplied facilities. These facilities include power, water, telephone, computer communications services, mail delivery, vendor servicing, and food supplies. The most physically secure facility can be affected to some degree by interrupting these supplies if the physical protection considerations do not extend beyond the obvious facility perimeter.

3.2.14 Human Factors

A final point to be made in this section is that, if human controls are used to provide intrusion prevention, human factors concepts must be carefully considered. For example, a London chemical company that had extensive physical security protection for its data tapes was victimized in 1977 by one of its own employees [5]. (As we have pointed out, this is not uncommon.)

The employee was a computer-operations supervisor who was passed over for promotion. He conspired, with a systems analyst accomplice, to remove the company's most valuable data tapes and disks. The supervisor was authorized to check tapes and disks out of their secure location, and he did so. He also checked out the backup media from a second site. With a total of 48 disks and 54 tapes, the men demanded a ransom payment from the company for the equivalent of half a million dollars. The company agreed and arranged to pay the men for the return of their data, but the deal was not completed. Scotland Yard, alerted to the proposed exchange, intercepted and arrested the men. The lesson is that the best security measures can be negated if the people responsible for their maintenance and use are not fully aware of the goals of the measures.

3.3   INTRUSION DETECTION

Since intrusion prevention is difficult, and must be considered to be a delaying action, intrusion detection is an important feature. Intrusion detection can be approached from the viewpoints of perimeter entry detection, room entry detection, and surveillance. Each involves guard and frequently local police forces, coupled in most cases with automated equipment.

3.3.1   Disturbance Sensors

There are several categories of perimeter detection devices. One is fence-mounted disturbance sensors. These can be electromechanical switches (such as position-sensitive mercury switches), piezoelectric transducers (which convert strain to electrical energy), geophones (to detect intrusion sounds), and electric cables (to detect position changes through impedance).

Electric field sensors detect changes in the electric field due to the geometry change between a field-generation cable and a field-sense cable. These systems have a workable length of about 1000 feet. Although human penetration attempts generally create higher amplitude and higher frequency disturbance signals than natural events, all of the above sensors are vulnerable to nonadversarial disturbances caused by, for example, blowing rain, sand, or sleet, or deformation due to ice accumulations.

3.3.2 Spurious Alarms

The preceding types of disturbances may cause spurious (invalid) alarms, a problem faced in using any intrusion sensor. A system that gives too many spurious alarms tends to be discredited as a source of valid alarms. There is generally a tradeoff between the probability of detecting an adversary and the probability of spurious alarms (see Problem 2). This tradeoff is frequently embodied in the sensitivity of the sensor, which requires judicious and frequently reevaluated setting. Another enhancement that helps in working this tradeoff is "signature analysis," which means automated processing to try to distinguish the characteristics of a true adversary from a natural occurrence.

3.3.3 Barrier Detectors

Another perimeter detection device, called a "barrier detector," creates a beam of energy, which, when interrupted, enables penetration sensing. Businesses commonly use these detectors implemented with light beams to alert employees to the presence of customers. The same principle is applicable to a variety of less-obvious sensors. For example, microwave or infrared beams, although detectable with the proper instruments, are not detectable by human vision. One of the problems associated with the high-frequency sources (e.g., infrared) is that high-frequency (above the GHz range) electromagnetic energy is absorbed significantly by fog, rain, snow, and dust.

One of the limitations of barrier detectors is the line-of-sight geometry required. If there are no obstructions or dead spots, these types of sensors can span about 1000 feet. The false alarm vulnerabilities include animals; blowing rain, sleet, and sand; and vegetation that may be moved by the wind. Signature analysis capabilities are again important enhancements.

3.3.4 Buried-Line Sensors

Buried-line sensors are underground devices or wires that sense seismic, pressure, or magnetic signals. The range is limited to at most about 100 feet, and the seismic and pressure transducers receive lower signal levels if the ground is frozen. Animals and nearby vehicular traffic are the main false-alarm threats.

3.3.5 Capacitance Sensors

Capacitance proximity sensors are another useful device, especially if the area to be protected is not too great. The change in capacitance due to a nearby physical presence (which changes the dielectric characteristics in the field between the capacitor plates) is sensed by circuitry in the same way (but on a much larger scale) that many elevator floor selection buttons respond to the immediate presence of a person's finger.

3.3.6 Active Sensors

There are several types of perimeter penetration alarm devices that are "active" (emitting continuous energy), such as millimeter-wave radar, laser radar (sometimes called "LIDAR"), and closed-circuit TV (CCTV). CCTV may have sensitivity in the visual or infrared spectrum. Although human surveillance of the returned signal is feasible, automatic processing (for example, with sensitivity to the presence of Doppler shifts) is common. Human interaction with these sensors will be explored at the end of this section when we examine surveillance. For "monostatic" systems, the source and the receiver are at the same location. This is almost always the case for CCTV, but radar systems can be monostatic, bistatic (source and receiver separated), or multistatic (multiple interacting sources and receivers).

A monostatic radar and most CCTV surveillance systems have ranges on the order of a kilometer. Doppler signatures of about 0.1 m/sec are discernible. Multistatic radar systems use a grid of transmitters and receivers to "bathe" an area with energy, thereby considerably extending the range potential and reducing the instantaneous directional limitations of monostatic systems.

Laser radars have inherently better resolution than millimeter-wave radars because of the high (near optical) frequencies but suffer the attenuation limitations of high frequencies in the presence of rain, snow, sleet, and dust. Common Doppler frequency sense capabilities are in the range of 0.01 m/sec.

3.3.7 The Doppler Effect

In order to understand the Doppler frequency sensitivity ranges, it is useful to express the Doppler effect mathematically. Relativistic considerations require Lorentz transformation for an exact solution, but a simplified approach is used here to illustrate the principle. First, consider motion with a velocity v toward a source of frequency f. Note that the wavelength is dependent on the propagation velocity of electromagnetic energy c, and the apparent wavelength of the reflected energy is reduced by the motion. The expression for the wavelength of the reflected energy can be formulated in terms of the time t for a complete cycle of energy to contact the target:

$$\lambda_r = ct - vt \tag{3-3}$$

where λ_r is the wavelength of the reflected energy, v is the velocity of motion, and c is the velocity of propagation.

Assume that the source wavelength is the sum of ct and vt, that is, $\lambda = ct + vt$. Substituting into Equation 3-3 and solving for the difference frequency (the Doppler frequency), we obtain:

$$f_d = c/\lambda_r - f \approx 2vf/c \tag{3-4}$$

For timely and efficient processing, Doppler frequencies must be on the order of 10 Hz or more (only about 10 cycles would be available for processing in an elapsed second). At radar frequencies (e.g., 10 GHz), the solution of Equation 3-4 for v results in a limiting value of about 0.1 m/sec. At infrared frequencies (e.g., 3×10^{11}), the limiting velocity is about 0.5 cm/sec. These calculations show that the required frequency depends on the desired sensitivity to motion.

Signal processing is not the only area to which automation has been applied. The current interest in robotics has made "security robots" feasible. The aim of these devices is to create a mobile platform on a tanklike vehicle that will convey sensors around an area, similar to a guard on patrol. The advantages of human judgment are incorporated in the processing of sensed information, communication is provided with the human guard force, and the personal safety of the guard force is enhanced.

3.3.8 Communication

For all of the perimeter sensors mentioned above, secure communication of the signals from the sensors to the guards' control center is important. The approaches generally used are to make the communication media as inaccessible as possible, and to incorporate tamper alarms and live monitoring by personnel. Another concern is reliable operation, which demands tolerance to environments (such as extreme operating temperatures) and requires periodic maintenance and testing. Power reliability is often attained by incorporating battery or Uninterruptible Power System (UPS) backup. The subject of UPS will be examined in detail in Section 3.5.4.

3.3.9 Room Intrusion

The second category of intrusion detection to be considered is room (or building) entry. This family of devices is based on principles very similar to those for home or automobile penetration alarm devices.

Room intrusion detection can utilize some of the same types of sensors as perimeter detection (capacitance sensors, disturbance sensors) and some of the same types of devices commonly seen in home systems (magnetic window and door switches, ultrasonic motion detectors). Ultrasonic detectors typically operate in the 20–30 kHz range and sense Doppler frequencies in the 20–700 Hz range. Ultrasonic sensors can be active (radiating energy and sensing Doppler shifts in the returned energy) or passive (listening for sonic frequencies in the 20–30 kHz region).

Pressure mats are frequently used, since they are simple, effective, and inexpensive. However, they are also easy to defeat if their presence is known.

Passive infrared sensors are also available. These have the capability to detect the warmth of a human, when human infrared radiation is added to the background infrared spectrum.

As was the case for perimeter sensors, these room intrusion detection systems are not perfect. Spurious alarms due to mice, window blinds, etc., moving in the wind, etc., must be considered. The false alarm probability must be balanced against the detection probability. The tradeoff can be made more profitable by utilizing appropriate signal processing. Also in ways similar to the case of perimeter sensors, considerations regarding communication, tamper resistance,

power, and reliability are important. But environmental requirements are inherently less severe because of the inside environment.

3.3.10 Surveillance

The final intrusion detection category we will consider is surveillance. Although surveillance can be automated, we will address the
topic under the assumption that real-time human interaction is involved. As previously mentioned, the monitored image can be created
through the use of radar or CCTV. Some of the considerations for
both are illumination level, sensor sensitivity, dwell times on each
"scene" or direction, magnification level of displayed scene, power,
communication, and maintenance.

One of the most important periods for surveillance is night time.
Since CCTV depends on reflected energy, some form of illumination
must be furnished. The most common type (unless psychological
deterrence is an objective) is "black light" or infrared. This frequency
range is not detectable by the human eye, but can be readily
processed electronically to provide a display image. This technique
has the advantage of furnishing complete information to surveillance
personnel, with no obvious warning to adversaries that they are
being observed.

Enhancement features on CCTV systems include sensitivity enhancement and phase locking circuitry. Phase locking prevents roll-
ing images due to switching cameras (and thereby losing
synchronization) in multicamera display systems. As another enhancement, source signatures are useful to help identify the image
under view.

3.3.11 Penalties

A final note on this topic is that alerting security personnel is not
the only response to intrusion detection. It is also possible to invoke
penalties, frequently under automated control. These may include
penalties against the intruder, such as capture; penalties prohibiting
subsequent barrier penetration of any kind; and penalties against
the possible target, for example by destroying protected data.

3.4 INFORMATION DESTRUCTION

It may seem anomalous to many who spend time protecting information and finding ways to prevent its destruction, but a commonly exploited vulnerability is created by failure of an information custodian to properly destroy information. Some of the ways in which this failure can lead to information compromise are outlined here.

Information is retained in nonvolatile memory media such as magnetic tapes until overwritten (and sometimes beyond that point, as discussed below). If a long file is overwritten by a short file, information may remain beyond the end-of-file marker that is not obvious but can be retrieved. Similar reasoning shows that information in memory that has been given an "erase" command is not really erased from most computer memory (e.g., hard disk or diskette). The logical pointers to the memory locations are merely removed. This fact has enabled development of the widely used Norton utility routines for the recovery of apparently lost data. Similar techniques can also allow unintended information compromises.

It is tempting also to consider information disposed of in a waste basket as "destroyed." Many compromises of valuable information have occurred because of this misconception or because of lack of any thought about the matter. In a widely publicized case that developed during the 1970s, a southern California telephone company was seriously damaged financially because too much useful information was exposed to an adversary through improperly discarded information.

The principal was a teenaged proprietor of an electronics business who found items in the telephone company trash bin. He picked up damaged equipment for resale by his company and noticed operating instructions for the company's automated parts ordering system. He also observed that equipment was delivered to the incoming dock and left there with almost no physical security safeguards. Combining this information with facts gathered through telephone calls and by touring the company (posing as a reporter), he began placing bogus orders through a touchtone telephone card dialer to the company computer. He then picked up the ordered equipment on arrival at the dock and sold it through his own company. In the final stages of the operation, the phone company was covering its shortages by ordering equipment from the perpetrator's company (not realizing that it was buying its own equipment). When the scam was broken, the phone company admitted to $65,000 in losses, but this is almost certainly a great underestimation [29].

An illustrative example of insecure disposal by personnel of a Las Vegas bank in the early 1980s was publicized [46]. Confidential information displayed on computer printouts was intended for disposal. An accident during the disposal process resulted in the information being strewn down heavily traveled Desert Inn Road and being turned in to local newspapers.

In both of these cases, attention paid to information destruction techniques would have prevented the losses. Some of the techniques are discussed below (overwriting, degaussing, burning, and shredding).

3.4.1 Overwriting

Information destruction by overwriting is common, and automated software routines (e.g., Norton Utilities "Wipedisk") are available to aid the process. Overwriting typically involves multiple overwrites of alternating magnetic polarity signals, for reasons discussed below.

It seems straightforward to destroy information by overwriting. However, there are subtleties to consider. The first problem is to be certain that the overwrite does not stop short of the end of information. A magnetic tape may well have information written beyond the current end-of-file mark, and disk media may have information beyond any current file pointers. Therefore, it is not appropriate to merely change existing information to all "zeros," for example. A safe approach is to overwrite the entire medium. Disk "formatting" does not safely obscure all information. Since overwriting is time-consuming, other approaches are more commonly used (see below), except for hard-disk assemblies. Before addressing these other approaches, it is important to consider the potential for residual information that may survive an overwrite.

Many forms of memory media retain a latent image of the preceding bit value following a write insertion of a new bit value. This is basically due to inability to achieve complete saturation of the magnetization or charge state that is being written. A changing bit may be driven slightly less into saturation than an unchanging bit. Although this effect has no consequence in the basic operation of the system, it has the potential for exploitation by an adversary with sophisticated equipment. This is the reason for the common requirement that overwrite involve a repeated (e.g., three times) pattern of alternation between one and zero.

3.4.2 Degaussing

Because of the time required for overwriting magnetic storage media, especially in security environments that require repeated overwrites, bulk erasure devices are popular. Where used within their specification limits, they are also secure [30]. Magnetic fields in the storage medium of 1500 Oersteds may be required. These bulk erasure devices are called "degaussers," and they are available for degaussing magnetic tapes, diskettes, fixed disks, some types of disk packs, cartridges, and drums. The basic principle is to drive the storage medium repeatedly (through a strong oscillatory magnetic field) to saturation.

Some development work shows promise for the ability to degauss large hard-disk assemblies. It is feasible to produce field intensities up to 1700 Oersteds throughout a five cubic foot volume [44].

3.4.3 Burning

Burning can be used to destroy information recorded on paper, punched cards, magnetic media, and semiconductor memory. Obviously, one disadvantage of burning is that reuse of the storage medium is denied. One caution is that information can sometimes be recovered from a nondestructive or incomplete burn. For example, physically intact paper ash can be examined by sophisticated technology to recover printed information not visible to the eye.

3.4.4 Shredding

Shredders can be used to cut paper, microfiche, diskettes, and similar relatively soft materials. Shredding devices are available in various size, capacity, cost, and volume-handling categories, all of which have security implications [31,32]. Cutting strategies include straight-cut or stripping, cross-cut or particle producing, "disintegrators" (repeated cutting until particles pass through a small screen), and "pulpers" (wetting and grinding of particles). More complete destruction is generally associated with better security. However, since time and cost are also factors in a balanced approach to security, another series of tradeoffs must be considered.

Most cut sizes available range from 1/4 inch to 1/32 inch. Below this size, the product may be called "dust" or "mulch." A variety of throat sizes, simultaneous page count capacity and feet per hour rates are available. Weights for the devices range from tens of pounds to thousands of pounds.

The smallest and simplest models are light-duty cutters called "electric wastebaskets" or personal or office shredders. These are available for a few hundred dollars. Heavy-duty floor models or volume shredders generally handle more volume of material per hour and cost a few thousand dollars. "Bulk" or production shredders can cost between $10,000 and $20,000.

Human factors features have also been considered by shredder designers. Noise abatement, safety, handling of staples, paper clips, etc., and displays for communication to users about problems such as full receptacles are common design features.

3.5 POWER PROTECTION

The remaining aspects of physical security to be considered in this chapter do not directly involve personnel as threats. The threats to be considered here are part of the environment (which includes air conditioning, humidity, presence of quality power, and freedom from damage due to fire, water, earthquakes). Computers and the other electronics involved in communications are very sensitive to the environment.

The overall electrical environment includes current and voltage delivered to the hardware in a variety of ways. We have chosen to defer most of these until Chapter 6 on hardware security. The discussion here will be limited to problems conveyed on the power system.

In addition to the effects mentioned above, other entities requiring environmental protection include operating, support, and user personnel; supporting equipment, such as supplies and tape libraries; the equipment housing or physical enclosure; and management personnel.

In this chapter, we will emphasize power quality and continuity, fire protection, water protection, and contingency planning, although air conditioning, humidity control, and earthquake-resistant construction [41,42] are also important.

3.5.1 Power Problems

Power quality in the United States is excellent, when measured for its support of general home and business needs. Outages are rare and the voltage uniformity is demonstrated by, for example, almost continuously uniform light illumination. Considerable effort is expended to keep utility power within 10% of nominal voltage. However, this quality is not always sufficient for computers, even though most computers tolerate at least 10% deviations from nominal voltage.

Some of the problems are:

1. Connections from the utility lines sometimes carry power over a considerable distance before it reaches a computer. These intrafacility routes can lower voltage unacceptably close to the design margin. The American National Standards Institute (ANSI) specifies that nominal 120 V power can drop by 8.3% by the time it reaches the user's entrance and by an additional 3.4% due to normal intrabuilding impedances (within cables, connectors, and circuit breakers or fuses) [9].

2. Load switching under unusual conditions can lower voltage significantly as the power company tries to keep as many users in service as possible. For example, a crucial switch or transformer failure can cause a large number of facilities to be switched onto an already heavily loaded grid. This was the general scenario that led to the massive northeastern U.S. and Canada power grid collapse in 1965. A power failure in an Ontario plant triggered a series of load distribution switchovers that could not be supported by the grid capacity. Parts of eight northeastern states and two southeast Canada provinces were blacked out for a considerable time [6]. Similar situations continue to develop [28], but sensitivity to grid collapse has resulted in provisions to withdraw utility sections from the grid upon signs of overload. Unfortunately, the withdrawal switchover can also cause transient quality problems (discussed subsequently).

3. In 1975, New York City suffered a loss of utility power due to two lightning discharges [43]. Most of Seattle was without power for four days in 1988. Although blackouts (complete loss of utility power) are rare, some computing functions are of such crucial nature that any blackout probability is of concern. Examples are national defense computers and air traffic control computers.

4. There are many sources of electrical transients (short-duration deviations) that a utility cannot completely prevent from entering a facility. These sources include lightning, transient loads

due to heavy-current-use equipment and electromagnetically coupled energy from sources such as radars.

In situations where any of these problems cannot be tolerated, secure operation is jeopardized, and protective measures must be sought. This section will address some of the techniques that can be considered. The tools we will examine are line monitors, voltage regulators, uninterruptible power systems, surge protectors, isolation transformers, grounding, and filters.

3.5.2 Line Monitors

Line monitors are not intended to provide direct protective measures, but they can be crucial in the overall scheme of protection. These devices can be used to identify the source of intermittent computer errors and to determine specific needs for other types of protective equipment.

The cost of line monitors varies from about $300 to $2000 [14], depending on the accuracy, number of parameters to be measured, sensitivity, amount of memory, degree of automation, etc.

Although line monitors are useful to obtain data pertinent to particular facilities, monitors have been used to compile data that is of general interest, and some of the most pertinent results will be reviewed here.

IBM data reveal [20] that power anomalies on a typical power line occur nearly twice daily, and IBM and AT&T data suggest [7] that approximately 50% of computer downtime is due to power problems. An AT&T Bell Laboratories study of Bell Operating Companies, Western Electric, and the AT&T Long Lines Department reported that 87% of the electrical anomalies measured were voltage sags. Another study [13] found that 11% of the measured electrical problems were voltage sags exceeding 10% of nominal voltage. Blackouts are reported to cause about 1–5% of the problems. Although it is not uncommon for blackouts to last 10 minutes or more, 50% last six seconds or less. These data suggest that computers can be and are affected greatly by the insufficient (or nonexistent) voltage of utility-furnished power.

When computer problems occur, they include RAM memory loss about 75% of the time, disk crashes about 25% of the time, and erratic hardware execution or hardware failure about 20% of the time

[47]. Overvoltage is possible, but rare (approximately 1% of the deviations). One of the greatest consequences of overvoltage is electronic hardware damage.

Other irregularities revealed by monitor data are generally called "impulses," "spikes," "transients," or "noise." These are relatively high-frequency deviations in the form of pulses or damped oscillations. The frequency content of these irregularities is typically in the kHz to MHz range. Power utility control cannot ordinarily go beyond the 100 Hertz range (i.e., no appreciable compensation is possible for high frequencies). Some of the specific data reported [13] show that a few spikes in the range of several thousand volts can be expected on a line during the period of a year. These transients can upset memory, cause hardware malfunctions, and damage electronics. Of course, there are techniques to lessen these potential problems, and these will be discussed in the following sections.

3.5.3 Voltage Regulators

Voltage regulators are useful in controlling power deviations (surges, sags, transients). The basic regulating operation depends on utilizing negative feedback to maintain voltage uniformity. This is most commonly done through electronic circuitry, but may also involve constant-voltage transformers (CVTs). CVTs have nonlinear response to current demands through ferroresonance, which can control output voltage within ±2% for most applications.

The cost of voltage regulators depends on the power capacity and the regulation quality. The general cost range is in the vicinity of 25 cents per VA (volt-ampere) of capacity, for the most basic regulators. More controlled regulation and noise isolation can be incorporated for about 50 cents per VA [13].

The goal for voltage regulators is generally to keep the voltage within about 8% of nominal ("static regulation") for supply voltages ranging up to 15% higher than nominal and down to 25% lower than nominal. Most regulators have sufficient capacitance to carry through a few milliseconds dropout and provide some noise attenuation.

Another measure of interest is the response of regulators to sudden voltage changes. This "dynamic" regulation is usually targeted to hold voltages within about 10% of nominal until the transient condition stabilizes to static regulation conditions (approximately 10 milliseconds).

3.5.4   Uninterruptible Power Systems

Sometimes power loss is disastrous, even if for only a few milliseconds. Logic failures can occur that alter programming steps and electronic damage can occur. "Disk crashes" (disk read/write heads damaging disks through contact) are a threat. Disk heads typically ride a small fraction of a millimeter above the disk surface. Power loss of 5–10 milliseconds can cause the head to contact and damage the disk surface. Up to 30% of power failures may cause disk damage in unprotected systems [10].

Personnel security systems can also be affected by power loss, but the time of loss is not as crucial as for computing equipment. This vulnerability is the reason that burglar alarm systems, for example, have backup power sources.

For these reasons, uninterruptible power systems (UPSs) are important to the integrity of computer operations. A UPS is a power system that has the capability to maintain power to a system when the utility power fails. UPS protection can now also be applied to LANs (see Chapter 8) [48].

Since generators (e.g., diesel-fueled generators) and inverters (e.g., dc-battery-to-ac-voltage converters) are also means through which power can be generated, it is important to make a distinction between these sources and UPS sources. The distinction is, simply stated, that the UPS is designed to minimize the time, risk, and effects of switching to an alternate source of power. The intent of the UPS is also to provide interim power until utility power is restored, until graceful shutdown is accomplished, or until a long-term source is brought on line.

There are two basic designs for UPS configurations. The most useful, and in a sense the most pure, is portrayed in Figure 3-3. This UPS system is intended to provide continuous power with no interruption in the event of utility failure. The key concept in Figure 3-3 is that an inverter is kept continuously online, furnishing power to the computer or other protected system. The dc inverter input is available from either of two sources: an ac-to-dc converter (rectifier) or a bank of batteries. The purpose of the converter is to obtain power from the utility source; the purpose of the batteries is to provide power in the event of utility failure. By diode gating, these two sources have exactly the same effect on the downstream components, and there are no noticeable changes in phase, frequency, or voltage if the utility power fails. Furthermore, this isolation helps reduce the effects of spikes, surges, and brownouts. The purpose of the reverse transfer switch is to disconnect the UPS from the load in the case of

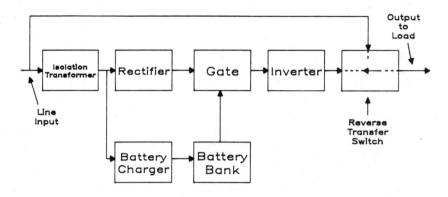

Figure 3-3   Online UPS system.

a load fault, such as a short, which would destroy the UPS and possibly the powered equipment. Under these conditions, reconnecting to the utility source is considered the best strategy for obtaining restored power as soon and as safely as possible.

Waveform quality is important for a UPS. For example, any dc component can saturate and possibly incapacitate fans and transformers.

Sufficient "in-rush" capability (startup output current capacity) is also necessary. Since the initial load may exceed by more than an order of magnitude the steady-state load current, it is crucial that a UPS have a strong starting capacity.

The system diagrammed in Figure 3-4 is frequently called a "standby power system (SPS)," an "interruptible power system (IPS)," or a "standby UPS." In this type of system, the power is furnished, as long as possible, directly from the utility. The loss of utility power triggers the inverter (typically idling at no load) as a power source and moves the forward transfer switch to replace the utility power. There is an associated power dropout time and a random change in phase. However, systems of this type are less expensive and have longer life than the online UPS. The most critical issue is whether the switchover time is sufficiently small to prevent disk damage. At present, this is difficult to accomplish, but faster switching technology and better disk systems are closing the gap.

Inverters built with ferroresonant technology (square wave or quasi-square wave driving a ferroresonant transformer) are commonly limited to systems furnishing a few kVAs, because of the size and weight involved.

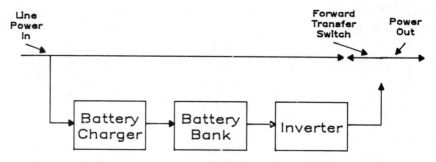

Figure 3-4   Standby UPS.

Converters and inverters can be based on rotary or solid state technology. Rotary technology means motors and generators; solid state technology means sine waves are synthesized. Rotary technology is predominant in the high power (above 50 kVA) range. Various forms of electronic inverters are used in lower-power-range systems. These usually utilize pulse-width modulation or stepped wave generation techniques.

The use of UPSs is increasing at a dramatic rate. Vendors claim that sales are growing at a rate of about 25% yearly. About 20% of financial institutions now have UPSs. Lower Manhattan is said to have the largest concentration of UPSs in the world, because of the crucial nature of Wall Street transactions [12]. Reversing earlier concentration of the UPS market, industrial companies now represent only 10% of the market and the military represents only 3% [21].

Important developments in battery technology have contributed substantially to UPS capabilities. Wet lead-acid/cadmium batteries (previously used almost exclusively) require special ventilation and periodic maintenance. These batteries generally cost about $250 each (500 Amp-hour capability) and can have 25-year lifetimes. Sealed maintenance-free batteries now have competitive performance [21]. For example, spiral Nicad and spiral lead-acid batteries have about a 10-year lifetime at a cost of about $100 each. Some, however, have Amp-hour ratings of little more than 10. Figure 3-5 shows a bank of UPS batteries.

The cost of UPS systems runs from about a hundred dollars for small-application systems such as video display terminals (VDTs) through a few hundred dollars for a microcomputer system and to tens of thousands of dollars for large systems. As a general rule of thumb, costs are in the $2.5–$3.5 per VA range [10,13].

Figure 3-5 UPS battery bank. (Photograph courtesy of Sandia National Laboratories.)

As in most other security measures we consider, the entire system must be evaluated along with the power system. For example, quality power continuity may be of no value if a power failure causes air conditioning system failure. From a risk-analysis viewpoint, the effect of power problems that could be prevented by a UPS must be weighed against the cost. This issue is becoming more important and complex because of local-area networks, file servers, and powerful new microcomputers.

3.5.5 Surge Protectors

Surges result from, for example, lightning in the vicinity, fluorescent light ballasts, and high-power loads such as welders, air conditioners, heaters, and machinery. All of these are especially likely to cause surges during transient conditions (e.g., turn-on).

Various forms of overvoltage protection are available such as arc-breakdown devices and metal-oxide varistors (which have extremely nonlinear resistance characteristics with increasing voltage).

Two frequently neglected or misunderstood characteristics of surge protectors are their energy capacity and speed of response. Energy capacity requirements depend upon the source. For example, a near-by direct lightning strike would deliver much higher energy than a passing mobile CB source. Generally, surge protectors are selected for high-energy-handling capability (approximately a thousand joules) where the overall power transmitted is high (e.g., at the power service entrance point). A personal computer (PC) may be protected by a much lower-energy device (a few hundred millijoules).

Manufacturers frequently specify power and time rather than energy, but the conversion is calculated by: energy (Joules) = power (Watts) × time (seconds). Most devices that handle less than a hundred millijoules are of marginal value, even for a small PC.

Arc-breakdown devices handle energy well, but suffer from slow response. This is because the voltage at which breakdown occurs is affected by the rate of application of the voltage (the "impulse ratio" effect). A very fast rising voltage may begin to initiate an arc break-down, but can increase to a much higher voltage before the break-down completes the protective diversion of energy (see Problem 4). This effect is very apparent in air-breakdown or gas-breakdown devices. For effective protection, response time should be approximately a nanosecond.

The impulse ratio effect can be well mitigated by "dielectric stimulated" breakdown [27], where the surface of a dielectric with a relatively high dielectric coefficient is used to increase electric field concentration in air or a gas. The protective mechanism in varistor devices depends on resistive conduction and therefore gives faster response. Varistor protectors suffer somewhat from aging, however, and therefore must be monitored. This is the reason that a colored indicator is usually provided. Varistor protection for computers will receive further attention in Chapter 6 under the topic of hardware security.

3.5.6 Filters

Filters are similar to surge protectors in that they divert unwanted energy toward a harmless path (usually to "ground"). Most filters combine capacitors with inductors (or inductive transformers). However, the specific selection of components and configuration depends on the characteristics of the unwanted signal. In addition to energy, the important characteristics are spectral frequency content and "mode" of entry to the system. The mode of entry is commonly referred to as "common mode" (CM) or "differential mode" (DM).

In order to assess the difference between CM noise and DM noise, one can picture three lines for the delivery of single-phase power, as is typical in commercial power systems. The "high" side is the black "hot" wire, the "low" side is the white wire (nominally at ground potential), and the ground wire is the green wire, which is most closely associated with ground potential (see subsequent grounding discussion). CM noise appears on both the high and low side, referenced to ground. DM noise appears between the high and low side.

One common misconception is that CM noise is easily removed by transformers (which are typically used at various points in the service route). However, the effect of transformers is limited to relatively low frequencies (typically less than one MHz) and may be subverted by recreation of the noise in the secondary. Nevertheless, transformers are useful in low-frequency CM noise suppression.

Some of the problems that must be dealt with in using transformers or inductors are magnetic saturation at high current (in which case the coupling and filtering properties of the device are seriously degraded) and size (especially if high power must be handled).

One of the most effective ways of achieving CM filtering without saturating an inductive core is to wind high and low lines onto a core together [22]. This means that the DM fields will cancel, essentially eliminating the saturation problem. This type of winding attenuates CM noise without affecting DM noise, and a device of this type is therefore called a CM inductor. In contrast, DM filtering can be accomplished by line-to-line capacitance and ordinary series inductance. CM filtering is also possible through line-to-ground capacitance, but this is generally not as effective as a CM inductor and is therefore usually unnecessary.

Effective overall filtering depends on the characteristics of the noise present. However, a good general approach is to use line-to-line capacitance for high frequency DM noise, DM inductance facing the line input in order to filter low-frequency DM noise, and a CM choke on the load side of the filter to attenuate CM noise (see Figure 3-6).

Another important consideration is physical configuration. The filter should be afforded a low-resistance mounting to a conductive bulkhead so that coupling around the filter is unlikely.

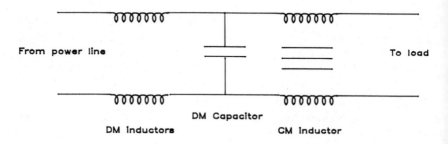

Figure 3-6   CM and DM filtering.

3.5.7 Grounding

Grounding configuration is a common problem because there is typically a relatively significant impedance between multiple "ground" points. The result is that currents induced by EM (electromagnetic) sources, signal and power return currents, and filter-diverted currents cause voltage and noise between different grounds. Although this situation is unavoidable, the consequences can be minimized by careful design.

In order to discuss grounding, we will first establish terminology. A facility ground is the ground point for the facility's primary input power. Earth ground is a metal structure sunk into the ground with a low-impedance connection to the local earth. A no-noise ground is a central point established for "star" connections to other grounds in use. This strategy helps prevent ground currents from affecting signal processing [25]. Structure ground is the equipment frame. In order to establish a star connection to no-noise ground, instrument circuitry may have to be isolated from the instrument case. Power ground is the power secondary ground where power is delivered to a facility through an isolation transformer. Signal ground is the reference point for digital and analog processing.

From a noise viewpoint, it seems attractive to use single-point (star) grounding; from a personnel safety viewpoint, it may seem best to use multipoint grounding to prevent any voltage buildup. However, it is usually possible [26] to meet safety standards in a way compatible with low noise. A strategy for accomplishing this is to run a robust ground conductor (equivalent in wire size to current-carrying conductors) within the line bus structure, where power is used by different loads. This is called a "feeder" structure [25]. Power filter displacement current can be eliminated by an isolation transformer.

Establishing an effective earth ground often requires electrolytic supply to the ground connection in such a way as to maintain low-impedance conduction over a long period of time [24]. Using natural salts that extract moisture from the air, it is possible [24] to get impedance improvements of more than a factor of 10 over a period of about 25 years.

The topic of electrical protective techniques will be revisited in Chapter 6, where hardware vulnerability to the electrical environment is addressed.

3.6 FIRE PROTECTION

Fires are one of the most serious problems in the physical security environment because of the magnitude of destruction possible and because of the frequency with which they occur. It is important to consider ways in which fires can be prevented, ways in which early detection is possible, and ways in which they can be suppressed if started. Since computers, peripherals, and communication equipment are sensitive to heat, smoke, particulate matter, and water damage, the overall environment is a severe threat. A contributing factor to the threat is the large amount of flammable material (e.g., paper listings, magnetic tape reels, and closure bands) and the sources of toxic gases in a high-temperature environment (e.g., plastics).

There are several well-known "peripheral" techniques for fire protection, such as the use of fire walls, construction with fire-resistant materials, door and vent closure systems, and location selection to avoid neighboring hazards. It is surprising to note that a crucial telephone switching center near Chicago, which suffered devastating fire damage (see Chapter 8, Section 2), had no fire walls [45]. Although these preventive techniques are important and interesting topics, we will concentrate on issues of special importance: water extinguishing, fire detection, hand extinguishers, flooding systems, and personnel evacuation.

3.6.1 Fire Fighting with Water

The most familiar method of extinguishing fire is to use water. Unfortunately, computers and peripherals are extremely sensitive to water damage, especially if under active electrical power. Automatic sprinkler systems are very attractive for protecting personnel and physical structures, but are extremely hazardous to computer equipment.

However, it is important that sprinkler technology not be discounted, even in a computer environment. These systems have been used and refined since 1878, and as a result, many safety and reliability features have been incorporated. For example, pipes and heads are subjected to hydrostatic tests prior to installation, and valve control systems to prevent filling with water until necessary are available. The result is that the use of sprinkler systems need not result in significant additional threat to computers. It is possible (and desirable) to design systems so that water is used only as a last resort to save people or the physical plant after electronics damage has become inevitable.

This leads to an interest in fire-protection techniques that are *not* threatening to computers, since everything possible should be done prior to water release. Common approaches include procedural measures to assure attentive and informed personnel, who understand and abide by important measures such as minimization of flammable materials, prohibition of smoking, and proper use of alarm and fire control equipment. Government agencies, insurance companies, and the National Fire Protection Association (in NFPA 75 [40]) specify some of these measures.

3.6.2 Detection

Fire and smoke detection alarms are familiar to most of us because of the availability in recent years of low-cost home devices. The technology for computer facilities is similar. The basic techniques used fall mainly into three classes: ionization detection, light-scattering smoke detection, and heat sensing. Ionization detection is the most commonly used. These devices use a small amount of radioactive material that ionizes the air molecules in a sensing chamber. A level of conductivity is established through the ionized medium. The presence of smoke particles results in ion attachment, reducing the ion mobility and hence the conductivity through the chamber. This reduction in conductivity is the basis for the detector alarm threshold. The devices are very sensitive to particles generated by open flames, even where smoke is not visible to the eye.

Detectors based on the principle of light scattering are less sensitive to invisible particles, but perform well in detecting smoke. The basic operation depends on transmission from a light source to a photoelectric detector. The most common physical arrangement is to aim the light source so that no direct path to the detector is possible, and therefore no light is detected in a transparent medium. The presence of smoke causes scattered light to reach the detector, and the alarm is triggered when the scattered energy exceeds a preset threshold.

Heat detectors are also useful in a computer environment, for example, to indicate when the temperature is too high to withhold water any longer. Heat sensors are the usual basis for triggering sprinkler systems. Heat detection is usually based on bimetal strips (two adjacent types of metal with differing thermal coefficients of expansion that thereby deform under temperature increases, closing an electrical contact), diaphragm-vented chamber covers (based on air expansion with temperature), leaf springs retained by eutectic metal (based on physical release by the low-temperature melting of the eutectic), thermocouples or thermopiles (based on conversion of heat energy to electric energy across the boundary of two or a series of pairs of dissimilar metals).

On detection of a fire, several responses are possible. These include use of hand extinguishers, "flooding" of the facility with an extinguishant that is not harmful to computers, and personnel evacuation.

3.6.3 Hand Extinguishers

A fire small enough to be controlled by personnel should be fought with hand extinguishers. The most common types are water, CO_2, dry chemicals, and a gas called Halon 1211. Water works well on fires involving wood, paper, and plastics (Class A fires), but is dangerous to use on electrically energized systems (Class C fires) because of the hazards of electrical shock and equipment damage. Dry chemicals are popular for home extinguishers but are inappropriate for use on computers because of the material deposited on the target. CO_2 extinguishers are useful for fires around electrical equipment but do not work well on fires involving paper and plastics.

Halon 1211 extinguishers are relatively expensive, but they are generally the best overall approach to fighting localized fires in computer facilities. They are effective against fires involving wood, plastic, and paper. They are safe to use in an electrical environment. They leave no residue. These considerations explain why Halon extinguishers are commonly seen around computer facilities. The general properties of Halon will be examined more closely later.

3.6.4 Extinguishant Flooding Systems

"Flooding" systems may imply water flooding to some, but in the fire-fighting context, the term describes the use of any gas or liquid that is applied throughout an entire area to be protected. Flooding systems are used only when it is apparent that the fire situation is beyond control by portable extinguishers.

Since water spray has damage potential for electronics, it is generally considered to be a last resort. However, it is possible to minimize water damage if time allows, for example, by covering equipment with plastic sheets prior to water release (see next section on water protection). For this reason, plastic mounted on rollers for ready dispensing is seen in some computer rooms.

CO_2 flooding is potentially hazardous to personnel because of its suffocating properties and because it substantially reduces visibility. These considerations often lead one to consider Halon flooding systems for systems having stringent protection requirements.

Halon is a trade name for a halogenated hydrocarbon (hydrogen atoms are replaced by atoms of the halogen chemical series) that has flame-extinguishing properties. When the ratio of Halon to air is kept suitably small, Halon is safe for flooding rooms being evacuated by personnel.

Two forms of Halon are commonly used for extinguishing fires. One is bromotrifluoromethane (CF_3Br), called Halon 1301, and the other is bromochlorodifluoromethane (CF_2ClBr), called Halon 1211. The numeric designation is a shorthand designation of the atoms in the chemical combination used. Halon 1301 is the usual choice for flooding systems because it is less toxic than Halon 1211. It is mandatory in the United States to not use Halon 1211 in flooding systems [33], although it is used in some other countries. Halon 1211 is usually preferred over Halon 1301 for portable extinguishers, because it is a slightly more effective extinguishant.

Halon is discharged as a gas in flooding systems. In large concentrations, Halon can suffocate fires. However, for the sake of safety, it is used at much lower concentrations than required for suffocation. The extinguishing properties of the gas at low concentrations are believed to be due to chemical inhibition of the combustion process. This leads to a potential problem, in that there is no cooling force introduced as would be the case, for example, using water. Char material or the combustible vapors evolved from the char may reignite if Halon is removed too rapidly, so it is important to maintain something close to a seal on the area to be flooded, thereby allowing ordinary convective cooling to occur.

Gas-to-air ratios of less than 15% are the usual design goal for flooding systems, since 15% is the limit within which short-term human exposure is not harmful. Extinguishant requirements are generally in the range of 5% or slightly higher, so flooding system design requires care to assure 7–10% concentrations. The supply for a Halon flooding system is shown in Figure 3-7.

Halon 1211 is discharged as a gas–liquid mixture and works by cooling, smothering, and chemically interfering with the combustion process. Halon 1211 is toxic at 4–5%, which accounts for its usual restriction to portable extinguishers.

Nitrogen is commonly added to Halon flooding systems to increase pressure and thereby speed the delivery of the Halon. Halon 1301 is extremely volatile. Halon 1211 is relatively low in toxicity, noncorrosive, nonconductive, and discharged at slightly below freezing temperatures. It has more deleterious effects on plastics and elastomers than does Halon 1301. Halon gases can react with fire to produce Halogen acids (hydrogen bromide, hydrogen fluoride, free bromine, and in the case of Halon 1211, hydrogen chloride and chlorine). These acids can be dangerous to humans and equipment. These disadvantages of Halon are mentioned as cautions, but are not substantial deterrents to the use of Halon as a computer facility fire extinguishant.

3.6.5 Personnel Evacuation

Judgment enters into the strategy of personnel evacuation, because there are a variety of fire conditions to be considered. The proper response to a small localized fire is to use hand extinguishers. In this case, it would not be likely to need evacuation. A widespread fire, on the other hand, might require Halon flooding and personnel evacuation. The use of Halon is expensive, and personnel evacuation is disruptive, so the judgment to use Halon must not be too hasty. The usual method of handling this problem is to incorporate a time delay (e.g., 30 sec) between detection/alarm and dumping of Halon. This allows time for human assessment of the situation in case Halon flooding and personnel evacuation are not necessary. Figure 3-8 depicts a typical overall fire-response strategy.

Figure 3-7   A Halon flooding system supply. (Photograph courtesy of Sandia National Laboratories.)

3.7 WATER PROTECTION

Water protection was mentioned above because of the threat posed by fire-protection sprinkler systems. However, there are many other

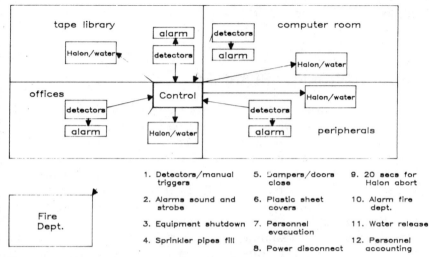

Figure 3-8   Fire-protection implementation.

1. Detectors/manual triggers	5. Dampers/doors close	9. 20 secs for Halon abort
2. Alarms sound and strobe	6. Plastic sheet covers	10. Alarm fire dept.
3. Equipment shutdown	7. Personnel evacuation	11. Water release
4. Sprinkler pipes fill	8. Power disconnect	12. Personnel accounting

ways in which water can threaten computer facilities. Some of these are burst water pipes in the building structure above the computer facility, roof leaks allowing rainwater to enter the facility, water flooding due to high outside water level relative to low-level computer facilities, and personnel-generated accidents involving cups of water, water hoses being used in the vicinity, etc.

In 1983, a U.S.-based Japanese automaking company had a roof collapse during a rainstorm [33]. The roof was flat, and debris clogged the drains. Ten thousand gallons of water and five tons of air conditioning equipment fell through the roof, decimating the data center.

The idea of plastic covers mentioned above for water protection is surprisingly useful for computers of all sizes. Although a 24-hour a day computer facility is unlikely to do more than make rolls of plastic available in the vicinity (as mentioned above), small computers may be routinely covered when not in use. In fact, custom-fit covers are readily available for most personal computers (PCs). This affords protection against water and also restricts the entry of dust and dirt into the computer system.

Another simple and effective protection technique is to use water detectors. These are widely available in a variety of models ranging from small standalone detectors and cable sensors to complete systems for alerting personnel and pinpointing location of moisture. The detection is usually based on detecting increased conductivity across an electrical gap located in a low-lying area likely to accumulate water.

3.8 CONTINGENCY PLANNING

In spite of the best protective efforts one can afford, disaster will overcome the protective barriers some perplexing percentage of the time. It is prudent to assess the action that should be taken beforehand, since a large number of preparatory measures can be pursued that may make the difference between a temporary disaster and a permanent disaster. These efforts are called contingency planning, and include backup (hardware, software, and communications), prioritization analysis (to make advance decisions about temporary partial operating capabilities), disaster insurance, and disaster recovery (to aid in the transition from a disaster back to normal operation).

3.8.1 Backup

Since a disaster may destroy valuable hardware, software, and communications resources, it is important to consider whether or not to back up these assets by providing duplicate or similar assets that are either less vulnerable to disaster, or at least not likely to be vulnerable to a common disaster. This is the reason that copies of operating systems, applications software, data, and instructions are commonly stored at an archive site. In a more restrictive sense, the same idea can be applied to hardware. In both cases there are important questions about what should be backed up, how often the backup should be updated and what forms of security should be implemented for the backup assets.

Communications backup is most effectively implemented through redundant communication modes. Following a 1988 central office switch failure in Massachusetts [49], one major computer company was able to make software changes within 20 minutes that allowed rerouting local and long distance communications through an alternate company microwave network.

An unsettling number of PC users copy diskettes representing valuable data or applications software and store it in diskette cases side by side with the original. This is convenient but imprudent. The principle is the same for any size facility: One of the most important reasons for backup is to avoid loss due to a disaster. This argues for storage in a remote location, although some companies use robust on-site vaults (made, for example, from reinforced concrete). The obvious tradeoffs are that remoteness causes cost in terms of time and effort to physically move the backup and in terms of additional security required for a backup site.

Some of the options commonly used for remote backup storage are commercial archive sites (which will provide, for a price, transportation and security), other locations owned by the same company or other companies (sometimes through reciprocal exchanges), or other parts of the same facility (on the premise that minor remoteness is paid for by lower auxiliary costs).

Commercial archiving costs for "medium-to-large" companies [38] range from $8000 to $15,000 per year, including handling of exchange cycling (new updates in; old copies out) on a daily basis. Similar charges for "small" companies cycling weekly range from about $3000 to $5000.

Another option is to use special storage techniques such as "data safes" [36] that may be co-located, but are intended to be more resistant to a subset of the threat environment (e.g., fire and theft). These are different from fire safes because of greater temperature tolerance. A typical fire safe will protect papers by limiting inside temperature to 350°F for outside temperatures of 1700°F. Such safes are called "class 350" safes and are also specified as to exposure time in hours.

Data safes, on the other hand, are typically specified as "class 150" (150°F limiting temperature for film, micrographics, and magnetic tape) or "class 125" (125°F limiting temperature for diskettes and similar low-tolerance media).

Although hardware backup could be treated in a manner analogous to software backup, it is usually handled much differently. Hardware backup typically is accomplished in one of several ways:

1. By service bureaus
2. By using "redundant" computer and communications systems
3. By identifying underutilized hardware that can be used in an emergency
4. By reciprocal agreements, which allows constrained processing by a disaster victim on the partner's hardware
5. By membership in a commercial "hot site" or "cold site"
6. By securing replacement hardware from immediately available supplies

Service bureaus are available to do limited types of processing for companies during recovery. They provide computing service for applications that are not heavily dependent on application software (e.g., standard statistical processing). An advantage of this approach is that no up-front costs are incurred unless a disaster strikes.

Redundant computer systems include dual processors, where processing can be handed off from one to the other in case of a problem, and high-reliability or fault-tolerant computers that are available from some manufacturers. These strategies are intended to prevent, insofar as possible, any downtime. This is a common requirement for crucial systems such as air traffic control, national air defense surveillance systems, and even airline reservation systems.[*]

Underutilized computers are computers that a company has cost-justified on the basis of partial-shift operation (not used 24 hours a day). Owners of such systems are sometimes willing to allow off-use processing as a good-will gesture, in reciprocal agreement, or for a price.

Reciprocal agreements can also be established between companies that operate 24 hours a day. The concept is that the partners agree to share the available processing time in case of a disaster, although the disaster victim may be relegated to second- or third-shift operation. It is important to periodically test processing at reciprocal sites, because no matter how well the initial compatibility is established, custom modification to operating systems and peripheral requirements is common and expected.

Hot sites are computer facilities designed to be occupied in an emergency. There are many hot sites in the United States ranging in size from about 2000 square feet to over 100,000 square feet of floor space. They have complete and operational computing facilities that are usually idle but ready for use.

These sites typically furnish (in addition to computing capability) physical security features, fire detection and protection, quality power, air conditioning, peripherals, and communications. Membership must be limited (typically 10 to 100) and geographically distributed, so that the probability of multiple member needs is minimal. Important considerations are compatibility of computer and operating system with applications to be run, relatively nearby location to minimize operating employee travel, level of security, and cost. Membership typically costs from a few hundred to several

---

[*]   A major airline can suffer losses nearing $50,000 per hour for downtimes in the peak 3 to 6 P.M. period.

thousand dollars per month, with increased fees during facility use. Time of use is usually limited (six weeks to 90 days is typical).

Cold sites are "shell" facilities, computer-ready, but containing no computers. The concept depends on the ability of a disaster-struck company to secure a computer and install it at the cold site. This is usually not difficult, because most computer manufacturers will deliver a new computer with high priority to one of their customers in trouble. Although this is usually the policy, some foreign customers have been delayed in receiving computers from U.S. manufacturers, apparently because of recent U.S. concern over uncontrolled technology transfer that may eventually reach undesirable destinations (see Chapter 5).

Typical cold sites range from about 1000 square feet of floor space to about 50,000 square feet. Fees range from about $200 per month to about $2000 per month, with increased fees for facility usage. Membership limitations are similar to those for hot sites, and usage period limitations are generally in the range of several months.

The final strategy mentioned (securing replacement hardware from immediately available supplies) requires that space be obtained on a temporary basis, either within the company or from a cooperating company. In the case of the automaker disaster mentioned above, full operation was restored in eight days, with the aid of a company specializing in this type of restoration [35]. Within four days, 1500 square feet of office space had been refurbished to become a raised-floor computer facility, and replacement equipment had been obtained. In another four days, complete operation had been restored.

3.8.2 Prioritization Analysis

Analytical assessment of the constituents of an operation (such as applications that are running on a computer system) is important in case operation must be curtailed. This curtailment is almost certain following a disaster.

One type of analysis used is called "criticality analysis." This is a method for establishing a quantitative measure of priorities for use in selective processing. Some factors in criticality analysis are listed below:

1. Time criticality of applications run. This can include direct financial loss (as mentioned in the airline reservation system situation), ill will with employees (as, for example, if payroll

functions were suspended), and ill will with customers (e.g., ATM downtime).

2. Effects on others. It is possible that downtime in a large computer facility could drive small dependent businesses to bankruptcy (if, for example, invoices were not paid, and therefore needed capital were denied).

3. Loss of real-time opportunity. Processing tied to some event (e.g., NASA processing of space shuttle flight data) may be needed in real time, with lost opportunity if delayed.

One common approach to criticality analysis is to use weighted rankings. Since much subjective judgment is involved, it is usually helpful to get management participation and/or approval of the results.

Another useful technique is called the "Delphi approach" (coined at the Rand Corporation). This involves two or more iterations of the judgmental decisions with feedback on the overall scores to help remove discrepancies that are due to incomplete background information.

Sensitivity analysis may also be required prior to disaster recovery because of security considerations. For example, security at a remote site where recovery processing will be done may not be equivalent to the home facility. There also may be questions about hardware and software threats that are extremely hard to control in such a situation (e.g., hardware "bugs" and software "Trojan horses"). For these reasons, applications to be selected for recovery processing may be influenced by level of sensitivity to such effects.

Sensitivity analysis is similar to criticality analysis, except that the factors of importance are financial or business loss jeopardy created by compromise of information, legal jeopardy, potential for future disruption (e.g., due to "virus" implants), and national security risk.

3.8.3 Disaster Insurance

Insurance is another component of contingency planning that can be helpful [37]. Insurance is available against natural disasters, against human attacks of many types, against employee misdeeds, against software failure, and against fraud loss. Fidelity insurance applies to a company's own employees. Blanket insurance covers all employees, more reasonably priced scheduled insurance names particular persons or job functions. Media insurance includes coverage for the cost of reconstructing software and information.

Insurance rates are generally improved by evidence of protective measures such as no smoking signs, training programs, Halon extinguishant systems, etc. An indication of rate structure can be obtained by considering typical situations (with the caveat that coverage details can cause large variations). For $500,000 fidelity insurance, covering 100 (blanket) employees, the cost may be $50,000 per year. A typical comprehensive insurance coverage for a $10 million data center may cost $25,000 per year with $25,000 deductible. A general comprehensive cost guideline [39] is 20 to 30 cents per year per $100 coverage.

3.8.4 Disaster Recovery Plans

Disasters don't always happen to someone else. In addition to fire and water incidents, which are familiar threats to computer facilities, one must consider some of nature's most dramatic displays of power. In 1971, a disastrous earthquake centered in the San Fernando Valley damaged numerous computer facilities in Los Angeles. In 1980, computer facilities in the Livermore, California, vicinity and other northern California communities were damaged. In 1985, a Mexico City earthquake damaged more than 20 computer facilities. Twenty thousand census tapes were lost, and four government mainframes were destroyed. A major bank, Banamex, was situated in an "earthquake-proof" structure, and lost no computing capability, but did lose all communications links. The Mount St. Helens eruption in 1980 was fortunately located in a remote area, but the dust emitted fell widely enough to create disk pack damage in surrounding areas.

Statistical studies of incidents reported as disasters vary widely, but the most significant classifications are usually water problems, fire problems, and power problems, each providing about 20% of the incidents. Earthquakes and communications failures provide about 15% each.

Software bugs can also cause disasters. The New York Stock Exchange suffered a serious shutdown in 1985, apparently due to a problem in a well-known operating system [34]. Not long afterward, one of the largest banks in the United States was shut down by a software failure, forcing a Federal Reserve loan of $24 billion.

Disaster recovery plans are a method for laying out a plan of action in advance that will be followed in case of a disaster. One reason for doing so is that the immediate requirements for action in case of a disaster are too great to be met efficiently under the time pressures involved. Another reason is that persons responsible for action in various areas are known by all, and there is no question in their minds or in those of the interacting parties about whether or not they should be making decisions. A relatively new reason is legal or regulatory requirements for contingency or disaster recovery plans (see Chapter 5). A final reason is that preparing in detail for disaster recovery is extremely helpful in identifying weaknesses in backup strategy, criticality analysis, or decision-making structure.

The basic elements of a disaster recovery plan are:

1. Responsible personnel. These usually include a recovery chief, who is the central focus for running the recovery operation, an upper management representative for policy guidance, a security representative for considering security implications of decisions made, an operations representative for questions about operating logistics, a users' representative, a plant engineering representative, a computer vendor representative, a communications representative, an auditing representative, and appropriate alternates.

2. Sequence of steps to be taken in a variety of possible scenarios. These cannot be all-inclusive, but should cover the major variations possible. These include utilization of previously established resources such as backup software, operating system and data copies, and criticality and sensitivity evaluations for applications that are candidates to be run. Some steps frequently specified are:

   a. Postdisaster meeting and assessment
   b. Determination of software, data, operating systems available or to be obtained
   c. Determination of hardware and communications equipment available or to be obtained, and contact with other companies involved (e.g., hot sites or computer manufacturers)
   d. Determination of personnel available (or replacements) and interim personnel needed
   e. Logistics of travel and obtaining needed supplies
   f. Initiation of activities to restore the physical environment (building, hardware) and any personnel lost

3. Techniques for evaluating the plan. This step includes mechanisms for periodic review, feedback of experience during disasters by the involved company or others, and methods for testing. Disaster-recovery testing is difficult because of reluctance to shut down any operations, but is a high-payoff technique when used. Even paper tests or scenario exercises have proved useful when applied.

Disaster recovery plans may be a subset of a formal general contingency plan that includes all of the elements in this section. Contemporary security considerations make this sort of planning absolutely essential. Fortunately, most organizations are now addressing the issue, and the overall contingency planning posture is improving.

PROBLEMS

1. Assume that the probability of protection by barriers is given by $p = f(c)$, a mathematical function of c (cost), where c is constrained to values such that $0 \le p \le 1$. Determine whether single barriers or multiple barriers are more effective for the following:

   a) $p = c$
   b) $p = c^2$
   c) $p = c^{1/2}$
   d) $p = sin(\pi c/2)(0 \le c \le 1)$

2. Assume that for an intrusion alarm the probability of false alarms, p_f, and the probability of detection failure, p_e, can be related to sensitivity, s, where s is a variable with values between 0 and 1. The equations are:

   $$p_f = s$$
   $$p_e = e^{-2s}$$

   For a measure of attribute, $p_e p_f$, how can the system be optimized?

3. Repeat problem 2, but with the goal of maximizing $(1 - e^{-2s})/s$.

4. For an arc-breakdown protector, derive an equation for voltage
    sensitivity (voltage at which the arc is completed), where the
    voltage is applied as:

    $$v = rt$$

    and the breakdown starts at 1000 V, taking 50 nsecs to com-
    plete. What is the voltage sensitivity if $r = 10^{10}$?

5. Design an electronic combination lock. The lock has a push-
    button and a light, and is to be operated by inserting a three-
    number combination. The operation is initiated by pushing the
    button, after which the light turns on for four seconds. During
    the four-second interval, the first digit is entered by the num-
    ber of times the button is pushed while the light is on. Then
    the light turns off for four seconds, during which time the
    second number is entered by pushing the button. The light
    then turns back on for four seconds, during which time the
    third digit is entered. If the combination is successful, the lock
    is opened by a solenoid for four seconds to give the user oppor-
    tunity for entry.

    The design requires showing indicative block diagram
    hardware interconnection for the button, the light, a
    microprocessor, RAM, and ROM. The program for the
    microprocessor is to be indicated in flowchart form.

6. The voltage delivered to a computer is 115 $sin2\pi ft$, where $f =$
    60 Hz.

    a) What is the average voltage delivered?
    b) What is the average of the absolute value of the voltage?
    c) What is the rms voltage delivered?
    d) What is the power delivered if the computer impedance is 1
        ohm?

7. The voltage delivered to a computer is 100 $sin2\pi f_1 t$ + 15
    $sin2\pi f_2 t$, where $f_1 = 60$ Hz and $f_2 = 400$ Hz.

    a) What is the average voltage delivered?
    b) What is the average of the absolute value of the voltage?
    c) What is the rms voltage delivered?
    d) What is the power delivered if the computer impedance is 1
        ohm?

DILEMMA DISCUSSIONS

1. A computer room has a push-button combination lock, and procedures prohibit "tailgating." Users argue that it is inappropriate to close the door in the face of a fellow employee,
   especially if known to them. The second person may expect
   tailgating as a courtesy, and both people may feel that the cost
   in terms of efficiency does not warrant strict adherence to the
   policy in cases where it is an obvious formality. What should be
   done?

2. Halon is considered by most people to be the ideal fire-fighting
   extinguishant. There is no other known compound that is color-
   less, essentially odorless, relatively safe, and nonconducting.
   However, chlorofluorocarbons (CFCs) are used in Halon systems. These compounds have been implicated (when released
   into the atmosphere) in damaging the earth's ozone layer (a
   protective upper atmosphere region that significantly reduces
   the earth's exposure to the sun's ultraviolet rays). In September 1987, a group of 24 nations (including the United States)
   signed an international protocol, agreeing to limit production of
   CFCs. Halon was given special treatment, because of its fire
   protection value. According to the protocol, Halon production
   will be held at 1986 levels, effective in 1992.

   Long-range forecasts by meteorologists cannot be guaranteed, but most warn that ozone destruction can lead to global
   warming, polar ice melting, coastal flooding, droughts, and increased cancer rates. You have the option of purchasing Halon
   systems as contingency against when supply might be limited,
   or of some protective sacrificing for the long-range good of the
   earth's environment. What would you do?

REFERENCES

1. Parker, Donn, *Fighting Computer Crime*, Charles Scribner's
   Sons, New York, 1983.
2. Higgins, Clay E., "Site Specific Perimeter Protection," *Security
   Management*, February 1986.
3. Owen, James W., "Setting Sensitivity Standards for the
   Facility Intrusion Detection System," 1985 Carnahan Conference on Security Technology.

4. Hunt, Allan R., and John A. Vanderslice, "Detection and Assessment Requirements Definition for the Small ICBM Physical Security System," 1985 Carnahan Conference on Security Technology.

5. *Computer Security*, Understanding Computers Series, Time-Life Books, Alexandria, VA, 1986.

6. *The 1987 Information Please Almanac.*

7. Rechsteiner, Emil B., "Clean, Stable Power for Computers," *EMC Technology*, July–September 1985.

8. Massaro, Kevin, "Guidelines Clarify Backup Needs in UPS Systems," *Computer Design*, July 1, 1985.

9. Wilson, Dave, "Designer's Guide to Uninterruptible Power Supplies," *Digital Design*, August 1984.

10. Bernstein, Amy, "UPSmanship," *Business Computer Systems*, July 1984.

11. Brill, Kenneth G., "Keeping Up your UPS," *Datamation*, July 15, 1987.

12. Wood, Lamont, "Uninterruptible Power Supplies," *Government Computer News*, January 20, 1987.

13. Tucker, Ruxton, "The Glitch Stops Here," *Computer Design*, February 1982.

14. Kimball, James D., "Interest in Power Protection Surges as Supply of Clean Power Sags," *Data Communications*, March 1985.

15. Edman, James, "Selecting a UPS for Today's Systems Requirements," *EMC Technology*, July–September 1985.

16. English, John D., "Safeguard your Microcomputers Against Costly Power Problems," *Office Systems*, October 1985.

17. Kellner, Mark A., "Protecting Data from Power Outage Problems," *The Office*, August 1985.

18. Pryor, Douglas, and Amy Smith, "Power Line Protection," *Business Computer Systems*, December 1983.

19. Fredell, Eric, "Peace Activist Found Guilty of Wrecking DOD Computer," *Government Computer News*, January 8, 1988.

20. Severinsky, Alex, "Coping with the Electronic Achilles' Heel," *DEC Professional*, June 1988.

21. Kolodziej, Stan, "The Ins and Outs of UPS," *Computerworld Focus*, April 6, 1988.

22. Queen, Ralph H., "Common or Differential-Mode Noise? It Makes a Difference in Your Filter," *EMC Technology*, July–September 1985.

23. Glancy, Donald, "Preventing EMI in ATE Systems, Part 1: Grounding and Shielding," *Test and Measurement World*, January 1987.
24. Kellow, Karen, "Low-Resistance Electrolytic Grounding System Improves Conductivity," *EMC Technology*, January–February 1987.
25. Gruchalla, Michael E., "Power Distribution and Grounding Safety in Instrumentation Systems," *EMC Technology*, January–February 1987.
26. National Fire Protection Association, *National Electrical Code*, (ANSI/NFPA70), National Fire Protection Association, Quincy, MA, 1983.
27. Cooper, J. A., and L. J. Allen, "Lightning Arrestor Connector Feasibility Study," Sandia Laboratories Research Report SC-RR-71 0180, April 1971.
28. Quittner, Joshua, and Nancy Harbert, " 'Pulling Plug' Spares State from Major Power Failure," *Albuquerque Journal*, Albuquerque, NM, March 1, 1984.
29. Parker, Donn B., *Crime by Computer*, Charles Scribner's Sons, New York, 1976.
30. Ensman, Richard G., Jr., "Information Disposal: A Vital Company Need," *The Office*, March 1986.
31. Kuflic, Terry M., "Shredders Meet Demands of Information Security," *The Office*, April 1986.
32. Pilla, Lou, "Shredders Cut It for Office Security," *Today's Office*, January 1986.
33. Colby, Wendelin, "Disaster Recovery Plan? Nah — It'll Never Happen to Us!" *Infosystems*, October 1985.
34. Schindler, Paul E., "Data on Computer Failures Should Not be Buried," *InformationWEEK*, November 4, 1985.
35. Beeler, Jeffry, "Destroyed Data Center Up a Week Later," *Computerworld*, March 21, 1983.
36. Metzner, Kermit, "Data Safes Can Take the Heat to Preserve Film and Magnetic Media," *Office Systems*, February 1986.
37. Wheeler, Richard, "Insurance Coverage for the Computer Age," *Office Systems*, January 1985.
38. Schlosberg, Jeremy, "Out of Site," *Digital Review*, March 1985.
39. Stamps, David, "Disaster Recovery: Who's Worried?" *Datamation*, February 1, 1987.
40. *National Fire Codes 1983* National Fire Protection Association, Quincy, MA, 1983.

41. Subcommittee on Science, Research and Technology of the Committee on Science, Space, and Technology, House of Representatives, "Whittier Narrows, CA, Earthquake: Lessons Learned," dated November 10, 1987, printed by the U.S. Government Printing Office, 1988.

42. Tarr, Arthur C., and A. M. Rogers, "Analysis of Earthquake Data Recorded by Digital Field Seismic Systems, Jackass Flats, Nevada," USGS-OFR-86-420, U.S. Geological Survey, 1986.

43. Wilson, G. L., and P. Zarakas, "Anatomy of a Blackout," *IEEE Spectrum*, February 1978.

44. Cohan, Lloyd, "Hard-Disk Assembly (HDA) Degausser," *Center for Computer Security News*, U.S. Department of Energy, July 1986.

45. Menkus, Belden, "Progress Makes Phone Outages More Damaging," *Government Computer News*, October 10, 1988.

46. "Bank Baffled over Printouts," *Las Vegas Review-Journal*, August 21, 1982.

47. Mandell, Mel, "If Climate Prevails," *Computerworld*, November 30, 1987.

48. Mehler, Mark, "UPSs Flourish as LAN Protectors," *Datamation*, July 15, 1988.

49. Brown, Bob, and Bob Wallace, "CO Outage Refuels Users' Disaster Fears," *Network World*, July 11, 1988.

4

The Personnel Security Environment

The term "personnel security" implies, to many, protection *against* the actions initiated by people. This is indeed important, but not nearly as important as protection *for* people. In this chapter, we will address security of people before turning to security from people. On this latter topic, we will address the types of behavior that threat personnel exhibit. Finally, we will consider techniques that are applicable to personnel security in general.

4.1 PERSONNEL AS ASSETS

An interesting question commonly asked in security seminars is "What is the most important asset requiring computer security protection?" [1]. After considering computers, operating systems, information, and the physical facility, one realizes that the obvious answer is people. It is common to overlook the importance of people assets, since we are conditioned to think about physical assets and information. A little reflection, however, makes it obvious that no asset approaches the value of people.

Some of the reasons for this value judgment are:

1. Employees hired for computer-related operations are typically well trained. This training may range from years of college education through years of on-the-job training (frequently both). An employee who is lost through failure of security measures to protect personnel well-being cannot be replaced without significant perturbations to the company operation. It should be noted that employees can also be lost because oppressive security makes working conditions too unpleasant to tolerate.

2. Cost is associated with every new employee hired. This cost includes advertising and other recruiting expenses, background investigation or screening, which is almost always done to some extent, and training expenses.

3. There is a significant potential, considering the propensity of society for litigation, that failure to adequately protect personnel from harm may result in legal action. Harm includes damaged reputation and improper working conditions in addition to physical trauma.

4. People who feel protected within the security environment are generally more productive and more likely to contribute to the overall security program. It follows, then, that protecting people as an asset enhances their value to the organization.

5. Our society places a high value on the moral aspects of protecting people. We place a premium on personal well-being that transcends required actions.

Many of the threats to people are identical to the physical threats considered in the previous chapter, resulting in identical protective strategies. Some threats are unique to people. It is informative to consider both types.

4.1.1 Threats Shared by People and Physical Equipment

A basic threat against people and physical equipment is damage caused by people. This includes acts by terrorists, saboteurs, vandals, and careless people. All of these may cause personal harm, either accidentally or intentionally.

Reported statistics [2,3] indicate that these types of incidents are frequent. Recent Data Processing Management Association (DPMA) data show that about 20% of computer crimes are committed for revenge. Revenge can be directed at or at least affect people. The

European Information Technologies and Telecommunications Task Force statistics show that 30% of the computer security incidents studied involved sabotage and bombs. A 1983 United Kingdom Bureau of Information Systems (BIS) Applied Systems survey ("BIS Computer Crime Casebook") reported that 48% of the cataloged incidents involved fires and explosions, most apparently caused intentionally. A 1984 study of Australian computer abuse showed losses due to sabotage as being on a par with losses due to fraud. Stanford Research Institute (SRI) statistics for the United States show about 15% of the security incidents reported involve vandalism. Donn Parker, SRI researcher, has recorded five incidents of guns fired at computers [3], and there is an incident of damage from a liquid (apparently urine).

During the past 10 years, terrorist activities have grown substantially [4]. Worldwide losses from terrorist incidents average well over $100 million per year. Terrorism is a pervasive threat against computer facilities worldwide.

An organization in France calls itself Comité Liquidant ou Détoumant les Ordinateurs (CLODO). This means "The Committee to Liquidate or Deter Computers." During a nine-month period in the early 1980s [22], CLODO was involved in four attacks on computer facilities in Toulouse, France. There have been about 30 terrorist attacks on computers in Europe during the past 10 years. There have been about 22 attacks against American computers abroad. At least four attacks in the United States have been attributed to "activists."

In Italy in the 1970s there were 27 computer attacks by the Red Brigade. The Red Brigade document "Resolutions of the Strategic Directorate" referred to computerization as a sinister plot to maximize social controls. Red Brigade members have attacked at least 10 computer facilities since publication of the document. In Ireland, the Belfast Cooperative Society, Ltd. computer facilities were destroyed by bomb attacks in 1972. Scotland Yard has uncovered recent evidence that the IRA (Irish Republican Army) is planning to target computers in England. Other computer bomb attacks have occurred in Japan and Brazil. To date, terrorists and activists have bombed more than 600 computer facilities.

Accidents caused by carelessness can be as serious as intentional attacks. These generally result from inattention, disregard, ignorance, or misinterpretation. The aforementioned DPMA statistics show that 27% of computer crimes are a result of ignorance and unprofessional conduct, much of which fits this category of threat. Most fires are caused accidentally. One computer facility incident involving personal injury resulted from heavy equipment being dropped from a crane through a roof. Electrical shock hazard cannot be discounted, although it is much less threatening today because of the proliferation of low-voltage equipment. Electrical hazards can also be created by miswiring, natural effects (e.g., lightning), and temporary exposure during repairs.

4.1.2 Threats Unique to People

Many threats to people are unique and not part of the physical threat environment. However, these threats warrant serious consideration. These include murder, assault, rape, robbery, theft of personal items, entrapment, harassment, slander, and character assassination.

Two threats that have received considerable publicity are VDT (video display terminal) hazards and low-frequency EM fields. The VDT threat is postulated because of recent studies that are indicative (although probably not conclusive) of physical harm (including miscarriages) due to either stress or (less likely) an accumulation of radiation. Eye strain, headaches, physical strength drain, and joint problems (including back) have been reported. In the state of New York, the Suffolk County legislature has instituted legal requirements for protective measures against these effects.

EM radiation from power lines has recently been associated with increased risk of leukemia and some other forms of cancers. At one time, the low frequencies (60 Hz) and low field strengths (tens of volts per meter) involved were thought to be harmless because much higher frequencies are required for the ionizing effects associated with radiation damage. Although some heating is known to result from these ELF (extra-low-frequency) fields, the effects, if substantiated, may involve more complex interaction of EM fields with biological cells.

4.2 PERSONNEL AS THREATS

It is interesting to consider personnel as threats to security, both from a viewpoint of types of personnel that provide threats and motivations that cause people to behave improperly.

4.2.1 Types of Personnel Threats

Traditionally, espionage agents have been considered a major threat to all forms of national security. According to the U.S. Department of Justice Federal Bureau of Investigation (FBI), this threat continues to become more serious. The FBI attributes most espionage to the U.S.S.R., with significant additional activity due to Soviet Bloc (allies) Eastern European countries, Cuba, and the People's Republic of China. The FBI estimates that the number of espionage agents in the United States has doubled since 1972. About one third of the communist country officials in the United States appear to have espionage duties as at least part of their assignments. It should be noted that computer data handling and data communication provide new opportunities for espionage agents.

Apparently, espionage results in significant information transfer to the U.S.S.R., if one can judge by the cases uncovered and prosecuted. Two men were convicted in 1977 of selling to the Soviets highly sensitive data on U.S. satellite systems. In 1978, a man was convicted of selling the Soviets a technical manual on an important spy satellite. In 1981, a conviction was obtained for a man who gave the Soviets information on a top secret communications system. An American and a Polish intelligence officer were arrested in 1981 and convicted of espionage because of a significant transfer of military-related technology information to Warsaw (and probably to Moscow). The CIA (Central Intelligence Agency) estimated that this compromise was worth hundreds of millions of dollars to Poland and the U.S.S.R. In 1986, a former NSA (National Security Agency) employee was given a life sentence for giving cryptographic information to the Soviets. The 1988 arrest of a retired U.S. Army sergeant in West Germany apparently uncovered a plot to sell NATO defense plans and details of missile sites to Hungary and Russia.

In 1985 two men, along with the brother and son of one of the men, were caught in an extremely critical compromise of Navy communications security. The Navy estimated that recovery from this incident would take several years and cost millions of dollars. Inestimable damage also resulted from the potential to decode previously recorded encrypted messages. The central figure in the case, a 20-year Navy career man named John Walker, was given a life sentence, and his associate, Jerry Whitworth, was given a 365-year prison term.

The espionage interests have traditionally been centered on classified national security data. However, recent activity suggests appreciation of the value of unclassified technology information in shortcutting expensive development efforts. Two employees of a firm that manufactures supercomputers and minisupercomputers were arrested in 1987 for attempting to sell company technology to the Soviet Union [10]. The emphasis on this relatively new area of activity is so great that the U.S. government security and legal procedures have gone through considerable turmoil and restructuring during the past few years. This topic will be addressed in the next chapter.

Another significant area of espionage activity that is mostly unrelated to classified information is industrial espionage. In a widely publicized case two years ago, two Japanese companies were charged with offering $500,000 to key personnel who had information pertaining to the technology used by a major U.S. computer manufacturer (IBM). There are at least two schools for industrial spies, one in Switzerland and one in Japan.

A second category of threat personnel is saboteurs. This will be broadly interpreted to include terrorists, activists, and personal grudge-holders. In contrast to espionage personnel, the intent of saboteurs is usually to achieve publicity for some cause by causing noteworthy damage. Computer and communications facilities make attractive targets because of the publicity value of damage to entities having a prominent public image. Unfortunately, this same motivation sometimes causes personnel to be included as targets. There is no doubt that sabotage is a serious threat.

A third type of threat personnel is criminals. Although all avenues of attack are criminal in some way, the category addressed here is associated with career criminals or organized crime. The motivation for criminals to turn to attacks on computer and communication entities is strong. For example, there are more than 10 billion ATM transfers per year in the United States. There are also more than 10 billion interbank transfers per year. There are four major transfer systems that move $500 billion per day in domestic transfers and $800 billion per day in international transfers. United States financial institution networks transmit about $1 trillion daily, an amount equal to 25% of the gross national product [23]. Although most ATM losses are not a result of sophisticated attacks, they are currently running over $100 million per year [13]. Computer crime-related losses may be running into billions of dollars per year [5]. Data on computer crimes investigated by the FBI show that the average loss is about $600,000. Banks have for many years been reporting more computer-related crimes than have any other form of business [14,6].

Hackers are a well-known threat to computer and communications security. This type of person usually depends on grapevines of information and tireless trial and error to penetrate computer networks through dialup connections. Hackers may be malicious, but are usually characterized as adventurous. Unfortunately, the resultant damage can be equally serious in either case. This subject is covered in detail in Chapter 8.

Insiders may provide the most common threat [7]. The well-known security consultant Robert Courtney estimates [18] that 90% of computer crime is instigated by insiders. Most other estimates exceed 75%. This is an especially serious category because insiders are people who have the advantages of access to valuable information that makes penetrations and compromises easier; at the same time, they often have, by virtue of their employment, a special measure of trust. Insiders can include computing personnel (operators, systems analysts, programmers, users), security personnel (security designers and security implementers), management (not only highly trusted, but highly likely to go unchallenged if deviating from expected procedures), and other employees (workers located in proximity to computing operation or sources of information, maintenance and cleaning personnel). Telling examples of the potential power for misdeeds available to insiders are the 1987 Ivan Boesky insider trading scandal and the 1987 $259 million insider fraud at Volkswagen AG in West Germany [24]. There are also many examples more directly related to computers [3].

In June of 1988, two small computers were stolen on two successive nights from the Strategic Defense Initiative Organization (SDIO) in the Pentagon. The area struck was under stringent physical security protection, including a guard, a security card-locked door system, and videotape surveillance. Investigators believe that the security bypasses accomplished could have been done only by an insider.

In 1981, a major state lottery was victimized by insiders with information on unclaimed winning tickets. They printed duplicate tickets containing the proper information in order to claim winning shares.

An unusual but important category is imposters. These are outside people who masquerade as inside people. This category is becoming significant enough that the FBI has had to modify its record-keeping procedures to prevent accumulating derogatory information about people whose identity has been assumed by others [11]. This group can include people who forge badges or other credentials or who succeed simply by lying. An interesting case [9] involved a job applicant who misrepresented his identity, degree, and experience, and managed to provide a glowing reference (from his wife) to company investigators seeking a company personnel reference. Once accepted by the company as a trusted employee, he exploited lack of controls to embezzle nearly a million dollars.

Recently, a 25-year-old unemployed, self-professed hacker used an impersonation ruse to order a used IBM 9375 computer for a valid company for delivery to a warehouse. Following an authenticity check on the company, but not the person, the computer was delivered prior to payment. It was then easily stolen. Unfortunately, the perpetrator committed suicide just prior to apprehension.

A final category is temporary personnel. This includes consultants, service personnel, temporary hires, and visitors. A danger involving this category is that there is generally more room for error in evaluating personal integrity during a short-term exposure. On the other hand, these people may be on-site long enough to become familiar to other workers, who then begin to accept their authority as they would that of long-term employees.

4.2.2 Motivations

It is interesting and useful to study motivations, because it helps us understand why people behave improperly and what preventive measures may prove effective. The motivations addressed will be financial gain, information acquisition or alteration, emotion-driven violence, love, challenge, and poor judgment, which includes carelessness.

A common motive for computer attacks is financial gain. People having this motive range from criminals whose way of life involves illegally seeking money, all the way through basically honest people who suffer from momentary temptation. Some people seek money out of desperation; in some cases they may even be altruistic. For example, one incident involving embezzlement from a U.K. bank [16] resulted from a woman's attempt to soothe her husband, who had lost his job. In another case, a senior accounting clerk in a department store chain used embezzlement to finance treatment for an alcoholic wife. An information supervisor in the Washington State Department of Health and Social Services apparently used computer crime to provide help (and drinks at a local bar) for broke and unemployed bar patrons. A grandmother stole more than $400,000 in order to help her daughter, who was struggling through nursing school following a divorce, and her son, who couldn't afford furniture for his house.

Financial gain may apply to company gain rather than personal gain, as, for example, in the case of industrial espionage. The gains are not always sought. Frequently they are offered, for example, through bribery. Many times they are offered accidentally through fortuitous discovery of crucial information.

A second motivation is based strictly on information. The motive may be simply to learn, for reasons ranging from information usefulness through curiosity. There are also many reasons for modifying information. Some involve financial gain, others may not. For example, it might be desired to modify grades or records of derogatory information. In 1975, an Ohio police chief was discovered to have deleted his reckless driving record from a computer database.

As previously mentioned, acts of violence are usually associated with the motivation of publicity for a cause. Some of the causes that have been most prominent in recent years are the anti-nuclear movement, the anti-war movement, anti-computer (and technology in general) sentiments, anti-company feelings, and anti-Americanism. Another cause for violence in general that has apparently had no role yet in computer security is influencing decisions, such as hostage release. One of the most common (and least obvious) causes involves personal feelings (revenge, disgruntlement, mental instability).

Love is one of the most powerful of all human motivators, so it should be no surprise that love plays a role in computer crime. One fraud [28] was initiated because of a romance and revealed to authorities because of spurned love. A woman employee of a computer peripherals company conspired with her boyfriend to create payments to a fictitious company. Credentials for the company were established through a birth certificate obtained for a child who had died shortly after birth. The man continued a relationship with his ex-wife, and this eventually drove the woman to turn in both herself and her boyfriend.

In separate incidents during an 18-month period [29], three computer executives in Sweden were caught giving defense secrets and classified information to the Soviets in return for relationships with female espionage agents. In approximately the same time period, a Japanese bank clerk, at the urging of her boyfriend, used fraudulent computer accounting to divert $500,000 to bank accounts under assumed names. The couple fled, but the woman was apprehended six months later.

A motivation that is especially apparent in hackers (but not exclusive to hackers) is meeting a challenge. Many perpetrators seem genuinely motivated by a desire to see if they can overcome the barriers in place. Closely associated with this motive is the desire to perform for peer recognition. Many hackers have been driven over the line of propriety by these pressures. One example occurred at a national laboratory when a scientist perceived a need by a gambling ring to computerize its operation. He agreed to develop and demonstrate the applicable computer routines through a dialup connection to one of the laboratory computers. By coincidence, this incident was uncovered through FBI wiretaps that were in place for investigation of the gambling operation. Also uncovered by virtue of the wiretap was evidence of a major college recruiting scandal.

One motivation associated with espionage is national loyalty, although there are usually many other factors behind espionage. In any event, there can be no doubt that this motive is powerful.

A final category of motivation is poor judgment. This comprises rationalization, insignificance, and accidental happenstance. Many perpetrators are convinced (or at least try to convince others) that their actions are not improper. One example [13] involved an ex-employee of a London (and Paris) company that offered numerical control programs for automatic milling machines through an international time-sharing service.

The man had worked as an applications engineer, helping customers evaluate and use the computer routines. He left the company and moved from London to Los Angeles. There were no field engineers for the company in Los Angeles, and company customers apparently continued to seek out the man for consultation. His computer password had been canceled by the company following his termination. However, he rationalized that he would actually perform a service for the company by continuing to consult and by demonstrating the routines through computer usage. He was not willing to deal with the "complication" of seeking the company's formal approval. He knew and began using the international password of another company employee in order to demonstrate the programs. Although charged with forgery and grand theft, he claimed to believe that he was performing services that the company would have wanted performed anyway, had there been a company applications engineer in the Los Angeles area. The company, whose income was derived from sales of its time-sharing service, felt differently.

The insignificance motivation is subtle. Some people believe their actions are too insignificant to be discovered. This belief is similar to petty theft, where the perpetrator believes that the risk of being discovered or prosecuted is small because the transgression is not serious. An example is afforded by employees who violate company rules against using computers for personal business, but do so sparingly, with care not to arouse attention.

Sometimes a transgression that appears at first to be small grows until its significance is inescapable. A gambling pool was the basis for a growing operation at a major automobile company [30]. It began with word-processor-assisted organization and documentation and grew to involve more serious computing support. The operation apparently involved 300 employees and $5000 per week payments.

Accidental motivation may actually be no motivation at all, although some people seem inexplicably accident-prone. This means the tendency to be careless or make mistakes. While not something that ordinarily leads to prosecution, it is certainly a tendency that needs to be recognized and met with appropriate protective measures.

The IRS was at the center of a 1985 controversy when 26,000 delinquency notices were erroneously mailed to mid-Atlantic companies [31]. The cause turned out to be a tape containing records of payments that had an unreadable header. During delays in handling the tape, the computer processing delinquency information found no record of the payments and as a result created the dun notices.

4.3 PERSONNEL INGENUITY

Before examining personnel security techniques, it is useful to consider the unique problems presented by reasoning personnel. When we described risk analysis in Chapter 2, we discussed probabilistic assessment of risk based on statistical predictability of threat frequencies. The situation for personnel is quite different. Although human reasoning is predictable to some extent, the approaches people have demonstrated in security have frequently been unconventional.

The best approach for dealing with intelligent personnel threats is to present an overall security environment that is as uniform as possible. The theory behind this is that a thinking adversary will seek the weak links in the protective armor. Although it is not possible to completely prevent weak links, studying the approaches that might be used and specifically identifying the approaches that have been used is the best way to get the information necessary to structure an effective protective environment. It is worthwhile considering some uncommon approaches in order to develop wariness about what to expect.

A commentary on human reasoning can be derived from the story of the Gordian knot [15]. The story says that "A complicated and difficult knot was tied by Gordius, king of Phrygia. It was said that whoever could undo the knot would rule over all Asia. Alexander the Great cut it with his sword." The success of Alexander the Great says something about unexpected approaches.

An early example of ingenuity [21] has been referred to as the "salami" (small slices) technique. An example [19] is the "round-down" system. Assume a savings account balance of $15.86. Applying 5.2% interest would add $0.8472 for a new balance of $16.68472. The actual amount to be entered as the account balance is $16.68. The accounting for the remaining $0.00472 can be carried or dropped with the statistical expectation that round-down amounts will be balanced by round-up amounts. A culprit, however, can accumulate all rounded down amounts in a controlled account without affecting any account holder's balance. Small amounts accumulated over many operations result in large sums (see Problem 3).

A computer operator in an Australian state-run betting agency changed the computer clock by three minutes so that race completion would occur before the computer time reached the actual time the race finished [29]. The interval allowed the man, with help from his girlfriend, to secure a bet on the winning horse and enter it in the computer with a legitimate-appearing time stamp. Romance again played a role in breaking the case, as the girlfriend became jealous of the man's relationship with another woman and revealed the scam to the authorities.

One of the first widely practiced ATM (automated teller machine) crimes involved ingenuity outside the computer processing [3]. It was made possible by machines that allowed ATM card removal prior to terminating a transaction. A perpetrator posing as a repairman would approach customers just after they had entered their PIN (personal identification number). The "repairman" would tell the customers that the machine was malfunctioning and was being serviced. Most would take their card and walk away, leaving the machine operational and in control of the perpetrator.

The asynchronous attack technique [3] can be applied in networks that process individual jobs in sequence. In this scenario, separation from one user's job stream to the next is essential. Unfortunately, a knowledgeable adversary can subvert the separation mechanism so that a privileged user's session is maintained for a subsequent user. One way that this can occur is where port contenders are used to connect a sequence of users to individual computer ports. At the end of a job, the computer must signal the port contender to switch to the next user. This allows a knowledgeable adversary to signal the port contender without the computer's participation, thereby connecting a new user (the adversary) to the old job stream.

One of the most publicized examples of ingenuity during the past few years has been the software virus (Chapter 7). This is a technique that involves planting an unwanted surreptitious code within an application program (the "Trojan Horse" technique). The purposes of the code are to do something unexpected by the user (for example to erase memory space) and to transfer copies of the code into other programs as part of a reproductive growth.

Another well-publicized strategy has been called the "terminal masquerade" (among other names). The attack consists of a message from the terminal of the perpetrator to the terminal of a user with higher use privileges. We will term this user the "authorized user." The targeted terminal must have "block mode transmission," which is the ability to transmit all or part of the contents of terminal display memory to the host computer when the terminal receives a special command from the computer. The attacker's message consists of command interpreter instructions intended for the host computer. The message is followed by the block mode send command for the authorized user's terminal. The receiving terminal automatically retransmits the command interpreter instructions to the host computer, which executes the instructions as if they came from the authorized user. The effect of this sequence is to enable an attacker to masquerade as the authorized user and to take advantage of the attendant privileges.

An interesting approach was publicized as the winner of a £100 (then about $130) prize offered in 1980 by the Computer Fraud and Security Bulletin in a contest seeking innovative approaches. The technique involved tapping telex lines carrying financial transfers between banks, and calculating the appropriate "standard test key" (STK) in order to insert fictitious transactions while avoiding the detection that would result from an improper STK. The calculation used only open literature descriptions of the STK algorithm. The contest winner exploited a weakness in the algorithm in order to change transaction digits without changing the STK. The weakness has since been repaired.

A few years ago a new rapid transit system began operation in a major U.S. metropolis. Encrypted debit cards were issued, with confidence that the encryption would prevent alteration of the data, which specified the remaining rides allowed. Some people discovered that decryption was not necessary, since the cards were easily duplicated. Replicating newly purchased cards allowed rapid multiplication of the perpetrators' purchasing power.

A major Lake Tahoe casino introduced ROM-controlled electronic slot machines with the expectation that the microelectronics were tamper-proof. The clear indication that they were not was a $3.25 million payoff (over three years) engineered through surreptitious replacement of memory data (ROMs).

Readily purchased electronic equipment [18] can be attached relatively inconspicuously to telephone lines that carry computer communications. It is possible to monitor for and record the sign-on sequence of a valid computer user. Later, the sequence can be played back in order to establish access to the computer. This technique can defeat passwords, cards, fingerprint, or signature identifiers and other access control techniques that are repeatable. The technique was used by a computer engineer in Japan [20] to steal 1.33 million yen (then about $7500) from a major Japanese bank. Only encryption, one-time passwords, or physical protection of the communication channel can prevent this type of attack.

A trick that has been used during electronic bulletin board and communication service interactive sessions is for one person in the communication session to send a message to the other person that causes password compromise by appearing to be a system message. An example is to send information such as "System temporary failure. Please re-enter password." Following reception of the password, the message can be sent: "System going down. Please sign off." At this point, the adversary knows the other person's password, and the person who has been victimized does not usually suspect the compromise. As we will see later (Chapter 8), variations on this technique can also be used to defeat some network encryption techniques.

Inadvertent electromagnetic emanations have been discovered to have the potential to convey computer and communications intelligence over surprising distances. Knowledgeable adversaries with proper equipment can detect the information (see TEMPEST, Chapter 6).

One of the early secure computer systems intended for handling classified military data was compromised by a "Tiger Team" testing for security weaknesses. The breakthrough was accomplished by mailing a rigged updated operating system release, which the computer operators unwittingly installed.

The list of techniques similar to the above is long. Although it may be entertaining to visualize the surprise generated by the discovery of each of these incidents, the message is serious. That is, it is difficult to predict the approaches that will be taken by an ingenious adversary. One should assess every possibility and should not assume that planned security measures are protection against every possible avenue of attack.

4.4 PERSONNEL SECURITY TECHNIQUES

Although many of the preventive techniques discussed throughout this book are effective against the actions of personnel, we will address in this section those that seem the most oriented toward the behavior of personnel. The discussion will be segmented into the subjects of prehiring investigation, termination, checks and balances, deterrence, monitoring, and administrative procedures.

4.4.1 Background Investigation

It is important [12] to know as much as practical about the background of personnel being considered for hiring as this background pertains to security risks. Background checks can range from cursory screening checks to full assessment of lifetime background. This latter approach is essentially the aim of procedures during consideration of personnel for national security clearances.

Many security breaches could have been prevented through background investigation. Frequently the investigation need not be thorough to be beneficial. For example, a London-based U.S. subsidiary suffered a $12 million loss in an "appraisal, sale, and leaseback" scheme. The perpetrator, who had been hired claiming "seven years experience with a major leasing company," actually had seven months experience. This false information could have been easily uncovered, and would have been indicative of the dishonesty displayed in the scam.

An assessment by the U.S. Department of Health and Human Services (HHS) showed that 20% of the people caught in computer crime have a prior criminal record, and 3% of the HHS employees who had access to money and benefit transactions had arrest records [8]. An assistant director at a Maryland hospital was indicted for embezzling nearly $200,000 in a scheme that was developed on the main hospital computer. It was then found that he had previously served a jail sentence for embezzling in Baltimore County.

There are several reasons for background investigations prior to hiring an employee. This is the best time to get information from the person, their previous employers, and their references. It is also easier to not hire an employee than to fire one. For similar reasons, a probationary period is useful. This allows more time to learn about a new employee with the bilateral understanding that derogatory information uncovered may be cause for dismissal.

The information available includes educational record, possibly a military record, previous employment, and personal data (marriage, divorce, bankruptcy, litigation, court actions, credit reports). Personal references are important, especially if potential biases can be removed (e.g., by cross-checking with neighbors, lawyers, doctors). A personal interview either for or including security objectives is indispensable.

An important warning flag is raised if a potential employee gives contradictory or erroneous information. Prospective employees can be informed that false statements will be cause for not hiring, or if discovered after employment, for dismissal. Another danger sign is discovery of any information that might be used by someone to blackmail an employee (e.g., covert homosexuality).

4.4.2 Employee Termination

Many companies that have not made termination a careful security procedure have paid for the mistake. This is especially true if there are any signs of discontent or duress. Some of these or similar procedures may also be appropriate in the event of a transfer.

Common termination procedures include revoking authorizations (passwords, keys, badges, cards), changing security information known to the employee (PINs, combinations), and reviewing legal obligations or signed agreements (e.g., nondisclosure).

Under signs of duress, it is advisable to immediately remove any physical or logical access to computers and data. It is better to pay an employee during a severance period with no productive effort than to suffer a disaster or crippling loss.

4.4.3 Checks and Balances

Separation of duties has been a widely used security concept. The idea is to reduce opportunities for people to carry out security compromises unilaterally. The implementation of this concept can be, for example, to have one person prepare a voucher, another approve payment, and a third issue the check in order to pay for a service. In addition to having different people involved in individual activities, it is helpful if they are as independent as possible (e.g., in different departments). This is a form of the strategy of checks and balances. Although carefully structured collusion can overcome checks and balances (Donn Parker observes [1] that about half of the cases he has studied involved collusion), an onerous burden is placed on the perpetrators.

A basic contributor to this strategy is the structure of the organization. In addition to contributing to separation of duties, another security reason for giving defined organizational responsibilities is to restrict physical access. For example, there may be little or no reason for systems analysts to be in areas containing operations personnel or vice versa. While it may not be forbidden, organizational structure at least makes it apparent to casual observation if employees are spending time in areas outside their job definition. Some of the other separations that make sense in an organizational structure are (Figure 4-1) systems analysts from programmers (to separate user interests from computer interests), development from maintenance (to establish bilateral configuration control), maintenance from operations (to separate programming from hands-on operation), and production control from project control (to separate data from operations).

More subtle separations involve assuring that close relationships (e.g., husband and wife) do not appear in functions that are being separated for security reasons.

Other useful controls [17] include 1) input controls (using batch totals or check sums in order to assure that entries are authorized and made only once), 2) change controls (assuring that changes are authorized and reviewed), and 3) testing controls (establishing system performance before use, including documenting results).

A large state motor vehicle department suffered extensive problems after converting to a new computer system in 1985. According to a state audit report, most of the problems that have plagued the system have been the result of failure to implement internal controls.

A warning about controls is that they should not be too highly parameterized. This means that thresholds of concern should be protected information or, better still, be varied somewhat randomly. In one highly publicized case [20], a bank fraud depended on changing data prior to computer entry and avoiding audit checks. The pertinent audit checks were triggered at a threshold of one million dol-

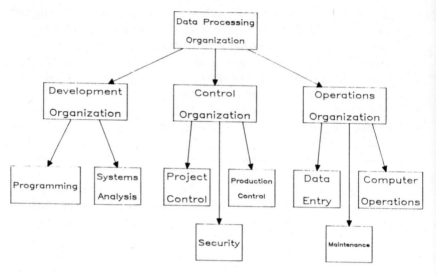

Figure 4-1   Organization for functional separation.

lars, so the perpetrator kept all transactions below the threshold. A mistake finally triggered the audit procedure, and the thief was caught.

4.4.4 Psychological Deterrence

There are several ways in which personnel can be discouraged from attempting misbehavior. None of these give absolute assurance, but some people will be completely dissuaded and most will be at least less likely to attempt improper action. The techniques are basically to publicize security measures, to publicize penalties for those apprehended, and to publicize prosecution.

4.4.5 Monitoring

Monitoring implies continuing to keep a watchful eye on personnel. In a way, most of us find monitoring displeasing because it is often associated with mistrust and police-state surveillance. However, experience demonstrates that the necessity far outweighs the tendency for distaste. One of the most widely used monitoring techniques is auditing. Another is simply supervisory awareness. Monitoring can sometimes involve actual video surveillance, but this is usually done only in response to evidence suggesting that surveillance data are needed.

An important technique is periodic personnel investigation. In the case of the retired U.S. sergeant in West Germany mentioned earlier, a Top Secret clearance had been given the individual in 1978, and there was never a reinvestigation.

A major point on this subject is that vigilance and awareness to information can contribute to uncovering activities that would otherwise go unnoticed. An examination of known computer crimes shows that most were discovered accidentally because someone noticed something out of the ordinary and someone followed up on the information. Sources for these types of information can include personnel from security, auditing, management, users, and, in general, tips from disassociated parties. An anonymous hotline may be useful for tips. All information derived will not be meaningful, but the potential usefulness is too strong to overlook.

Besides obvious tips involving incidents, other types of information that can provide warning signs include excess absenteeism, unwarranted excessive overtime worked, persistent tardiness to work, sudden low-quality work or low productivity, excessive complaints, and unwillingness to take vacations or job rotations.

4.4.6 Administrative Procedures

Administrative procedures are frequently neglected [27], and this is a common source of problems. There are many ways in which administrative procedures can contribute to security. Policies about what is allowable and what is not are useful for people to know, in addition to the deterrent factor mentioned previously. Management involvement in these policies sends a message about how strongly management feels about attempts to maintain appropriate behavior. In addition to the deterrent that this provides, employees frequently are influenced by a desire to emulate behavior of management. Furthermore, the advantage works both ways in that management involvement helps sensitize management to security, making managers more supportive and more responsive. "Security plan" documents help apply policy to specific facilities or computing areas and contribute to comprehensive evaluation of parochial security situations.

Procedures such as separation of duties, enforced vacation, job rotations, and accountability through formal reports are also useful.

Signed agreements, such as codes of ethics in behavior and nondisclosure (during and following employment) agreements, are helpful. Most organizations find it necessary to provide complete policy information in clear, concise written form to all employees. Attention to currency of the policies is also necessary.

In the case of the Ohio police chief mentioned earlier, a basic procedure resulted in his apprehension. The procedure established that the operator entering data was the responsible party, who was therefore to be notified in case of any change to the record. So he was immediately notified of the police chief's action and reported it.

One of the most important administrative functions is training. The security benefits of training are substantial. The objectives of training are to make personnel aware of and provide understanding about policies and procedures. This contributes to deterrence and also to acceptance of the security environment. It is important that training be cost-effective for the trainers and the trainees. This is one of the reasons that training must be carefully matched to the intended audience.

Some training techniques are 1) new-hire indoctrination (introduction to company motivations, procedures, rules), 2) organization-specific sessions (seminars, problem discussions, new information presentation), 3) attention-grabbers (security movies, bulletin boards, newsletters, handouts, posters), and 4) publicity on pertinent incidents.

4.4.7 Comments on Analytical Selection of Protective Measures

The discussion in Chapter 2 provided specific guidance about selecting protective measures as barriers against threats that are predictive in a probabilistic sense. Many personnel actions do not correspond to this model. Also, historical statistics are not available on threats that are unique or the result of inventive approaches (see previous discussion on personnel ingenuity). For these reasons, it is important to supplement traditional personnel security approaches (e.g., risk analysis) with scenario analysis, exposure analysis, or similar "thought-process" evaluations. The intent is to prevent or at least reduce vulnerabilities that can be identified by reasoning (or lucky) adversaries.

PROBLEMS

1. Assume that a computer security specialist is to be hired for an insurance company. a) Estimate the total investment that will be made in this employee during the recruiting and hiring process and during the first five years of employment. Do this by computing costs for the functions you judge necessary. b) In addition to this investment, propose a method for quantifying the increase in value of the employee due to experience.

2. From the following scenario, list items that might warrant security concern or further investigation and give reasons for items listed.

   Joe Smith is a programmer who has been with the company for 10 years. He has developed a reputation for being a hard worker, frequently arriving for work early and leaving late. Occasionally, he returns to work after supper and works well past midnight. Joe has ambitions for promotion, but his raises have become very small and he is not considered a candidate. Joe is unmarried and has no apparent social life. He sometimes travels to another city to visit his mother, who is in a nursing home. Joe's only other idiosyncrasies are that he purchases a new Porsche yearly and spends an unusual amount of time on the telephone. The background screening done on Joe prior to hiring yielded no negative information. Friends and neighbors knew little about Joe, but saw nothing detrimental in his personal conduct.

3. Assume that a bank sets up daily interest computations for each of 10,000 accounts. An attacker uses the salami technique to accumulate round-down amounts in a private account. What is the expected annual amount that the account will receive?

DILEMMA DISCUSSIONS

1. An accounting firm has a stringent policy against using company computers and software routines for personal or outside business. There is an internal company debate about how to treat transgressors who are apprehended. One faction argues that since the policy is stringent, the violators should be

punished and/or fired and the actions should be publicized to all employees as examples. The other faction argues that the violators should be warned that they will be under surveillance but will not be punished in exchange for not informing other employees of the misbehavior and not repeating it. The advantage cited is that there is less likely to be publicity that gives a police-state atmosphere to company employees and that might give potential customers misgivings about the integrity of the information handled by the company. What would your approach be?

2. Considering personnel screening, how much weight should be given to negative information from the distant past? On the one hand, negative incidents are good predictors of future negative incidents. Therefore, this type of information might be considered sufficient reason for not hiring into a position that might involve opportunity to violate computer security. On the other hand, our society's penal system is based on paying one's debt to society, after which further debt payment is unnecessary. In fact, some states (including California) allow one to petition the court for dismissal of some records following satisfactory completion of a sentence. If the petition is successful, the petitioner can then legally claim not to have been charged. The reason for this measure is to assure that rehabilitation is not impeded. Would you take the conservative position to minimize risk to your computer program or the liberal position of giving a person who may have made a mistake the benefit of the doubt?

3. We are conditioned in our society to not spy on or report on negative information about others. However, we may be asked in the interest of computer security to report incidents or behavior that seems improper or suspicious. How would you react to this request?

REFERENCES

1. Parker, Donn B., *Computer Security Management*, Reston Publishing Company, Inc., Reston, VA, 1981.
2. Wong, Ken, "Computer Crime—Risk Management and Computer Security," *Computers and Security*, Elsevier Science Publishers (North Holland), New York, 1985.

3. Parker, Donn, *Fighting Computer Crime*, Charles Scribner's Sons, New York, 1983.
4. Lamb, John, and James Etheridge, "DP: the Terror Target," *Datamation*, February 1, 1986.
5. Ball, Leslie D., "Computer Crime Is a Growth Business," *Across the Board*, June 1982.
6. Mayo, Ken, "Fingering Data Thieves," *Business Computer Systems*, November 1985.
7. Giglio, Lewis, "Computer Security Priority: Protecting Against Inside Jobs," *InformationWEEK*, August 19, 1985.
8. Flanders, Vincent, "Security in an Insecure World," *OnLine Data Access*, September 1985.
9. Hyatt, Joshua, "Easy Money," *INC.*, February 1988.
10. Gullo, Karen, "Security Is Loosely Practiced at Young Supercomputer Firms," *Datamation*, January 1, 1988.
11. McGraw, Tim, "Board Hashes Out Proposal for FBI's NCIC System," *Government Computer News*, January 8, 1988.
12. Brandon, Dick, "Employees," *Computer Security Handbook*, Douglas Hoyt, Macmillan Information, New York, 1973.
13. Barentine, Gene, et al., "Keeping the Lid on the Cookie Jar," *Security Management*, September 1985.
14. Parker, Donn B., *Crime by Computer*, Charles Scribner's Sons, New York, 1976.
15. *VLSI Systems Design*, January 1988.
16. Cornwall, Hugo, *Datatheft*, Heineman Professional Publishing, New York, 1988.
17. Van Duyne, Julia, *The Human Factor in Computer Crime*, Petrocelli Books, Princeton, NJ, 1985.
18. Schrager, Barry, "Outwitting 2-bit Thieves and Arresting Computer Crime," *Data Communications*, November 1982.
19. Baker, Richard H., "Lining Up Computer Crooks," *Micro Communications*, May 1985.
20. Perry, Tekla S., and Paul Wallich, "Can Computer Crime Be Stopped?" *IEEE Spectrum*, May 1984.
21. Browne, Malcomb W., "Locking Out the Hackers," *Discover*, November 1983.
22. Campbell, Douglas, "Targets for Destruction," *Security Management*, July 1988.
23. Hafner, Katherine M., "Is Your Computer Secure?" *Business Week*, August 1, 1988.
24. Ball, Michael, "To Catch a Thief: Lessons in Systems Security," *Computerworld*, December 14, 1987.

25. Greene, Richard M., Jr., *Business Intelligence and Espionage*, Dow Jones-Irwin, Inc., 1966.
26. Cohan, Lloyd, "Hard-Disk Assembly (HDA) Degausser," *Center for Computer Security News*, U.S. Department of Energy, July 1986.
27. Carlone, Ralph V., "Agencies Overlook Security Controls During Development," U.S. General Accounting Office Report to the House of Representatives Committee on Science, Space, and Technology, May 1988.
28. Bartimo, Jim, "Love and Death Figure in $155,000 DP Scam," *Computerworld*, May 3, 1982.
29. "Love, Money Drive International DP Crime," *Computerworld*, December 26, 1983.
30. Bartimo, Jim, "Three WP Typists at Ford Named in Betting Operation," *Computerworld*, January 10, 1983.
31. Betts, Mitch, "IRS Blames Computer Tax Tape Snafu on Human Error," *Computerworld*, March 18, 1985.

5

The Regulatory Security Environment

Many of the features of a security program depend on the behavior of people. This includes protective behavior as well as adversarial behavior. In both cases, it is important for all involved to understand what behavior is expected. It is also important that people understand what will happen if the specified behavior is not followed. For these reasons, security programs must involve specific regulations. These can range from organizational rules and policies to national or even international laws. The objective is to present users, operators, managers, and adversaries with information about what is allowed, what is not, and what response may be expected if behavior deviates from that allowed.

In this chapter, we will first examine the regulatory environment from the standpoint of national security, with particular emphasis on the current U.S. posture. Next, we will consider privacy issues. Then, we will address the U.S. legal environment. Last, we will assess the international legal environment.

5.1 NATIONAL SECURITY

Some information is deemed important to the national security. As one might expect, there are degrees of importance. The first categorization we will examine is based on determining whether information is "classified" or "unclassified."

5.1.1 Classified Information

Information that is identified as important to national security is "classified" in order to provide mechanisms for appropriate security (special protection, handling, and labeling procedures). This is true regardless of whether the information is in printed form, in computer memory, or in transit across communication media. Classifying information is not always an easily defined process. There are various levels (e.g., Top Secret, Secret, Confidential) and categories (e.g., Crypto, Restricted Data). Adding to the difficulty of definitive treatment is the fact that aggregations of unclassified information can be deemed classified.

In the United States, Executive Order (EO) 12356 (a fairly recent update of previous similar EOs) prescribes a uniform system for classifying, declassifying, and safeguarding national security information.

Classification decisions are made by people who have been authorized to classify by proper authorities. Implicit in this authorization is suitable training and responsibility. Classification guidance documents are approved by proper authorities for use and are made available for those who must make decisions regarding the classification and handling of information. There are also mechanisms for reviewing and possibly modifying decisions that have been made.

In order for people to be given access to classified information, they must be certified as "cleared" personnel through detailed background investigation by government agencies. Their clearance level must be at least as high as the level of classified information they require, and they must have a "need to know," including access to "Categories." This helps prevent indiscriminate access to all classified information of a particular classification level, even by people having clearance at that level.

The handling of classified information in computers and communications systems depends, as it does for data outside these systems, on the particular classification or classifications involved. Procedures for marking, transporting, reproducing, and destroying memory media are carefully defined. Obviously, computers and communications systems that handle classified data must possess security features that are of high quality. The challenges that have been presented in the national security arena have been met with some of the best technology and techniques that can be applied.

Although the U.S. government encourages the use of risk analysis, and even requires its use by government agencies and contractors, it is not considered proper to place a dollar value on classified information assets. For this reason, quantitative risk analysis is not applied to the protection of U.S. classified information. This does not remove the requirement that protective features must be selected in a cost-effective manner. The tradeoffs are accomplished by the judgment of those responsible for the systems, with review by controlling government agencies. This review process affords checks and balances to the system and also helps assure uniform approaches throughout the government.

The details of handling classified information are of little direct interest to those who do not deal with national security information. However, most of the techniques that have been developed for computer and communications processing of classified information are applicable to the security of unclassified information. For this reason, we will be interested in many of the security developments that have been made or sponsored by the U.S. Department of Defense (DoD).

5.1.2 The National Computer Security Center

Because of the difficulty of handling classified information in a computer environment, especially where all users of the computer system might not have the same level of clearance or need to know, the DoD introduced a Computer Security Initiative in 1978. The development of "trusted" computer systems (systems having features that enabled separation of levels of classification and levels of personnel clearances on the same system) was pursued through this initiative. Subsequently, the DoD established a Computer Security Center (DoD CSC) within the National Security Agency (NSA) in 1981. The function is now carried out by the National Computer Security Center (NCSC).

NSA was established by President Harry S. Truman as an agency of the DoD in 1952. Although the NSA mission has traditionally emphasized communications security (breaking encryption systems and designing encryption systems), NSA security expertise has been helpful to the NCSC. The DoD CSC and NCSC effort has included sponsoring research, establishing a system of evaluation for security systems, evaluating products against these evaluation criteria, and carrying out independent research. Most of the results have been made publicly available. We will examine this body of information in detail in Chapter 7.

Although much of the security assistance provided by the U.S. government is done as a public service, there is a strong national security motivation that provides much of the impetus. Since the benefits derived must frequently be weighed against some constraints, some of the government initiatives have been sources of great controversy. One such controversy might be called "the saga of the 145s," since it involved the National Security Decision Directive (NSDD) 145 (issued by President Ronald Reagan in 1984) and House Resolution 145 (signed into law as the Computer Security Act of 1987 by President Reagan in January 1988). Understanding these actions requires some background. We will begin by discussing sensitive unclassified information.

5.2 SENSITIVE UNCLASSIFIED INFORMATION

Until the early 1980s, there was a clear delineation of computer and communications security responsibilities within the U.S. government. The DoD CSC was working to improve classified computing; NSA continued to work on classified communications security; and the National Bureau of Standards* (NBS), under the Department of Commerce, provided public information on unclassified computer and communications security techniques. The NBS role had been specified by the Brooks Act (initiated by Representative Jack Brooks of Texas) of 1965, which made the Department of Commerce responsible for unclassified federal computer standards.

In the late 1970s, it was becoming clear that the United States enjoyed a comfortable advantage in computer technology (as well as several other technologies) over the countries considered political adversaries. The result of this imbalance was that foreign espionage was obtaining unclassified technological information that would shorten and reduce the cost of their own development times. Since many of the areas in which computers are applied (e.g., national early warning systems, anti-ballistic missile systems, encryption) are critical to national defense, a need was seen to protect a category of

---

*   Formerly known as the National Bureau of Standards, the agency has now been renamed the National Institute of Standards and Technology (NIST) [42].

information that had previously been unprotected. This category was called "sensitive unclassified."

Many incidents bolstered the concerns. *Parade* magazine published a description of a Soviet link that led through several countries and terminated in a Lockheed Sunnyvale computer. The U.S.S.R. had attempted to acquire a chain of banks to gain computer access to a bank known to have Silicon Valley links. There was no evidence of attempts to obtain classified information; the effort was apparently entirely directed at obtaining unclassified technology.

A Soviet physicist was known to have an extraordinary interest in the use of U.S. supercomputers. He was granted 100 hours of use of a Cray computer. Later, he made attempts to link into the computer remotely. His persistence was so frustrating that his visa was eventually marked "restricted from supercomputers."

A Defense Department study [19] found that Soviet intelligence agents had acquired NASA documents dealing with airframe designs (including computer programs on design analysis) and flight computer systems. It is interesting to note that the U.S.S.R. space shuttle vehicle now has many similarities to the U.S. space shuttle. The resultant savings to the Soviets were estimated at several years of research and testing and several million rubles (several million dollars).

Admiral Bobby Inman, then NSA director, was one of those urging that action to stop the drain of technology information be taken. A government study identified 100 areas [19] that were considered vulnerable to hostile intelligence. Computer information was targeted for special attention because of the large, organized accumulations of information available in computer databases and because of the potential for automated searching and sorting. A decision was made to issue a presidential directive to assure protection for these types of information and to specify steps to initiate corrective actions. The result was the presidential directive NSDD 145, issued in 1984, which contained both classified and unclassified portions.

5.2.1   National Security Decision Directive (NSDD) 145

The main features of NSDD 145 were to formally combine government computer and communications policy under the oversight of one agency (NSA) and to control sensitive unclassified (critical to national defense) information. A cabinet-level steering group was established in order to oversee the implementation of the directive, to provide policy guidance, and to assure budgeting. The group was chaired by the assistant to the president for National Security Affairs. Other members of the group included the Secretaries of State, Defense, and the Treasury; the Central Intelligence Agency (CIA) director; the Attorney General; and the Director of the Office of Management and Budget (OMB). The high-level positions of the membership indicated the emphasis that the administration was placing on the effort.

A Security Committee was also established to institute policies, to determine priorities, and to undertake evaluation. It was chaired by the Secretary of Defense. A subcommittee on telecommunications was established, chaired by the Assistant Secretary of the Treasury for Electronics. Another subcommittee on information systems was chaired by the Director of the Computer Security Center. As part of the expanded role of NSA prescribed by the directive, the name of the DoD Computer Security Center was changed to the National Computer Security Center.

The results of this initiative were to deemphasize the role of the Department of Commerce, specifically NBS, in providing guidance to the private sector on unclassified computer and communications security, and to enlarge the role of NSA to include jurisdiction over at least some private-sector security prerogatives. These changes were not popular with many in Congress. "Information-gathering" visits by NSA personnel and a movement (Project Overtake) to replace the widely used DES encryption algorithm (see Chapter 8) also increased ingrained private company suspicion of the agency and how it might use its new power. Some raised questions about how cost-effective the restrictive programs were [18] and whether U.S. scientists were being hampered more than foreign scientists by the restrictions (see Problem 5).

A series of incidents had served to heighten concerns. In 1979, the Atomic Energy Act had been used to prevent a magazine from publishing an article on nuclear weapons based entirely on information from public sources. NSA had canceled an encryption conference at MIT because of concerns about publicizing cryptology information. In 1982, the DoD had ordered more than 100 papers withdrawn from a Photo-Optical Instrumentation Engineers technical symposium because the papers threatened to "export critical technical data." In 1985, the DoD had made similar claims about papers given at a radar conference. In 1986, the Commerce Department's National Technical Information Service (NTIS) had issued a contract revision requiring private sector vendors of unclassified information to supply names and addresses of domestic and foreign customers, and required that no data be released to anyone "deemed likely" to give it to a foreigner. These requirements were removed in response to strong protests.

Finally, in 1986, a memorandum was issued by Admiral John Poindexter, then National Security Advisor, which empowered the DoD to restrict public disclosure of sensitive unclassified database information, even within the private sector. A group of congressmen decided that the movement had gone too far.

5.2.2 The Computer Security Act of 1987

A period of battles and negotiations took place in 1986 and 1987. Admiral Poindexter fell out of power during the "Irangate" turmoil, and his replacement, Frank Carlucci, rescinded the 1986 memorandum. The administration was gradually persuaded to support a strengthened role for NBS. This repositioning was enunciated in House Resolution (HR) 145 (a numbering coincidence) which was introduced by Representative Dan Glickman of Kansas working with Jack Brooks of Texas. The legislation passed both houses of Congress and was signed into law (P.L. 100-35) by President Reagan in January 1988. In addition to NBS, specific roles are spelled out for NSA, OMB (Office of Management and Budget), and OPM (Office of Personnel Management) [14,16]. Subsequent to the Computer Security Act, the National Bureau of Standards was renamed the National Institute of Standards and Technology (NIST).

The Act requires NIST, with technical assistance from NSA, to establish security standards for civilian agency computer and communications systems. It mandated that security plans are to be produced by government and government contractors for review by NIST, NSA, and OMB, and sensitive unclassified data must be identified. Other associated activities are that OMB has issued Bulletin 88-16 on security plans, and OMB Circular A-130 mandates civilian agency user training plans.

Although the intent of NSDD 145 remains unchanged, it now appears that the required security policies will be implemented in a manner that is acceptable to a wider range of people and organizations.

Implementation of this act has not reduced the effect of other government security programs. The Operations Security (OPSEC) program, and the Information Security (INFOSEC) program, which encompasses the Commercial Communications Security (COMSEC), Computer Security (COMPUSEC), the emanations security

(EMSEC), transmission security (TRANSEC), physical security (PHYSEC), and personnel security (PERSEC) programs are intact.

5.3 PRIVACY ISSUES

The term "privacy" implies personal privacy to most people. We will consider both personal and company privacy. The kinds of personal information we are most sensitive about vary, but a typical selection is medical condition and history, financial condition and salary, school record and grades, criminal record (including charges and arrests), marital status and history, family problems, and work evaluations. The general need for privacy was recognized in the U.S. Constitution, which forbids unwarranted searches of citizens and their homes. Early in this century, Supreme Court Justice Louis Brandeis wrote that "the right to be let alone is the right most valued by civilized men." Recent events demonstrate that these sentiments still persist. In this section, we will address this human need, which leads to specific computer and communications problems.

Four decades ago, George Orwell published a futuristic warning against loss of privacy and the other dangers of socialist collectivism: *Nineteen Eighty-Four* [given a contemporary assessment in Ref. 5]. Ten million copies have been sold, and 1984 has come and gone with much discussion about whether or not the U.S. government and other free-world governments are accumulating so much information about their citizens that they could become "Big Brothers."

Orwell's message has been widely misinterpreted as warning only against activities such as those the U.S. government is pursuing in database accumulation. Orwell's 1984 has become identified with contemporary threats to individual privacy, but a fair assessment would have to note that few people today feel that they must have blind allegiance to their leaders, that they have no access to public writing, or that pleasure is denied them. In fact, one of the most important differences between Orwell's society and ours is that there is a strong international movement to assure that individual privacy is properly protected. However, many authors feel [6,8] that privacy is linked to freedom from government oppression. Whether or not privacy encroachments are a threat to our way of government, there are legitimate needs for individual privacy to be balanced against society's increasing needs for computerized information. It is not an easy balance to achieve, as we shall see.

5.3.1 Threats to Privacy

The public, especially in free-world countries, is sensitive to any threat that may decrease privacy [3]. In 1965, a proposal for a Federal Data Center that would consolidate information about U.S. citizens was strongly opposed and eventually dropped. Some are convinced that the concept has only been postponed, and may in fact be implemented through nationally required personal identification cards [26].

Recent surveys by Louis Harris & Associates, Inc. and by the Institute of Electrical and Electronics Engineers (IEEE) confirm public concern. These surveys both showed that three-fourths of Americans are concerned about the current privacy situation. Almost 90% believed that a master file on each individual could be easily assembled, and more than three-fourths believed that this would be an invasion of privacy [25]. About half believed that computers represented a direct threat to privacy.

There are many consequences of this public concern about computer privacy that go beyond personal privacy. For example, state laws are now in effect [4] that require mandatory reporting of all state residents testing positive for the human immunodeficiency virus (HIV), which can develop into the acquired immunodeficiency syndrome (AIDS). AIDS preventive programs based on voluntary blood testing could be severely hampered if people at risk of exposure to HIV avoided testing for fear of lack of privacy for computerized records.

USA Today (October 16, 1987) reports that the federal government now maintains 3 billion computer files containing personal data. More than 3000 databases are available to the public over some 500 value-added networks. Data on each U.S. citizen appears, on the average, in about 100 computer files.

One of the most widely used private database applications is the credit record data maintained by credit bureaus. The threats to these data include exposure (wide distribution, relatively weak security), errors (data submitted in error or maintained in error), and linking (possibility of associating with other databases to accumulate information improperly).

Several illustrations of the problem have been recently given. CBS TV's *60 Minutes* detailed the extensive trail of information bits left by almost everyone as they use credit cards. Accumulations of junk mail show all of us how information proliferates. During the 1987 confirmation hearings for Supreme Court nominee Robert Bork, a listing of some of his videotape rentals was revealed.

Noting the accumulation of personal data in databases and potential links between these databases, *Washington Post* writer Pete Earley constructed an information-gathering scenario. The first step was identification of a license plate number. Many agencies have access to motor vehicle department files, in which license plate numbers are linked to the owner's personal data (address, sex, height, weight, date of birth, social security number). Further information on the owner is available through the social security numbers from state agencies such as compensation and tax offices (employer, length of employment, job title, salary). The Deeds Registry office links the owner's address to information including the owner's housing situation (ownership, date built, assessed value, deeds, loans). Divorce and marriage records are available that can be linked to the owner. These may include information about children and other relatives, in-laws, and ex-in-laws. Although data from most of these databases are rarely made public, they are not leak-proof. Many people have authorized access to each, and the security measures in place do not give complete assurance of personal privacy.

All U.S. states must now maintain income verification programs to enable social workers to check a welfare applicant's finances through records that even include some IRS data. Considering current abilities to link databases, information about individuals might today be in a situation close to that proposed for the Federal Data Center.

Much of the data management and much of the threat to privacy portrayed above can be linked to social security numbers. Franklin Roosevelt, who pledged social security number confidentiality in 1935 while urging implementation of the social security program, would probably be incredulous. Although the government does not strictly require social security numbers to be associated with data entered in databases, it usually makes it difficult to not comply. As a result, the government now uses social security numbers for a variety of initiatives, including identifying 18-year-olds and notifying them of their requirement to register for the draft, along with a threat that failure to do so is a felony [9]. Social security numbers are also used to track down delinquent student loan recipients.

The advantages of these types of data links are that compliance with national laws can be encouraged and taxpayer money can be saved, at least potentially. The disadvantages are that data can be misused or misinterpreted. Some examples will illustrate this danger.

Joseph Califano, Jr., Secretary of (then) Health, Education, and Welfare, announced "Project Match" in 1977. This was a database-matching program to track welfare cheats. The initial "matching" was between welfare recipients and federal employees. The intent was to identify federal workers who were illegally on welfare rolls. The program appeared to conflict with The Privacy Act of 1974 (see Section 5.4.2), but the provisions of the act were dodged by a liberal interpretation of the wording, since the objectives of matching seemed so worthwhile. In order to protect against abuses, computer-matching rules were developed by the Carter administration, requiring demonstrated cost-effectiveness and prenotification to OMB and Congress. The Reagan administration supported and continued the program, but removed the prenotification requirement.

The program has had both successes and failures. One couple was caught after collecting $60,000 over four years by using three aliases and fictitious children. Fifteen HEW employees were indicted during the first year of this program. However, the American Civil Liberties Union (ACLU) claimed that five of the indictments were dismissed, four persons pleaded guilty to misdemeanors (theft under $50), and six pleaded guilty to felonies. There were no prison sentences among the 15, and the total repayment ordered was less than $2000.

Some of the problems encountered were:

1. Errors. One woman quit work after being diagnosed as having cancer. After a few months of cobalt radiation treatment, she returned to work and notified the welfare agency. Welfare checks continued to be sent, in spite of her second notification to the agency. She decided that after two failures by the agency to acknowledge her requests, she had exercised sufficient effort. A judge agreed with her and ruled against the prosecution's case alleging fraud.
2. Timing. A person changing status from "welfare" to "employed" showed up on both lists by virtue of timing. Even if the two lists had been updated simultaneously, there was risk that the welfare list would be sent before the change and the employment list after the change.
3. Misinterpretation. People listed as employees, but working part time, could be eligible for welfare. In this case, they would legitimately show up on both lists.

In response to the obvious weaknesses in computer matching, the Computer Matching and Privacy Protection Act of 1988 established protective mechanisms, including formal review policies. Declaration of the matching purpose and legal basis is now required. The matching controversy will no doubt continue, but the message for those of us interested in security is that privacy protection has complexities that go beyond the black/white protection of data from unauthorized disclosure. There will usually be situations that raise questions about whether a particular operation is an infringement on intended use.

It has been demonstrated [e.g., Refs. 10,11] that databases can be constructed for independent purposes and with complete personal identification without using common linking identifiers such as social security numbers. One technique for accomplishing this depends on "smart" cards and public-key cryptography. These subjects are covered in Chapters 6 and 8, respectively. The basic concept is that individuals can select (or be given by a trusted process) separate "pseudonym" identifiers for each organization to which they furnish data. A "credential" (smart card containing data) can carry a credit certification issued by one organization under one identifier that will be honored by another organization under a different identifier. The linking process depends on the one-way transformation properties of public-key cryptography, along with some logistic strategies to prevent tracing based on data accompanying transactions. The conclusion is that untraceable business transactions and unlinkable databases are technically feasible.

5.3.2 Privacy Protection

In addition to the complex political problems of how far privacy protection should be carried and how private data should be used, there are some questions concerning how to best assure the protection of private data. Some protective measures are those that apply to any type of data (physical security to prevent destruction and unauthorized disclosure), logical forms of access control (to restrict those who can use, modify, or examine data), and encryption (to make the meaning of the data obscure to unauthorized people). The unique protective measure that can be applied to private data is regulatory protection (providing for rules on how to handle private data and penalties for violating the regulations).

These regulations can be in the form of requirements from company management; from a regulatory agency with jurisdiction over the company; or from local, state, and national governments. We will pay particular attention to national laws concerning privacy in the next section.

There are many similarities between private data protection and proprietary data protection. Proprietary data are generally considered to be data that are vital to a company's interests (design information, strategy information, financial information) because they would offer a competitive advantage to another company. This similarity can extend to legal protection.

5.4 COMPUTER AND COMMUNICATIONS SECURITY LAWS

We have suggested that legal measures serve as deterrents, help reduce confusion about what is and is not allowed, help punish offenders, and encourage uniformity among computer security approaches. In this section, we review some of the most significant features of the legal environment and discuss some specific legislation.

5.4.1 Background

There are two basic legal approaches of interest in computer and communications security. One is civil law, and the other is criminal law. One branch of civil law is "torts." A second involves breach of contract. In civil law, the aggrieved party is the plaintiff. The institution of a civil legal action is possible for negligence, intentional acts, and statutory wrongs. In criminal law, the government is the party that institutes litigation. The institution of a criminal legal action is possible for violations (which usually require intent) of criminal statutes (e.g., for fraud, larceny, embezzlement, extortion, sabotage, invasion of privacy). Included are committing an act forbidden by law and omission of a duty prescribed by law.

Negligence is endangerment of the interests of or injury to another person or persons through failure to exercise due care (that a "prudent" or "reasonable" person would exercise), including precaution and vigilance. Negligence can result in product defects or services improperly performed. Proper care is that which would "ordinarily" be expected.

Fraud is essentially misrepresentation. Specifically, fraud is a perversion of truth for the purpose of inducing another in reliance upon it to part with some valuable belonging or to surrender a legal right. This includes false representation of facts and concealment of facts so that another is caused to incur legal injury.

Invasion of privacy is intrusion, interception, misuse, or aggregation of information that infringes on personal desires to protect thoughts, sentiments, and emotions.

Four factors generally contribute to the "intent" to commit a computer crime. These are:

1. Knowledge. Computer crime requires an awareness of what the person committing the crime is doing. This awareness need not necessarily extend to the actual consequences of the action, as long as the results are not extraordinary.
2. Purpose. Many computer crime laws require that the person charged be shown to have had a particular objective to commit a crime.
3. Malice. Malice is the specific intent to do harm. Some laws are now in place to punish nonmalicious computer access (e.g., in New Jersey and California).
4. Authorization. Some statutes protect only against unauthorized computer access.

As might be expected, these factors are not always easily decided by the courts. A case involving two programmers employed by a Los Angeles food wholesaler illustrates the point [43]. The couple used the food wholesaler's computer to perform their own independent computer services under contract to a competitor company. They apparently made no significant attempt to hide the activity. When charged with fraud and misrepresentation, they argued that their open use of the company computer proved lack of intent to commit a crime. The pair was also charged with theft of computer time. Since the computer was leased, the defendants argued that the cost to the company was the same, whether or not they used the computer. Court rulings on these types of issues are always subject to individual interpretations.

Computers are always a tool in computer crime. They now usually provide a tool for law enforcement against computer crime [17]. Software tools are available that help compile lists of stolen property (including ATM cards), tabulate data on modus operandi, provide personal information on known criminals (types of crimes committed, associates, aliases, fingerprint data), and provide analysis of data such as telephone usage.

Computers may be directly involved in litigation in two basic ways. During the "discovery" (evidence gathering) aspect, computer-based evidence (e.g., audit trails) can be used. During the "trial" aspect, computer records may be admissible. The validity of computer evidence requires strong conditions [27] in order to not be considered "hearsay." The computer recording process must be shown to be secure and robust, and the accuracy of the evidence must be demonstrated. Specifically, the computer records must be made pursuant to established procedures for systematic and timely reconstruction and preservation, records must be made in the normal course of business, and the recording and storage processes must be shown to be trustworthy, accurate, and complete. In addition, the storage processes must be protected against human errors and mechanical breakdowns.

Some legal protection mechanisms of interest include copyrights (protection for the work or creation of an author, including computer programs), licenses (permission granted by an authority for an intended action, like software use), patents (protection for novel inventions, now having some application to software), and contracts (an agreement capable of being legally enforced).

5.4.2 Privacy Legislation

In the previous section, we reviewed a history of concerns about personal privacy. These concerns have been greatly heightened by technological developments in computing, communications, and databases. In 1969, a U.S. committee, the Committee on Scientific and Technical Information (COSATI), was established as an effort of the Federal Council of Science and Technology to examine the legal aspects of information systems. In 1972, Eliot Richardson, Secretary of (then) Health, Education, and Welfare, commissioned an advisory committee on personal data systems, seeking recommendations for legislation. A special study group was also formed at IBM. As a culmination of these efforts (along with similar studies in other countries looking at privacy issues), a generally accepted set of principles evolved. These principles provided the basis for The Privacy Act of 1974 and were embodied in many similar legislative initiatives in other countries [4].

The basic principles are 1) that the organization maintaining private data is responsible for the timeliness, accuracy, and security of the information, 2) the individual subject of the information must have a chance to learn about the information and correct it if necessary, and 3) the information cannot be used for a purpose other than the one for which it was gathered without the individual's consent. In addition to The Privacy Act of 1974, these basic principles have also been enacted into law in many other countries, including Sweden, Belgium, Norway, Denmark, West Germany, France, Austria, Iceland, Luxemburg, Hungary, Israel, and Great Britain.

The Privacy Act of 1974 applies specifically to agencies of the federal government and to custodians of data maintained for the federal government. This includes federal executive departments, the military, regulatory agencies, government corporations, government-controlled corporations such as Federal Reserve Banks, and the Federal Home Loan Corporation.

Under the provisions of the act, individuals are permitted access to their records and may request amendment in case of inaccuracy. Since there may be differences of opinion about accuracy, refusal to change a record results in a requirement for both sides to file a statement of the disagreement for arbitration.

Information maintained by an agency must be relevant and necessary (or required) and must be collected as directly from the individual as possible. On request, the agency must inform the individual of the authority for obtaining the information and whether such information is mandatory or voluntary. The agency must also state the principal purpose for which the information is intended, the routine uses that may be made of the information, and the effects of not providing all or any part of the requested information.

Agencies must maintain accurate, relevant, timely, and complete records. They must establish rules of conduct for personnel who have contact with the data. An agency must establish appropriate administrative, technical, and physical safeguards for the records. Notice must be served when any record is disclosed under compulsory legal process.

Any officer or employee of an agency who willfully discloses individually identifiable information is guilty of a misdemeanor. An individual's name and address may not be sold or rented by an agency.

In conjunction with the Privacy Act of 1974, a seven-member Privacy Protection Study Commission was formed in order to study databanks, automated data processing programs and information systems, and to survey standards and procedures. The commission makes annual reports to Congress.

The Right to Financial Privacy Act (1978) added to the privacy legal environment by prohibiting the government from obtaining financial records of customers or institutions without due legal process. The 1966 Freedom of Information Act offered a different type of public protection by allowing access by the public to many forms of government information. The Electronic Funds Transfer Act (a parent of the Right to Financial Privacy Act) provided for consumer protection in the access of Electronic Funds Transfer (EFT) systems by banks and financial institutions. The Fair Credit Reporting Act provided a means for credit bureau database subjects to check and correct credit records. The Buckley amendment provided the same rights for educational records. The Crime Control Act of 1973 provides for criminal justice records protection.

Communications privacy has been addressed by The Electronic Communications Privacy Act of 1986. This legislation updates The Wiretap Act of 1968, which restricted voice wiretaps but did not apply to computer and digital communications traffic. The new legislation specifically addresses electronic mail and cellular telephones, including computer communications. Protection is provided against interception and disclosure of personal and business data. The law essentially makes protection the key element, with communication technology being relatively insignificant. The foregoing list of legislative measures makes it clear that legal privacy protection has not been ignored.

A caution should be noted about assuming that quantity legislation means quality privacy. There is a danger that organizations swamped in paper compliance [8] will emphasize the mechanics of compliance over the intents of the legislation. Company management should not overlook the real objectives of privacy regulations while assuring formal compliance.

5.4.3 Procedural Legislation

Congressional deliberations on computer and communications security laws have been extensive during recent years. One of the early motivators was a 1976 study by the General Accounting Office entitled "Computer-Related Crimes in Federal Programs" [39]. Senator Abraham Ribicoff cited this study as influential in his introduction of The Federal Computer Systems Protection Act (1977). Although the bill did not pass, it provided a widely copied model for subsequent legislation, such as The Computer Fraud and Abuse Act.

One of the most significant pieces of procedural legislation was the Foreign Corrupt Practices Act of 1977 [12]. The law applies to most corporations, corporate managers, and directors. It requires that a corporation make and keep books, records, and accounts detailing transactions and dispositions of assets. Security is required to prevent disclosure of records, to detect crimes, and to recover from errors.

It also requires that internal accounting controls be maintained to assure proper authorization and recording of transactions, and to assure access control and data integrity. Cost-effective controls and risk assessment are mandated. Adequate funding and staffing of security programs are required.

The law establishes personal liability for noncompliance and provides for punishment of up to $10,000 in fines and up to five years imprisonment. It also provides for corporate fines and permits civil suits from stockholders. This legislation has been extremely helpful in impressing corporate management with the importance of computer and communications security programs.

Other procedural measures are:

1. The Communications Act of 1934 (and subsequent amendments), which established the Federal Communications Commission (FCC) to regulate interstate communications, control frequency allocations, and regulate licensing. As a subset, the Public Utilities Commission was tasked with intrastate communication not covered by the FCC [1]. The 1974 antitrust suit against AT&T was largely based on Title II, Section 215, of The Communications Act, which implies that telephone companies should buy their equipment based on price rather than relying on owned companies [38].
2. Professional standards that exist to assure a proper environment for people and equipment. These include the U.S. National Electrical Code, the U.S. National Safety Code, and the U.S. National Fire Protection Code.
3. The Computer Fraud and Abuse Act of 1984 (strengthened and expanded under the Computer Fraud and Abuse Act of 1986), which includes legal protection against unintentional acts.
4. A requirement for U.S. banks to report crimes to the federal government. This law was enacted to prevent banks from covering up incidents in order to protect their public image as reliable financial managers.

5.4.4   Copyright Legislation

The Copyright Act of 1976 provided little protection for computer programs (e.g., applications programs). It was intended to cover literary and artistic works. This shortcoming was addressed by software amendments and the Patent Act of 1980, which defined a computer program and gave rights to authorized owners (as opposed to authors). This act essentially authorized the owner to use the programs for intended computer operation and to make an archival copy, both without the consent of the copyright owner. Copies are permissible provided that the copy process is an essential step in the utilization of the program, or that the copy is for archival purposes only and that all archival copies are destroyed in the event that right of possession of the program ceases.

A software copyright protects the product, but not the algorithm. This is the main reason that applications programs were usually available only in object code. The source code was protected by copyright as an "unpublished work." In these cases, the copyright could actually be lost if the source code were published without a proper copyright notice. In 1983, the U.S. Court of Appeals ruled that object code (whether in operating systems, applications programs, or ROM) is copyrightable. In 1984, The Semiconductor Chip Act gave more specific protection against "reverse engineering" of logic designs.

For most software, illegal copying ("software piracy") is one of the most common and hard-to-control computer crimes [29–32]. For the software vendor, illegal copies may mean considerable loss of revenue, since these copies may take the place of software purchased legitimately. It is estimated [33] that about half of the personal computer software in use today has been illegally copied, and that the probable cumulative loss to software vendors is now in the billions of dollars.

There have been several approaches by software vendors to the software piracy problem [31–34]. A series of copy protection techniques have been used, and these have proved effective against the average adversary. However, commercial programs are available that allow one to circumvent most copy protection schemes, usually with purportedly legitimate motivations (backup, recovery of data from damaged diskettes). Legal pursuits of companies that either intentionally or unintentionally allowed copying has been attempted. In the mid-1980s, several multimillion-dollar suits were initiated. Most were settled out of court for substantial amounts. Public education regarding the stakes for vendors and the purchasers (who ultimately pay the price increases caused by software piracy) has been extensive. For example, the Association of Data Processing Service Organizations (ADAPSO) has distributed information in many forms, including the diskette look-alike booklet, "Thou Shall not Dupe." Most application software is delivered to the user with a notice of responsibility and a "shrinkwrap" license. The license statement claims that the purchaser is not the owner of the software and, by opening the package, acknowledges that the contents will be protected in the interests of the software developer.

The shrinkwrap license may be more a psychological deterrent than a legal deterrent. Court challenges to the validity of the license have not often been successful [23]. The problem is that most purchased products become the property of the purchaser. The intent of the shrinkwrap license is to make the consumer a licensee instead of an owner.

For several years, some major software vendors vigorously pursued legal action against companies within which software piracy could be identified. Very little recent legal action of this type has been initiated [37]. However, there have been a significant number of recent legal actions against developers of clones of well-known software products, with the contention that copyright laws were being violated. These actions are based on copyright features that were introduced into the legal system in 1985 and 1986.

5.4.5 Liability

There are legal requirements for due care in the development of software, the maintenance of physical facilities, and the use of information. Failure to meet these requirements can result in legal action charging liability.

Almost everyone has had an experience with "computer error," and almost everyone knows that it wasn't the computer that made the error. Lack of personal attentiveness can cause serious problems for others. In order to protect the interests of those who may be affected, legal measures have been enacted.

A large number of incidents ranging from trivial to deadly serious have occurred. *USA Today* reported (October 16, 1987) that a Michigan man was arrested five times based on erroneous computer information. Each time, he attempted to correct the incorrect data. A Dallas executive on a business trip was stopped for a minor traffic infraction [22] and identified by a computer record as an escaped convict. He was arrested and jailed; it took a week to correct the error.

One notable case found its way to the U.S. Supreme Court. An employee of a multimillion-dollar data vendor mistakenly identified a major construction firm as bankrupt. Subscribers to the data service also received the incorrect information. The construction firm sued for damages; the data vendor claimed First Amendment (free speech) protection and absence of malice. The court ruled that a data vendor could not be given the same protection that might be appropriate for the news media. The ruling stated that the business of furnishing information carried an obligation to assure that the information was correct.

Unfortunately, some mistakes endanger human lives. One of the most serious and tragic examples was a software error that led to the deaths of two patients undergoing therapeutic radiation treatment. Several other people were seriously injured [20]. The problem occurred in the control of a linear accelerator radiation source in a cancer treatment center. The first incident occurred when a patient receiving routine treatment following successful removal of a shoulder tumor was apparently given a severe overdose of radiation while the accelerator was being controlled to deliver a small dose. Within three months, the man was mostly paralyzed. Three months later he died. His wife filed a suit against the treatment center, the oncologist, and the manufacturer of the radiation source. A second patient was given a similar dose within a month of the first. Within another month, he died. Similar suits were filed. A woman was so badly burned in a similar incident at another cancer treatment center that her left breast had to be removed. At a different center, another patient was badly injured.

It was determined that the problem responsible for these and other incidents was a software control error that occurred under an unusual sequence of operations. The machine was designed for two different types of therapy, X-ray and electron, each intended for different types of cancers. The X-ray source was a high-intensity beam that was attenuated by a tungsten target. The electron beam was 100 times less intense and was delivered with the target removed. During a particular sequence of editing controls, the software failed to coordinate the insertion of the tungsten target with the use of the high-intensity beam. Although all indicators available to the operator portrayed a small dose, absence of the target increased the actual dose by a factor of 100.

Cases of the type described are not easy for courts to weigh. If software is viewed as a service, software producers can be found liable only if they can be shown to be negligent. If software is viewed as a product, the manufacturer can be held strictly liable. The manufacturer of machines controlled by complex software is faced with a dilemma. Since it is very costly and might be impossible (see Chapter 7) to develop perfect software, the cost of continuing assessment must be balanced against the potential of liability. Manufacturers of systems controlled by complex software can expect that unpredicted behavior may occur. They can also expect legal action in response to software behavior that causes harm.

Another threat created by failure to exercise due care can result from poor contingency planning. Contingency planning quality is necessary to avoid conflict with the Foreign Corrupt Practices Act, but it is also receiving emphasis from the banking community. The Office of the Comptroller of the Currency (OCC), an agency of the U.S. Department of the Treasury, has issued several banking circulars mandating contingency planning by national banks. The first requirement by the OCC was issued in 1983, and covered data center operations. It has gradually enlarged its requirements to include other operational areas and microcomputers. Although these actions apply to the banking industry, similar requirements are in place for government agencies and government contractors. As a result, company management is being sensitized to the contingency planning responsibility, with special notice that legal action may be successful if contingency planning is flawed [15].

5.5 INTERNATIONAL TOPICS

As illustrated during the discussion about privacy protection, there have been many similarities in objectives and results of the legal environment of the "free" (democratic) governments. This is probably due, in large measure, to similar political structures. Generally (see Figure 5-1), the leadership personnel of these countries are elected by the populace; the wishes of the people influence the legal structure; there is a relative independence between the judicial, legislative, and executive branches; and legal approaches to computer and communications security are considered important. These similar backgrounds have led to the recognition that working together is advantageous for many reasons, not the least of which is the necessity for transborder computer data communication. Many of the resultant issues have been addressed by international forums.

5.5.1 International Forums

Countries in Western Europe, Canada, the United States, Japan, Australia, and Turkey have participated in the Organization for Economic Cooperation and Development (OECD). OECD computer and communications interests have included privacy, databank controls, computer communications, and transborder data flow. Recommendations have included regulatory commonality and encourage-

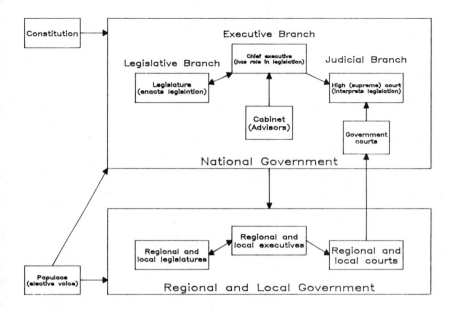

Figure 5-1   Legal structure of democratic countries.

ment of transborder data communication between countries having equivalent data protection.

Other activities include the International Bureau for Informatics (work on uniform protection for transborder flow by countries including France, Iraq, Iran, Israel, Italy, Jordan, Lebanon and Spain); a data protection group under the oversight of the European Economic Community (EEC or Common Market); the Nordic Council; the UNESCO International Commission for the Study of Common Problems; and the Council of Europe (which works through periodic conventions). All of these activities are encouraging the enactment of similar legislation, especially with regard to database privacy protection.

Privacy protection legislation applicable to computers has been enacted in many countries. For example, the Belgian Privacy Act of 1982 provides that people must be informed when their information is entered into a data bank. The West German Federal Data Protection Act of 1977 requires written consent prior to processing personal data. Countries that have been the most active in developing legislation applicable to computer and communications security include (in addition to the United States) Britain, Canada, France, and Sweden. The environment in these countries will be examined more closely.

5.5.2 The British Environment

Britain provided the primary legal models for most other democratic countries. The bicameral Parliament consists of a House of Commons and a House of Lords. The legislative control resides primarily in the House of Commons. The main day-to-day threats to Britain are perceived to be foreign espionage, international terrorism, the Irish Republican Army, criminals, and misusers of private data.

A major effort in formulating legislation in Britain was provided by the Committee on Data Protection, which led to The Data Protection Act of 1984 (discussed below). British legal security strengths include government data protection, anti-terrorist measures, protection against obscenity and defamation, and copyright protection.

A significant legal security development began with The Official Secrets Act of 1889. Major changes were made in 1911, 1920, 1939, and 1972. An interesting aspect of the act is Section 2, which makes it a crime for any crown servant to disclose, or for anyone else to receive, information learned on a government job. Interpretation is made by the Attorney General. This section has been a source of controversy. In the late 1970s, Philip Agee and Mark Hosenball were deported under the terms of the act, following Agee's revelation of CIA operatives in Britain and Hosenball's release of data on the Cheltenham communications interception center. Other similar incidents have raised questions in Britain about the appropriateness of the strictly interpreted provisions of the act.

There have been several incidents that point out differences between British and U.S. security regulations [28]. In one example, pharmaceutical data protected in Britain were furnished to the United States under the provisions of a trade agreement. In the United States, the data were revealed, subverting the British protection. The British Ministry of Agriculture, Fisheries, and Food exchanges data with the U.S. Food and Drug Administration, which does not afford equivalent protection. British shipping companies send protected data to the U.S. Public Health Inspections Office, which does not have equivalent protective requirements. A Parliamentary Report on the range of three missiles was being protected in Britain at the same time it was being released by the U.S. Joint Chiefs of Staff. These are examples that demonstrate the importance of ensuring similarity of protective legislation.

The Data Protection Act of 1984 was the first British legislation specifically addressing computers. Its main purposes were to preserve privacy and enable the enforcement of processing standards. It was intended to reduce misuse potential and allow secure international trade. Control of all U.K. data was intended, regardless of where the data were processed. Supporting bodies prescribed include the Data Protection Registrar (to handle registration, training, security measures, and enforcement) and the Data Protection Tribunal (to handle appeals of decisions by the Registrar). The act provides that personal data users must register intent to use the data, the purpose of the data, and its source. It provides for personal compensation for damages due to data destruction, disclosure, or inaccuracy. Home users (private, household, family, recreational) are exempt from the act's provisions.

The registration process includes identification of the individual, company, or organization using the data and details about the data use and to whom disclosure is planned. Registration is valid for three years (renewable) unless a shorter term is requested. Registration can be refused if furnished information is incomplete, false, or misleading; if there is evidence of poor security measures; or if there is evidence of failure to abide by defined protection principles. The protection principles are similar to those enunciated in the U.S. Privacy Act of 1974. Users are entitled (upon verification of identity) to learn of data held and to examine the data.

Exemptions from the provisions of the act can be granted for national security reasons, to avoid conflicts with other British laws, to avoid conflict with criminal prosecution, and to allow statistical and research studies (if done in a controlled manner).

5.5.3 The Canadian Environment

The Canadian legal system is modeled after Britain's. There is a bicameral legislative power, with the House of Commons providing the major legislative initiatives. The Senate members are appointed. The courts and the judicial system rely on appointed personnel. There are federal, provincial, and municipal police forces. The Royal Canadian Mounted Police (RCMP) is the federal force and serves many provinces. The RCMP has been an active organization in studying and developing computer and communications security measures. Canada is a NATO member and is influenced by NATO security measures. The main terrorist threat to Canada appears to be from the Quebec separatist movement.

The Canadian Human Rights Act of 1977 was a significant piece of privacy legislation. It is similar to the U.S. Privacy Act of 1974. Like Britain, Canada has an Official Secrets Act. It requires protection of government information and provides penalties for nonprotection. It has no measures that raise the controversy demonstrated in Britain. Canada's national security is enunciated in a 1963 Cabinet Directive (No. 35), "The Security of Information in the Public Service of Canada."

Like most other countries, Canada has found that legislative wording is sometimes out of step with current technology. One incident had especially clear implications about the relationship between crime and legislation [7]. A professor at a Canadian university had assigned a study of the university computer network control program, with the aim of identifying vulnerabilities. Under the study, a program was developed that could be used to modify the computer and terminal usage time charges. The program was not developed for actual use. However, a copy of the program was found in a wastebasket by another student whose motives were less honorable. The unprincipled student and two friends used the program to their advantage between four and five thousand times over a period of a few months before they were caught. The three were not prosecuted, but their computer privileges were withdrawn by canceling their passwords. Soon, all three had obtained new passwords and were again using the computer system.

Within a few months, vandalism of the computer system became evident. System crashes were occurring frequently. Computer files were being destroyed. Obscene and taunting messages were appearing on system consoles. Finally, the same three students were identified, apprehended, and arraigned. They were tried under Section 287 of the Canadian Penal Code for using a telecommunications service maliciously and without right.

A defense attorney argued that terminals and lines do not make a computer system a telecommunications facility. On appeal to the Supreme Court of Canada, the prosecution's Section 287 claim was invalidated on the grounds that the improper activity did not utilize a telecommunications system of the type intended under the law. As Minister of Justice Jean Chretian stated, the theft of computer data may require rethinking basic rules of criminal law that have their origins in history of a different type.

5.5.4 The French Environment

France has several unusual political features. It has a president elected by voters for a seven-year term under the constitution that was instituted by Charles DeGaulle. It has a bicameral parliament, with a National Assembly and a Senate. The presidential power is underscored by provisions that, in certain defined emergency situations, the president may assume full governing powers. The president also may dissolve the National Assembly, the more powerful branch of Parliament. France is a member of NATO, but has withdrawn her troops from the NATO military command. The government and the population are unusually concentrated (in Paris, where about one-sixth of the French people live). Five of the largest French companies are state owned, reducing the role of private capital. Most private banks in France were nationalized in 1981.

In spite of these unusual features, privacy legislation is not unlike that of other democracies. The Law Concerning Data Processing, Files, and Liberties (1978) provides privacy and human rights protection for computer and communications transactions. There is a National Committee for enforcement. Under the provisions of the law, no administrative decision resulting in a judgment on human behavior can be based on computer profiling of protected data. Any computer processing of protected data requires a declaration of intent approved by the National Committee. Data may be sent to another country only if the other country provides equivalent protection. Computerized data showing racial origins, politics, or religious beliefs are prohibited except for churches (e.g., membership lists).

5.5.5 The Swedish Environment

Sweden has followed up on a long history of privacy protection with a strong legal computer privacy base. The principle of free access to public records was apparently initiated in 1766. Now, approximately 90 laws control information disclosure, and approximately six laws provide for the right to examine database information. A comprehensive 1979 report of the Committee on the Vulnerability of Computer Systems (SARK) identified data, programs, computer and communications equipment, computer processing capability, and personnel as assets that should be afforded legal protection. National militarily significant information was specifically excluded as the responsibility of the Ministry of Defense (under the 1981 Secrecy Act). The SARK recommendations led to the Swedish Data Act with enforcement under the Data Inspection Board.

Under the Swedish Data Act, personal data files can be kept only by applying to and receiving a license from the Data Inspection Board. Restricted data requiring special justification include personal files on people other than organization members, employees, or necessary customer data; information that a person is suspected of or has been convicted of a crime or has suffered criminal penalties; information about illness, state of health, sexual life, receipt of financial aid, subject of Aliens Act action; and information about race, political views, religious beliefs.

Penalties and damages are defined for computer-related transgressions. Fines or imprisonment of up to a year are specified for setting up a personal file without a license, for unlawful dissemination, and for incorrect data transmittal. There are fines or imprisonment up to two years for unlawful procurement, alteration, or obliteration of personal data. Compensation to damaged parties is provided for in order to atone for suffering and monetary losses. It is apparent that personal privacy is well protected in the Swedish computer environment.

PROBLEMS

1. List the basic legal reasons that computer and communications crime is different from similar crimes not associated with computers or communications.
2. List the legal protections and avenues of restitution available for vendors of applications software.
3. List the differences, in your order of importance, between the military and civilian legal environments.
4. a) List five kinds of tort law violations involving computers or communications, each against the law for a different reason. b) List five kinds of criminal law violations involving computers or communications, each against the law for a different reason.
5. Assume that 400 U.S. scientists and 10 Soviet bloc scientists are attending a U.S. technical conference at which the presentation of potentially sensitive unclassified technical information is being considered. There is a 10% chance that the information will be useful to each American and a 20% chance that it will be useful to each person from the Soviet bloc. The expected value to each American who can use the information is $10,000, and the value to Soviet bloc scientists is $100,000. There is a multiplicative factor of about 10 for each U.S. scientist and 100 for each Soviet bloc scientist. This is the value of sharing or technological transfer to peers after the conference. a) Determine the expected value to the U.S. and the expected value to the Soviet bloc. b) Assume that the expected values are normally distributed with a standard deviation of $1 million for the U.S. and $6 million for the Soviet bloc. What is the

probability that the value lost to the U.S. by prohibiting disclosure of the information would exceed the value gained by the Soviet bloc if it were disclosed?

6. A typical sophisticated application program takes eight person-years to develop at a loaded cost of $70,000 per person-year. Subtracted from the retail price of $60 are distributor discount ($30), sales representative commission ($3), administrative overhead ($2), advertising ($3), and production cost ($7). a) How many units must be sold to recover the investment? b) Assume that double the investment is recovered. If the number of illegal copies is equal to the number of legal copies, and one-fourth of the illegal copies would have represented sales, what is the vendor's loss?

DILEMMA DISCUSSIONS

1. Computer matching has positive and negative potential. The positive potentials are that persons who have evaded legal responsibility may be apprehended, and in many cases taxpayer money may be recovered. The negative potentials are that some people may be wrongly identified, and personal privacy may be reduced. Would you favor computer matching or not? Why?

2. Since technology flow to foreign governments may endanger the relative strength of the United States, the U.S. government has imposed restrictions on sensitive unclassified information. The disadvantage of these restrictions are that the information becomes harder for U.S. scientists to share and use and that nongovernment companies are subject to a new set of government controls. Do you favor protecting sensitive unclassified information or not? Why?

3. Personal computer application software vendors insist that no unauthorized copies be made because free copies obviate purchased software. Some users insist that business criticality makes necessary more backup copies than authorized, and some users use multiple computers and argue that one person should not have to make multiple purchases. There is also resentment against vendors who charge high prices for software that is not thoroughly debugged. Monitoring copying by users would be extremely difficult. What should be done? Why?

4. You are an insurance executive and your company depends heavily on public reputation for your business. You have suffered a significant, but not crippling, computer embezzlement. The choice is to report the loss to the appropriate law-enforcement office and to prosecute the perpetrator, or to keep silent in order to avoid publicity. You know that publicity could cost you more loss in business than you could recover in prosecution. However, to not report the crime would result in losing an opportunity to discourage this individual and others from committing crime and would result in losing an opportunity to alert others in the business community to this type of crime. What would you do? Why?

REFERENCES

1. Sapronov, Walter, "Network Users Cannot Overlook the Legal Issues," *Data Communications*, January 1985.
2. Chabrow, Eric R., and Paul E. Schindler, Jr., "The Tug of War Over Corporate Data," *InformationWEEK*, June 10, 1985.
3. Neier, Aryeh, "Zealous Data Collection May Harm Personal Rights," *InformationWEEK*, October 26, 1987.
4. Moad, Jeff, "As AIDS Spreads, State PC Systems Are Reaching Limits," *Datamation*, August 15, 1987.
5. Podhoretz, Norman, "1984 Is Here: Where Is Big Brother?" *Reader's Digest*, January 1984.
6. Zimbardo, Philip G., "To Control a Mind," *The Stanford Magazine*, Winter, 1983.
7. Parker, Donn B., *Fighting Computer Crime*, Charles Scribner's Sons, New York, 1983.
8. Smith, Robert Ellis, "Privacy: Still Threatened," *Datamation*, September 1982.
9. Stibbens, Steve, "Privacy: A Nagging DP Problem," *Infosystems*, August 1982.
10. Chaum, David, "Security Without Identification: Transaction Systems to Make Big Brother Obsolete," *Communications of the ACM*, October 1985.
11. Chaum, David, "A Secure and Privacy-Protecting Protocol for Transmitting Personal Information Between Organizations," *Proceedings of CRYPTO 86*, Springer-Verlag, New York, 1987.
12. Parker, Donn B., *Computer Security Management*, Reston Publishing Company, Reston, VA, 1981.

13. Martin, James, *Security, Accuracy and Privacy in Computer Systems*, Prentice-Hall, Englewood Cliffs, NJ, 1973.
14. Power, Kevin, "Hill Might Punish Security Lapses," *Government Computer News*, July 22, 1988.
15. Sherizen, Sanford, and Albert Belisle, "Begin Contingency Planning or You Might Become an Outlaw," *Computerworld*, July 11, 1988.
16. Bloombecker, Buck, "On Capitol Hill, Loose Chips Sink Ships," *Computerworld*, December 14, 1987.
17. Balogna, Jack, "Software Applications Put the 'Byte' on Crime," *Computerworld*, December 14, 1987.
18. Power, Kevin, "Security Guidance near Final Stage," *Government Computer News*, June 24, 1988.
19. Howe, Charles L., and Robert Rosenberg, "Government Plans for Data Security Spill over to Civilian Networks," *Data Communications*, March 1987.
20. Joyce, Ed, "Software Bugs: A Matter of Life and Liability," *Datamation*, May 15, 1987.
21. Marshall, David, "Introduction to the Law on Software Licenses, Part 1: The Basics," *The Computer Law and Security Report*, May–June 1986.
22. Bequai, August, "Computer Libel: A New Legal Battlefield," *Digital Review*, May 18, 1987.
23. Swartz, Herbert, "Louisiana Bayou," *DEC Professional*, August 1987.
24. Bloombecker, Jay, "International Computer Crime: Where Terrorism and Transborder Data Flow Meet," *Computers and Security*, January 1982.
25. Perry, Tekla, "Readers Comment on Computers' Effect on Privacy," *IEEE The Institute*, April 1984.
26. Kilty, Larry, "A Security Consultant Sees Big Brother Lurking Around the Corner," *Data Communications*, July 1982.
27. McLeod, Ken, "Combatting Computer Crime," *Information Age*, January 1987.
28. Michael, James, *The Politics of Secrecy*, Pelican Books, New York, 1982.
29. Sterne, Robert Greene, and Perry J. Saidman, "Copying Mass-Marketed Software," *Byte*, February 1985.
30. "Can Software Makers Win the War Against Piracy?" *Businessweek*, April 30, 1984.
31. Freedman, David H., "Foiling Corporate Software Pirates," *High Technology*, July 1985.

32. Schiffres, Manuel, "The Struggle to Thwart Software Pirates," *U.S. News and World Report*, March 25, 1985.
33. Huston, Bill, "Self-Programmed Single Chips—The MC68705ss," Professional Program Session Record 29, Electronic Conventions, Inc., Los Angeles, 1982.
34. Albert, Douglas J., and Stephen P. Morse, "Combatting Software Piracy by Encryption and Key Management," *IEEE Computer*, April 1984.
35. Swartz, Herbert, "A Watershed Case for Copyrighting," *Business Computer Systems*, January 1984.
36. McCoy, Michael D., "Chip Pirates: Beware the Law," *IEEE Spectrum*, July 1985.
37. Steichen, Terry J., "Piracy Mania," *InfoWorld*, August 6, 1984.
38. Pearce, Alan, "Is a Radio Days Law Fit for the Information Age?" *Network World*, August 15, 1988.
39. "Computer Related Crimes in Federal Programs," General Accounting Office Report, 1976.
40. Nycum, Susan, and Donn Parker, "Computer Crime and Computer Technology," U.S. Department of Justice, Bureau of Justice Statistics, 1983.
41. Corley, Robert N., and O. Lee Read, *The Legal Environment of Business*, McGraw-Hill, New York, 1987.
42. Levine, Arnold S., "NBS Name Change Brings Expanded Mission," *Federal Computer Week*, August 29, 1988.
43. "The Case of the Daytime Moonlighters," *Computer Crime Digest*, February 1983.

6

The Hardware Security Environment

For most people, thinking of computers means thinking of hardware. This may include the mainframes, disk farms, printers, and other peripherals found in central computer facilities, and it may also include personal computers (PCs) and small business computer systems that are found in almost every office and business and in many homes. These are all of interest to us in this chapter.

From a security viewpoint, however, the hardware environment goes much deeper. Security is affected by the way components (as well as computers) are designed, processed, and manufactured. In any computer one can preserve operational integrity and introduce protective security features. Similarly, techniques for processing and communicating information are available that make such processing relatively immune to the intervening environment.

Hardware access control is also important. Hardware devices can contribute to verification of authorization and authentication through personnel identification. ROM-based security features are now commonly available.

Since most hardware is susceptible to electrical and electromagnetic effects, it is useful to understand threats posed by these effects and the appropriate protective measures.

Information tapping is another significant threat. Possibly even more important is the fact that information from electronic data processing and communication media emanates electromagnetically, even though such emanation is unintended. This makes passive remote information tapping an especially insidious vulnerability.

Personal computers have had a major impact on our society, as well as on security. Most people using these new tools generally have different backgrounds from the more traditional computer users. The implications for security are significant.

An increasingly important hardware security technique is "sealing" a device to prevent undetected tampering. The viability of the "smart card" concept depends on (among other things) the success of sealing.

These topics represent the substance of this chapter. We begin by considering various ways to ensure the integrity of data processing hardware and data processing capability.

6.1 HARDWARE INTEGRITY

Most of us have known the frustration of having the computer "down." Perhaps our work was delayed, or at least we were inconvenienced by having to obtain alternate processing capabilities. However, these minor frustrations are insignificant compared to the impact of downtime for some major computer systems. Airline reservation systems are crucial to the financial health of airlines. The reliability of electronic funds transfer (EFT) systems, including automated teller machine (ATM) processing systems, can be related to the banking industry profits. Air traffic control system outages can have serious safety impacts. Air defense, ballistic missile detection, and (eventually) Strategic Defense Initiative (SDI) systems are strongly tied to national defense. The stakes are certainly noteworthy.

Human error can also enter the picture. A major semiconductor manufacturer recently found [1] that its powerful microprocessor (being installed in large numbers of 32-bit desktop computers) had been affected by an error in the alignment of processing masks. The result was that tens of thousands of chips being delivered had the potential to make multiplication errors under certain limited conditions. The conditions were not seen during routine testing, but the existence of the error was intolerable. The company spent several million dollars to replace chips that may have been capable of errors.

Several techniques can be used for assurance that computers remain operational through crucial processing needs. The general concern regarding loss of processing capability was addressed in

Chapter 3 under the heading of disaster recovery. Here, we take a more detailed and hardware-oriented approach, with the recognition that the time to obtain alternate processing may have to be measured in minutes or even fractions of a second, rather than in days. For these types of requirements, component-level approaches, circuit-level approaches, information-level approaches, and system-level approaches are common.

6.1.1 Component Reliability

It is well known that techniques can be introduced in the manufacture of hardware components that make the components more reliable. These techniques include clean-room assembly areas, comprehensive testing, component selection to tight specifications, burn-in (operating the device for a period of time beyond the concentration of early lifetime failures called "infant mortality"), materials selection (e.g., gold-plated leads, which are less subject to corrosion than are cheaper alloys), potting (encapsulation), hermetic sealing (environmental protection), ceramic packages (instead of less robust plastic), careful soldering or welding of connections (instead of crimping), secure mounting (flat packs instead of dual in-line packages), and electrical protection (protective diodes, capacitors, and shielding).

Components that have been manufactured with an accepted degree of attention paid to these techniques are called "high-rel" (high reliability) parts. "Mil Spec" parts (manufactured and tested to military specifications) are a type of high-rel parts. A price is paid, literally, for such parts. A purchaser of components can also increase chances for improved reliability by "qualifying" parts to even more stringent requirements than those used in high-rel manufacture. Productive additional steps may include more restrictive selection, testing, and burn-in; the incorporation of peripheral protective surroundings (for electrical and physical protection); and generous "design margins" (circuit design allowing for component characteristics to change beyond the degree expected).

Some applications demand especially careful component production. Deep space probes and some weapon applications require that processing continue reliably under conditions of radiation and low signal-to-noise ratios. A satellite orbiting through the Van Allen radiation belts can receive a radiation dose of a million rads over its lifetime, an amount that, if not attenuated, would damage most electronics. (About 1000 rads would be fatal to humans.) Some techniques used in "hardening" semiconductors to radiation effects include the use of CMOS (complementary metal-oxide semiconductor) technology with very thin gate oxide structures, gold doping, tantalum silicide coating over aluminum conductors, and plasma-assisted silicon dioxide deposition. CMOS technology is also among the best available for ensuring noise immunity and low power operation, both of which are crucial to the success of deep space probes.

New technological developments in component manufacture have been exciting because of the small sizes achievable and because larger numbers of components on a "chip" (semiconductor substrate) have meant, in general, fewer connections (a notable source of reliability problems). In the early 1960s, integrated circuits contained only a few components on a chip; now a few million are possible.

However, this news has not been all good. As the size of the components in dynamic (recirculating charge) RAMs decreased, the charge representing a bit value decreased correspondingly. When sizes became small enough that charge amounts could be altered by anomalies in the ordinary environment, "soft" errors (bit changes) began to occur [2–4]. These errors are attributable to alpha particles that occur naturally and are enhanced by traces of radioactive elements (uranium, thorium) that are contained in integrated circuit packaging materials (gold-plated metal and ceramics). An alpha particle entering a silicon surface causes an electron-hole pair, resulting in a minute discharge. Soft errors occur when this discharge significantly changes the charge stored by a RAM data memory site. Remedies include using special geometries or material techniques to confine larger charge within the RAM memory element volume, refining material impurities, and using error-protection code techniques (Section 6.1.3).

Similarly, "vertical" magnetic bulk storage (with magnetic moments oriented perpendicular to disk surfaces rather than parallel) and optical storage devices have enabled extremely high memory densities [5]. Unfortunately, error rates are higher than those of less dense memories.

Winchester disk drives operate at about one error in 10^9 or 10^{10} bit transfers. Optical disks are about 1000 times more error-prone. Typical protective techniques are DRAW (direct read after write), which compares transferred data with a source copy, and signature analysis, checksums, and other error protection techniques.

6.1.2   Circuit Redundancy

A point of diminishing returns is reached in trying to produce perfect components. Fortunately, other techniques are known. One of these is to provide redundant components arranged logically in circuits so that faults that occur are either overridden or identified (or both). Fault identification enables repair, automatic alternate component selection, or discard of the data so flagged. These concepts can be applied during manufacture [6,7] in order to reject or repair components. One technique is to include spare components in component arrays. These spares can be made active in order to replace components determined to be faulty through testing. Typical amounts of redundancy for one-million-bit (1Mb) RAMs is about 1–2%.

Digital systems lend themselves particularly well to logical structures for fault detection, correction, and avoidance. The checking circuitry can be used to test the performance of a device during manufacture or in operation. Spare components can be activated in response to operational checks.

An example is "dual redundant" operation, where two equally capable components are operationally ready, but only one is active. The currently active component continually carries out self-tests and, at any sign of failure, hands the role of active component over to the other. One important implementation of this concept is in MIL STD (Military Standard) 1553B communication protocol, currently used on a wide selection of U.S. and NATO military aircraft (fixed-wing and helicopters), tanks, and ships. The protocol is oriented toward command/response transmission on a "bus" (see Chapter 8). There is a bus controller (frequently a computer) in command of all bus traffic. A bus controller of similar capabilities is in a standby redundant mode as a backup. The MIL STD 1553B system extends this concept to the entire bus, so that bus faults can also be circumvented.

"Built-in self-test" (BIST) is now in common use in complex circuits [81]. This capability is ordinarily implemented through examining data (e.g., shift register buffers) for bit pattern analysis. Many of the self-test capabilities pinpoint or localize faults.

Faults in digital systems fall into two general categories: intermittent and solid. Everyone who has tested electronics knows that intermittent faults are the most frustrating and the most frequent. The second category (solid faults) will be examined here, because it yields more naturally to logic-circuit fault diagnosis.

The theory of self-checking and self-repairing circuits can deal effectively with solid faults, especially under the assumption that there is no more than a single fault per circuit. Two warnings are appropriate. First, although redundancy can be used to temporarily mask faults, this only buys time. If the faults are not identified and repaired, the failure rate will eventually surpass the protective redundancy. Second, the addition of redundancy means that there are more components that may fail. The reliability gain through redundant logic must be balanced against the negative effect of additional components. Keeping these limitations in mind, we will consider some elementary examples in order to demonstrate the concepts. First, we consider fault detection.

Assume that solid logical faults result in a conductor being "stuck at one" (s1) or "stuck at zero" (s0). These faults are generally caused by shorts or opens. An open into an "and" gate is usually equivalent to s1; an open into an "or" gate is usually equivalent to s0. A short can be s1 or s0.

A test can be conducted by applying a sequence of combinational inputs (test vectors) and observing the outputs. As an example, consider a two-input (x_1,x_2) "and" gate with output $z = x_1 x_2$ (juxtaposition represents the "and" operation). An s1 fault in the x_1 line could be detected by the test vector $x_1 x_2 = 01$, since a "zero" output is expected, but a "one" output is generated in the presence of such a fault. This procedure is a form of E. F. Moore's "Gedanken" (thought) experiment strategy, where a "black box" (system to be investigated) is stimulated at its input terminals while its output terminals are being observed.

The logical approach described above is informative, but it quickly becomes intractable for large numbers of variables and large numbers of potential faults [8]. One of the most useful algorithms is the Roth "d-algorithm" [9] and its modifications. The basic aim of the d-algorithm is to first sensitize at least one path from the site of a potential fault to the output ("d-drive"). This is followed by a backward trace ("consistency operation"). An example will illustrate the basic ideas behind the algorithm. A tabular approach is usually presented in order to systematize the description of complex circuits. Here, we will follow a more tutorial approach based on a short, but descriptive, example.

Assume the logic circuit shown in Figure 6-1. It comprises "blocks," each containing a standard array of gates (shown within the dashed box). A testable fault is also shown. We will seek a test vector to identify the postulated fault.

A symbol, "d," is used for a potential fault-affected value that should be "one," but will be "zero" under fault conditions; and "d'" for a value that should be "zero," but will be "one" under fault condi-

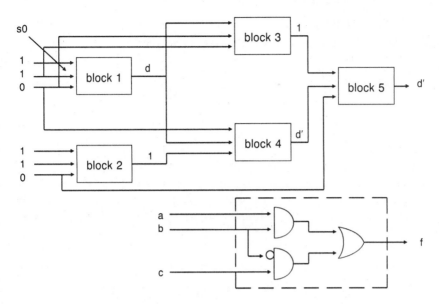

Figure 6-1   Application of Roth d-Algorithm.

tions. "Intersection" operations involving the "d" operand and the "d'" operand are similar to those used in ordinary Boolean intersection.

A representation of the faulty block is needed. This is called a "primitive d-cube of the fault." Other blocks in the path to the output must be "sensitized" to transmit fault information. The sensitization depends on representing fault-free blocks through "propagation d-cubes." Propagation d-cubes are shown by example below.

Before determining a "primitive d-cube" of the fault, a "singular cover" of the fault-free block is useful. This is similar to conventional logic simplification in that minimum-complexity prime implicant coverage is determined. This is done both for driving a "zero" to the output and for driving a "one." The results are:

inputs: $\underline{a\ b\ c\ \ f}$ (output)
$$
\begin{array}{cccc}
x & 0 & 0 & 0 \\
0 & 1 & x & 0 \\
\\
x & 0 & 1 & 1 \\
1 & 1 & x & 1
\end{array}
$$

(6-1)

where "x" represents a "don't care" (satisfied by either binary value). The result is called a "cover."

Now consider the block with a s0 fault at input "b." The performance of the faulty circuit can be described as:

$$\underline{a\ b\ c\ \ f}$$

$$x\ x\ 0\ \ 0 \tag{6-2}$$

$$x\ x\ 1\ \ 1$$

In order to determine test inputs that would reveal the fault, the "cubes" (such as $xx0$) can be viewed as "sets." Then, "intersecting" the conditions necessary for a good circuit to deliver a "one" with the conditions necessary for a faulty circuit to deliver a "zero," or vice versa, two meaningful (nonnull) conditions are obtained:

$$\underline{a\ b\ c\ \ f}$$

$$1\ 1\ 0\ \ d \quad \text{(normally "one"; "zero" under fault)} \tag{6-3}$$

$$0\ 1\ 1\ \ d' \quad \text{(normally "zero"; "one" under fault)}$$

This is the primitive d-cube of the fault. Note that $(110\ d)$ is obtained from the intersection of $(11x\ 1)$ and $(xx0\ 0)$, while $(011\ d')$ is obtained from the intersection of $(01x\ 0)$ and $(xx1\ 1)$. We will arbitrarily choose the first condition in Equation 6-3 and attempt to drive it through the circuit to the output without encountering unresolvable contradictions. This choice of inputs is indicated for block 1 in Figure 6-1.

The next step in the propagation is to consider block 3. The choice of a "zero" input for input "c" of block 1 assured that a "zero" would be placed on input "b" of block 3. For propagation of "d" through block 3, the "propagation d-cubes" are obtained from the "cover" (Equation 6-1). For propagation on "a," $01x\ 0$ and $11x\ 1$ intersect to give the propagation d-cube $d1x\ d$, which is not consistent with the "zero" on input "b." Therefore, no further propagation along this path is possible.

Now consider block 4. Propagation of the "d" on input "b" with a "zero" on input "a" must be compatible with the propagation d-cubes. Intersecting $x00\ 0$ and $11x\ 1$ from Equation 6-1, we obtain $1d0\ d$. Intersecting $01x\ 0$ with $x01\ 1$, we obtain $0d1\ d'$. Since the "a" input must be "zero," the latter propagation d-cube is required. This allows propagation to block 5.

The "a" input on block 5 must be "one" because of the inputs to block 3, and the "b" input on block 5 is "d'." Using Equation 6-1 and the input-b propagation d-cubes determined above, we see that the first propagation d-cube is required for propagation through block 5. Since the "b" input is "d' " (one for a fault), the output is "d'."

The drive to the output is now complete. Should it survive the consistency test, the "d'" output means that the output of a good circuit is "zero," while the output of a faulty circuit is "one" for the input vector that creates "d'."

For consistency, reverse conditions must be investigated. In this example, block 2 must be capable of creating an output "one" (for block 4), with a "c" input of "zero," as required for block 5. This is possible with the inputs shown, which satisfies the consistency check. The result can be obtained by using the cover cube $11x\ 1$.

This example gives an illustration of techniques that have been developed for efficient fault detection in combinational logic circuits. Similar techniques have been developed for sequential circuits, arithmetic circuits, and for data transmission channels. The latter will be addressed subsequently under the heading of information redundancy. An example of arithmetic fault detection will be given here.

Arithmetic fault detection is usually done in one of two modes: 1) separate coding and 2) nonseparate coding (Figure 6-2). In nonseparate coding, each operand is encoded and the coded result is computed by an operation on the coded operands. In separate coding, the main operation is computed in the usual way. Check symbols are carried along for each operand, and a separate operation is performed on these operands. A comparison is made between this result and a checking conversion on the result of the main operation. Separate codes are equivalent to residue codes. Nonseparate codes are "group" codes (see Section 6.1.3).

A widely used family of nonseparate codes is called "AN codes." These are applicable to addition, which can be the basis of all mathematical operations. AN codes depend on "modulo addition," which all computers use as the fundamental addition operation. Addition modulo M means that all results equal to or exceeding M are reduced by repeatedly subtracting M until a result less than M is obtained. An equivalent way of expressing numbers modulo M is to compute the remainder resulting from division by M.

The usual application of AN codes is to multiply sum operands by a number called the "check base," "A." Addition of the coded operands is performed modulo AM. This provides a check on the basic addition operation modulo M.

As an example, consider the addition:

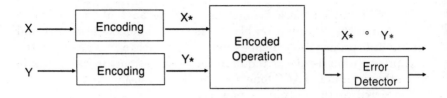

a) Nonseparate code

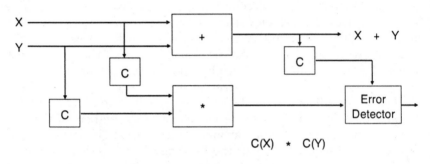

b) Separate code

Figure 6-2   Arithmetic coding.

$$s = 5 + 6 \text{ (modulo 8)} \tag{6-4}$$

where the checking is to be done using $A = 3$. The operands are to be encoded using multiplication by 3, and the check addition is to be performed modulo 24. The result is:

$$3s = 3 \times 5 + 3 \times 6 \text{ (modulo 24)} \tag{6-5}$$

The result can be checked by computing the residue (result) modulo A (modulo 3). A nonzero result indicates an error. This technique is based on the modulo arithmetic relationship:

$$A(x + y) \text{ (modulo } M) = (Ax + Ay \text{ (modulo } AM))(\text{modulo } A) \tag{6-6}$$

In residue codes, operand encoding is done by computing operands modulo A, where A divides M. The mathematical expression is:

$$C(x + y \text{ (modulo } M)) = C(x) + C(y) \text{ (modulo } A) \tag{6-7}$$

where $C(z)$ indicates computation of z modulo A. Checking the operation in Equation 6-4 with $A = 2$, we obtain:

$$11(\text{modulo } 8)(\text{modulo } 2) = 1 = (5(\text{modulo } 2) + 6(\text{modulo } 2))(\text{modulo } 2) \tag{6-8}$$

6.1.3 Information Redundancy

It is appropriate to consider other forms of testing, such as information testing, in addition to component testing. One of the most widely used applications of this idea results in what are called "error-protection codes." These codes are constructed so that information redundancy can be utilized for the detection of errors and even the correction of errors. This technique is especially appropriate for the class of soft errors.

In order to understand how error protection codes work, it is instructive to begin with some basic concepts. One of the simplest, and yet one of the most important, is the "parity" check.

A parity check is a redundant bit of information added to a block of bits in order to make the total number of ones in the information even (even parity) or odd (odd parity). Conceptually, the difference between even and odd parity is insignificant; in practice even parity is more frequently used because it can be related directly to the "exclusive-or" logic operation:

$$x1 + x2 = x1\overline{x2} \; v \; \overline{x1}x2 \tag{6-9}$$

where the + indicates exclusive-or and the operator v indicates Boolean "or."

A useful property of the exclusive-or operation is that it is a linear operation. This means that each operand can affect the result by the same amount, regardless of the values of the other operands. They can be combined in arbitrary order and in arbitrary groupings without changing the result. These features assure that parity implementations are relatively straightforward.

Mathematically, the exclusive-or operation meets the requirements of a "group." A group is a set of elements with an operation such that the elements have closure under the operation, the associative property obtains (order of multiple operations is immaterial), there is an identity element for the operation, and every element has an inverse under the operation. The first class of mathematically derived error-protecting codes used code words that were members of a group. The descriptive term was "group codes."

The system involving exclusive-or along with the "and" (multiplication) operation also meets the requirements for a "ring" and a "field." A ring satisfies the requirement for a group with the added restriction that the group operation must be "Abelian" (commutative). A second operation must maintain closure, must be associative, and must distribute over the first operation ($a(b+c) = ab + ac$). For a field, the second operation must be commutative, and every element except the identity of the first operation must have an inverse under the second operation. A field of p elements can be constructed for prime numbers simply by using modulo p addition and multiplication. The insight of young Évariste Galois [13] provided the key to *all* fields, based on mathematical systems using polynomial modulo operations. These fields are called "Galois fields." The properties discussed above allow productive analysis and synthesis of some useful properties.

First, assume that 48 bits are to be sent through an information channel where the probability of error for each bit (one changed to zero or vice versa) is 0.01, independent of other successes or failures in channel transmission. This description is known as the "binary symmetric channel" and the error rate is representative of a very noisy channel. The probability of successfully transmitting 48 bits through this channel is:

$$P_s = (0.99)^{48} = 0.617 \qquad (6\text{-}10)$$

The protocol associated with many information channels allows retransmission in the event that errors are detected. Since any error changes parity, a single parity check over the 48 bits has the capability to detect single errors and flag the need for retransmission. The mathematical expression for the parity check is:

$$p = b1 + b2 + \ldots + b48 \qquad (6\text{-}11)$$

In order to assess the effect of the additional overhead (parity check and retransmission), assume that a single bit will be returned from the receiver to the sender if an error is detected and that one additional attempt will be made to transmit the 48 bits. The probability of success in this case is the sum of the probability that 49 bits are transmitted correctly the first time (48 information bits plus 1 parity bit); and the probability that a single error is detected, a single bit is returned successfully, and 49 bits are transmitted correctly the second time. The equation for this situation can be approximated as:

$$P_s \approx (0.99)^{49} + 49(0.01)\,(0.99)^{48}\,(0.99)^{50} \approx 0.8 \qquad (6\text{-}12)$$

The result shows that a single parity check and some straightforward protocol can substantially improve the probability of successfully transmitting the information bits.

Further improvement can be realized by more frequent parity checks (shorter blocks). Assume that the 48 information bits are segmented into six blocks of eight, and an even parity check is added for each block.

$$
\begin{aligned}
p1 &= b1 + b2 + \ldots + b8 \\
p2 &= b9 + b10 + \ldots + b16 \\
&\;\cdot \\
&\;\cdot \\
&\;\cdot \\
p6 &= b41 + b42 + \ldots + b48
\end{aligned}
\qquad (6\text{-}13)
$$

The probability of success for each block is:

$$P_s' \approx (0.99)^9 + 9(0.01)\,(0.99)^{18} \qquad (6\text{-}14)$$

The probability of success for all six blocks (successful transfer of the 48 bits of information) is:

$$P_s = (Ps')^6 = 0.934 \qquad (6\text{-}15)$$

Although the probability of success can be made arbitrarily close to one by extending this process, it should be pointed out that the efficiency of the information transfer process is reduced with every improvement of this type. Communication efficiency can be important in many bandwidth-limited channels. Before addressing this concern, we will consider error correction.

The advantage of error correction is that retransmission of defective data is not necessary. All code checking and error correcting is done at the receiver. Since there is no reverse transfer, this process is commonly called "forward error correction," or FEC. As with the error-detection example above, a simple example is instructive.

An extension of the parity check process can yield arbitrarily reliable (approaching one) error correction. Assume that each bit is replicated m times (m even for convenience). The parity equations are:

$$p11 = p12 = \ldots = p1m = b1$$
$$p21 = p22 = \ldots = p2m = b2$$

.
.   (6-16)
.

$$p481 = p482 = \ldots = p48m = b48$$

The m-fold replication of each bit allows $m/2$ errors to occur in the transmission of each bit, and correction is still possible by a majority vote. The probability of success for each bit becomes:

$$Ps' =$$
$$(0.99)^{m+1} + (m+1)(0.01)(0.99)^{m} + \ldots + \binom{m+1}{m/2}(0.01)^{m/2}(0.99)^{m/2+1}$$

(6-17)

The overall (for 48 bits) probability of success is:

$$Ps = (Ps')^{48}$$ (6-18)

For $m = 2$, $Ps = 0.986$. For $m = 4$, $Ps = 0.9995$. This is a great increase in capability with increasing m. Unfortunately, as was the case for error detection, efficiency decreases rapidly for increasing m. For $m = 4$, five communication bits are being transferred across the channel for every single bit of information.

Until the late 1940s, this was an expected tradeoff. However, an analysis by Claude Shannon |10| first determined that any communication channel had a "capacity" for rate of communication. Then he showed that for any communication rate less than the capacity (no matter by how small an amount), error correction codes were possible that would force the probability of error to be as small as desired. In essence, this meant that it was not necessary to sacrifice information transfer rate in order to increase transmission accuracy. This existence proof did not show directly how to design codes, but it inspired interest in seeking codes that promised to be much better than those known.

Unfortunately, the search has not produced results as dramatic as might have been expected. In addition, the implementation of sophisticated codes has not been trivial. However, important results have been obtained. One of the most widely used families is called Bose-Chaudhuri-Hocquenghem (BCH) codes. In order to give a concise demonstration of some of the attractive features of these codes, especially with regard to implementation, an example based on restricting the BCH family to a fundamental case (equivalency with Hamming codes [11]) will be presented.

Assume that a single-error-correcting code is sought for transmitting four information bits. This requires a minimum "distance" of three between all pairs of code words. ("Distance" means the number of bit positions that have different bit values in the two words.) For distance three, any single error during transmission will result in reception of a code word that is distance one from the correct code word and at least distance two from all incorrect code words. This makes single-error correction feasible.

In general, distance-d BCH codes require a "generator" polynomial with d-1 consecutive $GF(2p)$ (Galois field of 2^p elements, where p is prime) roots. Such polynomials are well known and cataloged [e.g., Ref. 12, Appendix C]. Selecting $p(x) = x^3 + x + 1$, a seven-bit distance 3 (single-error-correcting) code is specified capable of transmitting four information bits.

Figure 6-3a shows a linear feedback shift register (LFSR) coder that matches the selected polynomial. The feedback connection on the left end of the shift register corresponds to the "x^3" term of the polynomial; there is no feedback connection to the line between the first two shift register elements because of the missing "x^2" term; the feedback connection to the exclusive-or circuit between the second and third shift register elements corresponds to the "x" term; and the feedback generation from the exclusive-or circuit on the right corresponds to the "1" term.

Starting in the reset (all-zero) condition, the sequence of states for the LFSR is shown as a function of four information inputs: $b1$, $b2$, $b3$, $b4$. The final result is that the three parity checks associated with the 4 information bits remain in the three shift register elements. Inspection of the result verifies the equivalence with Hamming codes, except that the code structure has been matched to an LFSR implementation.

Figure 6-3b shows a decoding circuit capable of identifying error positions. The decoder is also an LFSR, with connections determined by the same generator polynomial. The actual correction (complementing) of the identified bits is omitted. An example is shown, where $b1 = b3 = 1$ and $b2 = b4 = 0$. A transmission error is postulated in the second bit position, so the received code word is 1110001.

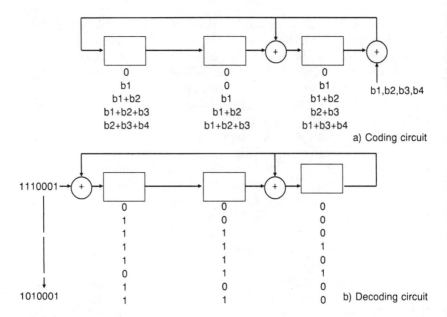

a) Coding circuit

b) Decoding circuit

Figure 6-3   Error coding/decoding example.

Starting with a reset (all-zero) decoder, the 7 bits are entered. The pattern remaining in the register is a "syndrome" (pointer) uniquely indicating an error. The error is determined to be in the second bit position of the received code word, because $b2$ appears in the parity check positions corresponding to where parity errors ("ones" in the decoding circuit) were produced. The decoding circuit has thereby identified the bit position that must be corrected to recover the original word, 1010001. More sophisticated coders than shown here are generally used, but the principles are similar.

The advantages of the mathematically based BCH codes are that error correction properties can be designed into the codes for a wide range of information block sizes, and that straightforward LFSR coder and decoder implementations can be derived directly from the mathematical structure.

A related technique is frequently used to check the accuracy of a message or digital pattern. The technique is to compute the modulus of a block of data relative to a polynomial. This result is appended to the block for checking by the receiver. The technique is called "CRC" (cyclic redundancy check), "digital signature," or "message authentication code." The similarity to "checksums" is also apparent.

As an example, consider a block of 15 bits: 110101100100101. Representing this bit stream by a polynomial (highest-order coefficient first) over GF(2), an algebra modulo, a polynomial can be structured. With the polynomial $x^3 + x + 1$ as the modulus, the result (remainder) is $x^2 + x$. This requires that the bits 0110 be appended to the information block. The polynomial chosen has the same "distance-three" property that was utilized in the previous BCH code example. This means that one or two errors will be detected by the checking process. For a degree-m polynomial, there are 2^{m+1} possible check patterns (remainders). This assures that randomly chosen data have only a $1/2^{m+1}$ chance of matching the check pattern.

Although these concepts are useful as data integrity checks, there are additional security considerations. In Chapter 8, we will return to this concept and add features that enable use as "digital signatures" (certifiable authority for an action) and "authentication" (verification that the sender is the person claimed).

6.1.4 Redundancy in Computers

Computer availability is typically limited to about 98% of the time [14]. Although this is a laudable figure, some applications demand better (national defense, personnel safety, business-critical). For many years, computer operational continuity depended on rapid maintenance or hot online backup computers. In 1976, a (commercially) new option called fault-tolerant computing was introduced by Tandem Computers, Inc. [15,16]. The objective was to incorporate sufficient redundancy so that available operating time percentages could be substantially increased. Today, a wide selection of fault-tolerant and high-reliability computers is available.

Fault-tolerant computers use multiple processors, some other extra hardware, and controlling software. Effort is expended to add the redundancy in an efficient cost-effective manner, so that the system can be made affordable. Typical prices are 30–60% higher than comparable conventional computers [15].

Fault-tolerant computer architectures [16] typically center on one of three strategies:

1. Transaction processing. Each task (an action involving, for example, entering an order, reducing a cash balance, changing accountability status) is considered a separate transaction. Processing state of health is determined by a check made be-

tween two processors independently executing the transaction. A need for self-test is indicated by disagreement; the self-test can identify a faulty component and indicate which copy of the transaction is valid.

2. Triple modular redundancy (TMR). Transaction processing is not well suited to general-purpose computing. A traditional technique used in these types of computers is triplication and majority voting on the output.

3. TMR systems are generally costly. For this reason, dual redundancy (DR) systems have been developed [14]. DR processing can detect, but not correct, errors. The benefit of the detection is that reprocessing or faulty component identification is possible. DR systems have less reliability than TMR systems, but may be a cost-effective approach for many applications.

Other techniques that have been used in fault-tolerant computers include error-protection codes, "watchdog" timers (assuring reasonable time windows for time-constrained processes), power supply and clock monitors, redundant component "masking" (arrays that do not depend on reliable performance by any single component), and software reasonableness checks (e.g., counting and timing the use of software modules).

Add-on components for fault-tolerant performance are also available. For example, personal computer (PC) fault tolerance can be achieved by installing interface boards and controlling software into two PCs that are interconnected [17]. The PCs operate simultaneously, exchanging data with each other in background during standard processing. The software evaluates the operation and assures that the most reliable data processing possible is obtained.

6.2 HARDWARE ACCESS CONTROL

Computer access is commonly restricted to authorized personnel through password authentication. This software-based technique is examined in the next chapter. One of the password weaknesses is that passwords are sometimes compromised. This is one reason that hardware access control techniques have been developed. The main four categories of hardware access control devices are card identifiers, biometric (individual characteristic measurement) devices, automated password generators (security keys, security code generators, or "see-through" security devices), and ROM (read-only memory) security controls.

6.2.1 Identity Verification

Anyone who pays for goods with checks or who cashes checks knows that the receiving party desires evidence that he or she is the person authorized to write the check. A driver's license, possibly in conjunction with other credentials, usually serves as satisfactory (but not foolproof) evidence. Applications of this principle are pertinent in granting access to computers, databases, communications networks, ATMs (automated teller machines), and physical areas.

The requirement for these types of applications is sometimes called "personal identification." In fact, guaranteeing personal identification is virtually impossible unless a person is closely monitored from birth. The pragmatic approach is to verify a link between a person and a claimed identity within the subset of people authorized to gain access. This much easier problem is called "identity verification." Within these constraints, identity verification is synonymous with authentication.

The traditional principle of identity verification has been that a person's claimed identity can be verified in three ways: 1) by a credential the person has (e.g., a key, badge, or card), 2) by something the person knows (e.g., a combination, a password, or a PIN), or 3) by something the person is (e.g., face recognition or fingerprints). Recent developments in biometrics not only emphasize the latter, but also have forced a new description for 3) above: something characteristic about a person (enlarged to include, for example, signatures, and typing and writing rhythm). We will consider hardware implementations of the three concepts, accommodating the more recent (and more accurate) extension to personal characteristics. Combinations of the three methods are useful in many cases.

6.2.2 Credential Identifiers

We are all familiar with credential identifiers. They include, for example, keys, cards, and badges. All of these were characterized in Chapter 3 as generally inexpensive and psychologically acceptable, but not highly secure. However, there are a number of technologies that have been applied to the credential concept in order to improve security and to introduce features such as audit records and duress signals.

The inherent low cost (approximately $1 to $100) and user ease associated with most credentials have motivated research on enhancing security without degrading the attributes to an unacceptable degree. There has been no obvious breakthrough in achieving this goal, but the results have been noteworthy.

Credentials utilizing technology can be partitioned in at least four convenient ways:

1. Reading technique. Automated assessment of a credential can be done in one of two basic ways. One is called "direct" reading (contact with a "reader" is required). The other is "remote" reading (the card need not touch the reader).
2. Operational characteristics. Operation can be accomplished in two different ways. Credentials can be "passive" (electrical, magnetic, mechanical, or optical energy is applied from an external source). Alternatively, they can be "active" (electrical energy is furnished within the credential).
3. Logical characteristics. Credentials can be described in two logical ways. Data storage credentials are merely repositories for data that are used in the authentication process. Processing credentials have computational power (usually accomplished by a microprocessor). "Smart cards" are an example of this type of credential.
4. Data storage capacity. There are three common categories of data storage: low-density, medium-density, and high-density. Data in low-density credentials occupy an area that is relatively large (an area that, if visible, would be noticeable to the eye). Examples of credentials in this category are cards with punched holes, bar codes, magnetic spots, "Wiegand-effect" wires,* infrared transmission/reflection spots, capacitance spots, resonant circuit spots, and metallic strips. Medium-density credentials include those storing data in magnetic strips and EPROMs (electrically programmable read-only memories). High-density data storage is common in smart cards and laser or optical cards.

The ability to alter or counterfeit cards is greatly reduced by using technology based on the Wiegand effect, infrared spots, capacitance spots, resonant circuits, or metallic strips.

Remote-read credentials have the dual benefits over direct-read cards of longer life (no contact wear) and hands-free operation. The

---

* A Wiegand wire is a specially treated ferromagnetic wire that produces a sudden change in flux when exposed to a changing magnetic field. The strong flux reversal is easily sensed by a detection coil.

utility of hands-free operation depends to a large extent on the degree of proximity required. Some remote-read credentials permit operation only within a few inches of the reader. Credentials that operate at a distance of at least one or two feet enable convenient door lock control and secure terminal control. In the case of door locks, hands-free credentials discourage tailgating (multiple persons entering in response to a single code entry) and lock disabling (e.g., propping doors open to avoid repeated combination entries).

An example of an extended-distance proximity credential is the Mastiff (Modular Automated System to Identify Friend from Foe) security system, developed in Great Britain. The credential (called a "token" by Mastiff Systems) sends a coded signal to a reader, so that the wearer of the credential need take no manual action beyond approaching the reader. A timer assures that a door cannot remain open.

On the other hand, the devices can be used for terminal enablement. The terminal remains operational as long as the possessor of a credential is present. However, if an authorized terminal user leaves the terminal, it is disenabled. This prevents an opportunistic unauthorized user from taking advantage of a terminal that has been used to initiate a job and then temporarily left unattended.

Most card credentials are passive. The Mastiff token is an example of an active device. However, to prevent improper use in case of loss or theft, the devices must be periodically charged using a special charger. The intent is that tokens remain on company premises after hours, and that unauthorized charging is difficult.

Current optical technology has enabled some companies to offer credentials [78] with high-density information storage (several MB* currently, with the potential for hundreds of MBs). Potential applications include storing medical records, biometric data, and personnel records.

6.2.3 Smart Cards

The term "smart cards" generally applies to cards that contain a microprocessor or equivalent means of logically processing data, a memory for storing data, and measures for ensuring security. The general idea of a smart card has been discussed at least as early as

---

* An MB is a million bytes (characters) of information. One MB is roughly equivalent to the number of characters in this book.

the 1960s, but the major impetus was provided in the early 1970s by a French inventor, Roland Moreno. He saw the need for many currently used features, including dedicated security logic [18]. Now, in addition to ordinary smart card features, some cards have keypads, a screen, and internal power.

Smart cards have been used as, or considered for use as, debit cards (immediate transfer of money from customer to merchant), self-verifying credit cards (eliminating the need for long-distance verification calls), telephone charge cards (immediate debiting, supplemented by telephone directory information), and records repositories (with immediate updating of medical, military, and business records).

France and Japan have been the leaders to date in smart card development, with the United States, Mexico, Canada, Great Britain, and several other European countries also participating. Groupe Bull of Paris has invested over $50 million in smart card development [19]. More than 10 million cards are in use in France. All French retailers are committed to have smart card readers by 1990. More than half of France's pay phones now accept smart cards [77].

In Japan, most smart card applications have involved debit shopping. However, there are also pilot projects on hospital medical records, personnel management, and inventory control. There are more than 80 vendors of smart card technology in Japan.

In the United States, Mastercard has promoted and tested smart cards (as self-verifying credit cards), and Visa has begun a joint program with Toshiba of Tokyo [54]. Visa's field tests involve a "super smart" or "very smart" card technology (cards containing a display and keyboard in the same size as conventional smart cards).

Marine recruits at Parris Island, South Carolina, are using smart cards instead of cash for base exchange and similar expenses. The U.S. Navy has been running a pilot experiment in purchasing based on smart cards. The U.S. Army has experimented with replacing personal "dog tags" (identification data tags) with smart cards. During the 1985 Reagan-Gorbachev Geneva summit, 3000 journalists were given smart cards to authorize telecommunication of news releases.

The ISO (International Standards Organization) has recommended standards to help assure smart card uniformity throughout the international community [20,21,33]. ANSI (American National Standards Institute) and NIST (National Institute of Standards and Technology) are also working on standards projects related to smart cards. The dimensions recommended by ISO are about 86 x 54 x 3/4 mm, to ensure size compatibility with current bank cards. Specifications also include clock frequency, serial I/O (input/output) rate, the number and location of interface connection points, power dissipation, and ESD (electrostatic discharge) tolerance.

Costs of smart cards are potentially less than $5. (Ordinary bank cards cost less than a dollar.) Smart cards with keying and display functions will probably cost about $20. Standalone readers cost about $600. Card readers that plug into PCs or point-of-sale terminals cost about $50 to $100.

Security is a crucial issue [22]. It is important that use of smart cards be restricted by a carefully controlled code (PIN or password) and that forgery be extremely difficult. This requires security codes for user authenticity and card authenticity. Since most cards are not intended to require a real-time link to a computer database, the reference codes must be stored in the cards in a nonvolatile memory area that is not accessible to unauthorized personnel. Other private information contained in nonvolatile memory has the same requirements for protection. Transaction records must also be recorded in nonvolatile memory. Tamperproofing is provided in a variety of ways (see subsequent section on seals), but common techniques include deactivation upon a selected number (e.g., three) of incorrect access attempts, memory destruction on attempts to bypass security controls, temperature-sensitive holograph sealing, and low-temperature debossing (delaminating). A significant effort aimed toward incorporating biometric (see following) access control into smart cards has attracted wide support. This would have a sense of completeness that is attractive in security approaches: A user would require a possession (the card), knowledge (PIN or password), and personal characteristic (biometric measurement).

6.2.4 Security Code Generators

A family of hardware access control devices is intended to deliver what amounts to a "one-time" password to a coordinating host. The advantage of these devices over conventional passwords is discussed in the next chapter, but basically it is to prevent observation and reentry of an intercepted password. These devices are given various names, including "security key generators," "see-through security devices," "hand-held keys," "decoders," "access-control encryption cards," and "security code generators." We will use the latter term.

The security code generator (SCG) process is a technique that effectively causes successive passwords entered by a user to differ in unpredictable ways. The user carries a hand-held device and uses it to generate or aid in the generation of security codes or passwords.

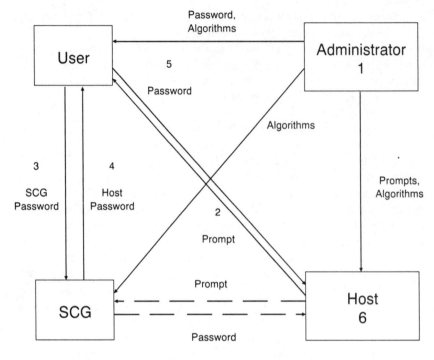

Figure 6-4   Security-code generator procedures.

The other component of the system is the software (or in some cases hardware) that communicates with the SCG or the user [23].

SCGs operate in a large variety of ways. The generic description of the approach is shown in Figure 6-4. The first step in the process is for an administrator to enter coordinating data in the host and into the SCG. This enables host identification of user/SCG inputs. The second step (following a user request for access) is for the host to display a prompt. The user then (step 3) activates the SCG (e.g., enters a password). The SCG communicates with the user (step 4), enabling the user to obtain a unique, but expected, password (step 5). The host, on successful comparison (step 6), grants access to the user.

Many variations are possible. In some systems, the host sends data directly to the SCG. In others, the SCG sends data directly to the host (through an interface box). These paths are shown in Figure 6-4 by dashed lines. Steps may be skipped (e.g., no entry of a user password into the SCG) or enhanced (e.g., the user may perform an algorithm or manual transformation of the prompt data to determine the SCG entry). The basic aim of the system remains to avoid unchanging passwords and the resultant decrease in security.

Devices that receive communication directly from the host may do so through special communication interface units, but a potentially simpler approach has been used [24]. For example, the operation of some devices depends on optical sensing of messages appearing within a designated area of the display. A CRT display is ideal; electroluminescent or plasma displays are not currently usable because of sensing difficulties.

At least one device depends on synchronized internal timing of the SCG and the host [25,26]. The device displays a pseudorandom code that changes following a selected interval (e.g., every 60 seconds). Different cards display different numbers. The correct number for a particular user is linked through the entry of the user's PIN. With the aid of quartz crystal timing, synchronization can be maintained for long periods of time (months).

It is possible for SCGs to incorporate biometric identification features and duress codes. The duress codes protect against a user being forced to use the SCG by notifying authorities of the alarm, while interacting with the user in a normal fashion.

Costs of SCGs [27] are in the $50 to $100 range. Software costs range from $5000 to $15,000. All SCGs that are not built to operate online are self-powered. SCG capability has been adapted to some software access control packages [25].

6.2.5 Biometric Access Control

Measuring a biological characteristic of a person is generally considered the potentially most reliable form of identity verification. In fact, law enforcement agencies have long considered fingerprints to be the most reliable form of personal identification. It follows that fingerprints and other biological measurements are the basis of biometric devices. It may be somewhat surprising, but biometric measurements can include measurements of personal *performance*, where the performance characteristics are unique to a person.

The most widely accepted definition of biometrics that includes the above features is [28]: "Automated methods of verifying or recognizing a person based on a physical or behavioral characteristic." The automation generally consists [29] of transducing some analog measurement of a physical or behavioral characteristic, converting the analog "signal" (voltage, current, optical, or infrared intensity) to a digital sequence, processing the sequence through some (usually proprietary) algorithm, and comparing the output to a catalog of reference records in search of a "match."

Since the algorithm used is basic to the competitive posture of the biometric system manufacturer, there is general reluctance to reveal the techniques used. The generic problem faced is a pattern recognition problem, which may be amplified by variations in image registration (position). Pattern recognition has never been an easily prescribed process. An example will be used to demonstrate that information need not always be obtained in conventional ways.

A classic technique for examining the characteristics of a temporal analog waveform is to perform a Fourier analysis of the signal (express the signal as a sum or continuum of orthogonal functions, each representing a particular frequency). In this way, frequency characteristics that would not otherwise be obvious are revealed. A similar technique for digital signals was apparently first described in 1923 [31]. Like Fourier expansion, the analysis utilizes a closed set of orthonormal functions. These are now usually called "Walsh" functions (sometimes "Rademacher-Walsh" functions). An example illustrates the concept and suggests a hypothetical application for pattern (possibly biometric) recognition. The basis for the technique is omitted, since the objective is illustrative.

Assume a logic function, f, of three variables, x_1, x_2, x_3:

$$f = x_1\bar{x}_2 \; \cup \; \bar{x}_1x_3 \; \cup \; x_2\bar{x}_3 \tag{6-19}$$

The function is shown in Table 6-1 in "truth table" (ordered binary counting sequence) form. The r columns in the table have the following logical equivalence:

$$r_{ijk} = x_i + x_j + x_k \tag{6-20}$$

where + indicates exclusive-or.

The function can be written as a weighted arithmetic sum of the r columns (Walsh expansion) as follows:

$$f = \sum F_k r_k \tag{6-21}$$

where the subscript k indicates considering all 2^n "r" functions for an n-variable function.

The computation for the F_k is:

Table 6-1   Tabular description of example function.

f	r0	r1	r2	r3	r12	r13	r23	r123
0	1	0	0	0	0	0	0	0
1	1	0	0	1	0	1	1	1
1	1	0	1	0	1	0	1	1
1	1	0	1	1	1	1	0	0
1	1	1	0	0	1	1	0	1
1	1	1	0	1	1	0	1	0
1	1	1	1	0	0	1	1	0
0	1	1	1	1	0	0	0	1

$F_0 = f_0$ (first value of f in the truth table)

$$F_k = \tfrac{1}{2}^n \sum (f + \bar{r}_k - f + r_k) \qquad (k \neq 0)$$ (6-22)

where the summation symbol and the minus symbol indicate ordinary addition and subtraction of the number of "ones" resulting from the "+" operations. The + sign indicates exclusive-or.

The results for the example in Table 6-1 are:

$F_0 = F_1 = F_2 = F_3 = F_{123} = 0; F_{12} = F_{13} = F_{23} = 1/2.$

This results in an arithmetic expression for f:

$$f = r_{12}/2 + r_{13}/2 + r_{23}/2$$ (6-23)

where the operations indicated are ordinary addition and division.

This expression is just as representative of the function as Equation 6-19, but the domain of orthogonal functions used has more pattern information. For example, consider the function displayed on a three-dimensional "hypercube."* The function f is shown in Figure

---

* An n-dimensional hypercube is a geometric concept for a function that is similar to a truth table in that all combinations of the variables are shown systematically.

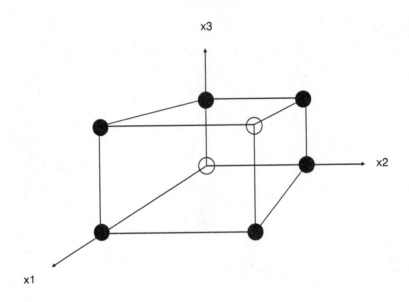

Figure 6-5   Hypercube representation of example function.

6-5, with "ones" shown by solid circles and "zeros" shown by open circles.

Geometrically, the function can be described as having two "zeros" at opposite corners of the hypercube. Three other functions besides f fit this description. All can be described by a Walsh expansion with three double-subscripted orthogonal functions with expansion coefficient absolute value of 1/2, and each member of the set has an even number (zero or two) of negative coefficients. A similar geometry could be derived by interchanging the role of open and closed circles (that is, with two closed circles at opposite corners of the hypercube). The Walsh expansion for this situation is the same, except that members of the set have an odd number (one or three) of negative coefficients.

This example is an indication of the subtle characteristics that are revealed when the algorithms used are tailored to the most recognizable features of a biometric signal. With this in mind, the motivation for treating many biometric algorithms as proprietary is clearer.

Our objective here will be to describe the general approaches used, while providing a minimal description of the relevant algorithms. There are currently seven relatively successful biometric techniques in use. These are:

1. Signature recognition. Signing one's name is a familiar form of identity verification. However, biometric signature recognition systems do not depend on the ordinary pattern visualized by persons.
2. Fingerprint recognition. The incredible uniqueness of fingerprints can be utilized by biometric systems, but the techniques used are sometimes different from law-enforcement recognition techniques.
3. Palmprint recognition. Palmprints are similar to fingerprints, but offer a larger area and larger (and hence easier to recognize) features for examination.
4. Hand-geometry recognition. Hands have several unique measurable physical characteristics that are useful for biometric devices.
5. Voiceprint recognition. It is common for persons to recognize voices over the telephone. Similar recognition is an objective for this type of biometric device.
6. Eye retina pattern recognition. Taking advantage of the viewpoint of an ophthalmologist, we find that retina patterns are very unique. This characteristic has been successfully used in one biometric device.
7. Typing rhythm recognition. A person working at a keyboard establishes some unique timing characteristics that are easily measured, especially since keyboards are so commonly used in computer systems.

Some general concepts are useful in considering the information presented below. Two performance parameters are generally cited as being representative of device performance. The first is called the "false reject" rate (Type I errors), which is the percentage of access rejections made to authorized personnel. The second measure is the "false accept" rate (Type II errors), which is the percentage of access acceptances made to unauthorized personnel.

Unfortunately, changes made to reduce one of the rates generally increase the other. The technical challenge is to design a system that gives inherently small rates of both types; then sensitivity adjustments allow tuning to an optimum (for the device and application) combination of error rates.

Performance data must be assessed with care, because the definition of an access attempt may vary as to number of tries, time spent in biometric evaluation, and even, in some cases, as to whether or not supplementary inputs (e.g., PINs) are considered part of the access procedure.

Another important factor is the ability of personnel involved in access tests. Experienced personnel do significantly better in achieving biometric acceptance than people who are unfamiliar with the process. This has special significance in applications like ATM transactions, where the general public would be required to operate the biometric devices. With these ramifications in mind, we will describe the seven types of biometric systems.

6.2.5.1 Signature Verifiers

It is commonly thought that signatures can be forged so well that even experts cannot detect the forgery. However, this is because the examiner sees only the pattern of *what* was written as opposed to *how* it was written [30]. Biometric signature recognition devices utilize signature dynamics (e.g., time, history of pressure, velocity, direction, and acceleration).

An IBM patent (U.S. patent 4 513 437) describes a biometric device that is based on an electronic pen. The pen contains three piezoelectric transducers, one for measuring pressure along the axis of the pen, and two for measuring transverse acceleration along two orthogonal axes. The implementation described in the patent processes 8-bit samples at a rate of 80 samples per second. About 1000 points are collected over 12.5 seconds. The processing algorithm incorporates a "dynamic reference adaptation" technique that allows for personal variations in style, and gradual changes in signature technique over time. Tests on the system over a two-year period indicated that the false reject rate was about 0.2%, and the false accept rate was about 0.4%. An ink cartridge is used in the IBM device, since people sign more naturally when they see what they are writing.

Sandia National Laboratories and Stanford Research Institute are also among those who have research and patent activity in the signature recognition field. Characteristics can be averaged over a signature, since it has been observed that individual portions of a signature may vary more substantially than the parameter averages. Total signing time, pen vertical motion (up and down relative to the writing surface), and rhythmic features have been evaluated. One device uses an ordinary ball-point pen, sensing pressure and velocity directly on the writing surface.

It is common to require several signatures for initial registration, and more than one measurement signature may be required for recognition. The main attributes of signature verification are user ease and familiarity, and fairly good accuracy.

6.2.5.2 Fingerprint Verifiers Remarkable accuracy and ease of measurement are attributes that attract the interest of law enforcement agencies, forensic examiners, and civil records custodians. The apparent uniqueness of fingerprints has attracted biometric verifier designers. Unfortunately, images derived from ink impressions on cards are not convenient for computer access control.*

Fingerprints are images of papillary ridges in the epidermal (outer) skin layer of the fingers [33]. Although the uniqueness of fingerprints was postulated by the early Egyptians and Chinese, the British government was apparently the first to classify, file, and use fingerprints for systematic identification. The basis for most of the classification techniques used is the "Henry System" (after Sir Edward Henry). This system, in expanded form, is now used by the FBI and police forces throughout the world.

The three basic features most often used by the FBI are the "arch," the "loop," and the "whorl." The arch is an upthrust in the flow of ridges in their path across the print. The loop is a near closure or "recurve" (change of direction of curvature) across a reference line. The whorl has a swirling appearance and has two or more "deltas" (triangular intersections), each associated with recurves. These are basic constituents in determining pattern "classes" (types) and "subclasses" (groups having been further segmented). Computer searches for prints with the best match to the features sought generally are used to narrow the possibilities down to a few prints, which are then examined visually.

Verification can also be made by locating "minutiae" (endpoints and bifurcations or splits of ridges), along with relative positions and angles. Biometric verifiers sometimes utilize the minutiae locations in an algorithm that allows for cleanliness variation and registration (placement) variations. A common method of capturing an image is to use light illumination on the backside of a glass platen on which the subject's finger is placed. The reflected light gives information based on the "frustrated total internal reflection" principle, whereby light does not reflect well from glass in contact with ·fingerprint ridges. A fingerprint verifier is shown in operation in Figure 6-6.

---

*   At least two devices have been marketed that require ink fingerprinting on a card, which is then inserted into the devices for identity verification.

Figure 6-6   A fingerprint verifier. (Photograph courtesy of Sandia National Laboratories.)

Because of the possibility that a person's finger may be injured or too soiled for recognition, it is helpful to register more than one finger.

6.2.5.3 Palmprint Verifiers   Biometric verifiers that utilize skin features on other parts of the body (such as the palm) are similar to fingerprint verifiers. However, there are differences, as one might suspect from observing one's own palm. The larger area and more extensive features of the palm have been used in at least one verifier.

6.2.5.4 Hand-Geometry Verifiers   The individual characterization of people's hands transcends differences in glove sizes. Hand-geometry verifiers have been widely used (see Figure 6-7). The illustrated device operates by measuring a three-dimensional image of the hand.

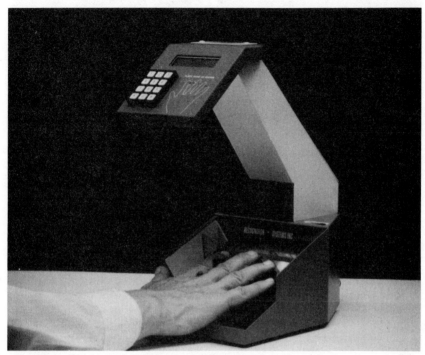

Figure 6-7   A hand-geometry verifier. (Photograph courtesy of Sandia National Laboratories.)

The operation depends on the reflected light image of a hand placed on a surface. Hand placement is guided by "dowels." Injured fingers or changes in fingernail length occasionally require reenrollment.

6.2.5.5 Voice Verifiers Our ability to recognize voices over the telephone suggests that automatic recognition is feasible. There are many current studies on biometric voice verification, and a few verifiers have been placed on the market.

One of the techniques used is to develop a time-history pattern of acoustic strength during the pronouncement of prescribed words. Refinements include frequency characterization (a spectrograph), linear predictive coding (a time-dependent correlation), and mannerism records. Basic features of voice patterns include "formants" ("bright spots" of frequency spectral concentration) and "phonemes" (smallest recognizable constituents of voice/sound generation).

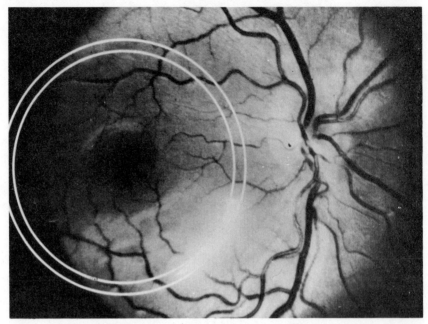

Figure 6-8   Scanning an eye retinal pattern. (Photograph courtesy of Sandia National Laboratories.)

Voice impersonators do not have notable success against verifiers, and techniques are available (e.g., randomly selected prompt words) to combat the use of tape recordings for spoofing.

6.2.5.6 Retinal Pattern Verifiers   Ophthalmologists routinely examine the pattern of blood vessels at the back of the eye, looking for signs of vascular damage. They also may observe what apparently is a unique pattern, usable for biometric recognition. The basic design of a retinal pattern verifier was conceived by the son of an Oregon ophthalmologist, based on these observations. The device uses an infrared beam to scan the back of the eye in a circular pattern. A detector measures the reflected light (see Figure 6-8).

The device uses 4096 values to assess the intensity of the reflection, and segments the scan into 320 points. The assessment of the pattern obtained is relatively straightforward if the measurement subject maintains correct visual orientation. This is accomplished by requiring the subject to use a viewer (see Figure 6-9) and look directly at a target dot.

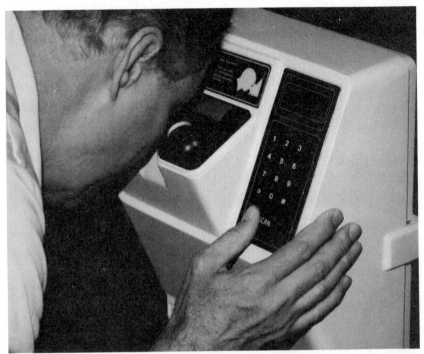

Figure 6-9 Using an eye retinal verifier. (Photograph courtesy of Sandia National Laboratories.)

Contact lenses do not interfere with device operation, but glasses do. A person can remove the glasses and use the device successfully if the target can be seen well enough to keep the eye properly oriented.

Retinal pattern verifiers have been installed for access control at the Air Force Consolidated Space Operations Center in Colorado Springs, Colorado [84].

6.2.5.7 Typing Rhythm Verifiers Most of us develop a distinctive technique and rhythm for typing passwords on a keyboard. It is possible to incorporate recognition of these characteristics along with recognition of the password. This is the basis for a number of software access control routines that incorporate a biometric measurement [28,34]. Although the achievable accuracy is not usually as good as that of other types of biometric verifiers, it provides a reasonable addition to security at a low cost.

6.2.5.8 Human Factors Many users of biometric devices have psychological concerns, and it is important to assess these effects on system operation. Some examples are listed below.

1. Some people are hesitant to use retinal scanners because of fear of the infrared source, which is merely a low-intensity LED (light-emitting diode).
2. Users have expressed discomfort with placing fingers in confined areas, such as might be required for fingerprint reading.
3. Techniques such as electroencephalography may be technically capable of identity verification, but the physical measurement requirements are incompatible with human comfort. The effect on styled hair is also a concern.
4. Devices that require electrical or electronic interaction, that cause physical discomfort, that require shared contact surfaces, or that raise suspicions about privacy infringement can be expected to offend at least some users.

6.2.5.9 Performance Assessment The development of biometric devices has been tedious, because systems at first (10 years ago) were very expensive (up to $75,000) and not extremely accurate. The result was slow sales, which hindered development funding. The present situation is greatly improved. Devices are available in the $1000 to $5000 range, and reasonable accuracy is achieved [36].

Available performance figures must be viewed with some caution, because there are not yet any industry standards for measurements [35]. Independent tests rarely confirm vendor-advertised data. However, with some caution in mind, an idea of the performance of biometric devices can be obtained through literature surveys.

Type I errors (false rejections) can be as low as one in a hundred for fingerprint recognition devices, and Type II errors (false acceptances) can be substantially lower, approaching one in a million for fingerprint and retinal scan measurements. Hand-geometry error rates (Type I and Type II) are less than one percent. Signature recognition error rates are usually more than one percent.

In addition to improvements in the basic technologies in use, effort is being expended on developing new techniques. Among strategies that have been considered are facial recognition, DNA fingerprinting, olfactory sensors, blood characteristics, dental characteristics, and ear geometry. Patterns of blood vessels have been assessed for the ear, wrist, and hand.

6.2.6 Memory Security Control

Memory protection is needed to prevent a user's programs from affecting the operating system or the processes of other users. A computer address space is the "primary memory" area referenced during program execution. This is distinguished from "secondary memory," which involves file space. There are two types of address space: "real" memory and "virtual" memory. Most systems use "virtual memory" to allow physical locations to vary for particular "virtual addresses." Virtual addresses are usually implemented through "pointers" that relate virtual addresses to physical location.

Early computers had no read protection in primary memory [82]. This meant that a user program running in one part of primary memory could read activity in any other part, including other users' programs and data.

There are valid reasons for placing a portion of security controls in a hardware device, such as a ROM (read-only memory). ROMs, although accessible to a determined physical attack, cannot be overwritten by software commands. Furthermore, hardware security controls have potentially high response speed, resulting in little system overhead. Basic hardware protection attributes now commonly available are "read-only" and "read/write." Many other attributes ("execute-only," "not accessible," "journal-taking") are possible [80]. ROM control can restrict user access or communication access through an internally stored "key" (number). By incorporating ROM control into the system boot process, initial conditions can be constrained.

Additional discussion on memory security is in Section 7.3.1.

6.3 ELECTRICAL AND ELECTROMAGNETIC THREATS

Hardware is susceptible to damage from various electrical threats. These include power anomalies, lightning-induced damage, electrostatic discharge (ESD), and electromagnetic (EM) energy. EM energy can be delivered from continuous EM sources (e.g., communications systems and radar), arc-generating devices (e.g., motors), and nuclear electromagnetic pulse (EMP) [52]. Strictly speaking, nuclear radiation is also an electromagnetic threat, but it is usually categorized separately. This is also true for alpha particles (mentioned earlier in this chapter). In this section, we will examine lightning, ESD, and conventional equipment-related EM sources. We will not address power anomalies (previously addressed in Chapter 3), alpha particles, or radiation effects.

6.3.1 Lightning

One of nature's most spectacular and most common phenomena, lightning has always intrigued people. Ben Franklin's early lightning research produced classic results (verifying the electrical nature of lightning and developing the lightning rod). The lightning rod currently remains an effective protective measure, although substantial improvements have been made in grounding and conductor routing [41].

Most lightning is generated in the cumulonimbus cloud structures (thunderheads) that are associated with thunderstorms. Although the generation mechanisms are not thoroughly understood, the charge separation of rising warm, moist air, and falling water and ice particles apparently separates electrons from molecules (which become positive ions) in a manner somewhat analogous to the charge separation that occurs when people walk across a carpet on a dry winter day (see following discussion on ESD).

The usual charge configuration is for the lower part of a cumulonimbus cloud to become negatively charged, and the upper portion to become positively charged. When the charge becomes great enough that the atmospheric dielectric properties can no longer prevent air breakdown (an "avalanche" of ionization), a conductive path is created, and a sudden massive discharge (or discharges) occurs. If the discharge is contained within the cloud, the lightning is termed "intracloud" lightning; if the discharge is between the cloud and the ground, it is termed "cloud-to-ground" lightning (or "ground-to-cloud" lightning). "Intercloud" and "cloud-to-air" lightning can also occur. Cloud-to-ground lightning is the most important in the context of computer security. Although airborne computer applications (those in aircraft and missiles) may be exposed to other types of lightning, the cloud-to-ground environment is the most severe. Therefore, hardening airborne computers to cloud-to-ground lightning gives protection during flight. Cloud-to-ground lightning has been widely studied and measured.

On the average, there are, at any time, about two thousand lightning storms in progress in the earth's atmosphere. Worldwide, there

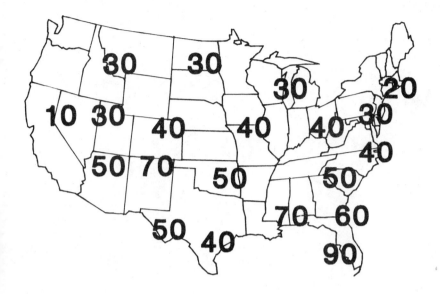

Figure 6-10   Thunderdays per year in continental United States.

are about 100 cloud-to-ground lightning flashes per second. Since most cloud-to-ground lightning lowers negative charge to the earth, one might wonder if the earth is becoming more and more negatively charged. The answer is that it is not, because negative charge can be measured during fair weather returning from the earth to the atmosphere. This charge flow is related to an easily measurable clear-weather electric field on the order of about 100 V/m (volts per meter). The outward flow of electrons results in a current of about 1000 A between the earth and the "electrosphere" (where the atmosphere becomes conductive to low-frequency signals). The voltage of the electrosphere is about 300,000 V (positive with respect to earth) [38]. The result is that a balanced charge flow is maintained for the earth's geosystem, with thunderstorms furnishing the "pumping" action for the charge motion.

Exposure to lightning varies widely with geographical location, with season, and even with time of day. Measurements of lightning activity are made by satellites and networks of lightning flash monitors. However, a graphic indication of lightning activity can be obtained from "isoceraunic" maps, which show "thunderdays" (days on which thunder is heard at a weather station). Figure 6-10 shows thunderdays per year as a function of general location within the

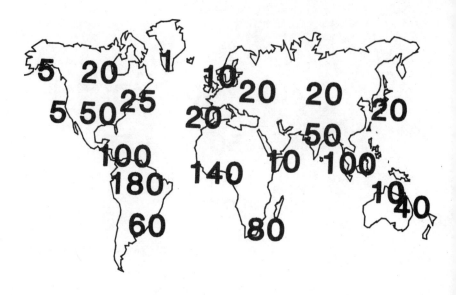

Figure 6-11   Thunderdays per year worldwide.

continental United States. Figure 6-11 depicts similar measurements taken around the world. The numbers shown in the figures are obviously integrated over wide areas, but a general indication of thunderstorm activity as a function of geographical location is apparent. Thunderdays per year convert almost one-to-one with flashes to the ground per square kilometer per year [40].

The electromagnetic effects of lightning are indicated by the static and bursts of noise heard on an AM radio during a lightning storm. Even at large distances (tens of miles), the effect is strong. The major source of this EM effect is the large current delivered during a lightning stroke. Items in the path of the current flow can experience much more damaging effects than radio static.

Lightning delivers huge currents in a short time. Peak currents of over 300,000 amperes have been measured, although the average cloud-to-ground lightning current is less than 30,000 amperes. The peak value is reached in times ranging from a few tenths of a microsecond to over 10 microseconds. Current rapidly decays over periods of tens of microseconds, although there may be hundreds of

Figure 6-12   Cloud-to-ground lightning. (Photograph courtesy of Dana Cooper.)

amperes of "continuing current" that last hundreds of milliseconds. Continuing currents are a special fire threat because of prolonged heating effects.

A lightning "flash" (discharge event) may comprise several individual "strokes" (pulses of current). The total duration of a flash may exceed a second. Figure 6-12 shows a multiple-stroke flash captured during a few seconds of time exposure. A typical flash may transfer a charge of about 20 coulombs and deliver an energy on the order of 10^{10} joules.

There are two major electrical effects due to lightning: 1) direct conducted current, and 2) induced current due to coupling or electromagnetic radiation. Most computer systems housed in buildings are relatively invulnerable to either effect, excepting currents delivered on power lines. This is the main reason that power line protection (Chapter 3) is so important.

An indication of the magnetic field generated by lightning is given by the Biot-Savart equation [45]:

$$H = I/2\pi z \tag{6-24}$$

where H is the magnetic field (A/m), I is the current (A), and z is the distance of the measurement from the source (m).

For a location 100 m from a 200 kA stroke with a 100 kA/μsec rise rate, the field is approximately:

$$H(t) = 360(e^{-0.02t} - e^{-0.9t}) \tag{6-25}$$

where t is in microseconds. This gives a peak value of about 320 A/m at a time of 4.3 microseconds. The corresponding electric field is about 120,000 V/m. The indicated field strength is hundreds of times stronger than that delivered by a clear-channel radio station. These values also approximate the field 10 m from a 20 kA stroke.

Airborne computer systems (e.g., aircraft computers) are generally the most likely to be affected when in the vicinity of a thunderstorm. Commercial airliners are often struck, with disturbance of the field caused by the aircraft frequently triggering the discharge. At times the entire aircraft may be in danger of destruction [39]. The Apollo 12 mission was nearly lost because lightning energy upset an inertial platform and caused fuel cell disconnects. The combination of sensitive digital circuits in aircraft and missiles and the replacement of metal structures with composites has increased concern over lightning protection for computers and other components in these vehicles. Contemporary protection includes "static wicks" to bleed off charge and fuel tank vent protection against spark initiation.

Protection against conducted current was the intent of Franklin's lightning rod, and he certainly had the right idea. Lightning current is delivered in a manner that suggests a high-impedance current source. This means, in effect, that insulation is not practical, since the current will be delivered without regard to the impedance of the target. The only reasonable protection against conducted lightning current is diversion. Lightning rods are intended to divert current away from a building structure.

Diversion is also basic (but on a smaller scale) to the operation of "lightning arrestors," "varistor" protectors, and "clamps."

Power line protection against lightning effects [51] is generally based on two principal techniques: 1) A grounded cable is provided above the current-carrying wires in order to intercept as much lightning energy as possible. 2) Arc-breakdown protectors, usually in conjunction with a varistor (nonlinear extinguishing resistor) are used to clamp extreme voltages, such as those induced on the lines by nearby lightning [49].

System-level protection against lightning effects also typically depends on arc protectors and nonlinear devices. An example is the "lightning arrester-connector" used in a number of hazardous situations [42]. Circuit-level protection against lightning is similar to ESD protection, described below.

6.3.2 Electrostatic Discharge (ESD)

Everyone has experienced the electrical jolt associated with ESD, for example, upon touching a light switch after walking across a carpet on a dry winter day. ESD is caused by a "triboelectric" charge separation (a person becomes charged with respect to the carpet [and ground] because of a frictional motion between dissimilar nonconducting materials). The discharge occurs when the voltage gradient (roughly proportional to the charge voltage and inversely proportional to the distance to a discharge point) exceeds the insulation breakdown capabilities of the air. It is common for a person to become charged to several thousand volts (35,000 V has been measured in a laboratory situation). Although the discharge current delivered is too low to harm a person, ESD currents are easily capable of damaging electronic equipment.

ESD effects are generally most severe in low-humidity conditions. Although the humidity in computer rooms is usually controlled, an increasing number of powerful computers require no special environmental conditions, and thus may be vulnerable to these effects. The potential seriousness of the problem is indicated by electronics industry losses of about $5 billion annually [43] and the loss of a Pershing missile and lives in an incident in Europe [44].

Sensitivity to ESD is indicated by the data from Ref. 43, shown in Table 6-2.

A common (but unsophisticated) model for the delivery of ESD is based on a critically damped series RLC circuit, where the ESD voltage is initially on the capacitor [76]. The equation for the current in such a circuit is:

$$i(t) = CVa^2 t e^{-at} \tag{6-26}$$

where the inductance, L, is $R^2C/4$ for critical damping, and a is $2/RC$. Typical values are 10-20kV for V; 100pF for C; 1000 ohms for R; and

Table 6-2   ESD susceptibility.

Device Type	Range of Susceptibility (V)
Bipolar transistors	380–7000
CMOS	250–3000
ECL	500–1500
Film resistors	300–3000
GaAsFET	100–300
Schottky diodes	300–2500
Schottky TTL	1000–2500
SCR	680–1000

25 microHenries for L. The resultant current is about 10 A peak in 50 nsecs (see Problem 9). More accurate models [76] indicate faster rates of rise.

ESD protection is afforded in the same way as protection against other electrical threats (lightning, EMP, EMR, EMI) [50]. Potential protective measures include [46,47] grounding, shielding, filtering, and voltage limiting (spark gaps, zener diodes, transorbs, varistors). In this section, we will emphasize varistors, since the other topics are covered elsewhere in the text.

Varistor material has a variable resistance that depends on the impressed voltage. One method of preparing the material is to heat treat silicon carbide in a ceramic binder. Another technique is to use semiconducting zinc oxide and a small quantity of other metal oxides to form a polycrystalline ceramic (metal oxide varistors). "Switching" (stressed nonlinear response) occurs at the ZnO grain boundaries, providing a distributed energy absorption. The protective voltage ("varistor voltage") depends on the grain size and the number of grain boundaries between the device electrodes. Low-voltage (3–8 volts) devices are now available, making varistors attractive for the protection of sensitive digital electronics.

The power-handling capabilities of varistors are consistent with ESD energy. Common capability is to carry tens of amperes delivered over tens of microseconds. Device capacitances are generally in the range of thousands of picoFarads.

Procedural protective measures [48] are used mostly in assembly, disassembly, or repair areas. These include humidity control, anti-static treatment (sprays, conductive fibers, conductive mats), and operating personnel measures (wrist straps, conductive chairs, cotton garments).

6.3.3 Electromagnetic (EM) Radiation

Radio static is an effect of EM radiation, most commonly being generated by lightning. Other sources of EM radiation include radars, radio and television broadcast antennas, motors, generators, arc welders, nuclear bursts, and even computers.

EM radiation is categorized as a function of the source. EMR is usually associated with radiation from radars and similar sources. EMI (electromagnetic interference) is associated with noise generated by equipment sources [53]. EMP (electromagnetic pulse) is associated with nuclear bursts.

The names associated with these threats differ, but the mechanism is essentially the same. That is, rapid transitions in current or voltage can cause "waves" of propagating magnetic and electric fields. The waves are maintained by the oscillation of the magnetic and electrical energy and the exchange of energy between magnetic and electric fields.

The relation between charge motion and field generation can be expressed as:

$$E = \sum qh/4\pi\varepsilon_0 z^3 + (d \sum qh/dt)/4\pi\varepsilon_0 c z^2 + (d^2 \sum qh/dt^2)/4\pi\varepsilon_0 c^2 z$$

$$H = (d \sum qh/dt)/4\pi z^2 + (d^2 \sum qh/dt^2)/4\pi c z \qquad (6\text{-}27)$$

where E is the electric field (V/m), H is magnetic field A/m, $\sum qh$ denotes the aggregate of charge pairs, each separated by distance h; ε_0 is the permittivity of free space (8.85×10^{-12}); c is the free space propagation velocity (3×10^8 m/sec); and z is the distance from the charge disturbance.

The first term of the expression for E is called the "electrostatic field"; the second term of E and the first term of H represent "near field" or "induction" field; and the last terms in the two expressions represent the "far field" or "radiation" field. Although the latter terms are inversely proportional to z, the reduction is slow enough to

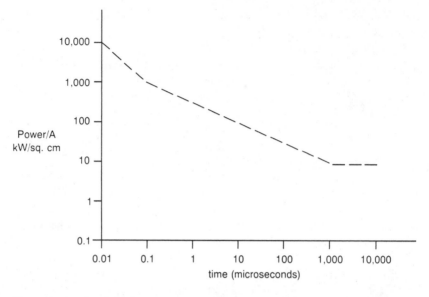

Figure 6-13   Semiconductor junction damage threshold.

allow propagation at large distances, as evidenced by AM radio broadcast ranges.

Conversely, energy can be obtained from EM fields, as waves are intercepted by wires, loops, separated plates, etc. The problem is that energy inadvertently intercepted in this way can overheat and hence damage sensitive components, especially semiconductor junctions.

The damage of semiconductor junctions has been extensively studied, measured, and modeled [55]. A straightforward model, the "Wunsch-Bell" model of damage threshold as a function of the power-time product of the impressed energy, is diagrammed in Figure 6-13. The figure shows the damage threshold for a square-wave application of power across a semiconductor junction for a period of time (shown on the abscissa). The threshold is specified in terms of power per unit area of the junction.

In the "A" region of the plot, energy is deposited so rapidly that it is confined to the junction area. This "adiabatic" heating region shows that the damage threshold is inversely proportional to the time of power application. In the "B" region, one-dimensional heat flow modeling results in a threshold inversely proportional to the square root of application time duration. Region "C" is the steady-state flow region, where the threshold is independent of time. Actual component measurements [55] rarely deviate as much as a factor of 10 from the line shown in the figure.

6.4 INFORMATION-TAPPING TECHNIQUES

Information tapping has many forms. We are accustomed to hearing about telephone taps, radio transmitting "bugs," and directional sound amplifiers. The U.S. Moscow embassy structure, a $22 million investment, has become unusable because of the information-tapping technology that had been incorporated by the Russians during its construction. The United States has installed encryption on many microwave telephone transmissions because of routine Soviet bloc interception and analysis of communication traffic.

All of the well-known tapping techniques are applicable (or have variants) in computer and communications security. In this section, we will survey common techniques in use today. These include direct connection to wires, passive coupling from wires, communication channel electromagnetic energy interception, fiber optics tapping, and "TEMPEST" (inadvertent intelligence-bearing information). ✳

may not be intel, information - see definition,

6.4.1 Direct-Connection Tapping

Direct-connection tapping of telephone lines is relatively easy. Low-priced tapping equipment is available in many electronics stores [61]. Tapping computer communications is only slightly more difficult. The most straightforward access is to the subscriber loop before it reaches the telephone exchange. An example of an access point is the pedestal box where local lines meet the main feeder cable. ✳

Frequently, lines and connection points are available in building wire chases, which are not always secured. The FBI averages about 400 reports each year of illegal telephone line intercept activities.

6.4.2 Passive Coupling

Passive coupling through inductive or capacitive response is another tapping technique. It has the advantages for the adversary of wider location options (not restricted to junction boxes), and less likelihood of detection. An inductive tap can be purchased for about $10 and a complete system (tap, signal-activated switch, and extended-capacity recorder) costs less than $200 [61]. The defenses against tapping include encryption, physical inspection, and equipment (e.g., time domain reflectometers) for pinpointing electrical connections.

6.4.3 Electromagnetic Energy Interception

Computer communications conveyed over land-based microwave links or over satellite links are vulnerable to interception from a wide variety of locations. This enables an adversary to be very inconspicuous. Much of the satellite traffic is on publicly disclosed frequencies. Telephone frequencies can be located by placing phone calls conveying a "tracer" (flag) signal. Encryption is the only practical defense against this threat.

6.4.4 Fiber Optics Tapping

Fiber optics communications are often cited as "secure" in that there are no emanations or passive coupling modes, and in that they are hard to tap because of small fiber size (comparable to or less than the diameter of a human hair). However, it is important to note that tapping is possible by skilled personnel. There is now some evidence that extremely difficult-to-detect taps are possible [79]. For these reasons, fiber optic interconnection should be viewed as a deterrent, rather than as assured protection.

6.4.5 TEMPEST

TEMPEST (not an acronym) was initially a term used to describe a government program to control "compromising emanations." Common contemporary usage of the term TEMPEST makes it now synonymous with compromising emanations. (Compromising emanations will be described in this section.)

The EM emanations involved in a TEMPEST assessment are similar to EMI (electromagnetic interference), except that the concern is the information conveyed, rather than the noise. EMI and TEMPEST both arise out of the phenomenon described in Equation 6-27, where charges in motion cause radiated fields. In the case of EMI [56], the fields are considered a nuisance (creating noise and masking data transfer). In the case of TEMPEST, where the emanations are related to data processing, the fields can create a security vulnerability [57,58].

6.4.5.1 The TEMPEST Vulnerability At first, it may seem incredible that any intelligence could be available in all of the signal flow taking place during computer and communications processing. Many "bookkeeping" circuits (e.g., clock and other timing circuits) are running continuously, and much of the data transfer takes place in parallel, where individual bits would seem hard to identify. However, intuition can once again be misleading. For example, some of the most energetic data processing is used to generate CRT (cathode ray tube) displays using a serial, repetitive format.

Another factor is that intelligence is frequently represented in computer and communications systems by English text. The redundancy of the English language is well known; it takes only about a third of the text characters read correctly to deduce most messages.

Radiated intelligence can occur in the form of two basic EM modes. The first is EM propagation from the source to a receiver. The second is EM coupling to conductors (e.g., power line, telephone line), followed by conduction along the lines.

The first mode of information transfer mentioned above is strongest in the immediate vicinity of the source. The conductive mode does not attenuate as rapidly and therefore may remain significant for a considerable distance.

In 1985, a dramatic demonstration of TEMPEST interception was broadcast on the British Broadcasting Corporation program "Tomorrow's World." A van equipped with a VHF antenna, a battery-powered TV set, and about $50 worth of peripheral electronics was driven to the vicinity of the tightly secured facilities of Holland's Post, Telegraph, and Telephone Service. Data being processed were read clearly during the experiment. Although the operation occurred in broad daylight, no one questioned the personnel involved about their activity.

A generic description of the type of equipment used in this demonstration [59] is shown in Figure 6-14. The cost depends on the sensitivity and selectivity required. A close-range interception can be accomplished for about a thousand dollars; a sophisticated system capable of detection at longer distances can cost hundreds of thousands of dollars.

It is informative to consider sensitivity to EMI for comparative assessment of TEMPEST signal levels. The FCC has established limits for emanated and conducted signal levels. The reasons for these limitations have nothing to do with TEMPEST. The purpose is to minimize noise generation by one piece of electronics equipment that will interfere with another (for example, by introducing noise into a TV display). The FCC limit is on the order of a ten millionth of a

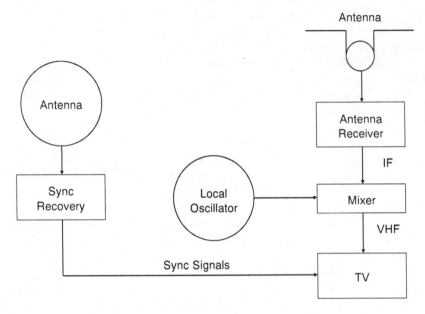

Figure 6-14   An emanations interception technique.

watt emanation at subgigahertz frequencies, and about a millivolt conducted noise up to 30 MHz. Both of these limits are exceeded by most standard 1-MHz TTL clock circuits. The result is that it is necessary to incorporate filtering, shielding, and grounding techniques into much of the equipment manufactured today, in order to meet the FCC limits.

Since the FCC limits are to prevent unintended reception of operating emissions, it follows [58] that by seeking transmitted energy and by providing for sufficient sensitivity, much lower levels of emanations and conducted energy than the FCC limits could be detected. Therefore, while the introduction of confinement measures for FCC compliance contributes to TEMPEST protection, it has no major security significance.

6.4.5.2 Protective Measures   There are a number of ways in which to reduce TEMPEST vulnerabilities. An obvious technique, especially for radiated EM, is to assure considerable distance between emanating equipment and an adversary. This technique is feasible where large controlled fenced areas enclose a facility. Location within the controlled area then becomes a potential protective measure. A re-

lated protective measure is to ensure separation distance from fortuitous conductors, such as telephone lines.

Circuit design can be useful since slower responding components
generally emanate less energy (see Equation 6-27). This means that
one should not "overdesign" speed of response; it should be only as
fast as required for timing constraints. Circuit layout is a factor in
that potential radiating loops should be kept as small as possible.
This is done by laying out short interconnections, with signal and
ground in close proximity to each other.

Metal shielding is potentially useful at the component, transmission medium, system, and room level. Shielding a small computer is
feasible, since shielding techniques are available for CRTs and vents.
Metal cases, metal paints, shielded cables, and shielded connectors
also contribute to shielding effectiveness. Room shielding requires
special treatment to seal around doors and other incursions. Conductive gaskets kept under mechanical pressure are commonly used in
these cases [60]. Filtering on power, communication, and signal lines
is also a frequently used measure.

Fiber optic signal transmission is helpful and avoids any problems
associated with grounding. Fibers and other optical techniques can
be used for intracircuit interconnection, and fiber optic cables can be
used for network communications. Fiber optic cables appear externally much like conventional cables (see Figure 6-15), except that the
actual fibers that carry the communication are roughly the diameter
of a human hair (approximately 100 μm). The energy containment
within the fibers is enhanced by a dielectric "cladding," and the
fibers are physically protected by sheathing.

Masking emanations with noise has been suggested, but is usually
not considered effective. The problems are that the generated noise
must be random to avoid filtering; that it must be spread over a wide
spectrum to cover all emanations, thereby requiring a large amount
of power; and that reliability of equipment in the vicinity of the noise
source is usually degraded.

Encryption can help reduce TEMPEST vulnerability in some
areas, but the CRT would probably not be included. However, a
similar technique has been used [59]. Instead of forming the CRT
image in the conventional, systematic manner, circuitry can be
designed to structure the display sequence in a keyed pseudorandom
manner. The person viewing the display sees no difference from an
ordinary display, but an adversary cannot directly reconstruct the
information from the emanations.

The ability to select "approved" equipment (minimal emanations)
is a procedural technique made available through the programs and

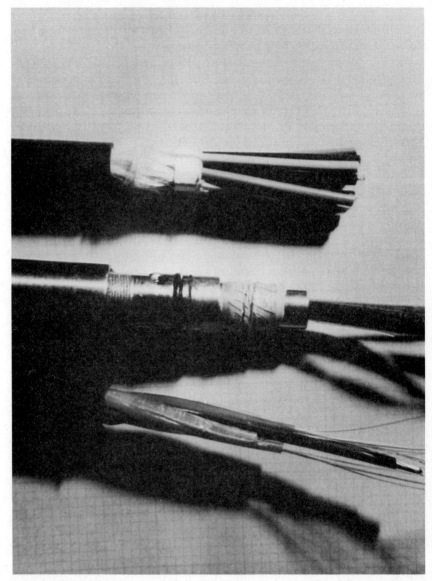

Figure 6-15   Fiber optic cables. (Photograph courtesy of Sandia National Laboratories.)

unclassified publications of the U.S. . government's Industrial TEMPEST Program (ITP) [61]. Approval is given to equipment that has been submitted by members of the ITP and which has passed stringent test requirements spelled out in a classified standard,

NACSIM 5100A.[*] Approved equipment is noted on an Endorsed TEMPEST Products List. Continued approval depends on periodic operational evaluation.

6.5 PERSONAL COMPUTER SECURITY

Although personal computers (PCs) operate under software instructions and can communicate over networks, their development depended on hardware technology. For this reason, the topic is treated here in a hardware chapter. Dramatic changes have appeared in the workplace since the "contemporary" PC was introduced in 1977. PCs are now more widely used than were calculators 15 years ago. Many engineers and scientists who felt, at that time, privileged to have any computer access now have more than one PC at their disposal. The implications for security are staggering. For example, security threats such as "hackers" and "viruses" would probably be insignificant were it not for PCs. ✳

Many changes have been introduced into the security environment as a result of PC proliferation [62]. Some of these are:

1. The type of people on which security depends is different. Many PC users have no detailed training in how hardware and software operates and the related security implications. Career "computer personnel" are not generally the people in control of PC operations.

2. The administrative control of PCs is less stringent and often nonexistent. It is rare to find separation of duties, auditing, supervision of computing operation, and enforcement of contingency planning (backup, recovery). Management is frequently unwilling to provide for, or unsuccessful in obtaining, resources to support PC security.

3. The overall value of the assets involved (hardware, software, data) is less significant. Therefore the overall security environment receives less attention.

4. PC users have a sense of independence and ownership of the resources, resulting in less sensitivity to organizational motives and policies.

---

[*]   There is a similar NATO standard, AMSG 720 B.

5. The operating environment is less oriented toward security. Physical security measures may be less stringent than in mainframe computer rooms; and power protection, fire protection, water protection, and environmental cleanliness may be inferior.

6. The software used is generally less secure. PC operating systems rarely have any significant security features, applications software usually is not provided with security features, and integrity may be harder to ensure because of less complete provision against data damage due to operational errors.

In this section, we will emphasize some of the specific problems created by these changes in the security environment. These include data exposure to unauthorized people, loss of data due to accidental destruction, indirect threats to mainframe security (e.g., introduction of dialup entry points), and misuse potential.

6.5.1   Data Exposure to Unauthorized People

One of the consequences of PC proliferation is that the people using computers have, generally, less exposure to the details of the overall computing environment, including security. They are more likely to think of the computer as a tool for increasing job productivity, without realizing the variety of security problems that may affect them. This can result in more exposure of data to unauthorized people.

The physical environment is of particular concern. Since PCs are usually located in office areas, control of the personnel that can be in proximity to PCs is less stringent than it would be for a typical computer room. This relative ease of physical access provides adversaries with enhanced opportunity to access data, whether stored on fixed disks, floppies, or cartridges. Hard-disk computers are potentially vulnerable to information being read by unauthorized personnel.

Lack of logical control also contributes to data-compromise vulnerability. The data are frequently available to an adversary without having to overcome any security measures. Where security measures are used, they are likely to be weak. An example is the ability to create "hidden" files (no directory listing). Recovery utilities such as the Norton routines [69] or "bit copiers" can be used to locate and read these files.

Another opportunity for data compromise occurs when information is improperly destroyed or improperly protected during servicing. Examples of improper destruction are reuse of diskettes without degaussing [65] and disposal of diskettes in "public" receptacles (e.g., wastebaskets). As an alternative to degaussing, systematic overwrite procedures can be used [63]. An example of servicing exposure is hard-disk servicing. Users have on occasion realized too late that protected data was on a disk that was exposed to service personnel either at the user's facility or at the service organization's facility. Unknown to many users, compromising information may be left on a hard disk with no indication to the user [64]. Many applications programs write temporary files on the hard disk. If not subsequently overwritten, these files can be read using the appropriate software.

A similar vulnerability is created by electronic mail (E mail) systems, to which many PCs connect. Most E mail systems create "archive" copies of all messages. These message copies cannot be erased by users, regardless of instructions given to the system. A large part of the detail in the Iran-Contra Tower report came from a secure computer system used by the National Security Council for E mail and word processing [83]. The messages read by investigators had been futilely "purged" by the users.

6.5.2 Accidental Data Destruction

Data generated by PCs can be inadvertently destroyed in a variety of ways. These include operational errors, system failures, diskette mistreatment, and environmental stresses.

A threatening operational error involves improper entry of the "Format" command. It is possible to misaddress a disk drive to execute formatting and unexpectedly lose data on the indicated disk. Most operating systems interpret "Format" as "Format C" (where "C" refers to a specific disk drive), and this can easily cause data loss.

One system failure that dogged early hard-disk computer users was failure of the hard-disk drive, with resultant loss of data. This problem, while now less likely, has not gone away. Other types of system failures can result in failure to write data to memory (for example on completion of an extensive graphics construction), with no indication given the operator.

Power anomalies are an indirect cause of system failure in that power protection may be considered a system responsibility. In any event, power fluctuations due to lightning and similar effects can cause data loss.

Diskettes have proved remarkably reliable in view of the treatment they receive, but there are limits to their tolerance of mistreatment. Diskettes are subject to heat damage at about 125°F, and while this seems like an abnormally high temperature, it can be exceeded within closed automobiles on summer days, in the vicinity of automobile heater ducts, and in proximity to heat sources such as ovens.

Magnetic fields of about 50 Oersteds will erase data on diskettes. Although this is a strong field strength, it is easily exceeded in the vicinity of magnets such as those that are used in paper clip dispensers.

Despite warnings on diskettes against writing on surfaces protecting the disk surface, this is often done. Diskettes can be corrupted by touching the recording surfaces with greasy or soiled hands. Diskettes have been bent, pressed with heavy objects, and subjected to unclean environments (smoke, liquids, dust).

Fire hazard must be considered. PCs are not normally in environments that are as well protected as computer rooms. Also, while mainframe computers usually have offsite backup storage, PC users may not even be aware of the necessity.

6.5.3 Degradation of Mainframe Security

The mainframe environment now usually includes terminal connections (hardwired or dialup) for PCs. The result is that mainframe computer security can be degraded by PCs in a number of ways.

A subtle problem involves failure to adhere to security policies. The mainframe environment has traditionally included mostly computer professionals, with a generally good understanding of—and a strong motivation to adhere to—security policies. The proliferation of PCs has somewhat lessened general security-conscious behavior.

One of the common applications for PCs on a mainframe-based network is the downloading and analysis of data. A problem created by this environment [72] is that decisions may be made based on PC records of a corporate database, records that may no longer be current at the time they are used. Where data can be changed by PC users, controls of the database privileges become more complex. These problems have now been amplified by the availability of multiuser PC operating systems [67]. This is one of the main reasons for the restriction on some networks to "diskless PCs," which force users to rely on the network for their data and software [85].

One of the most serious mainframe problems created by PCs is the capability of the PC to act as a dialup connection to a mainframe. A significant level of security confidence has been based on computers having no dialup connections, because this restriction allows physical control of terminal locations along with corresponding control of the community of personnel who can gain access to those locations.

For this reason, it is common to restrict computer systems to hardwired connections. However, the user of a connected PC can intentionally or unintentionally violate this restriction by installing an auto-answer modem. The existence of such a modem is usually difficult to detect with a cursory visual inspection. Therefore, the restriction against dialup connections to a network that incorporates hard-wired PCs is only as effective as are the PC users in adhering to the policy.

Another way in which PC users have subverted network management policies is to intentionally or unintentionally introduce a "pseudo-network" connection through another medium (e.g., handcarry). For example, a user who has access to two networks (whose interconnection is not allowed) can carry diskettes used on one network to the other network for use. Although no electrical connection has been introduced, the result can be just as damaging. An example of the problems that can be created by this type of data movement is spread of a computer virus (see Chapter 7).

6.5.4 Misuse Potential

"Misuse," as addressed here, means use of a company resource for noncompany business. The types of usage involved include personal business (income tax, database maintenance), game playing, school homework assistance, and outside organization or club support (mailing lists, databases). Many companies are sensitive to the misuse of PCs, because they feel compelled to control the use of a company resource or because resource acquisitions based on usage patterns that include personal use would be misleading. The result might be that the company purchases equipment to furnish a capability that serves no company function. Sensitivity to this issue varies greatly from company to company.

6.5.5 Protective Measures

A large number of protective measures are available that are effective against the problems described in the preceding text. These include physical security measures, personnel security measures, hardware security measures, and network security measures. Many of these fall into generic classes discussed elsewhere in the book. Here we will concentrate on measures that are generally aimed specifically at PCs.

Available physical security measures include power locks, keyboard locks, diskette case locks, and locking cabinets that also serve as operation consoles. The robustness of these locks is not generally great, but they are a cost-effective deterrent. The use of removable cartridge hard disks enables the memory units to be locked up in conveniently sized spaces. Removable cartridges are available in the 5–20 MB range for $1500 to $5000.

Making sure that procedures for timely backup are understood is mainly a procedural matter, but devices are available that encourage adherence to the procedures. For example, backing up the data on a hard disk is generally tedious and time-consuming. However, streaming tape cartridge backup devices are available for about $2000, and these can copy 20 MB in about five minutes.

Hardware security cards can be helpful in controlling computer access and memory access. These can be inserted into the computer and then must be physically locked in place.

Some of the software security packages available include capabilities for adding password access control (including multiple passwords for multiple users), file encryption capability, and auditing [70]. Other features sometimes included, or easily added by a user, include copy disabling and format query of users before proceeding. The recovery of apparently lost data (e.g., that which has been deleted by a system command) is possible using utility routines [69].

Hardware and software techniques are available for encryption of communication. Many of these incorporate DES encryption (see Chapter 8). Since DES is a national standard, interconnection with other users is generally facilitated.

At this point, it is appropriate to reiterate that cost-effectiveness is always an important consideration [71]. Since physical assets to be protected in a PC environment may be of lower value than we see in other environments, the cost of the security measures considered must be balanced against the reduction in risk and vulnerability. Information, on the other hand, may have value independent of the environment in which it is stored.

6.6 TAMPER-RESISTANT SEALS

Much current hardware uses technology that looks, to the casual observer, inscrutable. Integrated circuit (IC) chips contain hundreds of thousands of "gates" or transistors on a single piece of semiconductor the size of a fingernail. However, adversaries have demonstrated a remarkable facility for unraveling the IC morass. An example is the "chip pirates" that have plagued semiconductor manufacturers. Designs that appear extremely complex have been copied and sold, thereby obviating the chip development cost.

In addition, "bugs" have been planted in electronic equipment in such a way that they are extremely hard to detect.

There are a number of applications where it is desired to "seal" hardware against tampering. One motivation may be that physical control of a hardware item is temporarily lost. This loss of control could occur when another organization services the hardware, or when the hardware must be inspected for some other purpose (e.g., customs inspection during international travel).

The purpose of the seal is almost always to prevent undetected penetration. This means that tamper indication, not tamper prevention, is usually the objective. In practice, prevention is extremely difficult.

Some of the techniques that have been developed for sealing include [73] hard-to-duplicate mechanically scribed patterns, resin coating, fiber optic bundle cutting (see below), three-dimensional reflective particle arrays (see below), and ultrasonic seals.

The general aim of these techniques is to require that an adversary penetrate the device and to assure that the penetration will alter a reference pattern that is not feasible to duplicate.

One example is the fiber optic seal [74]. The seal is based on a cable carrying a bundle of twisted optical fibers. The cable is looped with both ends captured by a sealing and cutting device. The device is designed to cut approximately half of the fibers, so that light entering one end of the cable can be viewed at the other end as a pattern of cut and uncut (unlighted and lighted) indicators.

Another technique [75] is based on use of a clear epoxy coating, with the epoxy containing reflective particles. Multiposition photography records a three-dimensional pattern created by the particle positions, which becomes the "signature" or "fingerprint" of the seal.

PROBLEMS

1. a) Assume that twice as much production cost is necessary to produce a high-rel part. Would you expect the part to sell for twice the price? b) Assume that 1% RAM redundancy allows yield to increase by 1%. Is the redundancy a good investment?

2. What set of input vectors sensitizes the logic circuit $f = xy \lor z$ to all stuck-at faults?

3. a) Give nonseparate coding and code checking for the hexadecimal addition: B + 7, where the check base, A, is 5. b) Give separate coding and code checking for the same hexadecimal addition, where the modulus, A, is 4.

4. Do the two operations below represent a field?

+	0	1	2	3		*	0	1	2	3
0	0	1	2	3		0	0	0	0	0
1	1	2	3	0		1	0	1	2	3
2	2	3	0	1		2	0	2	3	1
3	3	0	1	2		3	0	3	1	2

5. Referring to the error-correcting code indicated in Figure 6-3, what would be the parity checks corresponding to the information bits 1011? If an error were made in the third bit during transmission, determine the pattern developed in the decoding circuit, and show how this pattern determines the necessary bit correction.

6. The set of vectors below can specify an error-protection code constructed by linear (bit-by-bit exclusive-or) combinations. How many code words can be generated from the set? How many information bits does this imply?

$$
\begin{array}{cccccc}
1 & 1 & 1 & 0 & 0 & 1 \\
1 & 1 & 0 & 1 & 1 & 0 \\
0 & 1 & 1 & 0 & 1 & 1 \\
0 & 0 & 1 & 1 & 1 & 1 \\
\end{array}
$$

7. Solve the following simultaneous equations of two variables over GF(4) as specified in the tables below.

	+ 0 1 2 3	* 0 1 2 3
2x + y = 3	0 0 1 2 3	0 0 0 0 0
	1 1 0 3 2	1 0 1 2 3
x + 2y = 3	2 2 3 0 1	2 0 2 3 1
	3 3 2 1 0	3 0 3 1 2

8. a) What is the transmission rate for the Hamming code that has three parity bits? Four? Five? Six? Seven? b) Assuming that the probability of a single bit error is 0.01, what is the probability of an uncorrectable error using the Hamming codes of part a?

9. A series RLC critically damped circuit charged to 10 kV is used to model an ESD discharge. R = 1000 ohms; C = 100 pF. a) What is the time to peak current? b) What is the peak current? c) What is the time at which current has decayed to half of its peak value?

10. If one watt of power is radiated isotropically at 100 MHz and is received by an antenna with a gain of 100 at a distance of 10 m, what is the received power? At 100 m? At 1000 m?

DILEMMA DISCUSSIONS

1. A security switch automatically disconnects a remote terminal outside of normal working hours to make sure that the terminal is not available to unauthorized personnel. However, employees frequently need to work late and wish to delay the disconnect until they leave work. The switching center does not have the personnel, the time, or the equipment to verify telephone requests from remote locations. It is considered inefficient business practice to automatically disconnect users at a prescribed time, but it is considered unacceptable security to leave the terminals connected at all times, and unacceptable

security to honor a telephone request without certain identification. What should be done?
2. Employees within a secure area frequently initiate long computer jobs from their terminals. The jobs typically run more
than an hour with no user interaction. The security rules state
that the terminals must be attended when active; users insist
that this is unnecessary inside a secure area and inefficient
from a standpoint of wasted time. The security rules recognize
the extent of the insider threat. What should be done?

REFERENCES

1. "Chip Maker Finds the Limits to Multiplication," *New Scientist*, June 11, 1987.
2. Redman, Capt. D. John, Capt. Ronald M. Sega, and Capt.
   Richard Joseph, "Alpha-Particle-Induced Soft Errors," *Military
   Electronics Countermeasures*, April 1980.
3. Cooper, James Arlin, *Microprocessor Background for Management Personnel*, Prentice-Hall, Englewood Cliffs, NJ, 1981.
4. Capece, R. P., "Alphas Stymie Statics," *Electronics*, March 15,
   1979.
5. Schieber, Stephen F., "New Memory Technologies Influence
   Test Data Reliability and Security," *Test & Measurement
   World*, October 1986.
6. Huber, William R., "The 64K RAM: A Fault-Tolerant Semiconductor Memory Design," *Bell Laboratories Record*, July/August
   1979.
7. Stewart, Donald M., "Lasers Fix Dynamic RAMs," *Electronics
   Week*, February 4, 1985.
8. Chang, Herbert Y., Eric Manning, and Gernot Metze, *Fault
   Diagnosis of Digital Systems*, Robert E. Krieger Publishing
   Company, New York, 1974.
9. Roth, J. P., "Diagnosis of Automata Failures: A Calculus and a
   Method," *IBM Journal of Research and Development*, vol. 10,
   1966.
10. Shannon, Claude E., and Warren Weaver, *The Mathematical
    Theory of Communication*, The University of Illinois Press, Ur-
    bana, IL, 1949.
11. Hamming, R. W., "Error Detecting and Error Correcting
    Codes," *Bell System Technical Journal*, vol. 29, 1950.

12. Peterson, W. Wesley, and E. J. Weldon, Jr., *Error-Correcting Codes*, The MIT Press, Cambridge, MA, 1972.
13. Rothman, Tony, "The Short Life of Évariste Galois," *Scientific American*, April 1982.
14. Kravetz, Gary, "Redundant Parts Keep Systems Running," *Computer Design*, May 15, 1988.
15. Eidsmore, Douglas, "Fault Tolerant Architectures," *Digital Design*, August 1983.
16. Horwitt, Elisabeth, "Fault Tolerance for the Masses," *Business Computer Systems*, August 1985.
17. Musich, Paula, "3Com Deals for Fault-Tolerant Ware," *Network World*, August 17, 1987.
18. Weinstein, Stephen B., "Smart Credit Cards: The Answer to Cashless Shopping," *IEEE Spectrum*, February 1984.
19. Latamore, G. Berton, "Smart Cards Get Smarter," *High Technology Business*, September 1987.
20. Barney, Clifford, "Smart Card: Will it Create a Billion Dollar Business?" *Electronics*, December 18, 1986.
21. Connolly, Harold, "Automating the Home—and Paying for It," *Computer Design*, July 1987.
22. Glazer, Sarah, "Smart Cards," *High Technology*, July 1986.
23. Anderson, Robert G., and David R. Wilson, "Foiling Snoopers: Use 'See-Through' Security," *Management Information Systems Week*, April 7, 1986.
24. Boulanger, Noel J., and Patrick Kenealy, "A Look at Lazerlock," *Digital Review*, March 1985.
25. McLellan, Vin, "The Future of Data Security Looks Credit-Card Thin," *InformationWEEK*, October 7, 1985.
26. Taft, Darryl K., "Time-Based System Promises Enhanced Security," *Government Computer News*, May 22, 1987.
27. Williams, Tom, "Access Control plus Data Encryption Adds Up to System Security," *Computer Design*, August 1, 1986.
28. Miller, Ben, "Biometrics: Getting Computers to Identify People," *Canadian Data Systems*, November 1987.
29. *Computer Security, Understanding Computers Series*, Time-Life Books, Alexandria, VA, 1986.
30. Wellborn, Stanley N., "Foolproof ID: Opening Locks with Your Body," *U.S. News & World Report*, December 17, 1984.
31. Walsh, J. L., "A Closed Set of Normal Orthogonal Functions," *American Journal of Mathematics*, January 1923.
32. McIvor, Robert, "Smart Cards," *Scientific American*, November 1985.

33. Martin, S. Louis, "Smart Card Development Expands as Standard Nears Final Approval," *Computer Design*, September 1, 1988.
34. Leggett, J., G. Williams, and D. Umphress, "Verification of User Identity via Keyboard Characteristics," Texas A&M University Symposium on Human Factors in Management Information Systems, College Station, TX, 1986.
35. Diamond, Sam, "Biometric Security: What You Are, Not What You Know," *High Technology*, February 1987.
36. Bakst, Shelley, "Biometrics: The Future in Security Methods?" *The Office*, July 1988.
37. Chameides, W. L., and J. C. G. Walker, "Rates of Fixation by Lightning of Carbon and Nitrogen in Possible Primitive Atmospheres," *Origins of Life*, November 1981.
38. Uman, Martin A., *The Lightning Discharge*, Academic Press, Orlando, FL, 1987.
39. Pitts, Felix L., and Bruce D. Fisher, "Aircraft Jolts from Lightning Bolts," *IEEE Spectrum*, July 1988.
40. Cianos, N., and E. T. Pierce, "A Ground-Lightning Environment for Engineering Usage," Stanford Research Institute Report No. 1, August 1972.
41. Stekolnikov, I. S., "Study of Lightning and Lightning Protection," U.S. Department of Commerce, April 1965.
42. Cooper, J. Arlin, and Leland J. Allen, "The Lightning Arrestor-Connector Concept: Description and Data," *IEEE Transactions on Electromagnetic Compatibility*, August 1973.
43. Matisoff, B. S., *Handbook of Electrostatic Discharge Controls (ESD)*, Van Nostrand Reinhold Company, New York, 1986.
44. Turner, C. David, "Electrostatic Discharge Primer," Sandia National Laboratories Report SAND87-2058, September 1987.
45. King, Ronald W. P., and Charles W. Harrison, Jr., *Antennas and Waves: A Modern Approach*, The M.I.T. Press, Cambridge, MA, 1969.
46. Huntsman, James R., "Proper Shielding Protects ICs from Electrostatic Damage," *Electronics*, July 14, 1982.
47. Violette, J. L. N., and M. F. Violette, "ESD Case History—Immunizing a Desktop Business Machine," *EMC Technology*, May–June 1986.
48. Impara, Carol, "Finding Static Control Solutions," *Electronics Test*, April 1986.
49. Peterson, Ivars, "In Search of Electrical Surges," *Science News*, December 12, 1987.

50. McLouglin, Robert C., and Randall J. Redding, "Protection of Electronics from Lightning and Other Large AC Power Pulses," *EMC Technology*, September–October 1987.

51. Frydenlund, Marvin M., "Lightning Protection Systems Must Fit Both the Purpose and the Structure," *EMC Technology*, November–December 1986.

52. Bloks, Huub, "NEMP/EMI Shielding," *EMC Technology*, November–December 1986.

53. Mier, Edwin E., "Static Builds over RF Emissions, *Data Communications*, October 1985.

54. Shogase, Hiro, "The Very Smart Card: A Plastic Pocket Bank," *IEEE Spectrum*, October 1988.

55. Antoine, Robert J., "How to Prevent Circuit Zapping," *IEEE Spectrum*, April 1987.

56. White, Donald R. J., Kenn Atkinson, and John D. M. Osburn, "Taming EMI in Microprocessor Systems," *IEEE Spectrum*, December 1985.

57. Schultz, James B., "Defeating Ivan with TEMPEST," *Defense Electronics*, June 1983.

58. Schultz, James B., "NSA and Industry Experience TEMPEST Growing Pains," *Defense Electronics*, June 1984.

59. van Eck, Wim, "Electromagnetic Radiation from Video Display Units: An Eavesdropping Risk?" *Computers and Security*, December 1985.

60. Grant, Peter, "Shielding Techniques Tackle EMI Excesses," *Microwaves*, October 1982.

61. "Information Systems Security Products and Services Catalogue," National Security Agency, July 1988.

62. "Microcomputers: Their Use and Misuse in Your Business," Price Waterhouse, New York, 1986.

63. "Personal Computer Security Considerations," National Computer Security Center, NCSC-WA-002-85, December 1985.

64. Krema, James F., "Personal Computers and the Matter of Security," *The Office*, August 1986.

65. Lu, Cary, "Defend Your Data!" *High Technology*, June 1986.

66. Seymour, Jim, "Hard-Disk Backup: A Step Forward," *Today's Office*, February 1985.

67. Giglio, Louis, "Hope Wanes for the PC as an Effective Corporate Device," *InformationWEEK*, January 20, 1986.

68. Beitman, Lawrence, "A Practical Guide to Small Business Computer Security," *The Office*, August 1982.

69. Ditlea, Steve, "Disk Doctor," *Science Digest*, May 1986.

70. Meyer, N. Dean, "How to Design a Nonrestrictive Microcomputer Policy," *Data Communications*, October 1985.
71. Walden, Jeffrey, "Cracking Down on Computer Crime," *Business Computer Systems*, October 1984.
72. Maglitta, Joseph E., "PCs: A Database Security Nightmare," *Digital Review*, January 26, 1987.
73. Harvey, G. L., J. M. McKenzie, and I. C. Waddoups, "Developments of Seals for Safeguards," 1981 INMM (International Nuclear Materials Management) Proceedings.
74. Perry, Tekla S., "Sealed With a Fiber Optic Kiss," *IEEE Spectrum*, July 1986.
75. Spice, Byron, "'Fingerprints' Could Deter Illegal Arms," *Albuquerque Journal*, July 18, 1988.
76. Fisher, R. J., "The Electrostatic Discharge Threat Environment Data Base and Recommended Baseline Stockpile-to-Target Sequence Specifications," Sandia National Laboratories Report SAND88-2658, November 1988.
77. Dillingham, Susan, "Cards Get Credit for Smartness," *Insight*, October 24, 1988.
78. Bains, Sunny, "Lasers Out-Think the Smart Credit Cards," *New Scientist*, October 29, 1988.
79. Bell, Trudy E., "Tapping Optical Fibers," *IEEE Spectrum*, June 1988.
80. Gasser, Morrie, *Building a Secure Computer System*, Van Nostrand Reinhold Company, New York, 1988.
81. Sheiber, Stephen F., "Building Circuits that Test Themselves," *Test & Measurement World*, November 1988.
82. Hsiao, David K., Douglas S. Kerr, and Stuart E. Madnick, *Computer Security*, Academic Press, Inc., New York, 1979.
83. Chalmers, Leslie, "Data Security and Control," *Journal of Accounting and EDP*, Fall, 1987.
84. Bass, Brad, "Automated Portals to Control Access to Space Center," *Government Computer News*, August 29, 1986.
85. "Diskless PCs Protect the Data," *High Technology Business*, July 1988.

7

The Software Security Environment

Software is the heart of the computing process. Almost all the actions taken by a computer system are controlled by software. Most of the computer operations not controlled by software are controlled by firmware, which is logically equivalent to software. So an examination of software is of great importance in security assessment.

In this chapter, we address six topics in which software is a primary consideration. The first of these topics is software-based threats (e.g., the virus). The second topic is access control (e.g., passwords). The software-oriented work of the National Computer Security Center (NCSC) is the next topic. This is followed by security concerns regarding databases. Structured software development is considered both as a methodology leading toward efficient and correct systems and as a vehicle for enhancing resistance to adversary attacks. The final, and very important, topic is electronic data processing (EDP) auditing.

7.1 SOFTWARE THREATS

The computer virus threat has been widely publicized during the past few years. As the name suggests, there is an analogy between a computer virus and a biological virus, since both are capable of spreading and infecting. The computer virus has the potential to force basic changes in the way computing is done because of the security measures that are now being considered and implemented to contain it.

The virus is one of a family of software threats that has been known for decades. We also know that they are more than theoretical concepts. The category includes "Trojan horses" (a general concept that is usually part of the virus attack), "time bombs," "logic bombs," "worms," "trapdoors," "covert channels," "asynchronous attacks," "tailgating," "superzapping," "browsing," and the "salami" attack. Other threats that have had less glamorous publicity, but often more serious results, include deleterious software features. These may be undocumented, in which case they are frequently the result of inadvertent software logic errors.

7.1.1 The Trojan Horse

Homer's description in *The Iliad* of a Trojan horse (taken to be a prize, although surreptitiously representing a threat) has a software analogy. Hence the name.

The intent of this type of threat is to embed a clandestine (usually malicious) software routine within a useful program. The execution of the program by a user results in the execution of the embedded Trojan horse routine (TH). The intent of the TH is to accomplish something under the auspices of the user that could not be accomplished as easily (or at all) by the adversary. For example, the user may possess database privileges the adversary does not have. A TH attack might be used to transfer data to an area accessible to the attacker. Another common motivation is memory destruction. The TH may be targeted to provide access to files the adversary would like to damage or destroy.

By being embedded in a privileged user's code, access controls might be changed to allow penetration by the adversary. An incident of this type is described below.

During the development of "Multics" (a relatively secure operating system described below), penetration tests were conducted by an Air Force "Tiger Team" (simulating adversaries). One approach used to penetrate the system was to send a bogus operating system update to the organization operating the Multics system. The operating system update contained a TH that allowed the Tiger Team to obtain computer access. The TH was so well done that the Multics developers could not find it, even after they were informed of its presence [1].

A CBS executive was victimized [6] by a TH that destroyed all information contained in his computer's memory. The TH was implanted in a graphics routine offered on an electronic bulletin board system.

It is not very difficult for an adversary to avoid detection by disguising or removing obvious traces of TH code. A source code execution that transfers the TH to the compiler binary code, then erases the copy from the source, and finally recompiles the TH in binary can be constructed to eliminate evidence of the TH in the source code [2].

7.1.2 Time Bombs and Logic Bombs

Destructive routines that are initiated at a specific time or under specific logical conditions are called "time bombs" or "logic bombs," respectively. Attackers have various reasons for incorporating delayed action in destructive programs. One reason is to time the destruction for maximum effect. Another is to use time delay to make it harder to allow a trace back to the "planting" activity. A third reason is to trigger the activity by some event (e.g., if the employee is no longer found on the payroll or in the password file). A fourth reason for delay is to allow a virus (see below) to migrate the corruption to backup programs. Then, if the virus is purged from a particular version of the system (before or after destructive action), the seeds of further destruction have been planted, ready for action when the backup copies are used.

There have been numerous instances of this type of attack. The Los Angeles Department of Water and Power was victimized in early 1985 [22]. The saboteur, apparently an insider, planted a time bomb in a routinely used department software program. When the attack was triggered, the department computer crashed repeatedly. For about a week, 20 people worked on the problem, and no orders for new water and electricity could be entered into the system.

In 1980, a money order fraud was based on the logic bomb technique [8]. However, the purpose of the routine was to suppress printing of a record that would have revealed the fraud. The fraud was perpetrated by a consultant helping to computerize money order accounting. The consultant, at least partially motivated by gambling debts, investment losses, and a failed business, saw an opportunity to "borrow" debt payment capital. He stole money-order blanks and cashed fraudulent checks. He coded the stolen checks with an "E" and inserted a logic trigger to assure that records of the cashed checks would not be printed out.

A combination time bomb and logic bomb has been implemented in their software by some vendors [29]. The conditions under which they are initiated generally are nonpayment and copying. The penalty is nonfunctioning software or a nonfunctioning computer. The user is usually given a message telling him or her to contact the vendor to defuse the bomb.

7.1.3 Viruses and Worms

The "worm" (memory-writing) and "virus" (program-infecting) threats are sometimes called "computer parasites" [3]. These threats are intended to grow, propagate, or replicate within a host program or memory accessible to the program each time the parasite is used. The AT&T Bell Labs and Xerox worm programs demonstrated the ability to move through a network [4]. The computer game "Core Wars" is based on two computer programs "fighting" each other to control computer memory. There is now an International Core Wars Tournament [16].

The most serious and pervasive threat of this type that now exists is usually referred to as a "virus" [4,20]. The groundwork for the virus was provided by John von Neumann in a 1949 paper titled "Theory and Organization of Complicated Automata," which extended his ideas regarding common memory for programs and data (von Neumann architecture). The virus technique has been explored for at least 25 years [5] and has been formally analyzed during the past 10 years [4]. A virus is defined [4] as a program that "infects" other programs by modifying them to include a (possibly evolved) copy of itself. In this way, the infection spreads. The intent of virus/worm programs is frequently to write into memory, destroying the previous contents. Another usage mode is denial of service by creating an endless loop. Occasionally, the intent is merely to display a message announcing penetration success, and to cause no harm. However, the capability to do harm ensures the need for protection against all viruses.

Virus routines are nearly always implanted as a TH. This was the method used in the Fort Worth, Texas, case that resulted from the 1985 firing of an insurance and securities employee [19]. Before leaving, the employee retaliated by deleting sales commission records and planting a virus set to activate two days after he left the company. Although the virus was found before it could take full effect, almost 170,000 records were destroyed, and the computerized issuance of company paychecks was incapacitated for about a month. The attacker was prosecuted and was convicted in 1988 under a Texas law that specifically identifies computer sabotage and electronic virus infection as felonies. This was apparently the first successful prosecution relating to a virus or any comparably sophisticated software attack [9].

A virus/worm/TH can also be sent within an electronic mail message, or it can be inserted in application software. Conceivably, it could be made a part of operating system software or even firmware. Delivery of a TH can be accomplished by an insider (e.g., network user or software developer). This was the case in November 1988, when a worm (which was frequently referred to as a virus in subsequent press accounts) crippled the operation of at least 6000 computers connected to Internet, an interconnection of networks including ARPANET (Advanced Research Projects Agency network), MILNET (a network of military computers), and the National Science Foundation network [5]. The worm took advantage of a "trapdoor" (see below) debugging feature in the Sendmail electronic mail routine. The program was 40 kB (kilobytes) long, and included automated password attempts with commonly used passwords. The worm was detected relatively quickly because of an apparent mistake that caused it to replicate rapidly and slow down the system by consuming memory [30].

The routines can also be inserted by an outsider if an insider can be made to use an "infected" piece of software. The "Pakistani Brain" virus, which has appeared at several U.S. universities, was apparently created and distributed by a software merchant in Lahore, Pakistan [18].

Viruses are now known to have affected well over 150,000 computers, and the number is no doubt much higher. Reports of computer viruses have come from countries including the United States, Israel, West Germany, Australia, Switzerland, Britain, and Italy. In addition to the incidents described above, viruses have struck at many companies, including IBM (on an electronic mail system), NASA, Boeing, Martin Marietta Corporation, McDonnell Douglas, NOAA (National Oceanic and Atmospheric Administration), Aldus Corporation, Miami University, Lehigh University, the University of Pittsburg, the University of Wyoming, Penn State University, the University of Houston, New Mexico State University, Hebrew University, Brown University, and Georgetown University [17,18].

Applications software from a major U.S. supplier and from foreign sources has been infected [10–15].

Some of the types of viruses that have been detected [30] are:

1. The Macintosh virus, a benign virus that appeared in commercial software and on electronic bulletin boards. Its apparent goal was to display a universal peace message.
2. The Lehigh virus, a malicious virus that resided in the COMMAND.COM portion of DOS microcomputer operating systems. It replicated itself on any other disk run on the system that contained an uninfected copy of COMMAND.COM. Zeros were written into the first 50 sectors of the disk attacked. Although it was hidden within the stack portion of COMMAND.COM in order to maintain the file size listed, its action was detectable by the date tag listed for the file, which changed with each execution.
3. The Pakistani Brain virus, apparently contained in some software sold by Brain Computer Services. It was in the disk boot sector. Any unlabeled disk accessible to the virus was given the label "Brain." Three disk sectors were created so that they were perceived as "bad sectors" by the system, and hidden files containing the virus were inserted in these sectors.
4. The Hebrew University virus, which invaded computers at the Hebrew University in Israel. It was cleverly written to evade ordinary security safeguards, and was "time bombed" to destroy all accessible files on May 13, 1988. Fortunately, its preliminary destructive actions and rapid replication led to its discovery prior to the set time.
5. The Amiga virus, which was found in commercial software. It appeared in at least three countries: England, Australia, and the United States.
6. The Flu-Shot 4 virus, an apparent attempt to trick users of a legitimate virus detection program into updating their protection. Instead of providing protection, it bypassed some common virus detection checks and corrupted hard disks.
7. The Christmas Tree virus, which created an innocuous Christmas greeting and caused a Christmas tree to be drawn on the system display. The virus was apparently hidden in a data file instead of within the more commonly utilized executable code.

The dangers of using software from unknown sources ("shareware," "bootleg" copies, electronic bulletin board offerings) are now substantial. This is the reason that most companies are now warning their employees to use only trusted software (see Section 7.1.11 for discussion of protective measures). Unfortunately, no software can be completely trusted (see below).

7.1.4 Trapdoors

A "trapdoor" is a short-cut technique that is frequently used during software development to bypass security access control procedures. The motivation is that the software developers do not want to be impeded by controls that do not apply to them and that only serve to degrade their efficiency.

The vulnerabilities that may result from this threat are that if trapdoors are not removed, or if similar capabilities are surreptitiously implanted, an adversary can easily bypass security barriers. This was the basic idea for the vulnerability portrayed in the movie "WarGames," and for the TH implant in the Multics attack described above. Auditors discovered a trapdoor in a commercial software product [36], in which the author's name served as the bypass password.

Surreptitiously implanted trapdoors are intended to be activated by a special command or unlikely sequence of events [7]. The intent is that the perpetrator can easily execute the trapdoor, but that no one else is likely to perform the required sequence of actions. If this were to happen, the existence of the trapdoor would be revealed.

The easiest trapdoor implant scenario involves an insider during software system development. However, as the Multics incident indicates, there are other ways of putting a trapdoor in place.

7.1.5 Covert Channels

An attacker working through a TH usually intends either destruction or information access. In order to acquire access to information, the attacker must either find a way to masquerade as a user authorized to read the information or must find a covert way for the TH to convey the information. This information transfer by an adversary is straightforward, except in multilevel secure systems (see Section 7.3). Features incorporated in multilevel secure operating systems give assurance that a privileged user will be prevented from sending privileged information to an unprivileged user. This blocks an obvious TH technique. A covert channel attempts to transfer the information in an unexpected way that is not prevented by ordinary multilevel security controls [21].

Since all information in a system that can be modified by one process and read by another is subject to covert channel attack, there are various approaches for an attacker. The information transfer rate (the bandwidth of the covert channel) must be high enough to be worthwhile for the adversary, and this tends to limit the usefulness of a covert channel.

Two basic approaches in establishing covert channels are [7]: storage channels (interpreting changes in information) and timing channels (interpreting the timing of observable events).

An example of a storage channel approach is to change file names or other file attributes (e.g., length, last date modified). If the existence of files can be confirmed or inferred from file access attempts or file creation attempts, the observation may then be used for information transfer. Shared resources (I/O devices, memory blocks) can be used if one process occupies the resource (e.g., submitting print jobs) in a way that can be observed and interpreted by another process ("printer unavailable, seven jobs in queue").

In a timing channel, the information-receiving process must calculate real time (based on a clock) between measurable events caused by the source process. As an example, one process could use a variable fraction of the available CPU time with a loop, while another process could attempt to introduce its own loops and calculate the amount of time available. A system that does not allow reading the system clock cannot prevent timing channels, because the reading process can introduce its own clock. Timing channels are generally burdensome to an adversary, because they are "noisy" (affected by other processes going on in the system). They are, however, difficult to prevent and hard to find.

7.1.6 Asynchronous Attacks

One of the logical attacks possible through software is based on utilizing the interval between the time at which an operating system performs security checks, and the initiation of a user process. A "classic" asynchronous attack involves a modification of the security parameters while they are stored in memory accessible to the attack process. This form of attack is sometimes known as the TOCTTOU (time-of-check-to-time-of-use) problem.

Another form of asynchronous attack is the "port contender" attack described in Section 4.3. This form of attack is sometimes called "tailgating" [35]. The problem, which may be inadvertent as well as intentional, occurs when a dialup or direct connection session is abruptly terminated and a concentrator, port contender, or packet assembler/disassembler incorrectly connects the next user to the previous user's job stream (and files). A similar version of this attack is possible on some call back devices (see Section 8.3).

7.1.7 Superzapping

Certain macro/utility programs sometimes are able to bypass normal restart or recovery procedures (e.g., in case of an unintended computer "lockup" state that prevents straightforward recovery to normal operation). These are called "superzap" routines, and unauthorized use to bypass security controls is called "superzapping."

A superzapping attack by a computer operations manager of a New Jersey bank was used to effect fraudulent account transfers of $128,000 [8]. The ordinary audit records were avoided by the technique, and the fraud was only accidentally discovered.

7.1.8 Browsing

Since many operating systems do not erase information in memory space reassigned to a new user, the potential for inadvertent information compromise exists (see Section 3.4). Browsing (sometimes called "scavenging" or "the residue problem") is an intentional search for desired information that may be in accessible memory.

Industrial espionage through browsing was discovered by personnel of a time-sharing service which had a number of oil companies as clients [8]. The attacker would request mounting of a scratch tape, which would then be routinely read before writing. The results of the attack were productive enough that the perpetrator was able to sell significant amounts of proprietary seismic data.

7.1.9 The Salami Attack

The "salami" (small slices) technique is intended to accumulate significant overall results without making individually noticeable changes. For example, a few cents of additional service charge on a large number of bank accounts might be unnoticed by customers or auditors. An example of a salami attack was given in Section 4.3.

7.1.10 Software Anomalies

All of the threats described above in this section are consciously implemented by personnel who intend to do wrong. There is another class of threats that can occur accidentally as well as deliberately. These are unexpected functions that occur when a system fails to perform as a designer expects. Although such unexpected behavior can be due to hardware or software, experience shows that software is the most common source of these problems, which we will term "software anomalies." The causes can be either software "bugs" or undocumented software features.

One of the most widely publicized of these problems occurred in early 1981, about 20 minutes before the scheduled launch of the first U.S. space shuttle [23]. The fifth (backup) flight control computer could not be initialized, and the launch was scrubbed. The problem was due to a delay time routine that had been introduced into the data bus initialization process two years earlier. The delay had been responsible for opening a 1-in-67 probability window that could allow a one-cycle missynchronization condition to occur between computers. This happened for the first time during the flight countdown, and correct initialization was impossible.

Although the space shuttle avionics software package is one of the largest flight software implementation efforts undertaken, many preventive steps had been taken, including extensive design checks, simulation, and testing.

In 1979, a simulation tape was misloaded on a NORAD (North American Air Defense Command) computer [24]. The computer read the simulation as an attack, and, in response, 10 aircraft took off from bases in Canada and the United States before the error was detected.

Twenty years earlier, the rising moon had caused an air defense system attack warning. In 1962, a Mariner 1 Venus mission was lost at a cost of $18.5 million because of a period in the software where a comma should have been.

In August 1988, a new air traffic control program was put into service on the East Coast, and erroneous sectors began to be printed out on a random basis due to a software bug. The computer was shut down, and more than 50 flights were delayed for up to an hour [25].

It has been widely speculated that programmed computer trading tends to make the stock market unstable, and contributed significantly to the October 1987 stock market plunge.

In 1988, a major airline put into service a software enhancement that, because of a bug, failed to show the correct number of discounted fares available for reservations [26]. The error resulted in travel agents being informed that bookings were not available, and the customers were then booked on other airlines. The company lost about $50 million because of the problem.

"Deadlocking" is a condition of suspended processing, where two or more processes wait indefinitely for resources that are held by each other and therefore never available. This condition usually results from a software bug.

During software development it is common for undocumented features to occur, either by accident or by intent [27]. From a security viewpoint, it is important to understand as much as possible about how a system will respond to undocumented inputs. Adversaries have a long history of discovering and taking advantage of these features.

Some examples [28] include the use of FORTRAN II in combination with a popular computer system of an early era to list the contents of any desired memory locations, and the use of a time-sharing system, without a front-end processor, that allowed capture of data (including passwords) from the I/O queue.

7.1.11 Protection

Cognizance of threats is the most important step in prevention. However, the software threats described in this section are especially difficult to prevent. We will summarize some of the most widely used ad hoc approaches. Section 7.3 will address a more comprehensive approach sponsored by the National Computer Security Center.

1. One of the most important procedures that can be followed is to attempt to ensure the integrity of software that enters a computer system from any source, especially electronic mail. Although easier said than done, awareness of the consequences encourages scrutiny of such software.

    There are several ways in which entry can be protected. One is to try to ensure that software vendors are known and reputable, and that the delivery channel through which the software arrives is as secure as possible. A technically sophisticated and effective technique is to include digital signatures (see Chapter 8) with the software. This also requires key management procedures, which account for the significant cost of this measure. On networks, protection mechanisms can be provided in gateways (see Chapter 8), so that source authentication is required before allowing transmission through the gateway.

Another technique is to screen personnel who could be in a position to pass software or electronic mail into the system. Striving to assure their integrity, providing auditing or monitoring of their activities, providing training on threats, and giving motivation for the security concerns is a worthwhile approach.

2. A significant number of commercial software "vaccines" (anti-infection routines) that provide protection against some forms of viruses, bombs, and other THs [32] are available. The strategies used depend largely on the attack techniques that are known. For example, the actions of writing to executable programs, device drivers, or boot blocks are testable danger signals. Some vaccine programs flag classes of memory-write action for user approval. Some vaccine programs perform book-keeping tests on file size and activity times, searching for anomalies. Some actually seek out and destroy code that has been identified as improper.

    These solutions are only partially effective. Perpetrators have inserted, into code, attack routines that masquerade as a vaccine. New techniques have been created by adversaries to bypass vaccine features. The contest between the attackers and the protectors will probably continue to escalate.

3. Write prevention is effective against a limited class of software threats. For example, a boot diskette can be write-protected. A good practice in DOS is to write-protect all diskettes containing .COM or .EXE extensions.

4. Network propagation of software threats can be slowed or eliminated by properly designed controls at network intercon-nect points (e.g., "gateways," described in Chapter 8) or in com-puter operating systems. There is a tradeoff between protection and user flexibility and freedom to use a network, but a price may have to be paid for ensuring sufficient security. Two U.S. agencies that are endeavoring to identify cost-efficient controls and to influence commercial suppliers to implement these con-trols are NSA (the National Security Agency) and NIST (the National Institute of Standards and Technology) [30].

5. Taking advantage of existing security features is a protection technique that is not always fully utilized. For example, rigorous password protection mechanisms (see next section) help isolate systems from outsiders who may be a source of software threats. Purging the memory of "public" computers be-

tween sessions involving different users affords reasonable protection.

6. Structured software development (described subsequently) provides a measure of protection against hidden attack software within legitimate software. The enhanced visibility of the logic of the routine contributes to correctly performing software, more readily evaluated software, and more effective auditing (described subsequently).

7.2 SOFTWARE ACCESS CONTROL

Access controls are barriers between users and protected resources. The classic decision that must be made in selecting access control techniques is how to assure, with cost-effective measures, that authorized users can pass the barriers with minimum expended time and minimum required skill, while unauthorized adversaries can be reliably blocked. The solution is not easy to implement, but software access control is one of the most important approaches for ensuring security.

There are two primary factors in the access control process: authorization and authentication. Authorization is a determination by a responsible individual regarding who should be granted computer use privileges. This is an administrative consideration. Authentication is the process of checking the identity that a user claims when attempting computer access.

Most contemporary computer security controls require both authorization and authentication. An example will help illustrate the distinction.

Assume that a company data processing computer is available for use by the financial organization. Assume that a single password is given to all financial department employees. In this case, authorization has been given to all financial department employees; there is no authentication. Now assume that unique passwords are given to all employees of a company. With proper password techniques, authentication can be obtained; authorization (within the company) is lacking. Ideally, both authorization and authentication measures should be in place. These concepts can be extended to file authorization and authentication. This will be addressed subsequently.

As discussed in Chapter 6, authentication can be based on something a person has, something a person knows, or some measurable characteristic of a person. The concept of personal knowledge is basic to the password access control technique.

7.2.1 Password Techniques

It is convenient, inexpensive, and logical to use computer processing power to evaluate the knowledge of a person requesting computer access. This approach is convenient, because it involves keyboard entries, which are basic to all other use of a computer. It is unusually cost-effective, because the required software is easily written. It is logical, because it uses the same processing capabilities that are available to serve users. In addition to the usual computer access application, password concepts are basic to the use of PINs (personal identification numbers) in ATMs (automated teller machines) and similar applications.

7.2.1.1 Basic Considerations Password authentication is the most commonly used computer access control technique. However, there is wide latitude in actual application. Some of the considerations involved are:

1. The generation of passwords can be by an administrator, by the users, or by an automated computer routine.
2. The passwords can be issued to the users through the mail, verbally, hand-carried, or as a CRT display message.
3. A record of the passwords can be kept by an administrator. The passwords must be represented in some manner in the computer, but the representation can be in "clear text" (undisguised), "encrypted" text (disguised), or in the form of an algorithm.
4. The passwords must be "recorded" by the user. This can be done by keeping a written or printed record, through memory, or through a combination of a written or printed record and an algorithm.
5. The construction of the passwords involves the character set used (alpha, numeric, upper and lower case) and the construction logic (random, dictionary words, phonetic, phrases).
6. Passwords can be changed at the instigation of users, an administrator, an automated computer routine, or in response to an "event" (termination, transfer, security incident).
7. Since the integrity of the password process depends on preventing exposure, exposure avenues must be addressed. These include administrators, personnel who may observe clear-text password files in system dumps, and personnel who may observe user records of passwords, or who may observe

passwords as they are entered at a terminal. The communication process between users and the computer provides another opportunity for compromise.

Each of the factors above must be weighed in terms of the security required for a system versus the capabilities of the computer, operating system, password routine, and communication system. The material in Refs. 42 (from the DoD) and 43 (from the NIST) is representative of an immense amount of advice on password management that is available in open literature.

The process of issuing passwords can itself create chances for exposure of the passwords. If issued by an administrator, the passwords are exposed (inadvertently and probably unwillingly) to at least that person. The administrator, no matter how trustworthy, then becomes one of the suspect personnel in case of a compromise.

Some favor user-generated passwords that can be communicated from the user to the computer directly, since this reduces the chance of administrative exposure. This appears to be an attractive concept, but there are significant problems. Users in general are incapable of generating (or unwilling to generate) secure passwords. This is not an indictment of users, but more a probabilistic assertion, as is addressed below.

Numerous studies [8,37] have shown that it is much easier for an adversary to penetrate a system on which there are user-generated passwords than on one using randomly selected passwords. Constraining controls on the user selections (minimum number of characters, maximum number of identical characters, etc.) are helpful, but this type of protection is at best a "patchwork" solution. It is more appropriate to address the real problem, which is the population from which the passwords are selected.

The population problem is that a good password routine can make a random selection from a large (millions to hundreds of millions) population of potential passwords. A good dictionary may only contain tens of thousands of usable words. The words that come to mind during a user selection process may be in the range of tens or hundreds, and the probability of selecting each one is not equally distributed. Thus, an adversary enjoys a significant advantage when attempting to breach a security system on which user-generated passwords are allowed (see Problem 9).

The basic equation for calculating password population (space) is:

$$N = r^s \tag{7-1}$$

where r is the number of possibilities for each character and s is the number of characters. Modifications to this basic concept are necessary, but straightforward, if the number of characters is variable, or if treatment of positions within the password is variable (see phonetic password discussion below).

The probability of guessing a password on one attempt is $1/N$, assuming the adversary has no information that would favor anything but a random selection. The probability of success goes up approximately linearly for small numbers, as the adversary tries multiple guesses:

$$P \approx nt/N \tag{7-2}$$

where n is the number of guesses per unit time and t is the time. This is the reason that password systems usually incorporate a "limited try" or "blacklist" feature (or both). The intent is to prevent the advantage of repeated attempts indicated by Equation 7-2 to exceed the desired security for the system. For example, a user may be disconnected after three consecutive incorrect tries in order to introduce an additional time delay. A user-ID (user identification) can be blacklisted after a large number (e.g., a dozen) unsuccessful tries, requiring some form of contact between the user and the system administrator to reestablish use privileges. Of course, an adversary can change user-IDs to avoid the blacklist, but the adversary's time is increased and the total number of attempts possible can be made significantly smaller than the password population.

It is also a helpful security measure to feed back information to the user on "last successful log-in" and "number of unsuccessful log-in attempts since then."

Attempts to link the frequency of password changes to password population are common but ill-advised [47]. The reason for password changes is related to the probability that a password will be compromised, either accidentally or through attack (see discussion of password compromise techniques in Section 7.2.1.4). Since this probability increases with time, password changes are used to reinitialize the process, usually with a period of once a year maximum (shorter for high-security applications). Password changes have no effect on the probability that an adversary will guess a password. This is strictly a function of the size of the password population and the rate at which attempts can be made (see Problem 10).

Passwords can also be issued to users automatically by a random-selection password generation routine. The advantages are secure password selection (assuming a good routine) and minimal exposure (usually only to the user). This technique is also applicable to PCs. Since the user may not find the password acceptable (e.g., because of difficulty to commit to memory), it is helpful to give the user options (e.g., accept or reject, choose from a list of selections). In this case, it is likely that the user will find a desirable password.

Administrator-issued passwords must frequently be conveyed to remotely located users. The most common technique is to print the password on a card and mail it to the user. This means that mail control as well as card control by the recipient must be considered.

The general handling of written or printed passwords must be strongly related to the handling of the information to be accessed. For example, a password that enables access to classified information must itself be classified, since knowledge of the protected information cannot be separated from knowledge of the password.

It is common for password administrators to store copies of the issued passwords. In this way, users can be reinforced of forgotten passwords. However, the procedure is unnecessary, since nearly all applications allow reissue of passwords. The user can therefore be given a replacement for a forgotten password, and no administrative record need be kept.

Storage of passwords in computer memory is generally more secure than administrative storage, but passwords are frequently "dumped" as part of routine system maintenance activities and hence must not be stored in clear-text form. There have also been successful computer attacks based on finding passwords in computer memory [28]. For these reasons, it is advisable to store passwords as one-way transformed representations.

7.2.1.2 One-Way Transformed* Password Storage Figure 7-1 shows the basic concept of one-way transformed password storage. When a password is "registered" in memory, it is entered in clear text (actual) form and is transformed into an equivalent representation by a one-way transformation. If done properly, knowledge of the transformed representation is of no value to an adversary, because the actual password is necessary for access. A user-entered password is transformed by the identical process, and the authentication is based on comparing the transformed value to the transformed representation in memory.

---

*   This concept is also sometimes referred to as "one-way encryption" in the literature. In the next chapter, the discussion of encryption will show why "one-way transformation" is more proper.

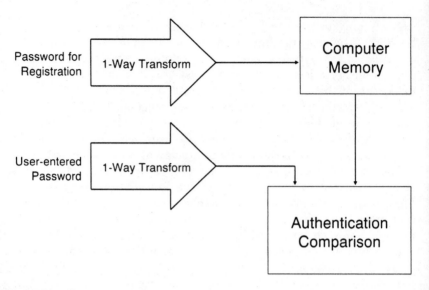

Figure 7-1   One-way transformed passwords.

The one-way transformation technique is intended to be robust enough so that there is no "trapdoor" that would allow the input possibilities to be narrowed down from all possible passwords. Of course, the correct input can be obtained by exhaustive search, but this does not degrade the security of the ordinary password concept.

The term "one-way transform," as commonly used, is based on the following mathematical concepts.

1. A "function" is an association or mapping of elements in a "domain" (source elements) to elements of a "codomain" (target elements) such that each element of the domain is mapped to a single element of the codomain. The set of elements mapped to by the function is called the "range" of the function (a subset of the codomain).

2. A "one-way function," f, is a function such that, for any argument x in the domain of f, it is computationally straightforward to compute y = f(x), but for all y in the range of f, it is computationally difficult to compute x deterministically (with less difficulty than exhaustive search) [39].

3. The terms "computationally straightforward" and "computationally difficult" are qualitative. However, considerable quantitative work has been done on the subject [40]. In brief, the

computational requirements of an algorithm can be measured in time and space. This means that the operations required can be measured and assessed for their computing load in terms of the time required for the computation or the number of processors required over a period of time.

Algorithms whose complexity is proportional to some power of the input length are said to have "polynomial complexity" (linear, if proportional to the input length; quadratic, if proportional to the square of the input length; cubic, if proportional to the cube of the input length, etc.). Algorithms whose complexity is proportional to some constant raised to a power proportional to the input length are called "exponential."

Problems that are known to be solvable by polynomial-complexity algorithms are called "P-class" problems. "NP-class" problems are problems for which the potential solution can be checked with polynomial complexity, but for which no deterministic solution is known with less than exponential complexity. "NP-complete" problems are a class of NP problems that appear exponential, but for which it has been proven that if any one is polynomial, then all NP problems are polynomial. These properties seem to make them the "hardest" of the NP problems.

Since NP problems are distinguished from P problems on the basis of "known" algorithms, there is always a chance that a problem thought to be NP (even NP complete) will be proved to be P. Therefore, one-way transformations that depend on computational complexity carry the same attendant threat as encryption techniques that depend on computational complexity. An analytical breakthrough may substantially weaken them. Nevertheless, the risk is frequently thought to be small enough that computational complexity is still depended upon. An example is Rivest Shamir Adleman (RSA) encryption [41], which depends on the difficulty of factoring large numbers (see Chapter 8).

A conceptual example of a one-way transformation that is useful for illustration (but poor from a security viewpoint) will be shown here; then a more commonly used one-way transformation will be described.

Assume that passwords are represented by bit patterns (e.g., ASCII) and can therefore be treated as numbers. A transformation of the numbers can be made through the equation:

$$T = P^n (\text{mod } m) \tag{7-3}$$

where P is the password number, n is a number for exponentiation, and m is the modulus. Note that for a Galois field mapping, P can be selected from the space $0, 1, \ldots m$, where m is prime. Since the mapping is not in general unique (one-to-one), the same transformed value will result from more than one password, unless the password space is limited. However, this is a secondary consideration. For now, we intend only to illustrate the concept.

Knowledge of T can lead to a solution for P in only two ways: 1) inversion of Equation 7-3 based on n and m, and 2) exhaustive search. The inversion requires significantly more sophisticated mathematics than the forward solution, and can be prevented altogether if n and m are unknown (i.e., are secret). Exhaustive search for a solution to Equation 7-3 is no easier than exhaustive search for passwords. It is not usually considered desirable to base a transformation on secrecy, because of "key management" (protecting secret keys; see Chapter 8). Therefore, the challenge is to find mathematical manipulations that are straightforward to perform, but that have no known straightforward inversion, even if all the parameters of the transformation are known.

An example of a one-way transformation that has no secret parameters and that is frequently used for password transformation is illustrated in Figure 7-2. Full understanding of the details of the transformation depend on knowledge of the description of encryption given in Chapter 8. For now, consider the encryption as a mapping of input bits to output bits based on a key. The decryption process is identical and uses the same key. The key is secret for encryption/decryption applications. For password transformation, the input is a value that need not be protected, such as an identifier for the user. The password is used as the key input. Since decryption can recover information only through use of the key, the password cannot be recovered directly.

Note that there may be ways to recover the information indirectly. This depends on the type of encryption used. For example, if the encryption were based on bit-by-bit exclusive-or, the password could be recovered by adding (bit-by-bit exclusive-or) the constant to the encrypted value. Therefore, it is important to scrutinize the properties of the transformation. One of the best encryption techniques for this application is DES (Data Encryption Standard; see Chapter 8).

It is interesting to note that most ATM cards carry a record of the PIN authenticator written onto the magnetic strip through use of a one-way transform. The advantage of recording the transformed PIN on the card is that users can change the PIN or make some types of transactions, even when a communication link to the host database

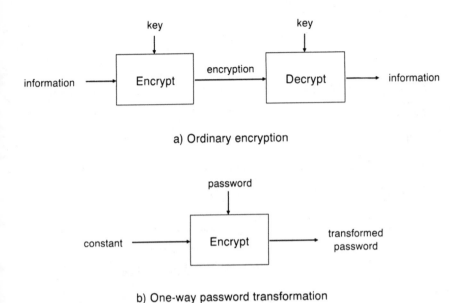

a) Ordinary encryption

b) One-way password transformation

Figure 7-2   Example technique for one-way transformation.

is not available. The one-way transform prevents an unauthorized person in possession of the card from reading the PIN with a magnetic strip reader.

7.2.1.3 Phonetic Passwords Computers may be penetrated by someone who reads a password that has been written on a blackboard, on a desk, or on an exposed card. In order to prevent this vulnerability, users must be diligent about not exposing passwords. However, a user is faced with the pressure of expediently accessing the computer without unlocking a repository. The obvious solution is for the user to memorize the password. This is difficult for randomly generated character strings, especially if a user is dealing with more than one computer. Many techniques are available for making passwords easier to remember (e.g., pass-phrases, algorithms, sentences where the first letter of each word is used, etc.). Multiple-word combinations of short dictionary words have also been used. Security code generators (Chapter 6) mitigate or eliminate the memory problem. However, by far the most commonly used technique is to utilize phonetic passwords.

Phonetic passwords are intended to be pronounceable passwords, because these are usually easily memorized. The words need not be

Table 7-1   A phonetic generator.

Constructions				
1. CVCVCVC	6. CVCPL	11. CVCVME	16. VCPCVC	21. VCVMZ
2. VCVCVCE	7. DVCVCE	12. DPCVC	17. VCVMVC	22. VMPL
3. CPCPC	8. CPCVCE	13. DVMVC	18. VMVME	23. DVMZ
4. DVCPC	9. CVMVCE	14. CPMVC	19. VMPCE	24. CPMZ
5. VCVCPC	10. CVCPCE	15. VMVCVC	20. VMVCZ	25. CVCVCZ

Descriptors	
C = consonant	E = end vowel
V = vowel	M = middle consonant digraph
D = beginning consonant digraph	L = end consonant digraph
P = vowel pair	Z = ending vowel pair

meaningful; in fact the number of meaningful pronounceable words is a small subset of phonetic words (see Problem 3).

A phonetic password generator coordinates "descriptors" (vowels, consonants, consonant digraphs, vowel pairs, etc.) into "constructions" (combinations of descriptors). The result is a "word" having a high probability of being pronounceable and memorizable. The operation of the generator is to first select a construction and then select the descriptors fitting the construction. We will find below that the security of the process is affected by how these steps are implemented.

As an illustration, consider the phonetic generator described in Table 7-1.

The specific characters or character pairs (elements) that are members of each set of descriptors are given in Table 7-2.

Note that pronounceability considerations cause elimination of Q, X, and Y from the set of consonants. There are other similar considerations in arriving at the set constituents. The passwords are also edited to remove any word ending in H, W, or J. In addition, the words are edited to remove words that are obviously offensive.

Table 7-2   Descriptor sets.

C = {B,C,D,F,G,H,J,K,L,M,N,P,R,S,T,V,W,Z}

V = {A,E,I,O,U}

D = {BR,CH,CL,CR,DR,FL,FR,GL,GR,KL,KR,PH,PL,PR,QU.SC,SH,
SK,SL,SM,SN,SP,ST,SW,TH,TR,TW}

P = {AI,EA,EE,IE,IO,OI,OO,OU}

E = {E,O,A,Y}

M = {{D},{L},BB,BC,BF,BK,BL,BM,BN,BP,BT,BV,CC,CD,CF,CM,CP,
DB,DC,DD,DF,DG,DK,DL,DM,DN,DP,DT,DV,DW,DZ,FB,FC,FD,FG,
FK,FM,FN,FP,FZ,GB,GD,GF,GJ,GM,GN,GP,GT,GV,KB,KD,KF,KM,
KN,KP,KT,KV,KZ,LB,LC,LF,LG,LM,LN,LR,LV,LZ,MB,MC,MD,MF,
MG,MJ,MK,ML,MM,MN,MR,MT,MV,MZ,NB,NC,NF,NG,SZ,TB,TC,
TD,TF,TG,TJ,TK,TL,TM,TN,TP,TV,VC,VG,VL,VP,NJ,NL,NP,NR,PC,
PD,PF,PG,PK,PM,PN,PV,PZ,RB,RC,RD,RF,RG,RJ,RL,SB,SD,SF,SG,
SJ,SR,SV}

L = {BS,CK,CS,CT,DS,FS,FT,GS,HS,KS,LL,LD,LK,LP,LS,LT,MP,MS
ND,NK,NN,NS,NT,PP,PS,PT,RK,RM,RN,RP,RS,SS,TS,VS,WS}

Z = {EE,OO,AY,EY,OY}

The number of possible words for each construction is the product of the number of elements in the set for each descriptor in the construction, minus the number of words removed by editing. Table 7-3 shows the number of words possible[*] for each construction and the total number of possible passwords.

The total number of passwords possible is large enough to be suitable for a password system. Individual words are readily memorized, and the generation process is easily implemented. However, there is another important consideration in phonetic password generation. The selection from the set of constructions should not be random. Since the number of possibilities for each construction is different, the probability of choosing each construction should be different. In fact, the probability should be exactly proportional to the

---

[*]   These calculations and the probability approach following were originally done by Charles Clark (Sandia National Laboratories), now retired.

Table 7-3   Number of words generated.

Construction Number	Number of Possible Words
1	10,827,189
2	2,898,020
3	311,040
4	291,120
5	969,000
6	450,585
7	870,664
8	930,240
9	6,068,616
10	930,240
11	6,071,664
12	290,520
13	1,898,209
14	2,031,066
15	6,325,590
16	968,400
17	6,316,915
18	3,546,564
19	543,744
20	423,275
21	422,950
22	263,376
23	127,095
24	135,990
25	724,505
Total:	54,636,577

construction population (cardinality of, or number of words in, the construction set).

Assume that a phonetic generator chooses constructions with equal probability, and then chooses elements for the types in the construction with equal probability. Assume that an adversary chooses passwords in exactly the same manner. The probability of the adversary selecting the same password as the phonetic generator is:

$$P_m = 1/n^2(1/n1 + 1/n2 + \ldots + 1/nn)$$ (7-4)

where n is the number of constructions, and ni is the population of construction i.

For the phonetic generator described above, $Pm = 1/13{,}291{,}157$. This means that an adversary taking no particular advantage of the properties of the phonetic generator is four times more likely to guess the generated password than if all passwords were equally probable.

An adversary who wishes to take optimum advantage of the phonetic generation technique would guess a password in the minimum-population construction. The probability of a correct guess would be:

$$Pm = (1/n)(1/nm)$$ (7-5)

where nm is the population of the construction with the minimum population. For the phonetic generator described above, the probability is $Pm = 1/3{,}177{,}375$. This means that an adversary would be 17 times as likely to guess a password than if all passwords were equally probable.

The solution to this obvious problem is to make the selection of all passwords equally probable. This is done by making the probability of selecting construction i equal to ni/N, where ni is the population of construction i, and N is the total password population. Under these conditions, the probability of an adversary correctly guessing a password is the same $(1/N)$ regardless of the strategy used. For example, assume that the adversary selects passwords in the same manner as the phonetic generator:

$$Pm = (n1/N)^2/n1 + (n2/N)^2/n2 + \ldots + (nn/N)^2/nn = 1/N$$ (7-6)

Assume that the adversary picks a password at random from the construction with minimum population:

$$Pm = (nm/N)/nm = 1/N \tag{7-7}$$

Assume that the adversary picks constructions with equal likelihood and picks a password at random from the population of the construction:

$$Pm = 1/n((n_1/N)(1/n_1) + (n_2/N)(1/n_2) +$$
$$\ldots + (n_n/N)(1/n_n)) = 1/N \tag{7-8}$$

Therefore, this phonetic generator selection process takes optimum advantage of the total password population.

7.2.1.4 Threats to Password Access Control

The threats to password access control mentioned above (exhaustive try, "intelligent guessing," fortuitous discovery) are the most obvious, but not the only techniques used. A large number of more technically sophisticated threats are known [45–47]. Some of these are summarized below.

1. Passive listening (tapping). The relative vulnerability of most computer communication lines makes tapping a significant threat. Unencrypted data, including passwords, can be recorded on tape and replayed to a terminal or printer using equipment costing about $150 [45]. A datascope or line monitor can directly display the clear text. Even passwords intercepted from encrypted traffic can be used to gain computer access. Although access through an encrypted link severely limits what can be done on the computer, it is not desirable to allow unauthorized access to a resource, thereby reducing capacity for authorized access.

2. Computer masquerade. An active line tap can be used to interrupt the normal connection between a terminal and a computer, and to "mimic" the interaction expected by the user. The user, seeing the screen display expected, will enter the ordinary log-on sequence necessary. An "unsuccessful attempt" message can be returned to the user from the adversary, and it is not completely unexpected. This technique allows the password to be "trapped," and then the normal system to be reconnected.

   The existence of and use of "computer simulation" programs for this type of attack are well known. One major credit card company was victimized through the capture of passwords allowing access to an important online customer accounting system [45]. A variation that does not require a line tap is to leave a terminal online to a computer, under control of an adversary's program. The sign-on procedure is then emulated, allowing passwords to be transferred to the adversary's file space. This technique was successfully used to collect passwords at a university in the United Kingdom [76].

A similar, but less sophisticated, technique was described in Section 4.3. Persons victimized by masquerades seldom are suspicious enough to report "unusual" behavior that they attribute to the host system. This problem can be addressed through training.

3. Interspersed entry. It is conceivable that an active line tap could be used to intersperse commands to a host in such a way that no effect is noticed by the user. This is accomplished by sending commands interspersed with the user's commands.

7.2.2 Software Security Products

Many computer operating systems are not as secure (for computer and data file access) as might be required for particular applications. However, it is not difficult to introduce software features that improve on the available security. Frequently this is done by systems programmers in order to provide the desired protective features. However, it is often possible to purchase software security products that augment operating system features with enhanced security. This is especially true for IBM and IBM-compatible mainframe computers and for most PCs. Some products are available for computers of other major manufacturers, such as DEC [48].

The generic types of software security features can be categorized as follows:

1. Multiple types of access control (particular restrictions applicable to individual users, individual terminals, and accesses to transactions, files, and programs).
2. Internal access controls (based on information such as date, time, terminal location, user-ID).
3. Restrictions against repeated unsuccessful access attempts. Examples are disconnecting the requester after a selected number of unsuccessful tries and blacklisting a requester after a selected number of unsuccessful tries. Another alternative,

progressively increasing time delays, is seldom found in security software products.

4. Timed automatic screen blanking and terminal deactivation (to prevent utilization of unattended terminals).
5. Automated audit trail assembly (including automated violation reporting to system administrators).
6. Support for hardware security devices (e.g., badge readers, security code generators, biometric devices).
7. Password features such as automatic expiration and disablement.
8. Authorization limitations on utilities (such as superzap routines).
9. File encryption.

The selection process for software security packages is strongly dependent on the existing computer environment [49]. However, some general selection guidance is appropriate. In addition to security features, there are easily overlooked administrative issues, including ease and accuracy of installation, motivation of administrators and users to support the operational environment, maintenance required, auditor expertise, and personnel training.

Specific comparative evaluations and user surveys occasionally appear in the literature [50,51]. The costs of security software products are generally in the range of tens of thousands of dollars for mainframe packages, thousands of dollars for minicomputers, and hundreds of dollars for microcomputers. Mainframe package lease costs range from $500 to $1000 per month.

7.3 NATIONAL COMPUTER SECURITY CENTER RESOURCES

It became obvious during the 1960s that at least some of the emphasis on information protection through physical security needed to be redirected toward hardware and software features internal to computers. A task force was formed under the auspices of the Defense Science Board in 1967 to seek computer security safeguards that would protect classified information in remote-access resource-sharing systems. Recommendations of this board were made in a 1970 report. Various agencies of the DoD subsequently sponsored research on security technical problems, with emphasis on controlling the flow of information in shared computer systems. NBS also led efforts on the subject, and sponsored two invitational workshops. Following recommendations resulting from activities at the second NBS workshop, the MITRE Corporation began work on security evaluation (see Section 7.3.5). A "Computer Security Initiative" was formulated and approved by the DoD in 1978.

The main intent of the initiative was to develop "trusted" multilevel processing capabilities (simultaneous use at different security levels by personnel having differing security clearances) for the DoD. This was to be provided within computer systems through hardware and software security and integrity measures.

In 1981, the DoD directed the creation of the Computer Security Center (CSC) at NSA to evaluate protective systems, to advise developers and managers on the suitability of processing techniques for DoD applications, and to assist in formulating appropriate requirements for acquisitions of systems for DoD use. In 1983, the CSC proposed a "Trusted Computer System Evaluation Criteria" which defined seven classes of security provisions. An expanded and updated document (the "Orange Book," discussed in Section 7.3.5) was published in 1985. In 1985, following the directives of NSDD 145 (see Section 5.2), the CSC was renamed the National Computer Security Center (NCSC). The two primary functions of the NCSC are to evaluate commercial security products and government computer systems, and to sponsor computer security research and development [52].

The concern of the DoD and the government regarding classified information protection is apparent in the work of the NCSC. Classified security information is protected through the use of security "levels" (degree of classification) and "categories" (or "compartments") determined by government specification of "need-to-know" areas (see Section 5.1). Our discussion will assume a philosophy that could be applied in the more general nongovernment atmosphere. Because of this direction, some terminology applies differently in government applications than in nongovernment applications. An example is "discretionary" security policy, which usually implies user discretion outside government applications and usually implies mandatory government need-to-know policy (which would be implemented as a system control) for government applications. In spite of such differences, the general usefulness of the NCSC activity is important to note. The concepts involved in the NCSC work are widely applicable, and most of the information developed is shared with private industry as a national service.

7.3.1   Secure Multilevel Software Development

Multilevel security is generally provided through both hardware and software features. However, the most significant developments have taken place in software. Here, we will emphasize the logic of the processes. The discussion appears in this software chapter because of the preponderance of software implementations of the logic. However, some of the ideas presented depend on the support provided by hardware features.

The basic ideas involved in designing secure systems are 1) to formulate a security policy model, 2) to design features that will implement and enforce the model, and 3) to verify that the model is correctly implemented. Some of the concepts involved are "mandatory" policy, "discretionary" (need-to-know) policy, "access specifications," "rings of protection," "reference monitors," "kernels," "execution domains," and "guards."

These concepts are discussed in the following material. Here, we will give a brief introduction. Mandatory policy defines inflexible associations between protection requirements for information having a particular classification level and information-access privileges of users having a particular clearance level. For example, information having a Secret classification level cannot be accessed by a user not having a Secret clearance level. Discretionary policy allows determination of rights of access to some "object" (e.g., an information file) by the "owner" of the object based on assessment of other users' "need-to-know." In government applications, the government "owns" classified information and determines the major segmentation of need-to-know rights by defining the "category" of an object. Many nongovernment companies have a similar policy. The result is that "discretionary" may be a misleading term, if it implies mandatory need-to-know policy.

A kernel is a manageably small software and hardware module that implements the reference monitor abstraction. The reference monitor concept requires that every request of a "subject" for access to an "object" be checked against access rules. Access rules may be lists or matrices defining rights (e.g., read, write, execute) of "subjects" (e.g., users, programs) to "objects" (resources such as files). Execution domains are necessary to separate more privileged code from less privileged code. There are always two or more execution domains. These can be visualized as concentric "rings" of protection for confined operating regions, where security restrictions increase with transition toward inner rings (the innermost ring surrounds the most highly protected entities).

Guards (a special case of the reference monitor concept) perform checks on interface processes such as database queries and responses. In some multilevel applications it is required that users at different security levels have access to at least some of the same data. The security of this process is frequently ensured by logical guards. One type of guard is a "one-way link" (a communication channel that allows data to move from a lower classification file to a higher one, but blocks the reverse direction of file movement). Another type is a "secure release terminal" (a means of assuring that transferred data are not in conflict with security requirements).

Probably the first system to be developed around a formally stated model was the ADEPT-50 system [53]. It was implemented on an IBM 360/50 in the 1960s, and was used for a number of years in DoD applications. It incorporated only limited features and was vulnerable to covert channels. The reason for the vulnerability was that the system enforced a "high-water-mark" policy, whereby a subject operating at a higher security level than that of an object being read would cause the object to be assigned the higher level of classification. Observation of object classification changes provided a covert channel.

In 1964, MIT and the Air Force (with help from AT&T Bell Laboratories and General Electric) developed the Multics (Multiplexed Information and Computing Service) operating system (a forerunner of the current Honeywell Multics system). It incorporated discretionary security policy, rings of protection, and access control lists.

The access specification concept was refined to identify "subjects" (initiators of action) and "objects" (receptors of action). An "access matrix" model was used to define privileges for each subject/object combination. Because access matrices are typically sparse, information is usually organized into an "access list" (specified privileges for each object).

The reference monitor, an abstract concept proposed in the early 1970s [21,54], provides for checking every request of a subject for an object against an access control specification stored in memory accessible only to the reference monitor. (This concept is illustrated in Figure 7-3.) The access control specification contains data such as security attributes and access rights. A reference monitor must always be invoked, it must be tamper-proof, and it must correctly enforce the desired security policy.

In the mid-1970s, work at Case Western Reserve and The MITRE Corporation resulted in development of a formal model (now called the Bell-LaPadula model [55]) for a secure operating system. Al-

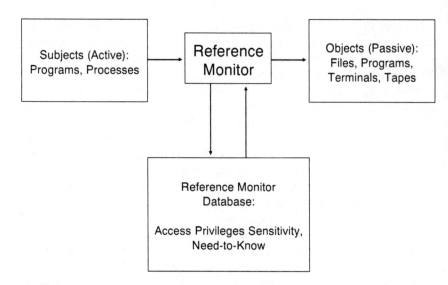

Figure 7-3   Depiction of a reference monitor.

though a complete description of the model is lengthy and complex, the two most well-known features of the model are the "simple security" property and the "confinement" or "star" property (often written as "the ∗-property"). The simple security property prohibits subjects from accessing objects having a higher security classification ("no read-up"), and the star property prohibits a subject from writing to an object having a lower classification level than the subject ("no write-down"). The latter feature prevents the TH attack that writes protected information into a less protected (or unprotected) file.

In the early 1970s, both MITRE and UCLA built prototype mini-computer (DEC PDP-11) systems that implemented security kernels. Both emulated the UNIX operating system as a base. MITRE's work was based on the Bell-LaPadula model. DARPA (Defense Advanced Research Projects Agency) supported the work at UCLA that led to a "Data Secure UNIX" (DSU) system. DSU implemented a mandatory security policy model that was formally specified and partly verified. The verification was partly automated, with substantial human involvement. Neither of these systems became commercially operational.

The Air Force and DARPA sponsored security work at System Development Corporation (SDC) in the mid-1970s based on the IBM Virtual Machine 370 (VM/370). The SDC system was named KVM/370 and ran experimentally on an IBM 4331 computer. The significant security features of the system were specified and verified.

The Multics system was restructured by Honeywell as Multics-AIM in the mid-1970s and has been successfully marketed since the mid-1980s. The "Access Isolation Mechanism," from which the name AIM is derived, incorporates the Bell-LaPadula model. Both discretionary and mandatory security policies are supported.

Multics has eight execution domains, called rings, that determine various levels of privileges and security required in a practical system. For example, the security functions may include initiating input and output, accessing all of main memory, and possibly recognizing exceptions to general security rules. Some "trusted" security functions need fewer privileges than the kernel, but more than a user.

The Kernelized Secure Operating System (KSOS 11), sponsored by DARPA, NSA, and the Navy and designed at the Ford Aerospace and Communications Corporation, was an attempt to develop a production prototype version of a "secure UNIX." The choice of UNIX was influenced by the structure of the operating system around a basic "kernel" that had memory management and I/O controls. Top-level formal specifications were successfully written and verified. The Bell-LaPadula model was incorporated, and a Boyer-Moore theorem prover was used.

NSA also sponsored the Provable Secure Operating System (PSOS) study. KSOS 11 and PSOS were not offered commercially, but the projects were useful in developing an understanding of secure systems development.

The Honeywell SCOMP (Secure Communications Processor) was based on a different approach to producing a secure version of UNIX. It was implemented on a Honeywell Level 6/DPS6 computer in UCLA Pascal. Hardware assistance to the SCOMP reference monitor functions is provided by a Secure Protection Module (SPM). The SPM is designed to mediate references between the main memory and I/O devices and between the CPU and the main memory. SCOMP has been available commercially for several years.

7.3.2 Memory Protection

Memory protection is essential in secure systems (Section 6.2). An early form of memory protection placed controlled memory into contiguous physical locations signified by a "base register" and a "bounds register" [7]. This technique enables the CPU to note the beginning and end of protected memory. Because large systems routinely swap address spaces of various sizes in memory, the fixed location for protected memory is a disadvantage of the base and bounds register concept. Efficiency is lost if blocks of memory are held fixed.

Contemporary memory management is usually achieved through "paging." In this concept, addresses are segmented into two "dimensions," a "page number" (high-order address bits) and an "offset" within the page (low-order bits). Paging facilitates "virtual memory" computers (an effective memory that is many times as large as the physical primary memory). Pages are moved between primary memory and secondary memory, as required. Since paging is controlled by the operating system, the mechanism is essentially transparent to the users, who perceive a large virtual address space.

Paged memory mapping requires "pointers" that can be provided by hardware "mapping registers." The mapping registers are preloaded under control of the operating system. This means that an instruction reference to memory can be restricted by the values (pages) allowed to be loaded into the mapping registers.

The virtual address space is divided into "segments," so that processes in one segment can be separated from processes in another segment. This is particularly straightforward under paged control. Segments usually comprise integer numbers of pages. Page numbers (and therefore segments) can be controlled by restricting the values loaded in mapping registers as a function of the process that is running. Segments can also be shared, where necessary.

As an example of the segment concept, a "user process" would not be allowed to write into the "system space" segment when running unprivileged programs in a user mode. Since "jump," "call," and "return" instructions can specify arbitrary addresses, memory control depends on whether or not the segment addressed has the proper identifiers (executable segment and segment available to the process). Either hardware or software (or both) can conceptually enforce the restrictions. The tradeoff is between software flexibility and hardware rigid security. Hardware is usually involved.

7.3.3 Execution Domains

The separation of processing into execution domains (rings) is independent of processing segments, since, for example, a given process may run in various domains, moving from domain to domain during execution. Domain separation is also usually controlled by hardware. Up to 2^p execution domains can be controlled with p "process state" bits. The implementation of reliable and efficient internal security controls of this type is much more easily accomplished with supporting hardware than through software alone [59].

The "capability-based system" concept provides multiple, dynamic execution domains. A "capability" is a special addressing mechanism (a pointer) for an object. The domain "possessing" the pointer to the object has the "capability" to access the object. A capability can only be created by the operating system, but once created, capabilities can be freely passed between domains. The intent is to allow each application to manage its own capabilities. Capabilities are signified by "tokens" associated with each user that signify the user's execution domains. Capability-based systems are not often built commercially because capability-passing freedom causes problems in creating controls against indiscriminate capability passing by a TH.

7.3.4   Models and Formal Verification

Many lessons have been learned during the development of multi-level system technology. One of the most fruitful approaches for designing multilevel secure systems has been the security "kernel" approach. The basic strategy is to separate the security-relevant functions of an operating system from the other functions. The purpose is to create as small a module as possible upon which security depends. In this way, the complexities of software analysis can be made manageable. The concept is facilitated by assuring precise specification and high-level language implementation. Although the security kernel approach is not universally accepted as ideal, it is by far the most commonly used approach for designing highly secure systems.

In practice, some security functions are placed outside the kernel. Discretionary controls, authentication, and audit records are common examples. Security functions that are outside the kernel are still considered to be within the "security perimeter." The totality of hardware and software features that support security functions is called the "trusted computing base" (TCB). The TCB includes the security kernel as a subset.

7.3.4.1   The Bell-LaPadula Model   The simple security rule of the Bell-LaPadula model relates directly to mandatory access control. Access classes, or classification levels, are readily represented by labels on information files in computer systems. Therefore restriction to users having a clearance equal to or greater than the file level is a

	Engineering	Manufacturing	Engineering & Manufacturing	No Discretionary Restriction
Secret	All—privilege user Secret engin. user	All—privilege user Secret manuf. user	All—privilege user	All—privilege user Secret engin. user Secret manuf. user Secret user
Private	All—privilege user Secret engin. user Private engin. user Private eng.& man. user	All—privilege user Secret manuf. user Private manuf. user Private eng.& man. user	All—privilege user Private eng.& man. user	All—privilege user Secret engin. user Secret manuf. user Secret user Private engin. user Private manuf. user Private eng.& man. user Private user

Figure 7-4   Example mandatory/discretionary security categories.

straightforward implementation of the "simple security" principle, and of mandatory access control.

The addition of discretionary access control (need-to-know compartments) makes the situation more complex. Consider an access control matrix[*] as illustrated in Figure 7-4. The rows of the matrix denote mandatory policy levels, and the columns denote discretionary policy possibilities. (In a government environment, the compartments would be categories such as NATO, nuclear, crypto, etc.). The matrix entries signify the clearance description of personnel who can have access to the indicated combination of level and compartment. Under the rules of this access control matrix, a person in manufacturing who has a secret clearance, for example, has no right to private engineering data because it is prohibited by need-to-know policy.

In order to better portray the interrelationships, some mathematical structure is helpful. We define a "dominates" operation based on a "partial ordering" relation. We will use the symbolic form $A \geq B$ to express A dominates B, where A and B represent set elements. This is a partial ordering relation (the elements are members of a partially ordered set) if:

1. It is "reflexive" ($A \geq A$),
2. It is "antisymmetric" (if $A \geq B$ and $B \geq A$, then $A \equiv B$),
3. It is "transitive" (if $A \geq B$ and $B \geq C$, then $A \geq C$).

---

[*]   Note that this matrix differs from the "access matrix" described earlier.

Mandatory security policy (the relationship between elements in different rows but the same column in Figure 7-4) is a partial ordering, and therefore it is a "dominates" operation. However, the addition of discretionary policy means that all pairs of elements (or security "classes") may not be related through dominance. Elements that are not related are said to be "incomparable."

Two additional properties fulfill the conditions of a "lattice" [60]. A lattice must be a partial ordering, and in addition it is required that:

1. In the set of all elements that are dominated by both A and B, there is a unique "greatest lower bound" that dominates all of the others.
2. In the set of all elements that dominate both A and B, there is a unique "least upper bound" that is dominated by all of the others.

In order to model the general security policy based on mandatory and discretionary control, there must be a unique "system high" class that dominates all other elements. This is always met in a government classification environment, and is usually met in private environments. There must also be a unique "system low" class that is dominated by all other elements. Although these conditions are not always strictly met, it is possible to model all of the classes, even though some may represent "empty sets."

As an example of a security policy access control lattice model, consider the conditions shown in Figure 7-5, which also correspond to the policy specified in Figure 7-4. The mandatory security policy is based on the classification levels "secret," and "private." Secret dominates private. Viewing the lattice as a cube, the vertices on the "upper face" of the cube represent the secret level, and the vertices on the "lower face" of the cube represent the private level.

The discretionary security policy is based on the fundamental compartments "engineering" and "manufacturing." Also implied are the possibilities "engineering and manufacturing" and "no discretionary restriction." The four vertical edges on the lattice "cube" represent these four situations. The lattice describes mandatory and discretionary access control through the domination property; a user can read data only from classes over which domination is possessed.

The Bell-LaPadula star property prevents success of a TH attack that is based on "writing down" information. For example, a TH placed in a text editor might copy information to an unprotected file. When being used at the secret level, this text editor would make information available for write-down without the user's knowledge.

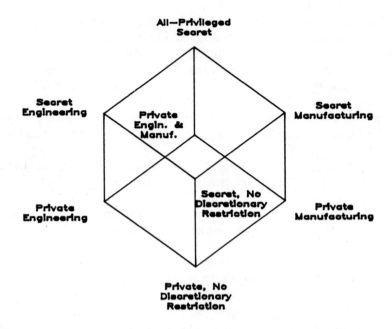

Figure 7-5 Sample security policy lattice.

Implementation of the star property assures that the text editor would be unable to carry out this TH command.

However, there may be a legitimate need to move information in a file to a lower classification level, such as when the information is of itself not classified and is needed for processing at the unprotected level. The star property would not allow this, but a set of rules might be used (e.g., a system administrator with proper authority) in order to satisfy the need.

Several other rules are associated with the Bell-LaPadula model. For example, the "tranquility" constraint [7] prevents the classification of active objects from being changed by a subject. Nonaccessibility to inactive objects is postulated to prevent a user from reading inactive files.

Since the Bell-LaPadula model was defined with only secrecy of data as a guiding principle, integrity issues remain. The Biba integrity model [61] mathematically describes read and write restrictions based on integrity access classes of subjects and objects. Integrity levels and compartments are based on corruption potential, and a lattice model applies to the protection conditions. A major difference is that the read and write conditions must be reversed for integrity:

1. A subject can write an object only if the integrity access class of the subject dominates the integrity class of the object.
2. A subject can read an object only if the integrity access class of the object dominates the integrity class of the subject.

7.3.4.2 Formal Verification The relationship between implemented code and the original security model is intended to be rigorously ensured through application of formal mathematical relations. This activity is called "formal verification" [82,86–89].

Following the development of the reference monitor concept, it was recognized [56] that seven steps would be necessary to verify the implementation specifications:

1. Create a mathematical security model that represents the desired security policy.
2. Write a formal specification for the implementation.
3. Prove that the specification is consistent with the model (and therefore with the security policy).
4. Write the specifications for the algorithms to be used.
5. Prove that the algorithm specifications are consistent with the top-level specification.
6. Write code for the algorithms.
7. Prove that the code is consistent with the algorithm specifications.

A number of tools have been developed to assist with the required verifications [53,56]. Verification is also strongly related to the choice of a structured programming language with a well-understood compiler. The relationships between the available tools and languages have been studied by the NCSC [57].

7.3.5 Trusted Computer System Evaluation

In order to focus the extensive and complex efforts required to produce trusted computer systems, considerable effort has been placed on security evaluation. As a culmination of the combined efforts of the DoD, the civilian government, private industry, and academia, the NCSC has published a specific set of evaluation criteria in a document known (because of the color of the cover) as the "Orange Book" [58]. The evaluation criteria are intended to provide an extensive assessment of overall system security as a function of well defined security elements. The criteria are useful as design guides, as measures of security performance of commercial systems, and as specification guidelines for ADP procurements.

The NCSC performs security evaluation of commercial products without regard to the application environment [82]. However, certification (technical evaluation of realization of security requirements) or accreditation (authorization to become operational) should include consideration of the application environment.

Four "divisions" are specified as a basis for the Orange Book evaluation criteria ratings. These are D, C, B, and A, with A signifying the highest degree of security and D the lowest. Within divisions C and B (there are also provisions in A), there are subdivisions called "classes." The classes are identified numerically, with number one indicating the lowest security class within a division. Each division and each class has been given a descriptive name, as shown in Table 7-4. The table also gives a hierarchical ranking from least secure (top of the table) to most secure (bottom of the table).

A brief discussion, with reference to the preceding material in this section, will provide a general description of the evaluation criteria. A detailed description of the criteria, together with rationale, is given in Ref. 58. The descriptions given are cumulative in the narrative below, with the requirements for each class including all requirements of the previous class.

Division D has only one class, Class D. This evaluation means that the system has been evaluated, but does not meet the requirements of any higher class.

The lowest class in the Discretionary Protection Division is C1. Class C1 requires that a degree of confidence in the hardware and software controls be provided. Users must be isolated from data (ordinarily through a reference monitor), and users must be authenticated. Demonstrated attainment of these specifications is based on functional testing. The environment is expected to be one of cooperating users processing data at the same level of security. Many major commercial operating systems (except PCs) meet these requirements.

Table 7-4   Division/class names.

Division D: Minimal Protection

Class D: Minimal Protection

Division C: Discretionary Protection

Class C1: Discretionary Security Protection

Class C2: Controlled Access Protection

Division B: Mandatory Protection

Class B1: Labeled Security Protection

Class B2: Structured Protection

Class B3: Security Domains

Division A: Verified Protection

Class A1: Verified Design

Beyond Class A1

The Controlled Access Protection Class (C2) has more heavily encapsulated resources. The most important objects must be well protected. Log-in procedures and explicit auditing capabilities must be in place. Most "add-on" security software products that have been designed and evaluated meet the C2 requirements.

In Division B, the Labeled Security Protection Class (B1) requirements specify that the system must have an explicit model for its protection techniques (e.g., the simple security and star property of the Bell-LaPadula model). There must be segmentation (execution domains), mandatory access control, and internal information file labels. Exported information must be labeled. A system security officer and documentation is required.

The Structured Protection Class (B2) must be developed around a formal security model. Systems meeting this evaluation are usually kernelized. Covert channel identification is required, and tracing of covert channel use must be possible. Mandatory controls must exist for all resources, including communication lines. Configuration control (for change identifications and rationale) is required. Multics-AIM is an example of a B2 product.

The Security Domains Class (B3) requires implementation of a simple central encapsulation mechanism that separates security-sensitive portions of the system from user services portions that are not directly related to security. The reference monitor must be shown to mediate all accesses, be tamperproof, and be analyzable and testable. System recovery procedures are required. Protection against authentication attacks such as those presented in Section 7.2.1.4 is required. Design implementation must be highly structured.

Systems meeting the A Division criteria incorporate extensive security considerations at all phases of development. Mathematical tools that use formal models with explicit security theorems are required for the Verified Design Class (A1). There must be a formal top-level specification and trusted distribution of the software. Configuration management is applied to both the specifications and the implementation. The Honeywell SCOMP received an A1 evaluation in December 1984.

Class A1 embodies the most secure set of criteria yet specified. The "Beyond Class A1" Class would require new developments. It is expected that the use of formal verification would be extended to the source level and that covert timing channels would be well identified in any criteria beyond Class A1.

The DoD has issued a directive [62] requiring that by 1992 virtually all computers that handle government classified or sensitive unclassified information must meet the C2 evaluation.

Because of normal requirements for security, and to introduce security measures in a cost-effective manner, the NCSC has also issued guidance on matching the evaluated security level to the requirements of the environment [63]. The results are summarized in Figure 7-6 and Table 7-5. Figure 7-6 displays a "risk index" as a function of the minimum user clearance and the maximum data sensitivity in a system. Table 7-5 shows the evaluation level necessary for the risk index obtained. The guidance is general; exceptions exist.

The term "categories" refers to a restrictive label, in addition to classification, that signifies compartmented access rights. The only categories of interest are those that exclude some users.

The conditions necessary for an environment to be considered "closed" instead of "open" are that 1) applications developers/maintainers have sufficient clearance (minimum of Secret) to assure that they have not introduced malicious logic, and 2) configuration control provides sufficient assurance that malicious logic has not been introduced prior to and during the operation of system applications.

Maximum Data Sensitivity

Minimum User Clearance	Uncl.	N#	C##	S	S1C	**	TS1C	TSMC
Uncleared	0	1	2	3	4	5	6	7
Sensitive Uncl. Only (N)	0	0	1	2	3	4	5	6
Confidential (C)	0	0	0	1	2	3	4	5
Secret (S)	0	0	0	0	1	2	3	4
Top Secret/Current Background	0	0	0	0	0	*	2	3
Top Secret/Special Background	0	0	0	0	0	0	1	2
One Category (1C)	0	0	0	0	0	0	0	1
Multiple Categories (MC)	0	0	0	0	0	0	0	0

* 1 for Secret, Multiple Categories; 0 for Top Secret, no Categories.
** Secret, Multiple Categories and Top Secret, 0 Categories.
# For Categories, Add 1 to First Two Rows.
For Categories, Add 1 to First Three Rows.

Figure 7-6   Security Risk Index.

A "dedicated" security operating mode is one in which processing is limited to one particular type or classification of operation (full time or for dedicated periods of time*). "System high" hardware/software configurations need only provide need-to-know protection between users. In "compartmented" operation, the system is allowed to process two or more types of compartmented information. Users must be cleared for at least Top Secret information for unescorted computer access. "Multilevel" operation allows two or more classification levels to be processed simultaneously while some users are not cleared for all information present. "Controlled" operation is a multi-level security mode in which there is a limited amount of trust in the hardware/software protection capabilities.

7.4 FILE AND DATABASE SECURITY

A common system file structure organization is the "flat" file system, where file names are maintained in a global name space stored in a single systemwide directory [7]. Flat-file structure is not designed to

---

* "Periods processing" requires special provisions for "cleansing" the system between dedicated activities. These provisions include repetitive overwriting of memory or replacing memory units and the operating system.

Table 7-5   System evaluation requirements.

Risk Index	Operating Mode	Minimum Class, Open Environment	Minimum Class, Closed Environment
0	Dedicated	No Minimum	No Minimum
0	System High	C2	C2
1	Limited Access, Controlled, Compartmented, Multilevel	B1	B1
2	Limited Access, Controlled, Compartmented, Multilevel	B2	B2
3	Controlled, Multilevel	B3	B2
4	Multilevel	A1	B3
5	Multilevel		A1
6	Multilevel		
7	Multilevel		

Notes:

1. Where there is no prescribed minimum class, C1 may be required for integrity and service continuity.

2. The requirement for C2 may be reduced to C1 if the system does not process classified or sensitive data.

3. The requirement for B1 is increased to B2 if a system processes classified or compartmented data and some users do not have at least a Confidential clearance, or if there are two or more types of compartmented information being processed.

4. Blank entries indicated that the requirements are beyond the current state of trusted computer system technology.

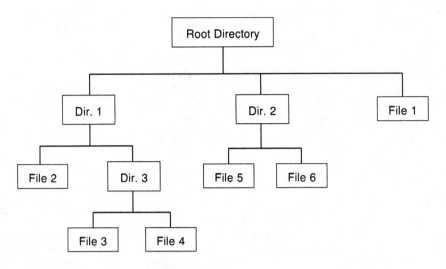

Figure 7-7   Hierarchical file structure.

hide file names from any user. **Preventing processes from choosing file names prevents covert channel signaling through file name generation.**

A "hierarchical" file structure is organized around "directories" (and directories within directories), where each directory refers to a collection of files. The resulting "tree" structure is illustrated in Figure 7-7. Files are accessed along "path" names (directory sequence, followed by file name within last specified directory). Access to directories can be controlled in a manner similar to that by which flat-file access is controlled. However, this structure incorporates better security attributes, because a user who does not have read access to a directory cannot infer anything about its contents or about the hierarchy below the directory.

Preventing the use of covert channels through file structures depends on preventing a process from modifying an attribute of an object (a file or a directory) where the object is in a lower-level directory than that in which the process is operating. An example involves name conflicts, where a message could be returned denying a file name request where the file name had been used at a higher level.

In addition to hiding files, file access can be controlled through file passwords. Since file passwords are usually used for less stringent security protection than computer access passwords, it is common to allow user-selected file passwords.

Database management systems (DBMS) are software routines that manage data entry, modification, readout, and security functions. Query languages allow user transactions to be prescribed concisely and in terms convenient to the users. Associations of various parts of the database can be made and relations between files can be utilized. A relational database system has data arranged by logical values instead of by physical positions in fields [77]. A commercial DBMS may cost from $50 for a simple PC system to more than $10,000 for a capable mainframe system.

A DBMS may contain a reference monitor subsystem to mediate access requests. It is possible to attach classifications to each data element in a file, to each record in a file, to each field in a file, or to "views" (abstract portions) of the database [83]. A DBMS "query" (request for information) is checked by the reference monitor for restrictions. For example, the DBMS may grant access to a view that has been restricted by the permission parameters in the reference monitor database.

Two subtle problems arise in providing information strictly by the defined file access rules. These are called "aggregation" and "inference." The aggregation problem occurs where an accumulation of information entities, each having no sensitivity, becomes sensitive in the whole. Sometimes information can be deduced from the total collection that could not be deduced from the constituents alone. As an example, consider a company whose level of effort on a project (say, the "Weather" project) is protected. The existence of certain divisions in the company (e.g., "Weather Research," "Weather Modification," "Weather Testing") is not protected. However, an aggregation of such division names is indicative of level of effort.

Inference situations arise when one can draw conclusions from available facts without seeing the conclusions explicitly. For example, assume that a company's salary information is protected, but that statistical parameters such as "average salary of Ph.D.s" are available. For a company with only one Ph.D., the inference of the person's salary would be direct.

One approach to these problems is to implement a "query monitor" to check on inference conditions and aggregation threats. These monitors are very difficult to design.

7.5 STRUCTURED SOFTWARE DEVELOPMENT

The development of quality software has proven to be an elusive goal. It is not easy to define software quality, to determine the best approach to achieve it, or to measure it. However, quality software is a major contributor to system security. Ideally, software should verifiably achieve system security specifications, should be free of anomalous behavior that could compromise security, and should be so easily examined and tested that hidden threats would be unlikely. The goal has not yet been achieved, but its pursuit has resulted in substantial improvements in software development methodology. Structured software development is the approach that has been the most successful.

Structured software development involves a planned effort to efficiently satisfy system requirements (including security policy); to perform reliably; and to be organized for logical design, analysis, and test.

Many guidelines exist to assist designers in structured design. An example is the ANSI/IEEE (Institute of Electrical and Electronics Engineers) Software Engineering Standards [64–67]. Well-known books [e.g., 68,69] are also available. Here, we will limit discussion to a brief summary of the topic.

Seven activities form a reasonable basis for structured software development:

1. Software quality assurance planning. It is important to provide well-defined quality checks for a product. These may include reviews and inspections (see activity seven). Software audits (independent examinations to assure compliance with stated criteria) are a traditional form of quality control and nearly always involve security checks. Audits may be used at milestones or during the product's life cycle. A time frame is agreed on for implementing changes based on audit findings.

2. Configuration management. There must be activities to assure that design and code are well defined and cannot be changed without full review of the reasons for the change and the implications of the change. After a software module is thoroughly reviewed and tested, it can be "baselined" and given an issue number. A copy of the issue is placed under control. This is an important feature for protecting security attributes of a system.

3. Software requirements specifications. System requirements specifications are necessary to assure understanding among developers, users, and management of the features that will be provided by the software. This may involve "rapid prototypes" to demonstrate expected system behavior. It is helpful to augment the textual requirements with "structured analysis" [74] (a formal method of defining and constructing a graphic non-

redundant model of the requirements). Structured analysis includes the development of "data flow diagrams" (portraying data interfaces) and a "data dictionary" (list of data flows, processes, and stores).

4. Software testing. Testing typically involves a plan, test case specifications, and documentation of results. The tests are essential to demonstrate that system performance satisfies the system requirements. Virtually all software has too many possible operation paths and conditions for exhaustive test [71]. For this reason, structured test selection for maximum test effectiveness is useful [72].

5. Software verification and validation. An independent verification and validation activity has two roles. First, it specifies methods for ensuring that each phase of the software development meets the requirements of the previous phase (verification). It also evaluates the software to ensure compliance with the requirements (validation). Testing security features is an important part of the activity.

6. Software design. The software design specifies the internal structure, the internal interfaces, and the processing details of the design. "Structured design" [73] builds on the structured analysis, adding a "structure chart" that depicts software modules, transitions between modules, and data passed between modules. Each module is implemented and tested independently, and then the modules are integrated. The source code is inspected to remove errors in logic or implementation, and to ensure security and integrity.

7. Software inspections. Designs of all but the simplest of functions are subject to errors in definition, design, or implementation. It is generally accepted that a design review process can reduce these problems by introducing peer synergism and fresh points of view. Early identification of problems is essential to cost-effective resolution. A formal software design review process called "inspections" has been widely used to review development phases [80]. The advantages of the inspection process are that it is structured for efficiency, and enables accumulation of data that can improve future designs.

The cost of finding and correcting errors in a design increases exponentially as the design and implementation proceed (see Figure 7-8 for typical costs). Thus, the early overhead due to incorporating inspections in the design process is more than repaid later in the program [85]. The inspections participants include a "moderator" (administers meeting), a

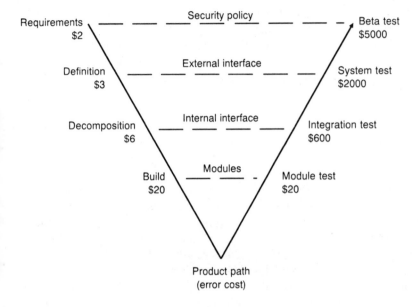

Figure 7-8   Structured software development.

"reader" (paraphrases line-by-line content), a "recorder" (records and classifies problems), and the "author" (for questions and clarification). All participants are "inspectors" of the product, without being judgmental of the author or the design. The intent is to provide a tool to help the author produce a better product without "grading" the product. Identified problems are scheduled for repair, and the final outcome is an inspected and approved product.

Structured software development is now supported by a variety of CASE (computer-aided software engineering) tools. These packages cost from about $1000 to $85,000 [81], depending on their capabilities.

The DoD has had an active interest in software development methodology. Three DoD programs have recently begun as part of a "Software Initiative" to improve software available for government applications [70]. One of these programs is the Software Engineering Institute, jointly supported by the Air Force Electronic Systems Division and the Carnegie Mellon Institute. A second is the STARS (Software Technology for Adaptable, Reliable Systems) Program. The goal of the STARS program is to utilize and improve the software engineering environment and to increase military software development productivity by a factor of 10. The third program is the Ada programming language (MIL-STD-1815A), currently mandated for all new mission-critical DoD computer applications. Ada is encouraged both as a "standard" and because it is oriented toward structured design.

7.6 AUDITING TECHNIQUES AND TOOLS

The verification of system security features and system security performance is a difficult task requiring constant surveillance of the system. One of the best known tools for achieving this goal is the EDP audit function. EDP auditing, if properly done, gives additional insight, identifies signals that point to security weaknesses or failures, and helps prevent security bypasses resulting from collusion.

The $30 million fraud described in Section 1.4 was possible only because auditing procedures were lax. Another case [83] demonstrates the importance of carefully selecting data for audit. A supervisor of a major city income tax refund section noticed that refund payments were assigned a reference number according to the case, with no direct tie to a person or business. The supervisor selected reference numbers, increased the check amount, and changed the name and address for payment to an accomplice. After the check was issued, he would change the data back. There were no authorization barriers except for the authority of the supervisor. The team received more than $120,000 before being apprehended.

During system development, auditors serve as advisors as to the effectiveness of internal controls, such as data logging, value totaling, and access restrictions. Auditors generally look for 1) the adequacy of internal control, 2) sufficient feedback procedures (measures for obtaining meaningful data), and 3) features that make data auditable with efficient use of resources. Auditors assist in the test process by helping check on the adequacy of controls. Operational audits help ensure compliance with standards on performance, media labeling, handling, and storage. Usually audits occur at the input, output, and internal level.

Auditing functions are generally performed at regular phase points or milestones during system development and at frequent but random times during operation.

The magnitude of the auditing function generally must be balanced between the degree of threat and the availability of auditing resources. Thus, while awareness of sophisticated threat potential is essential, the concentration is on routine controls. Depending on how much support the audit function receives, it may not be productive for auditors to search for THs and covert channels, for example.

For these reasons the audit approaches used tend to be oriented toward the most common problems. Some of the tools and techniques are:

1. User command log. This control is designed to detect unauthorized actions and monitor command activity by users.
2. Sensitive file access log. This tool detects unauthorized accesses to sensitive files and to monitor file access activity.
3. Crash log. This log is used to detect a "denial of service" attack.
4. Program change log. This log facilitates detection of unauthorized modification of programs.
5. Data adjustment/correcting log. This is to detect unauthorized modification of data.
6. Extended records information. This capability in an application program appends audit trail information to all transaction records. The intent is to detect unauthorized transactions.
7. Parallel simulation. Processing production transactions with programs that simulate critical aspects of application program logic helps detect programs that operate in a different manner than expected.
8. Code comparison. "Comparator" programs |75| that compare a production program to a control program are used to identify differences. The comparison is generally difficult, because inserts and deletes change program sequence numbers. The comparator logic depends on identifying the logic instead of the sequence numbers. The output is a list of changes for review. This technique has some limited capability to find a TH code.

    Checksums (see Chapter 8) also provide a means of detecting changes in programs or data. The checksum is a function of all of the bits representing the program or data. Some operating systems |78| have checksum utilities for this purpose.
9. Selected transactions. This is a logic procedure for screening transactions most likely to be of importance. It is generally aimed at finding improper transactions.
10. Data handling procedures. The intent of reviewing data handling procedures is to verify compliance with policies and standards during the preparation of data for input. This attention is important because of the high potential for misuse at the data entry point.

11. Selected area audits. Statistics are used to identify unexpected variations, such as a high level of uncollected receivables, for examination.
12. Test data sets. Application systems such as payroll or accounts payable can be tested with typical data in order to verify expected output.
13. Snapshot audits. Audits require routines embedded in application software to record memory states at critical application decision points. This permits the auditor to monitor detailed program logic.
14. Library usage record. This is to examine access to sensitive library modules. For example, an unexpectedly large number of accesses would be cause for attention.

In addition to the software security packages mentioned earlier, which nearly all include audit functions, there are a number of add-on audit software packages. An obvious requirement for all audit data recorded is that the storage files must be securely protected.

Audit procedures give a degree of protection against intentional attacks by making the perpetrator's job more difficult and by making the chances of detection high. The overall effect is a reduction in unintentional errors, control of mischief and fraud, increased productivity, and better management information.

PROBLEMS

1. Assume that passwords are selected from 4-character combinations of 26 alphabetic characters. Assume that an adversary is able to attempt passwords at a rate of one per second. a) Assuming no feedback to the adversary until each attempt has been completed, what is the expected time to discover the correct password? b) Assuming feedback to the adversary flagging an error as each incorrect character is entered, what is the expected time to discover the correct password?

2. Assume that the probability density function for passwords created by a community of users is known to be $p(word\ i) = \binom{10}{i}/P$ for each of 10 possible passwords ($i = 1,2, \ldots ,10$), where P is the total number of users. a) Solve for P. b) What is the chance of an adversary guessing a correct password for a user if the probability density function given above is known?

3. Assume a 3-character password generator that constructs combinations of the 26 alphabetic characters. a) How many passwords are possible? b) Assume that the words are constrained to be meaningful (to most people) English words. About how many passwords are possible? c) Would any of the words generated in a) or b) be objectionable?

4. Assume that a number (r^k) of source elements is mapped using a balanced linear transformation to a smaller number (r^p) of target elements. A particular source element, x_i, is mapped to a particular target element, y_j. a) What is the probability that a different source element, x_k, $(x_i \neq x_k)$ that results in the same target element, y_j, could be produced by an adversary? b) What is the probability that the correct source element can be selected? c) What is the probability that the correct target element can be produced by selecting a source element?

5. A password algorithm is in use. You are an adversary. Deduce the algorithm (the next response) for the following prompt/response pairs:

DCTAR/GXEV; BPQZE/RSBG; CRDLN/UGOQ; AHIMV/ ?

6. A phonetic password generator picks two segments randomly for each six-letter password. The form for each segment is: CVC (consonant, vowel, consonant), where V = <a,e,i,o,u> and C = $\overline{V}$. a) What is the total password population? b) What is the probability of an adversary guessing a password correctly?

7. Design a three-letter phonetic password generator by:

   a) Specifying construction forms
   b) Specifying sets of characters used

   Then calculate c) the probability of an adversary's success if random form selection is made by the generator and by the adversary, d) the probability of adversary success if the generator uses random form selection and the adversary knows the algorithm, and e) the probability of adversary success if the generator chooses forms with choice probability in proportion to the percentage of passwords for the particular form relative to the total population.

8. A phonetic password generator is used with forms $S_1, S_2, \ldots,$ S_n. Each S_i contains x_i words. An adversary knows the forms and the words. He assumes that the system will use optimum selection (choosing forms with probability proportional to the

number of words in the form), but the system uses random form selection. What is the probability of success for the adversary?

9. An adversary knows that the user of a system with user-generated passwords will pick a password from a population of 100 possibilities, where the probability of selecting possibility "i" is i/5050. What is the adversary's probability of guessing the user's password? [*Note:* K. F. Gauss calculated the denominator necessary for this problem in his head. Could you?]

10. Assume that computer interaction over a 1200 baud line allows 14 password guesses per minute. There are 100,000,000 possible passwords. a) How long would it take for an adversary to have a 10^{-3} probability of guessing a password? b) How long would it take if passwords are changed daily?

DILEMMA DISCUSSIONS

1. New operating system releases frequently arrive in the mail. It is known that there is potential for TH attacks through this avenue, but none have ever been detected. All possible authentication and verification techniques known would require substantial company resources. Should overhead be expended against the threat, or should one take a considered chance based on lack of any evidence that the threat really exists?

2. Company rules state explicitly that all computer users must have a unique password. The computer vendor argues for an exception, since there is a pool of service personnel from which different people are chosen for each job. The vendor does not want the overhead of maintaining individual passwords for a generic function being carried out by equally qualified people, all doing the same job, especially since the passwords may be used very infrequently, if at all. However, to compromise company policy applicable to all other users is an uncomfortable precedent, especially since audit data is linked to particular service personnel only through records kept by the vendor. What should be done? Why?

3. Information in the literature suggests that user passwords should be system-selected, since user-selected passwords are more readily guessed by skilled adversaries. Users argue that they should select their own passwords on the grounds that they are more easily remembered, and therefore less likely to be written down; and that they would be willing to follow selec-

tion criteria (no names, reasonable length, etc.). What should be done?

4. A computer that contains classified information must be accessed by two separate groups within the same company, and the two groups do not have a common need-to-know. A secure multilevel operating system is available, but the cost of obtaining it is burdensome. The option of installing the operating system is attractive, because it would assure that one group's information could not be accessed by the other group. However, it is not clear that the separation on the basis of need-to-know is cost-effective, since the two groups work in the same company, and there is no reason to think people in one group would gain from the other group's knowledge. What should be done?

5. Users who have access to several computers would prefer to have the same password for access to each computer. This has the advantage of minimizing demands on users' memories and thereby giving less likelihood of passwords being exposed through written or printed records. On the other hand, compromise of a single password could then give access to a number of computers. Would it be better for a user to have different passwords for each computer or not?

REFERENCES

1. Enger, Norman L., and Paul W. Howerton, *Computer Security*, Amacom, New York, 1980.
2. Thompson, Ken, "Reflections on Trusting Trust," *Communications of the ACM*, August 1984.
3. Morrison, Perry R., "Computer Parasites," *The Futurist*, March–April 1986.
4. Cohen, Fred, "Computer Viruses," *Computer Security: A Global Challenge*, Elsevier Science Publishers, New York, 1984.
5. Nordwall, Bruce D., and Breck W. Henderson, "Rapid Spread of Virus Confirms Fears About Danger to Computers," *Aviation Week & Space Technology*, November 14, 1988.
6. *Computer Security, Understanding Computers Series*, Time-Life Books, Alexandria, VA, 1986.
7. Gasser, Morrie, *Building a Secure Computer System*, Van Nostrand Reinhold Company, New York, 1988.
8. Parker, Donn, *Fighting Computer Crime*, Charles Scribner's Sons, New York, 1983.

9. Lewyn, Mark, "It Was a Tough Case to Explain to Jury," *USA Today*, September 22, 1988.

10. DiDio, Laura, "Viruses Plague Networks, Jeopardize System Health," *Network World*, July 4, 1988.

11. Daly, James, "Sparse Coverage for Viruses," *Computerworld*, August 15, 1988.

12. Brooks, Doug, "Let's Vaccinate Ourselves Against Computer Viruses," *Government Computer News*, June 10, 1988.

13. Murphy, Erin E., and Elizabeth Corcoran, "Contagious Computers," *IEEE Spectrum*, May 1988.

14. Ruiz, Frank, "DoD Fights Off Computer Virus," *Government Computer News*, February 5, 1988.

15. Ponting, Bob, "Some Common Sense About Network Viruses, and What to do About Them," *Data Communications*, April 1988.

16. Voelcker, John, "Virus vs. Virus," *IEEE Spectrum*, June 1988.

17. Hafner, Katherine M., "Is Your Computer Secure?" *BusinessWeek*, August 1, 1988.

18. Elmer-DeWitt, Phillip, "Invasion of the Data Snatchers," *Time*, September 26, 1988.

19. Savage, J. A., "Computer Time Bomb Defused; Felon Nailed," *Computerworld*, September 26, 1988.

20. Denning, Peter, "Computer Viruses," *American Scientist*, May–June 1988.

21. Lampson, B. W., "A Note on the Confinement Problem," *Communications of the ACM*, September 1975.

22. Sullivan, Kathleen, "Logic Bomb Brings Agency's DP Operations to Standstill," *Computerworld*, April 15, 1985.

23. Garman, John R., "The 'Bug' Heard Round the World," *ACM SIGSOFT Software Engineering Notes*, October 1981.

24. Bellin, David, and Gary Chapman, *Computers in Battle—Will They Work?*, Harcourt Brace Jovanovich, San Diego, CA, 1987.

25. "Boston ATC Center Software Error Causes East Coast Delays," *Aviation Week & Space Technology*, August 22, 1988.

26. Bozman, Jean S., "Airline Hurt by Faulty Fare Estimations," *Computerworld*, September 19, 1988.

27. Cordner, Russell A., "Undocumented Switches," *DG Review*, August 1988.

28. Herschberg, I. S., "The Programmer's Threat: Cases and Causes," *Computers & Security (3)*, 1984.

29. Blakeney, Susan, "Software Developers Planting 'Booby Traps'," *Computerworld*, July 12, 1982.

30. Munro, Neil, "Big Guns Take Aim at Virus," *Government Computer News*, November 21, 1988.
31. Highland, Harold Joseph, "Computer Viruses—A Post Mortem," *Computers and Security*, April 1988.
32. Joyce, Edward J., "Software Viruses: PC-Health Enemy Number One," *Datamation*, October 15, 1988.
33. Menkus, Belden, "No Vaccine to Ward Off Effects of Virus Attacks," *Computerworld*, July 11, 1988.
34. Cox, John, "After Virus Attack, Users Rethink Nets," *Network World*, November 14, 1988.
35. Baley, Alan, "Tailgating: A Dirty Little Network Security Problem," *Data Communications*, March 1988.
36. Goldstone, Bruce J., "A 'Backdoor' Password Problem," *EDPACS*, July 1985.
37. Tanenbaum, Andrew S., *Computer Networks*, Prentice-Hall, Englewood Cliffs, NJ, 1981.
38. Fak, Viiveke, "Characteristics of Good One-Way Encryption Functions for Passwords—Some Rules for Creators and Evaluators," *Computer Security: A Global Challenge*, Elsevier Science Publishers, New York, 1984.
39. Diffie, W., and M. E. Hellman, "New Directions in Cryptography," *IEEE Transactions on Information Theory*, IT 22, No. 6, 1976.
40. Aho, A., J. Hopcroft, and J. Ullman, *The Design and Analysis of Computer Algorithms*, Addison-Wesley, Reading, MA, 1974.
41. Denning, Dorothy Elizabeth Robling, *Cryptography and Data Security*, Addison-Wesley, Reading, MA, 1982.
43. "Department of Defense Password Management Guideline," CSC-STD-002-85, April 12, 1985.
44. "Password Usage Standard," National Bureau of Standards Federal Information Processing Standards Publication 112, May 30, 1985.
45. "How Passwords Are Cracked," *EDPACS*, September 1985.
46. Bynon, David W., "System Security, Part 1," *DEC Professional*, October 1988.
47. Brown, R. Leonard, "Computer System Access Control Using Passwords," *Computer Security: A Global Challenge*, Elsevier Science Publishers, New York, 1984.
48. Shannon, Terry, "Standing Guard," *Digital Review*, April 1986.
49. Eloff, Jan H. P., "Selection Process for Security Packages," *Computer Security: A Global Challenge*, Elsevier Science Publishers, New York, 1984.

50. McEnaney, Maura, "ACF2 Snatches Top Spot," *Computerworld*, December 3, 1984.

51. Johnston, Robert E., "Comparison of Access Control Software for IBM Operating Systems—ACF2, RACF, SAC, SECURE, & TOP SECRET," *Computer Security Journal*, Fall–Winter, 1983.

52. Faurer, Lt. General Lincoln D., "The Secrets War," *Government Data Systems*, November/December 1983.

53. Landwehr, Carl, "Protecting Stored Data Remains a Serious Problem," *Military Electronics/Countermeasures*, April 1983.

54. Ames, S. R., Jr., M. Gasser, and R. R. Schell, "Security Kernel Design and Implementation: An Introduction," *Advances in Computer System Security*, Artech House, Norwood, MA, 1984.

55. Bell, D. E., and L. J. LaPadula, "Secure Computer Systems: Unified Exposition and Multics Interpretation," MITRE Corp. Report MTR-2997 Rev. 1, March 1976.

56. Bonyun, David A., "Formal Verification: Its Purpose and Practice," *Computer Security: A Global Challenge*, Elsevier Science Publishers, New York, 1984.

57. Kemmerer, "Verification Assessment Study—Final Report" (five volumes), National Computer Security Center, March 1986.

58. "Department of Defense Trusted Computer System Evaluation Criteria," DoD 5200.28-STD, December 1985.

59. Wells, Paul, "On-Chip Hardware Supports Computer Security Features," *Electronics*, March 8, 1984.

60. Gill, Arthur, *Applied Algebra for the Computer Sciences*, Prentice-Hall, Englewood Cliffs, NJ, 1976.

61. Biba, K. J., "Integrity Considerations for Secure Computer Systems," Air Force Electronic Systems Division Report ESD-TR-76-372, 1977.

62. Munro, Neil, "Most DOD Computers to Meet C-2 Security by '92," *Government Computer News*, August 1, 1988.

63. "Computer Security Requirements—Guidance for Applying the Department of Defense Trusted Computer System Evaluation Criteria in Specific Environments," Department of Defense CSC-STD-003-85, June 23, 1985.

64. Institute of Electrical and Electronics Engineers Software Quality Assurance Plans, Std. 730, 1984.

65. Institute of Electrical and Electronics Engineers Software Configuration Management, Std. 828, 1983.

66. Institute of Electrical and Electronics Engineers Software Test Documentation, Std. 829, 1983.

67. Institute of Electrical and Electronics Engineers Software Requirements Specifications, Std. 830, 1984.
68. Brooks, Frederick P., Jr., *The Mythical Man-Month*, Addison-Wesley, Reading, MA, 1982.
69. Fairley, Richard, *Software Engineering Concepts*, McGraw-Hill, New York, 1985.
70. Stewart, James A., "Validation: A Moving Target," *Defense Systems*, October 1988.
71. Suydam, William E., "Approaches to Software Testing Embroiled in Debate," *Computer Design*, November 15, 1986.
72. McCabe, Thomas, "A Complexity Measure," *IEEE Transactions on Software Engineering*, December 1976.
73. Yourdan, Edward, and Larry L. Constantine, *Structured Design*, Yourdan Press, New York, 1978.
74. DeMarco, Tom, *Structured Analysis and System Specification*, Yourdan Press, New York, 1979.
75. Lancaster, Gregory M., "Code Comparison—An Inexpensive Approach to Security and Auditability," *Datapro Newsbriefs*, March 1981.
76. Norman, Adrian R. D., *Computer Insecurity*, Chapman and Hall, London, England, 1983.
77. Chester, Jeffrey A., "Demystifying Relational Database Systems," *Infosystems*, October 1985.
78. Zipp, Eric, "More Security Tips for VMS System Managers," *Digital Review*, April 1985.
79. Anderson, D. A., "Operating Systems," *IEEE Computer*, June 1981.
80. Fagan, Michael, "Advances in Software Inspections," *IEEE Transactions on Software Engineering*, July 1986.
81. Voelcker, John, "Automating Software: Proceed with Caution," *IEEE Spectrum*, July 1988.
82. "Information Systems Security—Products and Services Catalog," National Security Agency, April 1988.
83. Wilson, J., "Views as the Security Objects in a Multilevel Secure Relational Database Management System," 1988 IEEE Symposium on Security and Privacy, April 18–21, 1988.
84. Ball, Michael, "To Catch a Thief: Lessons in Systems Security," *Computerworld*, December 14, 1987.
85. Boehm, Barry W., *Software Engineering Economics*, Prentice-Hall, Englewood Cliffs, NJ, 1981.
86. Backhouse, Roland C., *Program Construction and Verification*, Prentice-Hall, Englewood Cliffs, NJ, 1986.

87. Loeck, Jacques, and Kurt Sieber, *The Foundations of Program Verification*, John Wiley & Sons, New York, 1987.
88. Nidi, Ali, *An Introduction to Formal Program Verification*, Van Nostrand Reinhold Company, New York, 1985.
89. Hoare, C. A. R., *Communicating Sequential Processes*, Prentice-Hall, Englewood Cliffs, NJ, 1985.

8

The Network Security
Environment

Networks are essential tools for computer users. Anyone who has ever used networks would find it hard to imagine a computing environment without remote access to mainframe computers, dialup access to computers, long-distance data transfer capability, distributed database collections, sharing of scarce or expensive peripheral resources, electronic mail, and electronic bulletin boards.

The growing use of networks has been driven partly by a desire for the obviously useful services that networks can provide and partly by necessity. One of the problems that timesharing systems have created is that they have so successfully met user needs that the number of users typically grows until the system response becomes annoyingly slow. An obvious solution is to purchase more timesharing computers, but this is not always the most efficient solution. It frequently makes sense to restructure computing around a shared-resource network environment as a cost-effective way to put more computing capability in the hands of the users. Networks are a cost-effective means of providing both increases in computing capability and access to a number of convenient services.

However, networks have resulted in new and serious security problems. Data flowing through networks or residing temporarily on network nodes may be especially vulnerable to interception, alteration, disruption, or masquerade. Frequently, there are many more ways for an adversary to attempt to access computers connected to a network than for standalone systems. Since network users typically have a large physical distribution, a large population, and are somewhat "invisible," administrative problems are also substantial.

In this chapter, we begin describing the network security environment by surveying network architectures and threats. Next, we emphasize the protective measures that are most widely applied to network security. These are port-protection devices, encryption, authentication, and dedicated network "administrator" computers.

8.1 NETWORK ARCHITECTURES

A network provides means for two or more entities to establish a connection so that information transfer can occur. It is usually possible for two entities to also exchange information interactively. The entities may be computers, operating systems, programs, processes, or people [1]. These entities are called "network resources." "Network nodes," which connect to the network, are computers and user terminals. The connection strategy is called the "network architecture." This strategy includes the physical interconnection structure (topology) and the logical communication structure. A number of logical interface functions are usually provided by a network. The functions include sending messages, receiving messages, executing programs, obtaining status information, and obtaining information on other network users and their status. A "protocol," or communication strategy, must be implemented by the users. Multiple "services" can be provided for network users. These are implemented by "layering" (embedding) protocols, with the position or hierarchy of the layer corresponding to the protocol involved. A typical protocol includes a "header" (address and/or type of data), a data word or words, and a "trailer" (e.g., a checksum).

8.1.1 Geography of Networks

Networks can be categorized in many ways, and all categorizations have fuzzy boundaries. One of the categorization techniques is to call networks "wide-area networks" (WANs) or "local-area networks" (LANs) depending on their physical dimensions. The general distinction is that LANs are for intrabuilding or neighboring building con-

nections, usually not exceeding a few hundred meters in dimension.[*]
A WAN, on the other hand, may extend over continental dimensions
or beyond. These are often called "long-haul" networks.

These types of terminologies are not crisp. The Yankee Group
defines a LAN as "an intraoffice, intrabuilding, intrafacility communications system that supports some type of communications
processing and transparent information transfer between users
and/or electronic devices" [6]. Some further distinguish a LAN from a
digital PBX (private branch exchange) system, since a digital PBX
transports, switches, and processes both voice and data [7], and a
typical LAN provides little segmentation of information (e.g., "need-
to-know" protection) from users. These variations in terminology are
generally a matter of choice and do not affect the performance or
security considerations to be addressed.

8.1.2 Satellite-Based Networks

Satellite-based networks have been successful largely because of the
availability of geosynchronous (stationary relative to the earth) satellites. Arthur Clarke, in a 1945 *Wireless World* article, proposed that
these types of satellites would be useful because they could be stati-
cally targeted (instead of tracked) by ground station antennas. The
orbital patterns are often called "Clarke orbits."

Following an international agreement and the U.S. Communications Satellite Act of 1962, the first geosynchronous satellite (Syncom
II) was launched in 1963. There are now more than 100
geosynchronous satellites used for communications of various types,
and many of them carry computer traffic. Data sent to satellites
(uplink) is received, amplified, and transponded onto a slightly lower
frequency for retransmission to the ground (downlink).

For any orbiting satellite, the force balance between gravitational
attraction and the inertial resistance due to orbital motion
(centrifugal force) is expressed as:

$$mr\omega^2 = GmM/r^2 \qquad\qquad (8\text{-}1)$$

where m is the satellite mass, r is the orbital radius, ω is the an-
gular velocity, G is the universal gravitational constant (6.673×10^{-20}

---

[*]   Sometimes LANs may be structured over a one- to two-kilometer local
environment.

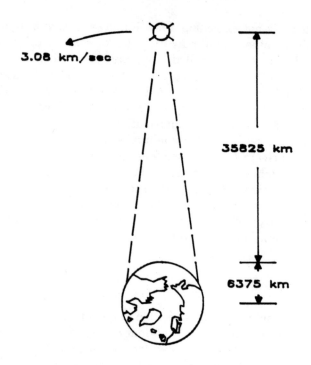

Figure 8-1   Geosynchronous satellite (polar view).

km³/kg-sec²), and M is the mass of the earth (5.983 x 10^{24} kg). The geosynchronous constraint forces ω to be equal to $2\pi/(24 \times 3600 \times 0.9973)$. The denominator is the time in seconds for the earth to make a complete revolution in space coordinates, which is a little less than 24 hours because of the earth's revolution about the sun. The solution for the required orbital radius is:

$$r^3 = GM/\omega^2$$

(8-2)

The result is about 42,200 km. Since this is about 35,825 km (approximately 22,300 miles) greater than the earth's radius, wide geographical coverage (18,000 km along the equator) is theoretically possible (see Problem 2). The geometry is depicted in Figure 8-1, where distances are shown approximately to scale. The orbital velocity of a geosynchronous satellite is:

$$v = \omega r \tag{8-3}$$

The result, as shown in the figure, is a little greater than 3 km per second.

Even though geosynchronous satellite coverage fringes are subject to geometrical obstructions, and though the antenna patterns used are more directional than isotropic, it is apparent that geosynchronous satellite transmission and reception is possible over a wide geographical area (the satellite communication system "footprint"). This is an advantage in usability. It is a disadvantage in security, since transmissions are easily intercepted and jamming would not be difficult for a determined adversary. The latter point was demonstrated effectively in 1986 by a man who called himself "Captain Midnight." Captain Midnight transmitted a signal to a geostationary satellite that temporarily overrode the programming signal of a major cable movie channel and replaced it with a message protesting signal encryption [5].

The distance of geostationary satellites from the earth causes some throughput problems due to the time required for data to travel from the transmitter to the receiver. Assuming a round-trip distance of 75,000 km, this time is 1/4 second. The problems caused by this delay are very serious for some commonly used network protocols and can be prevented only through carefully designing the protocol to meet the conditions of high response time. There is typically some loss in efficiency in reacting to detected transmission problems such as interference and bit errors. Because of the large transit times, it is essential that transmission errors (e.g., due to electrical storms) be corrected rather than flagged for retransmission (see Section 6.1). Therefore, forward error correction (FEC) is usually implemented in satellite data transmission systems.

International agreement on the specific location of satellite positions and frequencies is essential [8]. The International Telecommunications Union has provided the most productive forum for negotiations on specific satellite locations and frequencies. Most satellite uplink/downlink frequencies are in the ranges of 6 GHz/4 GHz (C band), 8 GHz/7 GHz (X/C band), and 14 GHz/11–12 GHz (Ku band). There is limited use of 30 GHz/20 GHz (Ka band). C band is generally considered to be the most attractive frequency because there is less rain attenuation and more technology base, but higher frequencies are becoming necessary to relieve congestion. Higher frequencies are also advantageous in applications where narrow antenna beams and directional steering are needed for security.

Until about 1983, satellite spacing was four degrees minimum, and five-meter ground station antennas were sufficient. Now, the minimum spacing has been reduced to as little as one degree. Larger antennas and cross-polarization are often required for low-interference data-handling. A typical ground station antenna (11 meters in diameter) targeted on a geosynchronous satellite is shown in Figure 8-2. Antennas on satellites generally have broad-beam coverage, but there is interest [9] in electronically steered "spot" beams.

Some communications satellites are placed in polar orbits. A particular strategy is called "sun-synchronous orbits," because the progression of the orbit around the earth is synchronized to a day (usually 12 hours). These types of communications satellites are particularly well suited to electronic mail (E mail) applications since they can receive messages and "store and forward" anywhere in the world in less than 12 hours.

The pervasive interest in communications satellites notwithstanding, there is a good possibility that most satellite communications will eventually be switched over to land-based (and sea-based) fiber optic networks (see Section 8.1.8.3).

8.1.3 Network Topology

The physical interconnection of networks is usually called a "topology," to correspond to the geometry of the connection scheme. There are four fundamental configurations, with combinations and "internets" (networks of networks) frequently used. The four are:

1. Star topology. The basic structure of the star topology has a central switch (see Figure 8-3) that is connected to every node. An example of a network with this topology is a single-switch-node digital PBX (private branch exchange) system. For most single-switch-node PBXs, the central node is a central switch (although sometimes circuit switch and packet switch capabilities are combined), which acts as a conduit for interconnecting nodes. This is called a "circuit switched" network. Another approach to a star topology is a "message switched" (store and forward) network. Examples of message switched networks are electronic mail and electronic bulletin board systems, where a central computer collects "messages" from users

Figure 8-2   Ground station antenna for geosynchronous satellite. (Photograph courtesy of Sandia National Laboratories.)

that can later be retrieved by other users. Security controls are appropriately embedded in the central switch of a star network.

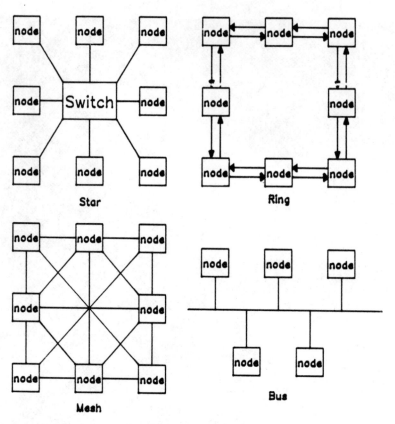

Figure 8-3   Basic network topologies.

A "tree" or "hierarchical" network (connections through progressive branchings) is topologically an internet of star networks.

2. Ring topology. A useful approach is to connect a sequence of nodes in a loop or ring (see Figure 8-3). This topology can be implemented with minimal cabling, and (if bidirectional) can continue operation even with a cable break. Logical switching can be used to bypass faulty nodes. A "synchronous" loop can be controlled by an administrative node that sends a particular control message around the loop containing a "token" (a token ring). The token strategy provides attractive response characteristics under a wide variety of load conditions. Self-generating token rings can also be implemented without an administrative node. In either case, the token "possession" is an indicator that a node has communication permission. Taking advantage of this permission, a node can write a message for

transmission, thereby "using" the token and preventing interference due to possible transmission from other nodes.

Figure 8-3 shows counterrotational ring capabilities, which provide fault tolerance enhancement. Rings may also be simple unidirectional rings. The use of the ring topology is almost always confined to LANs.

3. Mesh topology. In a mesh topology, each node can conceptually be connected directly to each other node (see Figure 8-3). This topology has integrity and routing advantages, because it is not easily subject to catastrophic failures, and because routing logic can be used to select the most efficient route through multiple nodes. For hardwire connected mesh networks, the amount of cabling is often burdensome, since each pair of communicating nodes must be connected by an individual cable. This is one of the major reasons that vehicles with complex communications requirements, such as aircraft and the space shuttle, have adopted bus communication topologies. The communication medium for the mesh topology can be either "open" (broadcast through widely dispersed EM transmission) or "closed" (confined to specific connection conduits such as cables).

4. Bus topology. The basic strategy of the bus topology is to provide a single communication conduit on which any node can place information and from which any node can retrieve information. Attachments to the bus do not (within practical limits) impact the other nodes on the bus. Similar to the case for mesh topology, the communication medium can be open or closed. A closed channel is usually used for LANs, and WANs may be open or closed. Token passing can be accomplished on buses in a manner similar to token rings (a "token bus"); however, a logical addressing algorithm must be implemented.

8.1.4 Information Formatting

Although terminals may communicate with computers on a character-by-character basis, network communications are almost always structured around transmission "blocks" (or packets). These blocks are formatted to contain a relatively large number of characters (or bits). Blocks are "framed" with start and end characters, and block transmission can be either in a continually synchronous mode or in an internally synchronous mode (information spaced regularly and contiguously following a reference position indicator). The information transmitted is digitized by representing data with bit patterns.

Character "coding" by bits usually uses ASCII (American Standard Code for Information Interchange) or EBCDIC (Extended Binary Coded Decimal Interchange Code) representation.

An efficient communication strategy for sending large amounts of information through a complex (e.g., mesh) network was developed in the early 1960s. It is called "packet switching." In this technique, the overall transmission is broken into small packets, each of which is appended with supplementary information that determines transmission identification, destination, and order of the packet in the transmission. At each network node (or switch), a routing strategy is determined for the particular packet and particular network conditions. Therefore, the packets can move through the network in a diverse pattern, each being handled independently of the others (and independently of other transmissions). At the receiving end, the sequence information associated with each packet is used to reassemble the transmission.

Routing efficiency is the main advantage of packet transmission where diverse routing algorithms are used, but there are also security advantages, in that information tapping is generally not very useful unless the tap is close enough to the source or destination that a significant portion of the message traverses the point tapped. Network integrity is also enhanced by packet transmission, because it is usually possible to route data around faulty nodes or circuits.

Covert channel potential (see Section 7.1) is a disadvantage of packet transmission. Packet headers and length provide information that could be controlled by a TH (Trojan horse).

DDN (ARPANET), Telenet, and DATAPAC are examples of packet switched networks. In 1976, the CCITT (Consultative Committee for International Telephone and Telegraph systems) adopted a packet switched transmission protocol standard, the widely used X.25.

In a "virtual circuit" operation, a "routing table" is used as a predetermined logical routing strategy. "Connectionless service" has no fixed routing constraints and no end-to-end handshakes for acknowledgment or error detection. "Datagram" services are normally connectionless.

8.1.5 Information Traffic Management

A fundamental network problem is that access between potential user-nodes must be mediated to prevent interference. This can be done in several ways. A straightforward channel access mediation technique is called "time-division multiple access" (TDMA). This is a static allocation of periods within a time frame during which each node may transmit. Interference is not a problem for TDMA systems, but efficiency may be low unless significant complexity is added. An efficiency improvement can be obtained by adding demand assignment to the protocol (TDMA/DA). This enables time allocations to be controlled dynamically in response to demand for channel capacity. "Frequency-division multiple access" (FDMA) is a similar technique that uses frequency bands instead of time slots.

Another transmission interference control technique is the ALOHA technique [2]. ALOHA transmission can be applied to satellite networks structured around a central node and a star topology. A node wishing to transmit on the network sends a packet transmission on the satellite uplink and listens for the downlink echo. About a quarter of a second following the transmission, the echo will be received by the central station and by the originating node(s). Coincidence in the time selected for transmission is detected by interfering reception of two packets from different transmitters. Both (or all) transmitters detecting interference randomly select a time delay for retransmission of the "damaged" packet. In this way, noninterfering packets are transmitted once, and interfering packets are retransmitted until interference is avoided.

An ALOHA network becomes inefficient if it is underutilized (because of wasted channel capacity) or if it is overutilized (because of retransmissions due to interference). A "slotted" ALOHA network decreases the probability of interference between packets by requiring that users transmit only at the beginning of discrete time intervals.

For compact networks (LANs), interference problems can be minimized by a technique called CSMA (carrier sense multiple access). The basic strategy is for a user node to listen to the channel for the presence of a carrier (signifying another user transmitting) before attempting to transmit. Upon carrier sensing, a randomly selected delay may be used before a retry ("nonpersistent" algorithm). Alternatively, transmission can be attempted upon loss of carrier detection ("persistent" algorithm). It is possible that two or more nodes will attempt to transmit at the same time (before any other carrier is detected), creating a "collision." Each transmitting node waits for an acknowledgment from the recipient. Lack of acknowledgment is interpreted as a collision, which requires retransmission after a randomly selected delay.

Collision detection can be incorporated to further minimize interference. Carrier sensing during transmission causes immediate cessation of transmission. This prevents wasting channel capacity, which would occur if colliding messages were each continued to completion. The name of this widely used LAN protocol is CSMA/CD (carrier sense multiple access with collision detection).

8.1.6 Information Signaling

Once a node has gained access to a network, there must be a means of representing information to be transmitted. Here, we discuss various techniques. The most basic categorization for information signaling techniques is the use of "baseband" (information coding sent directly into the channel medium) or "broadband" (information modulated onto a carrier that is compatible with the characteristics of the channel). Broadband systems are generally more complex than baseband, but the transmission distance capability is greater. It is common to extend broadband system range indefinitely by using amplifying repeaters. Broadband systems can have more flexibility than baseband, through channel assignment. Data and video signals, for example, can coexist on the same network.

From a security standpoint, broadband systems present more opportunities for an adversary, because more data are usually available on the communication medium. Also, the allocation of broadband channels allows a small overlap in frequency response characteristics, which requires careful crosstalk analysis.

Examples of commonly used baseband signaling techniques are "non-return-to-zero" (NRZ), where a change in level is distinguished from no change to provide binary information, and "Manchester II bi-phase level" (binary information represented by direction of change between levels in the center of a bit period).

Broadband systems utilize carrier modulation, which is the systematic variation of some parameter of the carrier. Digital modulation, required for computer communications applications, means that only specific values of the parameters are used. The most obvious parameters available are amplitude, frequency, and phase, which lead to three types of modulation: 1) "amplitude-shift keying" (ASK), 2) "frequency-shift keying" (FSK), and 3) "phase-shift keying" (PSK). PSK requires a phase reference value at the receiver. This is not as readily accomplished as amplitude and frequency references. The two ways in which a reference can be established are "differential PSK" (operating only on the amount of change in each phase transition) and "coherent PSK" (phase referenced to a phase-locked oscillator controlled by the incoming carrier).

8.1.7 Transmission Protocols

Transmission protocols are generally considered to be the mechanisms through which intercomputer functional communications take place. This includes most of the processing decisions that must be made. So much more is involved than the transmission of bits discussed above that bit transmission is usually neglected in protocol discussions. We have tended to do the same here by separating "information signaling" from "transmission protocol," but it should be noted that this is done only for convenience.

Embedded functions necessary to complete an accurate and useful information transfer may be arranged in a variety of ways (protocols). Many organizations have become involved in protocol work. Among these are the International Organization for Standardization (ISO), the Consultative Committee for International Telephone and Telegraph (CCITT), the Corporation for Open Systems (COS), the U.S. Department of Defense (DoD), and the Institute of Electrical and Electronics Engineers (IEEE).

8.1.7.1 The Open Systems Interconnection (OSI) Model

Partly to provide guidance on how to select information-handling protocols, and partly to provide a path toward standardizing network communications for possible interconnection, ISO began development of a protocol model in 1977. The model, first published in 1979, is the ISO Reference Model for Open System Interconnection (frequently called the "OSI model").

The OSI model framework is structured around "layers" of services, each of which is passed to another layer within the network function. As each data entity is received by a transmission layer, it adds the appropriate data for the service being performed (a "wrapper" on the received package). This is usually accomplished by adding a "header" and/or a "trailer" of information. The result is nested headers and trailers representing information about layer services. At the receiving end, the information is sequentially "unwrapped."

As Figure 8-4 shows, the OSI layers connect a source to a destination through seven source layers, a transmission medium, and seven destination layers, possibly with intermediate nodes. The function of the seven layers is described below, in order of the numbers assigned by the OSI model.

1. Physical layer. The physical layer has the responsibility for mediating direct access to the transmission medium. It includes information modulation techniques. Traffic management

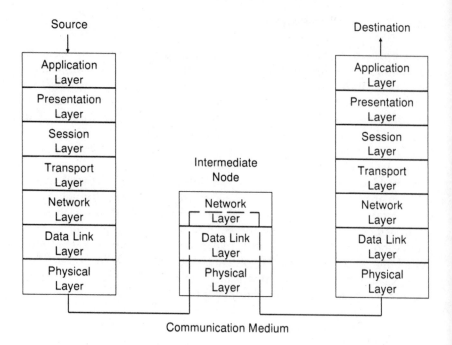

Figure 8-4   OSI model layers.

functions such as token ring, token bus, and CSMA/CD all operate at this level.

2. Data Link layer. The data link layer is responsible for enhancing the transmission quality of node-to-node data transfers. This can include checksums or error-correction, and synchronization features. "Framing" is also accomplished here. Link (node-to-node) encryption, usually done in hardware, is implemented in this layer. IEEE standards incorporating the functions of the first two layers are 802.3 (CSMA/CD), 802.4 (token bus), and 802.5 (token ring).

3. Network layer. The network layer is the controller that decides where to route data (e.g., toward the transmission medium or toward the user). It provides switching and addressing functions in a packet network. This is the highest layer involved in intermediate node functions. The security implications of correct routing are obvious.

   The network layer supports both intranetwork (communications services) and internetwork (internet) functions. The latter function allows "gateways" to be configured for translating from the lower protocol layers of one network to another.

4. Transport layer. The transport layer provides end-to-end inter-process communications facilities. This may involve multiplexing a number of independent message streams over a single connection, and segmenting data for matching the requirements of the network layer. End-to-end (source to destination) encryption is usually implemented in software within this layer.

5. Session layer. The session layer manages the overall connection through the network during a continuous user activity and provides for recovery in case of disconnection. Security depends on the process initiation and maintenance of correct connectivity.

6. Presentation layer. The presentation layer manipulates data syntax (code or format conversions such as ASCII, EBCDIC, and BCD) to convert between syntax that will be useful to a user and syntax that will be effective on the network.

7. Application layer. The application layer provides for specific applications or services to a user by mapping system commands (e.g., electronic mail messages, data file transfer, CAD/CAM/CAE entries) into a high-level network function.

The lower three layers (layers one through three) are usually implemented in hardware. Most of the necessary features in these layers are provided by widely used networks (e.g., Ethernet or Telenet). As was shown in Figure 8-4, these are the only layers involved in passing information through an intermediate network node. The upper four layers are usually provided by a host machine connected to the network, and therefore are usually implemented in software.

The security applications that fit within the OSI model architecture have been specifically addressed by the ISO [49]. Included are the differences between link encryption and end-to-end encryption (see below). However, security measures specifically needed in end systems (installations and organizations), including covert channel protection, are not addressed.

There are important distinctions between link encryption and end-to-end encryption. Link encryption means a separate encryption process for each node-to-node transmission link. Full text, including headers and routing information, can be encrypted on the links. This process involves only the first two OSI layers. At each intermediate node, decryption and reencryption takes place, thereby exposing the information to some node processes. End-to-end encryption (including packet or datagram encryption) protects information from source to destination. This may be essential if the source node and/or the destination node require protection within intermediate nodes because of concern over proprietary or sensitive data exposure or because the intermediate nodes may have less robust security features than desired.

End-to-end encryption is generally performed at the higher layers (e.g., the transport layer) so that address information necessary at intermediate nodes will not be packaged within the encrypted data. This usually requires software encryption. In case of misrouting, there will be no information compromise using end-to-end encryption.

Traffic analysis protection must be considered for end-to-end encryption. The intent of traffic analysis protection is to mask the frequency, length, and origin destination patterns of the message traffic [57]. If encryption were performed in the presentation layer, an analyst could determine which presentation, session, and transport entities could be associated with a particular traffic pattern. Performing encryption at the transport layer would limit the information association by not identifying higher-level entities. Additional protection can be provided by continually or randomly flooding the communication channel with dummy traffic. The price paid is lost channel efficiency.

8.1.7.2 The Integrated-Services Digital Network (ISDN)
The CCITT, an arm of the International Telecommunication Union of the United Nations, promotes the Integrated-Services Digital Network (ISDN). The intent of the ISDN standard is to allow a variety of services (telephone, computer terminal, facsimile machine, video display unit, alarm system) to be entered into a single interface. ISDN is intended to improve the economics of local and long-distance communications services. The OSI model is included as part of the specification. Standards for data transfer rates are defined at frequencies including 16, 64, 144, 384, 1544, and 2048 kbps (thousand bits per second) for various uses.

Supporting efforts are mainly in the U.S. and Europe, with Japan pursuing a similar and contributory "information network system" (INS).

8.1.7.3 The Corporation for Open Systems
The Corporation for Open Systems (COS) was formed in 1985 with several objectives related to protocol standardization. These include the encouragement of stand-

ardized implementations of the OSI and ISDN models. COS is a consortium of manufacturers and users of computer and communications equipment, funded through dues paid annually by each member. The inclusion of users is a key feature of the organization. Both technical personnel and upper management personnel contribute. An attractive benefit of membership may prove to be the prestige of COS testing and certification of member products [10].

8.1.7.4 Transmission Control Protocol/Internet Protocol (TCP/IP) Since the early 1970s, the U.S. DoD has supported substantial research at Stanford University and elsewhere in TCP/IP protocol for MILNET, Internet, and other networks associated with its ARPANET system. Many vendors offer TCP/IP equipment. Deficiencies in network management facilities and for security authentication in TCP/IP, as well as a desire to take advantage of standardized commercial products, have now resulted in the DoD's movement toward the OSI model.

8.1.8 Transmission Media

The medium through which information is transmitted from node to node on a network has both functional and security importance. Physical security measures (see Chapter 3) include enclosing and alarming the distribution system (locked junction boxes, underground cabling with locked access panels, protected (conduit) distribution systems, etc.). Some of the salient features of transmission media are described here.

8.1.8.1 Twisted Pair Wiring Typical twisted pair wiring consists of two small (22- to 26-gauge) copper wires encased in insulation and twisted together. The purpose of the twist is to cause cancellation of the magnetic fields that couple voltage from interfering sources onto the wires. The voltage coupled into one twist "half-period" is cancelled by a nearly equal and opposite voltage coupled into the adjacent twist half-period. Twisted pair wiring can be made relatively immune to more forms of interference by differential signaling or by shielding (with single-point grounding or double shielding) the twisted pair. Twisted pair wiring is easy to install and convenient to service. It is also easy to tap. The main performance limitation is rate of increase of loss (due to high capacitance) with increasing frequency.

If shielding is used between the wires of a twisted pair, the configuration is capable of carrying 10 Mbps (million bits per second) transmissions over limited distances (a few kilometers). Over short distances (a few hundred feet), it may be possible to use unshielded twisted pair wiring at 10 Mbps [4]. Twisted pair wiring is used almost exclusively for baseband transmission.

Twisted pair wires are used to connect telephone instruments, data terminals, and computers to PBX switches. However, most standard telephone circuits are four-wire (quad) untwisted cable, and consequently, quad performance is not as good as twisted pair. Standard telephone circuits have about three kHz bandwidth. Specially conditioned circuits are available at higher frequencies. For example, the commonly used "T1" channel supports 1.544 Mbps, with repeaters placed nominally every 6000 feet.

8.1.8.2 Coaxial Cable Coaxial cable (coax) is almost always configured as a copper inner conductor surrounded by insulation, which is in turn surrounded by a coaxial shield. An outer insulation cover is usually utilized. Coaxial cable is popular for local area networks because of its low attenuation and its ability to handle wide ranges of frequencies without degradation. Also, it is optimized to provide high propagation velocity. The wide frequency range is useful for both baseband and broadband systems. The high propagation velocity is especially important in CSMA/CD systems, where interference must be sensed as quickly as possible.

Coaxial cable is generally more expensive than twisted pair, and it is more expensive to install because of its greater bulk. Signal propagation distances can exceed a kilometer in baseband applications, and can exceed 10 kilometers in broadband applications.

8.1.8.3 Optical Fibers Optical fibers (sometimes simply called fibers) are becoming widely used in networks because of high performance and security features. They are less bulky than coax and have much higher bandwidth than twisted pair or coax. Ground current and electromagnetic interference effects and emanations effects are eliminated. Fibers are difficult to tap. Signal attenuation is a consideration, because a fiber transmission system is limited to LANs unless repeaters are used. Installation, splicing, and connector termination attachment require care, skill, and special tools.

Three basic types of fibers are used. Single-mode step-index fiber has an extremely small core (8–10 μm), intended to carry a single mode of polarized light. This type has very high bandwidth and very low attenuation. Multimode step-index fiber (approximately 50-μm

core) allows several modes and has more limited bandwidth than single-mode fiber. For this reason, its use is limited. Multimode graded-index fiber (approximately 60-μm core) has an index of refraction that falls off gradually from the center of the fiber toward the outside. It is the most commonly used fiber for LANs, having high bandwidth, low attenuation, and multimode capability.

An important contributor to the acceptance of optical fiber transmission systems has been the recent development of fibers with very low transmission loss. Fiber losses can now be as low as about 0.1 dB/km (single mode at 1300 nm), a factor of 100 improvement in a little more than a decade. Fiber communication systems have bit transmission rates of up to the Gbps range with very high bandwidth, bit-error rates (BER) as low as 10^{-12}, several kilometers distance between repeaters, and mean time before failure (MTBF) of more than a million hours. The outer diameter (including cladding) of fibers used is usually 125 μm (comparable to the diameter of a human hair). Cable bundles of hundreds of fibers are only a few centimeters in diameter. In many applications, fiber transmission systems are comparable in cost to coax systems. Fiber cables can be pulled into ducts as coax replacement.

Optical fibers degrade in a radiation environment by "darkening" to light transmission. Specially treated "rad-hard" fibers are less vulnerable, but all fibers are susceptible. For this reason, fiber communications links may not be appropriate in some applications, such as in the vicinity of particle accelerators.

Fiber optic LANs handle much higher data rates than cable LANs. In order to provide standards guidance for data rates and other parameters, the American National Standards Institute (ANSI) has worked on a fiber distributed data interface standard (known as FDDI). The standard FDDI data transmission rate is 100 Mbps, and a token ring mediation strategy is specified.

8.1.8.4 Electromagnetic Transmission Optical transmission through fibers is actually a form of electromagnetic transmission. The transmission of data electromagnetically is necessary for fiber networks and satellite-based networks, but is also used for land-based networks through open transmission (free-space transmission between buildings, or, in some cases, intrabuilding transmission through building materials). Electromagnetic frequencies used range from the kHz region through laser frequencies (approximately 10^{15} Hz). Powerful laser or microwave sources are usually used for open electromagnetic systems.

8.2 COMMUNICATIONS SECURITY THREATS

The physical span of networks creates a number of unique problems. The larger area requires more extensive physical protection, provides more availability for intercepters or jammers, results in more places from which TEMPEST emanations may occur, and assures more potential diversity of user backgrounds and their controlling security policies. Dialup networks introduce the potential that access can be attempted from most parts of the world. Networks traversing international boundaries usually accrue problems in coordinating laws, policies, and protocols. For these reasons, it is useful to take a specific look at communications security threats. These threats generally can be categorized as interception, alteration, jamming, and loss of integrity (intentionally or accidentally caused). Improper access attempts (including those of "hackers") are treated separately in the next section.

8.2.1 Information Interception

The interception of information by tapping is a common concern on an unencrypted network. As will be discussed in the encryption section, tapping is sometimes a threat (although of lesser importance) on encrypted networks. Tapping is conceivable within buildings, on overhead lines, or on underground lines (see Section 6.4). Direct-connection taps provide the greatest signal for the adversary, but remote inductive taps, which are harder to locate, are frequently feasible. As a security measure in addition to physical protection (Chapter 3), signal level detectors and/or standing wave interference detectors can be used to provide an alarm signal upon detecting a reduction in received energy. This is useful mainly on broadband systems [11], including fiber optics.

Electromagnetic signals can be intercepted with relatively small antennas, and the antennas can be easily camouflaged within electromagnetically transparent enclosures (e.g., fiberglass or wood). The source of interest may be an intended transmission (microwave or satellite link) or an unintended emanation (TEMPEST). Even intended transmissions on a closed network may be intercepted under some circumstances. For example, coaxial cable, although shielded, may still leak rf energy. Potential sources for leaks include faults due to damage or deterioration in the shield or in the connector mating configuration. Although some energy passes through shields at an attenuated level, most shielding provides sufficient attenuation that this form of leakage is insignificant [11]. Twisted pair is a medium that results in more serious emanation problems.

8.2.2   Alteration, Spoofing, and Denial of Service

Interception is a passive attack in the sense that information is not altered. Active attacks can be used to modify information, replay sequences, or to take advantage of another person's security access (masquerading). These types of attacks, described in Chapters 4 and 7, include using idle time on a terminal, intercepting a "sign-off" and continuing the session, and sending a valid user a fake message indicating that the session is being terminated by the host. The latter two attacks are called "masquerades," because one network device is disguising itself as another network device.

Satellite links are also subject to illegal resource appropriation through "bootlegging" [5]. Bootleggers operate through satellite transponders by utilizing the fringes of the transponder frequency response spectrum. The intent is to avoid any detectable effect on the authorized satellite service, while obtaining enough transponder energy to complete a transmission link.

Another important form of network spoofing is based on modems having "autoanswer" capability. The threat is that a network not intended to receive dialup calls can be remotely accessed by telephone lines, with no obvious external evidence. The method used is to connect the autoanswer modem between the telephone line and a line to the nondialup network. This connection is especially easy to hide within an A-B switch box that can connect a terminal to either the nondialup network or to the telephone line. The threat requires either participation by an insider or inside penetration. The motivation may be expediency of computer access for an authorized individual, whether or not the security implications are appreciated. One partial safeguard is to restrict the use of modems to those in which the autoanswer capability has been disabled. User education and motivation regarding this threat is essential.

User awareness and administrative control also play a role in preventing "interconnection" of partitioned networks through "hand-carried" software. Physically partitioned networks may be subject to internetwork transfers if users transport software (e.g., tapes or diskettes) between networks. This vulnerability can result in the insertion of a TH (Trojan horse) or a virus, for example, into a network thought to be immune to outside threats.

A network can be subjected to denial-of-service attack. The objective is to make the network, or a portion of the network, unusable. This can be done in many ways discussed in previous chapters, such as a software virus, sabotage, and improper actions by inside authorized personnel. A unique denial-of-service threat to networks is jamming, the next topic.

8.2.3 Jamming

Intentional disruption of a network link is a threat for which encryption can provide no protection. Satellite and microwave links are especially vulnerable because it is difficult to find a jammer that has extensive areas from which to attack. Sophisticated jamming sources can attempt to evade location determination, which is sometimes done using directional beam scanners. The jammer evasion technique is to selectively transmit into a sidelobe of the scanner antenna beam. There are a number of ways, however, to provide protection against jamming. Three of the most important are frequency hopping, spread spectrum processing, and antenna pattern nulling.

All three of these techniques force the power required for effective jamming to increase, potentially making jamming infeasible. Frequency hopping depends on a pseudorandom sequence of frequency selections, the sequence followed by the transmitter and receiver, but unknown to the jammer. The aim is to force the jammer to dilute its energy over a wide frequency spectrum, while the authorized communicators process at any one time only the selected frequencies. Spread-spectrum processing is similar to frequency hopping, except that phase varies pseudorandomly. Antenna pattern nulling requires high frequencies and switchable directivity for high directional definition and beam steering. The intent is to move the receiving antenna pattern geometrically so that a null (low gain) is directed toward the jammer, while usable antenna pattern (high gain) is directed toward the authorized ground station.

8.2.4 Accidental Loss of Network Integrity

In 1988, a fire in an Illinois local/regional telephone switching center caused one of the worst public telephone outages ever [12]. About 35,000 local circuits went down, more than 110,000 long-distance lines in a 20-mile area were cut, and 50,000 data circuits were severed. Some networks were disrupted for nearly a month. The massive and prolonged outages illustrate the threat to computer network integrity due to accidents or natural occurrences. Similar central switch disasters have occurred previously, and a major New England central office was shut down after the Illinois disaster [53].

Before the 1984 divestiture of AT&T, telephone lines were routed according to government guidelines on integrity [13], at least partly to enhance chances for survivability in case of war. Integrity through routing remains a network concern. These observations illustrate the importance of robust networks.

Satellites are included among integrity concerns. More than 7000 pieces of orbiting debris are now being tracked by the U.S. Space Command, and many more objects are too small to track [14]. More than 300 tracked objects are near the geosynchronous band. Communications satellites have actually been moved to avoid potential damaging collisions. Intentional attacks by adversaries using anti-satellite weapons would be a threat in a wartime communications environment.

In addition to resistance to failures, it is also important that recovery be considered. Threats to restoring operation include lack of maintenance resources (parts, skilled personnel, money) and lack of contingency planning (see Chapter 3).

8.3 DIALUP SECURITY AND HACKERS

Dialup network connections can be made directly from a terminal or computer modem (modulator/demodulator) to standard telephone lines, or an "acoustic coupler" can be used to signal through standard telephone hand sets. Networks that allow dialup access offer users the convenience of connecting from any location where there is a telephone line. Unfortunately, this same opportunity is available to unauthorized persons. This section will address the types of problems these persons represent for dialup networks, and the types of protection that can be employed against the threat.

8.3.1 Hackers

"Hacker" was once a term of admiration. It was easy for people (especially students, who had more opportunity) to become addicted to the power afforded by computers. Many of these people would spend long hours exploring the capabilities of computers and searching for ingenious ways to achieve unusual accomplishments. They were called "hackers."

As personal computers became available to more and more people, incidents of unauthorized accesses, data modification and destruction, and system disruption occurred through some of the same techniques that were once admired in hackers. Although probably unfair, the conventional understanding of the term hacker is now largely associated with these forms of misbehavior.

One of the early hacker incidents was the penetration of two networks, one in the United States and one in Canada, by the "Dalton Gang" ([15], also mentioned in Chapter 1). The fact that the leader of the participants was a 13-year-old eighth grader illustrated that very young people were among those who could assemble the equipment and knowledge to mount a threat to computer networks. The penetration was aided by "inside information" from the brother of one of the participants. None of the Dalton gang was prosecuted.

Because the "414" incident ([16], also mentioned in Chapter 1) occurred shortly after a popular movie portraying a hacker who nearly initiated a nuclear attack, and because one of the penetrations was at a national laboratory that developed nuclear weapons, the public became concerned about whether computer security was good enough for national security information. Although none of the computers penetrated had data that were classified or represented any threat to national security, the expense to the national laboratory and to the other organizations involved (for investigation and response) was substantial. The perpetrators took advantage of well-known standard passwords that were distributed on installation tapes and that had not been changed.

"Teens Got Pentagon Codes, Computer 'Hackers' 'Moved Satellites'," according to a headline of a major U.S. newspaper in 1985. Although a more accurate accounting [17] showed that no satellites were moved and no Pentagon information was compromised, the youths had bypassed telephone toll charges, had an unauthorized computer penetration, and had ordered merchandise using purloined credit card information.

In 1987, a group of West German hackers demonstrated in a widely publicized series of incidents [18] that geographical distance provides no protection. A variety of European and U.S. corporate and government computers were penetrated, including the U.S. National Aeronautics and Space Administration (NASA) Space Physics Analysis Network. Similar less publicized incidents have been occurring for several years. One U.S. national laboratory has detected intrusion attempts from several European countries and from the Orient [19].

A West German attacker was monitored during his activities in order to obtain information on the techniques used [19]. The intruder used commonly known (to hacker bulletin board users) security weaknesses in standard operating systems and tried well-known passwords that are often successful (not removed after installation or commonly selected by users). An interesting attack used was to download a file of one-way transformed passwords from a computer with an operating system that does not protect its transformation routine. A dictionary input to the transformation routine was then used to search for matching transformed passwords. Some successes were noted.

Some hackers express belief that breaking into computer systems is not harmful and may in fact be helpful in identifying security weaknesses for system personnel. It also may be claimed that avenues utilized should not exist on systems where security is a responsibility. One might wonder if the same reasoning should justify entry into an unlocked home, but a difference is perceived (by some hackers) between violation of personal property and violation of corporate property. Few security personnel and system administrators agree with this view. They are more likely to believe that a difference in risk of apprehension and punishment is more responsible for the perception that home break-ins differ from computer break-ins.

Sometimes the struggle between hackers and security personnel becomes extreme. The FBI, perhaps feeling frustrated over lack of legal coverage for dealing with hackers, has struck back at them by obtaining federal search warrants and seizing computers [17,20]. A correspondent who expressed contempt for the activities of hackers was deluged with hate mail and threatening telephone calls. He was also victimized by a computer-based appropriation of his credit card numbers [21].

8.3.2 Hacker Bulletin Boards

An electronic bulletin board is a computer system that stores messages furnished by users for retrieval by other users. The bulletin board computer is typically networked to a large number of users, usually through dialup lines. Electronic bulletin boards are not difficult or expensive to implement. Commercial bulletin board software can be purchased for $100 to $500 [22].

Hacker bulletin boards are electronic bulletin boards that are intended to spread information useful to hacking activities (e.g., software routines, dialup telephone numbers, system passwords, user account identification, telephone toll charge bypass techniques, security weaknesses) [23]. Some of the software programs commonly available are autodial routines (systematic telephone number sequencing in search of modem tones), automatic password generators (systematic sequence of letter combinations or words), and copy protection bypass routines. Some hacker electronic bulletin boards have restricted membership, and for these, background investigations may be conducted of potential network users.

One investigator [54] found a hacker bulletin board that contained a Pentagon computer phone number, the phone number for a computer at a U.S. Air Force base in Alaska (including what was claimed to be a valid password to the computer), and various data on a long list of U.S. companies.

8.3.3 Dialup Protection Alternatives

The protection of computer dialup lines, and network communications lines in general, can be provided in a variety of ways. The most widely used of these are shown as an alternatives tree [24] in Figure 8-5. The techniques fall into two classes: one-end alternatives and two-end alternatives, depending upon whether the protection can be provided at only one end of a communications link, or must be provided by cooperating devices, one at one end and one at the other. One-end alternatives can be provided at the host end or at the user end; two-end alternatives can involve "handshaking" authentication between a user-carried device (e.g., a security code generator) or hardware associated with a terminal, and host processing. Encryption and authentication are a special form of two-ended protection involving cooperating devices that obscure the information being exchanged from unauthorized observers.

"User devices," indicated in Figure 8-5, are most often implemented as security code generators (SCGs, described in Section 6.2). "Encryption and authentication" will be discussed later in this chapter. "Terminal devices" (a two-end approach) and "user-end alternatives" (a one-end approach) both involve terminal-end hardware that restricts user activity. The one-end user alternative is usually a "security modem" that incorporates call screening security functions

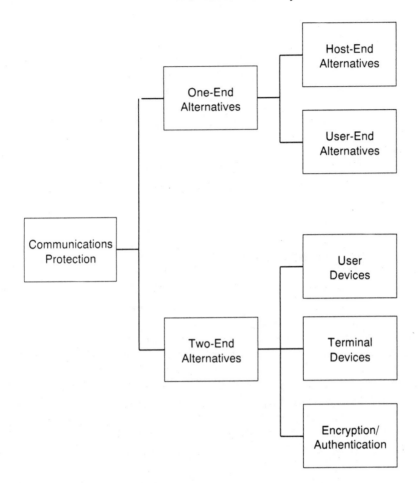

Figure 8-5   Communications protection alternatives.

into a single-user modem. The security furnished is not substantial, because the user-end hardware can be bypassed. The two-end terminal devices normally work on a challenge/response basis. This is a method of authenticating a particular terminal, at which, or within which, there is hardware that performs functions similar in most respects to those of SCGs (see Section 6.2).

The "host-end alternatives" include passwords, discussed previously, and "port protection devices," a term that includes callback modems and call-intercept modems (both discussed below).

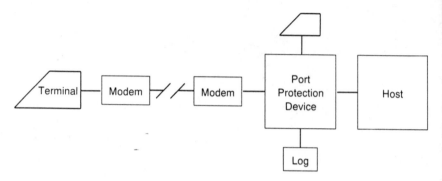

Figure 8-6   Port protection device.

8.3.4 Port Protection Devices

A port protection device (PPD) is intended to provide a host-end security barrier against dialup access attempts. The choice of capabilities available depends on the amount of security required, the flexibility and user convenience desired, the user throughput needed, and the size of the system to be protected (number of dialup ports).

The generic operation of PPDs is illustrated in Figure 8-6. A dialup connection is made to the PPD instead of to the host computer. The PPD provides an intercept function that requires additional security checks before connection to the host. Incorrect security data result in a disconnect after a small number of attempts.

The operation of PPDs is categorized into either "callback devices" (that disconnect the caller and return a call to the expected number) or "computer sentry" devices (that give neither a connection nor a modem tone until security information has been entered). Callback devices are intended to prevent access attempts from unauthorized locations. Computer sentry devices are intended to eliminate the modem tone (which most autodialer routines detect) and to add a security barrier, such as an additional password, prior to connection to a host computer. This additional barrier is usually also incorporated into callback devices. The PPD functions necessarily add time to the user activities.

Another distinction in the operation of PPDs is between analog (capable of accepting information entered on tone-dial telephones) or digital (capable of accepting ASCII information entered from terminals). As described below, callback devices usually operate as digital devices for accepting information and as analog devices for placing calls.

Analog devices are located in front of the modem (as opposed to the location shown in Figure 8-6). Some furnish synthesized voice messages to the caller; some are silent. Security checks such as passwords must be constructed from the 12 tones available (10 numbers, #, and *). Some analog devices allow code entry without using tone-dial telephones by recognizing voice response to synthesized voice prompts or by incorporating circuitry to enable acceptance of terminal entries.

Digital devices are located behind the modem (as shown in Figure 8-6). These PPDs depend on information entered from a computer terminal. This gives a larger population for passwords.

Since the PPDs must store data about users for use in security checks, they have some of the same requirements that a host would have for password security. The memory for security data must be nonvolatile, it should not be easily accessible physically, and system privileges should be required for access. In addition to password/PIN data, callback devices must store telephone numbers. A number of devices also allow time windows to be specified as a further access control measure. Figure 8-6 indicates a method (typically using a terminal) of entering data and a method of recording activity for audit purposes.

The recording of audit data is an important feature. Audit data can include successful and unsuccessful access attempts, access times, and activity durations. In addition to security scrutiny, audit data also provides system utilization data and telephone toll charge data. The latter is often necessary in order to compensate for telephone charges that are automatically billed to the unintended party. For example, administrators of a computer using callback mode may want to charge users for telephone connection time. Or an organization using computer sentry devices may wish to absorb telephone costs rather than expecting employees to pay charges for doing company work away from the company.

An obvious concern about a callback system is that users may be traveling on a somewhat unpredictable schedule, so authorized telephone numbers for callback may be unknown. There are several ways to address the problem [25]. Most callback devices provide for disabling the callback step for prescribed users. Some have a capability for allowing the user to enter the callback number from a remote location upon proper authentication.

An economical benefit of callback devices [26] is that they allow automatic options for call routing through the least expensive service available at the time. For example, a selection of services may be available at a central site. The least expensive service that is not saturated at the time could be selected. In addition, by pooling all charges against one location, it is frequently possible to obtain volume discounts.

There have been instances of callers reaching a line just as a callback dial was to begin, thereby connecting the incoming call to the host. (This is similar to the experience almost all of us have had in reaching a dialed party's phone just as they pick it up to place a call.) Protective measures can be taken to avoid this vulnerability. One is to dedicate a number of lines for incoming calls and code verification and a larger number of different lines for outgoing calls and computer use.

The availability of callforwarding has created another minor problem for callback operation. A host placing a call can dial an authorized number and reach an unauthorized forwarding number with no indication that the call has been forwarded. From an adversarial viewpoint, the requirements are that an authorized user's telephone (or telephone line) be used for forwarding to a number under the adversary's control. Also, in order to take advantage of the authorized user's passwords or other security credentials, either information would have to be obtained by tapping, or the user's log-on session would have to precede the callback dial. In the latter case, the user would have an indication that the callback operation was not successful. If the user were alert to the security implications, contacting a security administrator could help identify the adversary.*

The costs of PPDs are in the range of $500 to $1500 per port for callback devices that accommodate one line or a small number of lines [25,27]. Computer sentry devices are less expensive. Systems that handle a large number of lines cost from $250 to $850 per port.

8.4 ENCRYPTION AND CRYPTANALYSIS

Encryption techniques are used to safeguard information while it is stored within a network node or while it is in transit across communications media between nodes. Protection within a node is generally the less demanding of the two applications, because the

---

*   Although call tracing is still not trivial, it is now less tedious. Modern equipment, which can be put on line with proper authority, can provide immediate real-time traces.

confined nature of the node facilitates physical protective measures. For transmission between nodes, there is generally substantial opportunity for data interception, so encryption techniques that provide security in the communications environment are very important to network security.

8.4.1 Background

Encryption is a term that is commonly used to refer to the science of how information can be disguised so as to be conveniently recovered by authorized personnel and highly resistant to recovery by unauthorized personnel. This general subject is more correctly defined as "cryptology" [30], a word derived from the Greek *kryptós* (hidden) and *lógos* (word).

Cryptology includes "cryptography" (techniques for disguising information), a word derived from *kryptós* and *gráphein* (to write). Also included as part of cryptology is "cryptanalysis" (adversarial deduction of intelligence from encrypted text), a word derived from *kryptós* and *analýein* (to undo). Cryptography is synonymous with the formal definition of encryption. As shown in Figure 8-7, encryption is used to convert a message ("plaintext" or "clear text") into a "cryptogram" or "ciphertext," or a "cipher." An "encryption key" is almost always used in the encryption process in order to allow (periodic or aperiodic) changes in the process and/or to allow secrecy, even if the encryption algorithm is known to adversaries. An algorithm for encryption and decryption is called a "cryptosystem."

A "decryption key" is used in "decryption." The decryption key is the same as the encryption key in a "symmetric" or "single-key" encryption system. The keys are different (and one cannot be easily derived from the other by an adversary) in an "asymmetric" ("two-key" or "public key") system. The cryptogram must resist cryptanalysis.

A "cipher" is distinguished from a "code" by virtue of the secrecy implications. A code is a representation of information in some different form for purposes other than secrecy. Examples are ASCII (a group of bits representing alphanumeric characters), error-protection codes (representations of information that provide protection against the effects of random bit changes), and programming statements (higher "language" representations of computer control signals). A cipher depends on the representation being secret, most often through key secrecy, and sometimes through algorithm secrecy. A keyless one-way transformation is generally considered to be neither

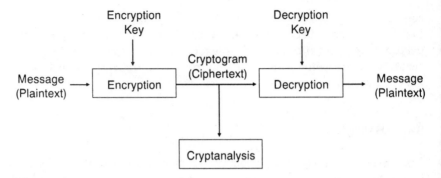

Figure 8-7   Basic cryptology terms.

a cipher nor a code, since it is not intended to allow recovery of the input information.

Although secret encryption algorithms are used in some applications, there are reasons for making algorithms public. One reason is that guaranteed secrecy of the algorithm is impossible. As time goes by, the danger of a compromise increases. Also, as personnel privy to the algorithm details leave the organizational environment within which the algorithm exists, they may be less motivated to protect the algorithm secrecy. Those who depend on secrecy of the algorithm can never be sure that the algorithm has not been compromised.

Another benefit of not protecting an encryption algorithm is that, if made public, the algorithm is exposed to a large community that can scrutinize it for weaknesses. The possibility of discovering security flaws in encryption algorithms is a strong motivator for encouraging thorough examination by cryptologists.

Two techniques are considered basic to encryption: transposition and substitution. Transposition is a reordering or permutation of the information "symbols" (e.g., alphabetic letters). Substitution is a replacement of the symbols with different symbols. During permutation, the symbols retain their identities but lose their position. During substitution, the symbols lose their identities but retain their positions. Combinations of transposition and substitution are common. Transposition and substitution need not be based on a tabular definition. They can be accomplished through mathematical algorithms.

The transformation of a group of message bits directly into a group of cipher bits is called a "block cipher" operation. Combining the transformations of transposition and substitution to produce ciphertext is called a "product cipher." Where a block product cipher uses transposition and substitution alternately and iteratively recirculates the output of the transposition/substitution pair for "rounds" of combined transformations, the operation is called a "recirculating block product cipher."

Historical evidence shows [30] that encryption techniques were used at least as far back as the early Egyptians, Hebrews, Babylonians, and Assyrians. The Spartans encrypted military communications, as did the Romans. An Arab encyclopedia written in 1412 contained a discussion of encryption.

Cryptology is an important national security issue. The Walker espionage incident (see Chapter 4) demonstrated the strategic importance of military communications security. Forewarning of terrorist activities is sometimes possible due to decrypted intelligence [33]. Certainly, cryptology has an important role in computer communications security.

8.4.2 Cryptanalysis

Cryptanalysis results have a long history of success that has far exceeded most people's expectations. In World War I, the outcomes of the Battle of Tannenburg and the battle for Paris were directly affected by intelligence derived from cryptanalysis of encrypted German messages. The United States entered World War I because of a decrypted message [31]. Isolationist sentiments were strong enough to keep the United States out of the war until the German foreign minister sent the encrypted "Zimmerman telegram," instructing his ambassador in Mexico that Germany's objective was to reach an agreement with Mexico as an ally in the war, and that "the lost territory in Texas, New Mexico, and Arizona" would be returned to Mexico. The effect was substantial, and the United States entered the war.

The Japanese were victimized in conference negotiations by a U.S. cryptanalysis break in 1921. This may have contributed to their attack on Pearl Harbor 20 years later. It certainly spurred their work on powerful rotor and telephone stepping switch encryption machines. However, most of the ciphers generated by the new equipment, typified by the "Purple" cipher machine, were broken by the United States.

In World War II, the Battle of Midway was won at least partly because U.S. cryptanalysts decrypted the Japanese plans for order of attack and also learned of a Japanese diversionary action. The architect of the Pearl Harbor attack, Admiral Yamamoto, was killed in the Solomon Islands as a result of his itinerary being decrypted, which allowed his plane to be located and shot down.

British World War II cryptanalysis effort (Chapter 1) was also beneficial in minimizing casualties during battles with the Germans. At least 70 German submarines were sunk during World War II because message decryption revealed their positions [32].

Given ciphertext, cryptanalysis approaches depend upon 1) some standard constraints that normally are imposed, and 2) free thinking and ingenuity. The standard constraints lead to four general classes of cryptanalysis techniques: "traffic analysis," "ciphertext-only attack," "known-plaintext attack," and "chosen-plaintext attack."

Traffic analysis is used where successful decryption cannot be achieved or where a decryption effort is not judged feasible. A lesser level of information still may be available from the amount of communications traffic to particular locations, the times of communications, and the observable conditions that can be coordinated with communications. Standard ways to combat traffic analysis are to use obfuscation strategies (make communications appear random) or to send constant data traffic, even if much of it is meaningless.

Ciphertext-only attack is the weakest position a cryptanalyst can have short of being confined to traffic analysis. The material available is the intercepted ciphertext, and usually some general knowledge about the communications system and operating procedures.

A known-plaintext attack requires that substantial amounts of plaintext and ciphertext be known, enabling study of the properties of the transformation used. Some of the plaintext may actually be "postulated," based on common assumptions. For example, computer sessions may commonly include the prompt: "Enter Password," letters commonly end with "Sincerely yours," etc.

Cryptanalysis becomes easier if one can cause known plaintext to be processed by the cryptosystem and can obtain the results. The procedure is called the chosen-plaintext attack. This was the technique described in the previous section used by a West German hacker to discover passwords.

Most major cryptanalysis breaks have come through the application of ingenuity and insight. One of the major reasons that cryptanalysis has been so effective is that cryptosystems may be designed based on one set of principles, and a cryptanalyst may discover another approach that effectively bypasses those principles.

Some fundamental understanding of this problem can be gained by considering some simple illustrative examples.

1. An elementary cryptosystem is constructed by shifting each alphabetic character forward in the alphabet K positions (wrapping around from Z to A), where K is the encryption key. This is widely known as a "Caesar cipher," because it was actually used for military communications by Julius Caesar (with K fixed at three!) [34]. An example cipher is:

    LZWJW AK FG GLZWJ DSFYMSYW TML XJWFUZ

    The potential task for an adversary who knows that a Caesar cipher has been used, but does not know the key, is to systematically try each of the 26 possible keys until a meaningful message can be read. Assuming English language, the mean number of tries before succeeding would be 13. However, a cryptanalyst would not have to work that hard. Notice that the Caesar cipher preserves "distance" (alphabetic sequence difference) between letters. That is, if A and C are put into a Caesar cipher, the corresponding ciphertext letters will be distance two apart, since A and C are distance two apart. This feature can be applied to short words in order to rapidly narrow down the potential keys. For example, consider the first two-letter word of the example cipher, AK. Since A and K are separated by distance 10, the cleartext input is also separated by distance 10. All two-letter words having distance 10 between the letters are conveniently displayed by two alphabetic sequences that are distance 10 apart, as shown in Table 8-1.

    Since the only English word in the list is "IS," the most probable key is 18 (I replaced by A, and S replaced by K, both differing by 18 alphabet positions). Aligning two alphabetic sequences shifted by 18 positions, we obtain:

    THERE IS NO OTHER LANGUAGE BUT FRENCH.

    This illustrates how a cryptanalyst may take advantage of a property not considered by the cryptographer.

2. Ciphers can easily be constructed to avoid the distance-preserving property of the Caesar cipher. Also, by removing the ordering constraint, there are 26! (more than 10^{26}) possible keys instead of 26. However, these ciphers have the same representation for a letter each time it is used, and are therefore easy to break by noting single-letter frequency distributions [34]. For example, "E" occurs about 13% of the time in the

Table 8-1   Distance-10 words.

A K	N X
B L	O Y
C M	P Z
D N	Q A
E O	R B
F P	S C
G Q	T D
H R	U E
I S	V F
J T	W G
KU	X H
L V	Y I
M W	Z J

English language. "T" occurs about 9%, "A" and "O" about 8%, etc. By matching the frequencies of occurrence of letters in ciphertext (and possibly including frequencies of digrams, trigrams, etc.), meaningful messages do not take long to deduce. In spite of the enormous size of the key space, only about 25 characters of ciphertext are needed on the average to cryptanalyze a simple substitution cipher. Formally, this result is expressed as substitution ciphers having a small "unicity distance" (the number of characters needed to uniquely determine the key, which averages 27.6 for English) [34]. The frequency analysis technique was basic to deciphering the cryptogram concerning buried treasure in Edgar Allan Poe's "The Gold Bug."

Distributions of other types of text can also be cataloged. An ASCII file in a Pascal program for computing frequency distributions, for example, has a different but distinctive characteristic [34]. The frequency distribution characteristic principle is the same.

3. One of the types of cipher machines used by the Germans during World War II was called the Lorenz. These machines used a "stream" cipher invented by Gilbert Vernam of AT&T in 1917. The Vernam cipher was designed to encrypt the Baudot code, a 5-bit per character code used for teletype transmissions. Each character code is added (bit-by-bit exclusive-or) to 5 bits from a key stream. The identical ciphertext/key stream addition operations recover the code for one in possession of the key stream.

The Vernam cipher resistance to cryptanalysis depends on the key stream. If the key stream were infinitely long, it probably could not be broken. Since infinite key streams are not practical,* Vernam cipher users tried to devise very long key streams that might appear infinitely long to a cryptanalyst. However, a cryptologist named William Friedman noticed that although two strings of randomly selected letters had only 4% matches (identical letters in the same position only 4% of the time), two strings of English text had 7% matches. The reason for this effect is the nonuniform frequency distribution of letters in the English language. It meant that if two streams of ciphertext could be aligned so that the key stream started in the same position for each, the number of matches would nearly double.

This observation, combined with available computing power, was sufficient to break the Lorenz ciphers [32]. Searching for the required alignment is tedious but easily programmed for computer solution.

Once the alignment is found, groups of letters thought to represent a word are picked out of one ciphertext stream and checked to see if the corresponding group of letters in the other ciphertext stream represents meaningful text. The validity of this approach is demonstrated by the equations below:

$$w1 + k = c1$$
$$w2 + k = c2 \tag{8-4}$$

where $w1$ represents the bits of a guessed cleartext word thought to be in one ciphertext stream, $w2$ represents the corresponding bits in the second ciphertext stream, k represents

---

* The goal of infinite key streams can be achieved by never repeating the key stream. For example, a one-time key was used for a number of years for "Hot-Line" communications between Washington and Moscow.

the corresponding key bits, c_1 and c_2 are the ciphertext, and $+$ denotes bit-by-bit exclusive-or. Adding Equations 1 and 2, we obtain:

$$w_1 + w_2 = c_1 + c_2 \qquad\qquad (8\text{-}5)$$

Since c_1 and c_2 are known, if w_1 is guessed correctly, w_2 will be revealed correctly. Eventually, a correct guess is made for w_1, and meaningful text is noted in w_2.

These types of computing demands led to the development of the British Colossus, described in Chapter 1.

The above observations concerning cryptanalysis are intended to serve as a caution about the hazards of depending on a cryptosystem that might be less secure than expected for a particular application. If robust security is an objective, ad hoc procedures are seldom appropriate. Even the use of well-known cryptosystems must be tempered with caution and care.

8.4.3 Symmetric Cryptosystems and DES

A large number of cryptosystems have been developed. Many of these systems have been acknowledged to be robust systems when properly applied. Until recently, there were no "standard" systems that were widely used and for which security tradeoffs were well known. The lack of standard systems made network connectivity a problem, because two parties using differing cryptosystems could not directly make a secure communications link. An exception has been in government handling of classified data, where standard government encryption gear was not only available but mandated.

A need for a standard system for unclassified applications was perceived by the National Bureau of Standards (now NIST). A call was issued in 1972 for proposals for a system that would be supported as a national cryptosystem standard. The response was unsatisfactory, so the call was repeated in 1974. Meanwhile, IBM had been working on a cryptosystem that combined substitution and transposition into a recirculating block product cipher (called "LUCIFER"), which was well matched to hardware implementation. The IBM system operated on 64-bit blocks of information and used a single 128-bit key. IBM proposed the LUCIFER system to NBS in 1975. The proposal was accepted by NBS, but evaluation by industry groups and by NSA was sought. Mostly because of the influence of NSA, the key length was changed to 56 bits, and some changes were made in the "S boxes" (described below). In 1977, this cryptosystem, known as the "Data Encryption Standard" (DES) became a federal information processing standard [35].

DES keys are actually 64-bit blocks, but 8 of the bits are parity checks and are not involved in the cryptosystem processing. Not all 2^{56} keys are usable; there are four known keys (weak keys) for which double encryption (twice with the same key) produces the original plaintext. There are six known pairs of keys (semi-weak keys) that yield mirror-image key extractions (see below for discussion of key extractions). Double encryption using these pairs also results in plaintext.

The basic operation of DES is shown in Figures 8-8 through 8-10. The input shown in Figure 8-8 is a 64-bit block of plaintext. The bits are transposed through a one-to-one transposition (permutation). The resulting block is split into a 32-bit "left half" and a 32-bit "right half." The right half is transformed by a key-dependent nonlinear function, f, and added (bit-by-bit exclusive-or) to the left half. Following this "round," the halves are interchanged and the process is repeated. After 16 rounds, a final permutation is applied to generate a 64-bit block of ciphertext.

The operation of the nonlinear f functions is described in Figure 8-9. The 32-bit input is given an expansion mapping to 48 bits, which is added (bit-by-bit exclusive-or) to a 48-bit "key extraction" (K_1, K_2, . . . in Figure 8-8). The result is compressed by "S-boxes," with 6 input bits producing 4 output bits. The resulting 32 bits are permuted to produce the function output.

The key extraction is shown in Figure 8-10. The 56-bit key is permuted and split into two 28-bit halves. Each half is subjected to a recirculating left shift of either one or two positions, the choice of which is prescribed by round number. After each round, the resulting halves are combined, and the 56 bits are compressed and permuted to give a 48-bit key extraction. In this way the 16 key extractions K_1, K_2, . . . , K_{16} are obtained.

The encryption and decryption operations are identical, except that the key extraction order is inverted during decryption (the order is K_{16}, K_{15}, . . . , K_1).

As described above, the cryptosystem performs "block mode" (sometimes called "electronic codebook") encryption (a block of input is transformed to a block of output, independent of any other blocks, as shown in Figure 8-11a). This mode is unsuitable for most communication applications because transmission of repetitive plaintext blocks will yield repetitive ciphertext. Therefore a block mode cryp-

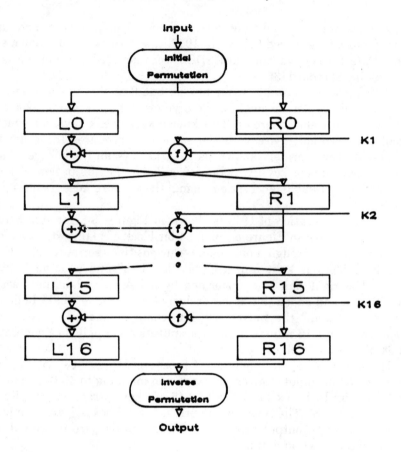

Figure 8-8   DES processing structure.

tosystem is vulnerable to a known-plaintext attack. Protection against this vulnerability is usually provided in cryptosystems by using "feedback," where previously generated cryptosystem output is mixed into subsequent ciphertext generation. In order to protect the first block of ciphertext generated in a stream, an "initialization vector," (IV) must be used in place of the feedback (Figure 8-11b).

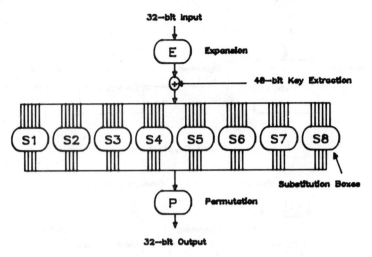

Figure 8-9   Keyed substitution/transposition function.

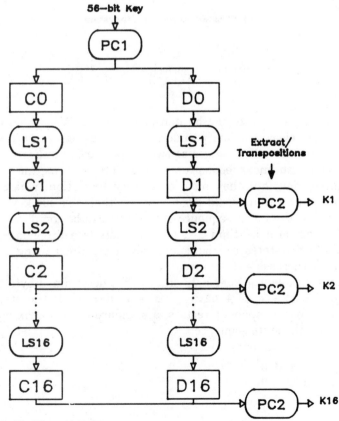

Figure 8-10   Key extraction.

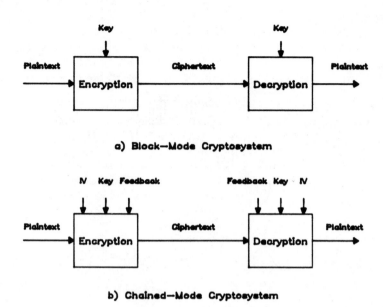

a) Block—Mode Cryptosystem

b) Chained—Mode Cryptosystem

Figure 8-11   Block encryption and chaining.

In order to minimize the burden of managing IVs, which usually are changed every session, pseudorandom IV generators are usually used to coordinate IV changes at two or more communicating nodes. Maximal length linear feedback shift registers are sometimes used in this application, but they have a security limitation, which is the same limitation that would argue against their use for key generation. That is, the LFSR sequence of 2^n-1 bits can be completely determined using no more than 2^n successive bits (see Problem 9). Also, all 2^n-1 LFSR states can be completely determined using no more than n + 1 successive states.

As an example, consider a 15-state LFSR determined by a polynomial $g(x) = x^4 + a3x^3 + a2x^2 + a1x + 1$ (n = 4). If the states are treated as four-component vectors, a standard-form matrix equation determines the state sequence:

$$\underline{s}' = \underline{s} \begin{bmatrix} 0 & 1 & 0 & 0 \\ 0 & 0 & 1 & 0 \\ 0 & 0 & 0 & 1 \\ 1 & a1 & a2 & a3 \end{bmatrix} \qquad (8\text{-}6)$$

where s' signifies the state following state s.

Assume that the following pair of successive states is observed:

$w1x1y1z1, w2x2y2z2$

Applying this information to Equation 8-6, the following equations are obtained:

$$w1 + a1z1 = x2 \tag{8-7}$$

$$x1 + a2z1 = y2 \tag{8-8}$$

$$y1 + a3z1 = z2 \tag{8-9}$$

For $z1 = 1$, these equations determine $a1$, $a2$, and $a3$. There can only be three successive states with $z1 = 0$, so no more than five total successive states are required for a solution. Concerns of this type are lessened by using nonlinear feedback shift registers for IV sequencing.

It is also possible for the transmitter to send the IV to the receiver unencrypted, since the IV does not directly provide a cryptanalyst an advantage. The problem is that the analysis posture is enhanced every time the IV repeats, which in practice it must.

The feedback process is usually called "chaining." Although chaining does not affect the number of keys required for an exhaustive attack, it substantially increases the protection against a known-plaintext attack. Chaining is used in a variety of cryptosystems and is specified as part of the information furnished by NIST on useful DES modes.

Synchronization between the sender and the receiver requires that both know the IV as well as the key and that they can both determine message and block boundaries.

The effect of communication errors is also a concern, because it is possible for a single bit error to render the rest of a message unintelligible. To address these concerns, several types of chaining have been developed.

In "cipher block chaining" (Figure 8-12a), the ciphertext for each 64-bit block is used as the feedback for the subsequent 64-bit block. With this technique, a bit error affects only two blocks. However, a missing or additional bit cannot be tolerated. There must be some

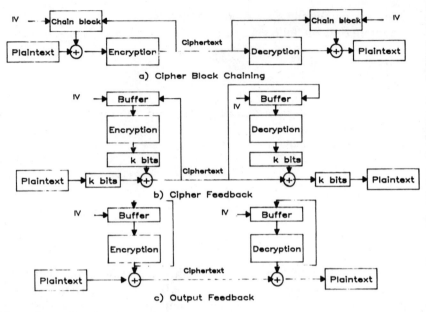

Figure 8-12   Feedback modes.

external mode of resynchronizing if framing cannot be reliably maintained.

"Cipher feedback" (Figure 8-12b) uses a buffer of k-bit characters within a block, and shifts one character (k bits) out of the buffer for each pass through the encryption algorithm. Only k bits of the encryption output are used for addition to each k-bit plaintext character. There are typically unencrypted start and stop bits at each character boundary, thereby maintaining framing. Although speed is slowed because of the number of encryption passes necessary, this technique is well matched to asynchronous lines where speed demands are not high and framing protection is useful.

In "output feedback," (Figure 8-12c) the output of the encryption process is both fed back and added (bit-by-bit exclusive-or) to the plaintext. Therefore, ciphertext is not fed back, although generated ciphertext still depends on previous information (cryptosystem output). An output feedback system is not self-synchronizing. The effects of transmission errors do not propagate beyond the position in which they occur. Note that although 64-bit block processing is depicted in Figure 8-12, k-bit processing (as described above for cipher feedback) is also possible.

8.4.4 Applications for DES

The DES cryptosystem has been subjected to more scrutiny than any other cryptosystem in history. No significant weaknesses have been found. It is used for unclassified data protection not only in the United States, but also in many foreign countries, and has been adopted as an ISO standard.

DES was intended to be implemented in hardware, and many of its operations are readily performed by hardware systems. Software implementations are also available. DES software has a potential cost benefit over hardware, because once written, it can be copied for multiple installations. If purchased, such copies may or may not be allowed, depending on the vendor requirements. However, software runs considerably slower than available hardware. A variety of DES hardware devices are available; some run as fast as 20 Mbps. Prices for DES encryptor/decryptors run from a few hundred dollars to tens of thousands of dollars, depending on speed, key management capabilities, physical security, and flexibility.

A vexing problem with any cryptosystem such as DES is that while it is becoming more widely used (more than 100,000 DES chips per year are sold), it is also being exposed to increasingly sophisticated threat technology. DES has been used for more than a decade, and in that time, computer power has increased from tens of MFLOPS (millions of floating point operations per second) to about a GFLOP (a billion floating point operations per second). Parallel and vector processing techniques have also increased substantially. Another disadvantage of an aging cryptosystem is that there is more time for some subtle weakness to be discovered and surreptitiously exploited. Also, if DES were broken, a very large number of users would be jeopardized.

The DES key space, determined by 56 bits as a little more than 7 $\times$ 10^{16}, is becoming less assuring.* Although multiple (reiterative) encryption is possible, it is not as effective as multiplying the key length would lead one to believe [47].

With these concerns in mind, and spurred by the emphasis of NSDD 145 (see Chapter 5) on the importance to government security of sensitive unclassified information, a partnership was formed between NSA and 11 electronics companies to develop new standard encryption devices (COMSEC devices). The effort was called "Project

---

*   Note that if keys could be tried at a rate of a billion per second, it would be expected to take about a year to discover the correct key.

Overtake." The algorithms developed and the implementations used are part of The Commercial COMSEC Endorsement Program (CCEP). "Type I" devices are intended to be TEMPEST shielded, tamper-sealed, and used for the protection of classified information. "Type II" equipment is for unclassified information protection (supplementing and possibly eventually replacing DES). These devices are tamper-sealed and may not be exported.

Under this initiative, NSA developed algorithms intended to replace DES. A major difference was that the algorithms were secret, requiring security-cleared vendors to develop hardware, and requiring protection against reverse engineering, since the devices were to be used in unclassified applications. NSA also provided a procedure for key distribution and "key tagging" to keep track of the keys issued.

Objections to the Project Overtake initiative included the threats of having to plan for replacement of present implementations of DES, as well as the NSA role in key control [36]. There were also concerns about the effects on international communications [37], since the new encryption hardware could not be exported.

While the DES algorithm was under consideration for renewal as a federal standard in 1987, HR 145 was under consideration as The Computer Security Act of 1987 (see Chapter 5). Some of the sentiment that led the government to reallocate computer security responsibility to NIST also influenced the eventual decision to reaffirm DES as a federal standard for another five years (in spite of a negative vote from NSA) [38].

The prognosis seems clear. In spite of its civilian-sector popularity, DES in its present form is likely to lose support for unclassified government-related applications by the mid- to late-1990s.

8.4.5 Public-Key Encryption and RSA

In order for two network nodes to interchange encrypted communication, they must exchange keys in such a way that an adversary cannot intercept the keys. At best an inconvenient constraint, especially in cases of large geographic distance between the two nodes, this problem is compounded by the need for periodic key changes. The number of keys in the key management process may be very large if every network node must have a unique encryption key with every other node, because there are a large number of potential pairs, P, in an n-node network (Equation 8-10).

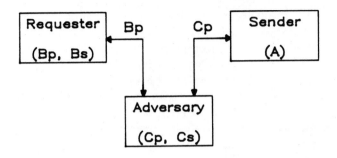

Figure 8-13   Public-key interception.

$$P = n(n\text{-}1)/2 \qquad\qquad\qquad (8\text{-}10)$$

Until the mid-1970s, it was generally believed that no encryption key exchange over public channels could be made securely.[*] The public-key cryptosystem strategy [39] changed many people's minds.

The public-key concept depends on the encryption key and the decryption key differing, but sharing a complementary property such that the input can be recovered by successive transformations based on the two keys. In all applications of the process, one key is secret, and the other is public. Protection depends on preventing the adversary from learning the secret key, although knowing the public key.

Assume that two network nodes each have determined such a key pair. Assume that each knows the other's public key, but neither reveals their secret key. We will name the two nodes "A" and "B," and denote the respective secret and public key pairs as "As" and "Ap"; and "Bs" and "Bp." In order for node A to use the cryptosystem for a secret transmission to node B over a public channel, the message to be protected is encrypted using node B's public key, Bp. Since node B is the only user who knows the matching secret key, Bs, only node B can decrypt the message. Public-key cryptosystems can be used for authenticity as well as secrecy (see next section).

It is tempting to conclude that node B could request a secret transmission by sending its public key Bp to node A over a public channel. Unfortunately, there is a serious problem with this idea. Referring to

---

[*]   A former NSA Director, Admiral Bobby Inman, has revealed that a public-key concept was developed at NSA in 1966.

Figure 8-13, assume that the requesting node sends Bp for A to use for secure transmission to node B. An adversary, C, with access to the public channel can intercept the transmission and masquerade as node B by sending an adversary public key, Cp, to node A. This enables the adversary to decrypt transmissions that node A believes to be secure. The adversary can also masquerade to node B as node A by reprocessing messages transmitted by node A. This is done by reencrypting node A messages using node B's public key.

For this reason, public-key cryptosystems do not eliminate the key management problem. The problem magnitude is reduced, however. Instead of the potential number of keys used on a network increasing nearly in proportion to the square of the number of nodes (see Equation 8-6), the number of potential keys (2n) increases linearly. For 1000 nodes, the reduction is from 499,500 keys to 1000 key pairs.

8.4.5.1 Diffie-Hellman Concepts The basic paper on public-key concepts given by Diffie and Hellman [39] included a proposal for a secure key exchange over a public channel through exponentiation of a primitive constant, C, in a field having a prime number, p, of elements. The primitive requirement means that $C^0, C^1, \ldots, C^{p-1}$ must range over all of the elements in the field.

In the procedure, user A selects an integer Xa from the field, and user B selects Xb. User A transmits $Ya = C^{Xa} \bmod p$, and user B transmits $Yb = C^{Xb} \bmod p$. Each exponentiates the received number using its selected integer, and both results are the same, which can be used as a secret key:

$$K = Y_b{}^{Xa} \bmod p = Y_a{}^{Xb} \bmod p = C^{XaXb} \bmod p \qquad (8\text{-}11)$$

An adversary attempting cryptanalysis would find the solution for Xa, given only Ya (or for Xb, given only Yb), more difficult than the exponentiation computation required of the nodes.

Although the illustrated key exchange is not in itself secure because of the threat shown in Figure 8-13, an important principle is illustrated. The objective of the work on public-key cryptology has been to find problems that are computationally infeasible to solve, using all known methods, but that are feasible to solve with additional information. For this reason, Diffie and Hellman suggested that NP-complete problems might be usefully applied to cryptosystems. However, the most productive work has been in factoring (see RSA cryptosystem in Section 8.4.5.3).

The public-key concept applied to a network depends on the availability of public-key directories, so that each node can be assured of knowing the public key of any other node to be engaged in communication. The security of the information in the directories requires further subsequent consideration.

8.4.5.2 Merkle-Hellman Knapsacks One of the first mathematical procedures that showed promise as a public-key cryptosystem was the Merkle-Hellman knapsack technique [40]. This technique is now known to provide minimal security against cryptanalysis [45]. Nevertheless, a short description of the technique will be given here, since it illustrates the potential for mathematical algorithms to have solutions through "trapdoors," which depend on additional information not available to an adversary. The basic Merkle-Hellman knapsack was broken in 1982, and the multiply iterated knapsack was broken in 1984 [45].

A "knapsack" is a mathematical result that must be precisely arrived at using a subset of operands. For example, a set of positive integers, $P = \{p_1, p_2, \ldots, p_n\}$, can provide potential operands for summing to an integer S. The knapsack problem is NP-complete. However, a special class of knapsack problems is called "simple knapsacks," because the solution is straightforward. For problems of this type, the members of set P are a "superincreasing" sequence (each element is larger than the sum of the preceding elements). An algorithm for solving a simple knapsack is to process the set elements in order, beginning with the smallest. A cumulative and tentative sum is formed: If the sum is larger than S, the element is not a member of the required subset; if the sum is smaller than S, the element is a member. In the first case, the element is not used in the accumulation; in the latter case the element is used. For example, a superincreasing set is:

$$P = \{1,3,5,10\} \tag{8-12}$$

The Merkle-Hellman technique is intended to convert simple knapsacks into "trapdoor knapsacks," so that adversarial solution is difficult, but information available to the recipient of the trapdoor knapsacks enables solution. This is done by choosing two integers, u and w. An inverse of w (mod u) is computed. The integers u and w must be relatively prime, and u must be at least twice a_n. For example, considering the set of Equation 8-12, u might be selected as 20 and w as 7. Set P is converted to a set P':

$$P' = wP \bmod u \tag{8-13}$$

In the set of Equation 8-8, using the chosen u and w, $P' = \{7,1,15,10\}$. An inner product of the message, treated as a vector, and the set P' produces the ciphertext. For example, a message (M), 1101, applied to the example information above produces:

$$C = (1,1,0,1) \cdot (7,1,15,10) = 18 \tag{8-14}$$

The recipient is provided u and w^{-1}, where w^{-1} is the inverse of w. Using the example values, $w^{-1} = 3$. The recipient produces C':

$$C' = w^{-1}C \bmod u \tag{8-15}$$

This can also be shown to be the inner product of P and the message vector:

$$\begin{aligned} C' &= w^{-1}P'M \bmod u \\ &= w^{-1}wPM \bmod u \\ &= PM \bmod u \end{aligned} \tag{8-16}$$

Using the example values, $C' = 3 \times 18 \bmod 20 = 14$. Since P is a simple knapsack, the solution for M is straightforward:

$$C' = 1 + 3 + 10 = (1,1,0,1) \cdot (1,3,5,10) \tag{8-17}$$

$$M = 1,1,0,1 \tag{8-18}$$

Many other knapsack cryptosystems have been proposed, but none are in widespread use.

8.4.5.3 The RSA Cryptosystem

The only widely used public-key cryptosystem is the Rivest-Shamir-Adleman (RSA) scheme [41]. Its security lies in the difficulty of factoring large numbers.

RSA processing is based on exponentiation modulo a number n, where n is a product of two large prime numbers:

$$n = pq \tag{8-19}$$

The Euler totient function of n, $\varphi(n)$, is computed:

$$\varphi(n) = (p-1)(q-1) \tag{8-20}$$

This is the number of positive integers less than n that are relatively prime to n. Since p and q are prime, the solution is straightforward, as shown in Equation 8-20.

Two numbers, e and d, are picked such that they are inverse, modulo $\varphi(n)$:

$$ed \bmod \varphi(n) = 1 \qquad (8\text{-}21)$$

Encryption of a message, M, is performed by exponentiation:

$$C = M^e \bmod n \qquad (8\text{-}22)$$

In an intriguing mathematical relationship, decryption has the same form:

$$M = C^d \bmod n \qquad (8\text{-}23)$$

Confirmation of this relationship can be seen from Fermat's Theorem, which states that for every M relatively prime to n:

$$M^{\varphi(n)} \bmod n = 1 \qquad (8\text{-}24)$$

From Equations 8-22 and 8-23, we obtain:

$$M = (M^e \bmod n)^d \bmod n = m^{ed} \bmod n \qquad (8\text{-}25)$$

Since $ed \bmod \varphi(n) = 1$, $ed = t\varphi(n) + 1$ for some integer, t. Inserting this information in Equation 8-25,

$$M^{ed} \bmod n = M^{t\varphi(n)+1} \bmod n \qquad (8\text{-}26)$$

Since $M^{\varphi(n)} \bmod n = 1$ (Equation 8-24),

$$M^{ed} \bmod n = M \qquad (8\text{-}27)$$

There are constraints on the choices of the parameters in the scheme. Both p and q should be large to make factoring n difficult. Rivest, Shamir, and Adleman recommend picking d (or e) relatively prime to $\varphi(n)$ in the interval $\{max(p,q)+1,n\text{-}1\}$.

8.4.5.4 Factoring The RSA parameters e and n can be released as a public key. The secret key would then be d. If d were available to an adversary, decryption would be trivial. Therefore, a plausible adversarial attack would be to factor n. Once p and q were found, $\varphi(n)$ and d would follow. This is the reason that factoring capabilities are so strongly tied to RSA security.

A feeling for the difficulty of factoring large numbers can be obtained by considering that, by trial divisions requiring a nanosecond each (assuming numbers up to the square root of 10^{70}), it would take a billion times the age of the universe to factor a 70-digit number. However, through a combination of sophisticated factoring techniques and ingenious matching of computer architecture capabilities to factoring algorithms, notable results have been obtained.

As shown in Figure 8-14, a number of achievements have been made in factoring over the past 15 years. During the mid-1980s, the "quadratic sieve" algorithm and a "special q variation" were implemented on a Cray 1S computer, taking advantage of the parallel architecture to allow an improvement in factoring capabilities by a factor of 300 in a single year. Using these techniques, it was possible to factor numbers of more than 70 digits in less than 10 hours [42]. Since the basis of the quadratic sieve involves dividing the factoring problem into a number of subproblems, and then combining the results, modifications were adapted to implement factoring techniques on a number of separate processors. This resulted in being able to factor numbers having 81 to 86 digits in 1986 on a Sun 3 network [43] and a Macintosh network. A 100-digit number was factored in 1988 [44] using a loose organization of approximately 50 small computers based in the United States, Europe, and Australia.

The implications for RSA are that key lengths should be chosen with some consideration of the size numbers expected to be factored over the lifetime of the keys. Much of the commercial RSA equipment available uses 512-bit keys, which equates to 154-digit numbers to be factored. Note that DES uses 56-bit keys. This is one of the reasons that RSA encryption equipment runs much slower than DES (thousands of bits per second, instead of millions).

8.5 AUTHENTICATION AND DIGITAL SIGNATURES

There are applications for which the authenticity of a message must be guaranteed. For many of these, secrecy of the message is not important. Authentication can be provided by adding a CRC (cyclic redundancy check) to a message, where the CRC (the remainder on

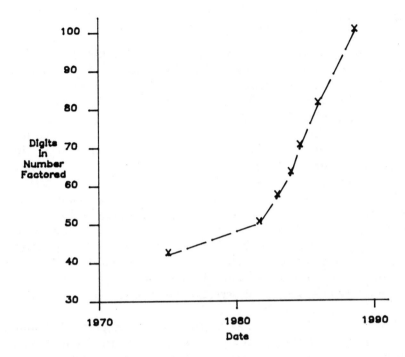

Figure 8-14   Factoring progress.

division of the message treated as a GF(2) polynomial by an ir-
reducible GF(2) polynomial) is a function of the data transmitted.
Any changes to the data have a high probability of altering the CRC.
This technique, called a "message authentication code" (MAC), is frequently used to authenticate financial transactions, because it is
simpler to implement than encryption. However, cryptosystems are
also widely used as data authenticators. In a single-key system, an
adversary cannot masquerade as a user unless the key is known or
the ciphertext to represent a user is known.

In some applications, a CRC is called a "digital signature." However, this type of signature only suffices to assure the recipient that
the transmission is authentic. It is sometimes necessary for the
sender to be protected against a recipient's claim that an action was
authorized by the sender. Using a CRC or single-key encryption, no
evidence exists as to whether or not a message displayed was actually from the sender, as opposed to being "forged" by the recipient.
Public-key cryptosystems solve this problem. In this section, we will
consider both authentication and unforgeable digital signatures.

8.5.1 Authentication

To ensure authenticity, an adversary (or natural occurrences) must have an extremely small probability of substituting a false message that the recipient will judge to be valid. Protection against adversaries also requires that the adversary not be able to determine the transformation used for authenticity, even if both plaintext and ciphertext are known. Where single-key cryptosystems are used for authenticity, authenticity cannot be separated from secrecy. However, in asymmetric cryptosystems, authenticity can be achieved without secrecy (or vice versa).

Assume that a message is transformed[*] using the sender's secret key, and it is transmitted to a recipient for authentication. The recipient can transform the received "ciphertext" using the sender's public key, thereby recovering the message. The only source of a meaningful message would theoretically be the sender, because no one else knows the secret key. Authenticity is thus assured. The transformed message is not secret; anyone who knows the sender's public key can produce it.

The RSA cryptosystem has a commutative property that allows both secrecy and authenticity to be provided in the same message. This requires two transformations by both the sender and the receiver. The sender incorporates authenticity through secret key transformation, and then affords secrecy by encrypting with the recipient's public key. The message transmitted is doubly transformed by the receiver by first applying the recipient's secret key to undo the secrecy protection, and then transforming with the sender's public key to reveal the authentication.

8.5.2 Digital Signatures

Although there are various possible ways to prevent the recipient of messages from making false claims against a sender (such as through a secure third-party escrow), public-key cryptosystems are well matched to the task. Assume that an order is placed by a sender by using the sender's secret key for authentication. The recipient uses the sender's public key for recovering the order. The recipient then records the order with the received ciphertext, the decrypted

---

*   "Transformed" is used instead of "encrypted," because there is no intent here to make the transmitted message secret.

plaintext, and the public key. Evidence is now in place that only the recipient who knows the secret dual key could have sent the message. The ability to certify the result to third parties makes this an appropriate digital signature.

The same procedure can be used to protect software against unauthorized modification. One way in which this can be done is by "signing" a transmission of software to indicate validity. To prevent the software from being modified during transmission while the authentication is in place, the transmission can be protected for authenticity and secrecy, using RSA encryption, as described above.

Another type of software protection is to prevent modifications to software by transforming the software with a secret key, and exposing it to adversaries only in ciphertext form. The system running the software would recover the program logic through public key encryption. After recovery (perhaps just prior to execution), the software would again have to be well protected. However, the overall protection burden would be substantially reduced.

8.6 AUTOMATED NETWORK ADMINISTRATION

The dispersed nature of networks causes a number of security problems. Network security controls are derived from two basic philosophies, as indicated by Figure 8-15. Control can be placed in a central network security controller (CNSC), in which case all access control, key management, and audit recording are done at this single administrative node; or control can be distributed, in which case security functions are handled independently by distributed network security controllers (DNSCs). In the latter case, administrative and security information exchanges among the DNSCs are necessary. Users who are authenticated on one node are generally accepted by other nodes based on authentication information exchanged between DNSCs.

Network security control is frequently structured as a combination of the two basic systems portrayed in Figure 8-15. The objective is to achieve both the flexibility of distributed processing and the security of centralized control.

One major problem of centralized control is that it is difficult in any network more extensive than a LAN to maintain current security and authentication data. Also, network efficiency is hampered by the central controller's potential to become a bot-

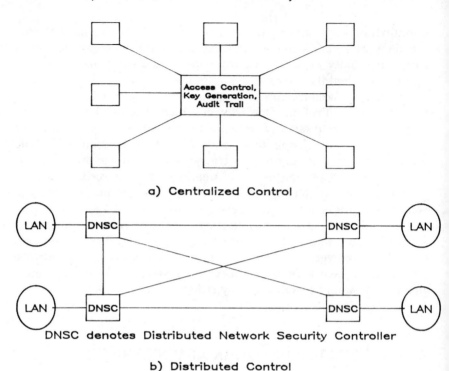

a) Centralized Control

DNSC denotes Distributed Network Security Controller

b) Distributed Control

Figure 8-15   Network security administration.

tleneck, and system reliability and integrity is totally dependent on the central node.

Distributed control is more likely to be inconsistent in policy enforcement, and the overall network tends to have security only as good as its weakest link. As an example, assume that security policy is not uniform, that, say, node A does not allow writedown (see Section 7.3) and node B does. A user at node A may circumvent the local control by sending a file to node B, writing down at that node, and returning the data to node A.

Networks frequently comprise networks of networks (internets) in which case "bridges" are required for protocol pass-through and "gateways" are required for protocol translation and buffering. Security interpretations may also be necessary. Since bridges and gateways generally have no need to directly service users, they are frequently restricted from running user code. The same restriction is appropriate for CNSCs and DNSCs. DNSCs may have the dual role of bridge/gateway processor and security controller.

Networks can meet essentially the same security controls as standalone computers if sufficient administrative mechanisms are in place. The DoD NCSC has extended its "Orange Book" criteria to network applications through a "Trusted Network Interpretation" (the "Red Book") [46].

The NCSC recognizes two means of accrediting networks. The individual systems can be independently created, managed, and accredited through a joint approval process, or the network can be treated as a single system and accredited as a single entity. The network security considerations include how security mechanisms are distributed and allocated to various network components. It is possible to structure multilevel communications channels and multilevel packet switches that connect hosts at different levels and different security evaluations.

Included among the functions of security controllers are key management functions. In order to securely distribute keys (even public keys), issue service can be requested of a "key distribution center" (KDC) or "key management center" (KMC), or key center functions can be incorporated within security controllers.* Key issue functions include secure authentication of key recipients, along with valid authentication to the recipients of the KMC or KDC authenticity.

The problems outlined above have been addressed through activities in six general areas: 1) network security standards, 2) network security architecture, 3) network key management, 4) network access control, 5) network auditing, and 6) network integrity management.

8.6.1 Network Security Standards

Network security standards activities are intended to promote interoperability and uniform security approaches throughout networks. Some of the previous standards activities described in the first section of this chapter, such as the OSI model, contribute to these objectives.

The major government organizations contributing to network security standards are the DoD, the Department of Commerce (specifically NIST), and the General Services Administration. In ad-

---

*   A KMC is used on system setup and infrequently thereafter. A KDC is used during each call or session setup.

dition to the NCSC work described previously in this Chapter and in Chapter 7, DoD sponsors the Secure Data Network System (SDNS) and the Government Open Systems Interconnect Profile (GOSIP) efforts [50]. SDNS and GOSIP both incorporate the OSI model for communication protocol. SDNS is a joint program with DoD and industry representatives to address services such as confidentiality, integrity, authentication, access control, and sender nonrepudiation. GOSIP specifies a selection of protocols at each OSI layer, as well as the requirements for conformance and security.

Federal Information Processing Standards (FIPS) are published by NIST. The publications are sent to government agencies, and most are available to the public. DES was issued as FIPS PUB 46. Federal standards are published by the General Services Administration (GSA). An example publication is Federal Standard 1027, "Telecommunications: General Security Requirements for Equipment Using the Data Encryption Standard," which specifies proper implementation and use of DES equipment.

Financial communications standards are provided by the American National Standards Institute (ANSI). These include techniques for message integrity (e.g., checksum, or message authentication code), confidentiality (DES), access security (e.g., password protection), and key management (e.g., the KMC concept).

8.6.2 Network Security Architecture

NSCs and DNSCs both serve a number of nodes or users. Service bottlenecks can be minimized by providing temporary security controller services (e.g., key management, authentication) through a star topology, and then providing user connections through (where authorized) a mesh or bus topology. This is a basic concept of the SDNS program.

System setup, using this strategy, requires a unique key from a key management center (KMC) for each node device that will communicate. Each node device must exchange credentials with other candidates for communication, and control restrictions must be determined. After the system has been configured, there is no need for further participation by the KMC, as long as access control restrictions have been determined and the proper security services are in place. These are assured by the node devices [51].

8.6.3 Network Key Management

Key management includes the generation, distribution, and accounting of cryptographic keys. Recovery must be considered part of key management because of the potential for failures to subvert the system generation, distribution, and accounting capabilities. User convenience is also an essential attribute.

When a node device is put into service, the KMC must securely issue keying information. Because of the wide geographic span of many contemporary networks, it is now becoming necessary to distribute keys through communications networks, rather than by personal conveyance. This requires protection against interception (e.g., physical control or previously keyed encryption processing). As long as the process remains secure, node devices authenticate each other and information is also exchanged to make access control decisions.

8.6.4 Network Access Control

Access control features depend on authentication of the communicating party. Once authenticated, each user must have a "profile" of network privileges established. This profile supports the security policy established for the network. Authentication is ordinarily established by a system carrying out the node or DNSC function. Once authentication is established in a distributed network, reauthentication at other network nodes is usually not considered necessary if the network is secure. "Peer access approval" (PAA) is required at initiation of a session of this type in order to establish what information may be communicated by each node. "Peer access enforcement" (PAE) can be maintained over the life of the connection. Under this condition, every data transfer and every use of a network resource is checked against the access control rules.

8.6.5 Network Auditing

Network auditing requires a set of records that provide documentary evidence of processing used, from the original transactions forward to related records and reports and backwards from records and reports to the corresponding source transactions [49]. It is not necessary that all audit records be recorded at one source, so long as an investigation can relate the records unambiguously through proper identification (e.g., user-ID, date, time). A uniform time standard throughout a network is essential in order to coordinate audit data. Providing precise time service is not trivial, however.

8.6.6   Network Integrity Management

Network integrity management includes 1) fault detection, isolation, and avoidance, 2) performance and status monitoring, 3) maintenance of system databases, and 4) recovery from failures.

Six aspects of management, identified in the SDNS program [51], are useful to consider: 1) connection management, which arbitrates the establishment of node connections, 2) key management, which provides lifetime support of key materials, 3) access control databases, which maintains profile information, 4) audit control management, which oversees the gathering of audit trail information, 5) health and status management, which maintains status records and performs self-tests, and 6) operations management, which provides network support such as contingency planning.

As networks become more complex, automated management of network functions that enforce security policy and facilitate key management become increasingly more important.

PROBLEMS

1. Assume that it is required to launch a "geo-daily-synchronous" satellite, such that it will be directly over every point on the equator once each day, and at the same daily time for each point. a) At what altitude should it be placed in orbit? b) Is the solution to part a) unique? Discuss the reason for your answer.

2. Assuming the geometry shown in Figure 8-1, describe the theoretical satellite coverage pattern on the surface of the earth. Give a quantitative measure of the pattern dimensions.

3. A Caesar cipher was used to produce the ciphertext below. Use the most efficient cryptanalysis you can to deduce the plaintext message.

    AOPZ PZ AOL LUK VM AOL WYVISLT.

4. Assume a public-key cryptosystem based on multiplication by the key, modulo 31. User A has public key 28 and secret key

10. User B has public key 7 and secret key 9. a) Show cipher-text and decryption for secret transmission from A to B of mes-sage, M, 25. b) Show ciphertext and decryption for authentica-tion from A to B of message, M, 25. c) Show ciphertext and decryption for authentication and secret transmission from A to B of message, M, 25. d) Show how a cryptanalyst who knows the encryption algorithm could compute the unknown secret keys of both A and B.

5. Given a CRC polynomial $g(x) = x^4 + x + 1$, compute the bit pat-tern that would be appended to 11010010110.

6. A double-iterated Merkle Hellman knapsack cryptosystem uses two knapsacks. User A has generated public keys $P1'$ and $P2'$. User B encrypts a message using these keys in the order shown. User A receives ciphertext 71. What was the message?

$P1$ = {1,3,5,10}, $u1$ = 20, $w1$ = 9, $P1'$ = {9,7,5,10};
$P2$ = {1,2,4,8,16}, $u2$ = 50, $w2$ = 11, $P2'$ = {11,22,44,38,26}

7. User A encrypts message 2 using RSA for transmission to B providing secrecy and authenticity, using the data below. What is the ciphertext?
A public key = 37, A secret key = 13, B public key = 17, B secret key = 53, n for both = 77.

8. Estimate how long it would take to try all of the words in an ordinary-sized dictionary as passwords at the rate of one try per second.

9. Given an LFSR output sequence, 10011010, determine the gen-erator polynomial.

10. For RSA encryption with n = 35, are there any key pairs that are not self-inverse ($d \neq e$)?

DILEMMA DISCUSSIONS

1. A computer that has dialup capability is protected by a callback system. Some users travel extensively and find it dif-ficult to know in advance from what telephone number they will need computer access. Since it is possible to bypass the callback feature for specific users, they request that when they are traveling, the callback feature be disabled for them. To do so degrades the security that the callback system was intended to provide. What should the approach to this problem be?

2. Rules state that there is to be no interconnection between partitions of a computer network. Some users find it convenient to move software and data manually between partitions, using tapes and diskettes. Strictly applied, this is a network interconnection, but the users are trusted personnel, and they carefully assess anything moved in this manner. Since they are aware of the potential hazards and since they are unlikely to intentionally create problems, they argue in favor of the practice. What should be done? Why?

3. A group of hackers has shown remarkable ingenuity in penetrating a network. They have been identified, but since there has been no damage, it was decided to not prosecute them. However, their penetration techniques are unknown and it is thought that knowledge of the techniques is important in repairing the security weaknesses of the system that are being exploited. The dilemma faced is that it may be possible to seek hacker cooperation, possibly even paying for information, but to do so would place value (possibly financial value) on wrongdoing. What approach should be taken?

REFERENCES

1. Gasser, Morrie, *Building a Secure Computer System*, Van Nostrand Reinhold, New York, 1988.
2. Rosner, Roy D., *Distributed Telecommunications Networks*, Lifetime Learning Publications, Belmont, CA, 1982.
3. McNamara, John E., *Local Area Networks*, Digital Press, Bedford, MA, 1985.
4. Stix, Gary, "Telephone Wiring: A Conduit for Networking Standards," *IEEE Spectrum*, June 1988.
5. Naegele, Tobias, "Bootlegging on Satellites Turns Out to Be Real Problem," *Electronics*, May 5, 1986.
6. Benjamin, Robert, "The Legend of the Ring, the Star, and the Tree," *Office Products News*, September 1981.
7. Reagan, Philip H., "Is It the PBX, or Is It the LAN?" *Datamation*, March 1984.
8. Gallagher, Robert T., "ITU Members Compromise on Satellite Slots," *Electronics*, September 23, 1985.
9. Lowell, Robert R., and C. Louis Cuccia, "NASA's Communication Program for the 1980s and 1990s—Part 1," *MSN & CT*, August 1986.

10. Davis, Dwight B., "Pulling Together on Computer Communications," *High Technology*, September 1986.
11. Squibb, Nigel J., "Preventing Data Theft on Broadband Local Area Networks," *Data Communications*, May 1988.
12. Strauss, Paul R., "Fiery Exposé: No National Authority Oversees Central Office Security," *Data Communications*, July 1988.
13. Horgan, John, "Safeguarding the National Security," *IEEE Spectrum*, November 1985.
14. Johnson, Nicholas L., and Darren S. McKnight, *Artificial Space Debris*, Orbit Book Company, Malabar, FL, 1987.
15. Golden, Frederic, "Superzapping in Computerland," *Time*, January 12, 1981.
16. Baruffi, Andrea, "Computer Security: What Can Be Done?" *Business Week*, September 26, 1983.
17. Bloombecker, J. J. Buck, "The Spread of Computer Crime," *International Computer Law Adviser*, May 1988.
18. Ball, Michael, "To Catch a Thief: Lessons in Systems Security," *Computerworld*, December 14, 1987.
19. Stoll, Clifford, "Stalking the Wily Hacker," *Communications of the ACM*, May 1988.
20. Gallant, John, "Raid Nets Computers Allegedly Used to Access NASA Files," *Computerworld*, July 23, 1984.
21. Sandza, Richard, "The Revenge of the Hackers," *Newsweek*, December 10, 1984.
22. Musgrave, Bill, "Bulletin Boards and Business," *Datamation*, January 15, 1987.
23. Landreth, Bill, *Out of the Inner Circle*, Microsoft Press, Redmond, WA, 1985.
24. Troy, Eugene F., "Security for Dial-Up Lines," NBS Special Publication 500-137, May 1986.
25. Colbert, Mary, "Ports of Entry," *Digital Review*, April 1986.
26. Durham, Stephen J., "Callback Modems Mean Security and Savings," *Data Communications*, April 1985.
27. Evans, Sandy, "What's New in Computer Security Accessories," *Security Management*, January 1986.
28. Steinauer, Dennis D., "Computer Security Products and Professional Organizations," *Hardcopy*, August 1986.
29. Troy, Eugene F., Stuart Katzke, and Dennis D. Steinauer, "A Technical Approach to Computer Access Control," *Security Management*, December 1985.
30. Simmons, Gustavus J., "Cryptology," *Encyclopedia Britannica*, 1986 edition.

31. Hellman, Martin, "Cryptography in the Electronics Age," *The Stanford Engineer*, Fall/Winter, 1978.
32. Zorpette, Glenn, "Breaking the Enemy's Code," *IEEE Spectrum*, September 1987.
33. Kahn, David, "U.S. Intelligence Races the Clock to Decode Terrorists' Messages," *Albuquerque Journal*, December 21, 1986.
34. Denning, Dorothy Elizabeth Robling, *Cryptography and Data Security*, Addison-Wesley, Reading, MA, 1982.
35. "The Data Encryption Standard (DES)," Federal Information Processing Standards Publication (FIPS PUB) 46, January 15, 1977.
36. Howe, Charles L., "Into the Night," *Datamation*, June 1, 1986.
37. Howe, Charles L., and Robert Rosenberg, "Government Plans for Data Security Spill Over to Civilian Networks," *Data Communications*, March 1987.
38. Munro, Neil, "NBS Reaffirms DES Standard for Unclassified Communications," *Government Computer News*, February 5, 1988.
39. Diffie, Whitfield, and Martin E. Hellman, "New Directions in Cryptography," *IEEE Transactions on Information Theory*, November 1976.
40. Merkle, R. C., and M. E. Hellman, "Hiding Information and Signatures in Trapdoor Knapsacks," *IEEE Transactions on Information Theory*, September 1978.
41. Rivest, R. L., A. Shamir, and L. Adleman, "A Method for Obtaining Digital Signatures and Public-Key Cryptosystems," *Communications of the ACM*, February 1978.
42. Davis, J. A., and D. B. Holdridge, "Factorization Using the Quadratic Sieve Algorithm," *Advances in Cryptology*, Plenum Press, New York, 1983.
43. Silverman, R. D., "The Multiple Polynomial Quadratic Sieve," *Mathematical Computing*, January 1987.
44. Ruthen, Russell, "Factoring Googols," *Scientific American*, December 1988.
45. Brickell, Ernest F., "Cryptanalysis of Multiply Iterated Merkle-Hellman Knapsack Systems," *Advances in Cryptology*, Plenum Press, New York, 1984.
46. "Trusted Network Interpretation," National Computer Security Center NCSC-TG-005, July 31, 1987.
47. Merkle, Ralph C., and Martin E. Hellman, "On the Security of Multiple Encryption," *Communications of the ACM*, July 1981.

48. Patterson, Wayne, *Mathematical Cryptology for Computer Scientists and Mathematicians*, Rowman & Littlefield, Totowa, NJ, 1987.
49. "ISO 7498/Part 2—Security Architecture," ISO/TC97/SC21/-N1528/WG1, September 1986.
50. Barker, L. Kirk, and Larry D. Nelson, "Security Standards—Government and Commercial," *AT&T Technical Journal*, May/June 1988.
51. Karp, Bennett C., L. Kirk Barker, and Larry D. Nelson, "The Secure Data Network System," *AT&T Technical Journal*, May/June 1988.
52. Eckerson, Wayne, "Brokerage Steers Clear of Disasters," *Network World*, January 9, 1989.
53. Brown, Bob, and Bab Wallace, "CO Outage Refuels Users' Disaster Fears," *Network World*, July 11, 1988.
54. Caputo, Anthony, "Increase in Computer Crime Points to the Need for Patching Vulnerabilities in Security Systems," *Communications News*, August 1986.
55. Meyer, Carl H., and Stephen M. Matyas, *A New Dimension in Computer Data Security: Cryptography*, John Wiley and Sons, New York, 1982.
56. Kahn, David, *The Codebreakers*, Macmillan and Co., New York, 1967.
57. Rutledge, Linda S., and Lance J. Hoffman, "A Survey of Issues in Computer Network Security," in *Computer and Network Security*, IEEE Computer Society Press, New York, 1987.
58. Hartmann, Michael, "FDDI Standards are Near for Fiber Optic LANs," *Government Computer News*, December 19, 1988.

9

Current Perspectives on Computer Security

Previous chapters have covered particular aspects of computer and communications security. These concepts must be integrated within the environment of specific types of organizations. In the first chapter, a systematic approach to security was suggested. In the second chapter, the concept of distinct security environments was presented, with Figure 2-1 portraying a two-dimensional view of security. In the figure, rows represented the systematic sequence of security considerations, and columns represented the six environments involved. The previous six chapters have addressed security issues within the context of each of these environments. Up to this point, the six environments have been essentially dichotomized; now we seek a consolidated and coordinated view. This adds a third dimension to our security view.

In this chapter, an overall perspective (the third dimension) is given using four different approaches. First, an organized method for coordinating the six environments is presented. Second, current security strengths and weaknesses are assessed. Third, current security research perspectives are examined. And fourth, an outlook for the future is given.

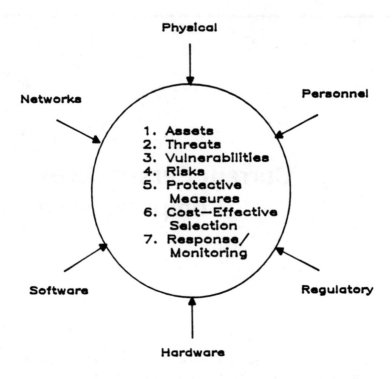

Figure 9-1   Security approach seen from six environments.

9.1 CONSOLIDATION AND COORDINATION

As shown in Figure 9-1, six different vantage points have been involved in studying Chapters 3 through 8. A few features could be recognized as the same from different viewpoints, but mostly the view seen depends on the environment assumed. Having completed this modular approach, it is now necessary to consider a unification. How does it all fit together?

Our contention is that the preceding material can be brought together, but the consolidated approach depends strongly on the nature of the business to which it applies. One might be tempted, at this point, to simply dismiss the problem as too organization-dependent to be meaningfully addressed. We prefer the contention that general guidance from several viewpoints is a useful contribution.

For illustration, and to make the problem tractable, we arbitrarily categorize companies into five types, each of which has different constraints and interests with regard to computer security. In working with an organization-specific approach, we cannot argue that the coverage is comprehensive. The proposal is simply a reasonable way to allow a general treatment with enough detail to be useful to those working within various environments. The five categories selected are:

1. Banking/financial—depends on investment transactions to make a profit. The public and other companies are sources of the finances.
2. Scientific/consulting—sells technical services to other companies; computers and communications are used.
3. Military/government—non-profit; funded by and directly controlled by the government.
4. Educational institutions—bring public personnel on site for education and training, charging tuition.
5. Commercial/business—use computers as a tool for accounting, bookkeeping, inventory, payroll; computers support mainstream business activity. Computers are not directly responsible for the business activity.

If security problems are viewed from each of these five organization types, the security environment emphasis appears different in each case. This is analogous to how the security structure within environments differs. The concept is illustrated in Figure 9-2. It is difficult to defend a uniform viewpoint for all organizations within each category. Nevertheless, we will attempt to give such a general view by ranking the importance of the six security environments to each organization type, with consideration of the constraints most commonly faced. A prioritized list of protective measures, derived from the organizational considerations, is also given. These suggestions are intended to be guidance for cost-effective budget allocations.

9.1.1 Banking/Financial

Investment decisions are intended to generate profit for banking/financial organizations. Network transactions involving finances are of crucial importance. Operational continuity of networks is important for customer relations and company image. For these reasons, network security is generally the most important considera-

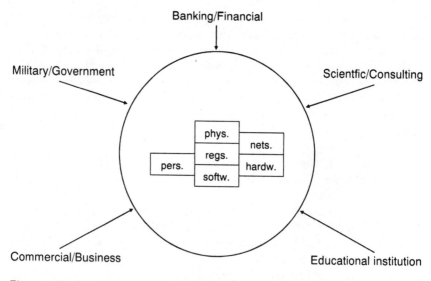

Figure 9-2   Environments seen from five business perspectives.

tion to banking/financial organizations. Because money transactions are so tempting to larcenous people, personnel security is also an important consideration. Ranking the six security environments in order of importance to the banking/financial industry, the following prioritized list of security environments is reasonable:

1. Network security
2. Personnel security
3. Regulatory security
4. Physical security
5. Hardware security
6. Software security

For each of these environments, vulnerabilities and protective measures can be addressed specifically for the banking/financial industry. This has been done in Figure 9-3. Each matrix in the figure portrays one of the security environments, and they are presented in the order given above. Rows in each matrix correspond to some of the most significant vulnerabilities (priority ordered) in that environment; columns correspond to some of the most significant protective measures (also priority ordered). The code at the bottom of the figure indicates the general effectiveness of the protective measures against the cited vulnerabilities. Some of the "vulnerabilities" are cited in

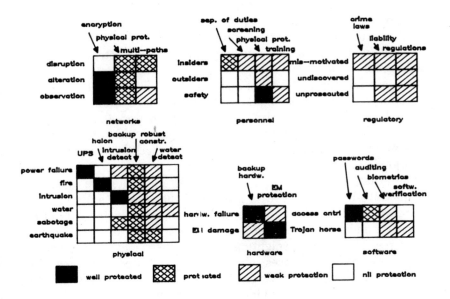

Figure 9-3   Banking/financial environments.

terms of threat agents, but in all cases, vulnerability of some asset to a threat is implied.

Some of the concise labeling in the figure warrants elaboration. For example, the "network" vulnerability titled "observation" means compromise of protected information (proprietary, private, sensitive). The protective measure "multi-paths" means use of alternate network paths for redundancy. Under the "regulatory" matrix, the "undiscovered" vulnerability refers to failure to detect incidents, while "unprosecuted" refers to incidents known to management that are not prosecuted. The "liability" protective measures include provisions for holding management responsible for effective prosecution. The "regulations" protective measure encourages general personnel vigilance and responsibility, which increases the probability of detection of incidents.

In the "hardware" matrix, "hardware failure" refers to ordinary component failure due to internal stresses or wearout, while "EM damage" requires an external source of energy. The "software" matrix includes "passwords" as a meaningful protective measure with the implication that passwords are used effectively, as opposed to merely being used. A similar provision applies to "auditing." "Software verification" refers to quality tests applied to software to help prevent threatening features. All of these elaborations are important in understanding the intent of the figure, which is to give a parochial view of the security environment as constrained by the banking/financial industry.

In this way, Figure 9-3 gives a snapshot qualitative "risk analysis" for the banking/financial industry. Assessing the overall picture, one can deduce a list of prioritized protective measures. Individual companies may or may not have these protective measures in place. However, the list can serve as a prioritized checklist made from the general viewpoint of companies within the category.

Note that arriving at a prioritized list of protective measures means considering the relative priority of the security environments, the relative priority of the vulnerabilities, the relative priority of the protective measures, and the overall effectiveness of the protective measures. The general weighting used here is a matter of judgment, and there are differences of opinion, even among experienced security practitioners. However, differences are not usually extreme. The list derived for the banking/financial industry (from the author's viewpoint) is:

1. Encryption for financial transactions
2. Network redundancy for operational continuity
3. Separation of duties for personnel handling financial transactions
4. Background screening for personnel handling financial transactions
5. Crime laws directed at wire and ATM fraud
6. Training for personnel handling financial transactions
7. Uninterruptible power system for operational continuity
8. Hardware backup for operational continuity
9. Effective passwords
10. Effective auditing
11. Halon fire protection for operational continuity
12. Intrusion protection to prevent transgressors

9.1.2 Scientific/Consulting

The product of scientific/consulting organizations is technical information. This typically involves computing and exchange of information over networks. Since technical information is being marketed, and since other types of information (e.g., proposals, bidding data) may be crucial to business health (and therefore sensitive), network

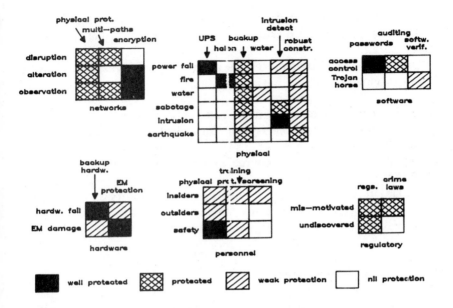

Figure 9-4   Scientific/consulting environments.

security is typically of utmost importance. Physical security and software security are also relatively important. The prioritized list of security environments is:

1. Network security
2. Physical security
3. Software security
4. Hardware security
5. Personnel security
6. Regulatory security

In the network matrix (Figure 9-4), disruption is shown as the most important threat, with the assumption that network communication is crucial. Alteration of data would be of almost equal concern. Observation applies to the types of protected (sensitive) data discussed above. The most appropriate protective measures for these vulnerabilities are physical protection for the network constituents, redundant network path options, and encryption.

The physical security environment has high importance because of the need for processing continuity. While hardware security is also a factor, it is more straightforward in this environment than physical security. Software security is important to prevent improper access and to assure that no disruptive software features, such as Trojan horses, are present.

The list of prioritized protective measures for scientific/consulting organizations is:

1. Physical protection for networks
2. Uninterruptible power system for operational continuity
3. Effective passwords
4. Backup hardware for operational continuity
5. Effective auditing
6. Halon fire suppression for operational continuity
7. Training in order to reduce the insider threat
8. Regulations to discourage mismotivated people

9.1.3 Military/Government

The aims of military/government organizations are to support national missions. There is no profit motivation, although cost-effective performance is expected. Personnel provide the key to security, because they are essential in the protection of sensitive or classified information and because they have duties that may be related directly to successes or failures of the government. Also, the main adversaries to government operations are personnel (espionage agents, terrorists, saboteurs).

A secondary concern is physical security. One contribution of physical security is to support government operational continuity. In some situations, operational continuity may be crucial to national security. Networks may also have a crucial role in communicating protected information.

The prioritized list of environments is:

1. Personnel security
2. Physical security
3. Network security
4. Software security
5. Regulatory security
6. Hardware security

The personnel threats are best met by physical security measures (see Figure 9-5). Physical security can be used to prevent outsider and unauthorized insider access to crucial facilities. Another impor-

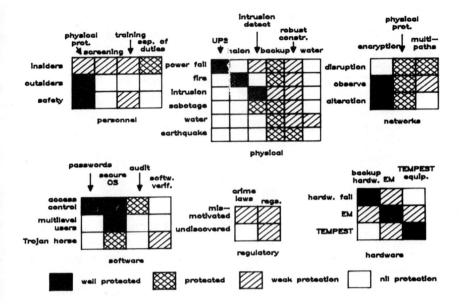

Figure 9-5   Military/government security.

tant measure is personnel screening. Personnel screening is important to control the types of insiders that have privileges.

Encryption is one of the most effective network protective measures for the military/government environment. Physical security for network constituents is another.

In the software matrix, an important access control technique is the use of kernelized secure operating systems (see Chapter 7). This is the most cost-effective technique for securely separating multilevel users.

The prioritized list for the military/government environment is:

1. Physical protection for computer facilities and for network constituents
2. Uninterruptible power system for operational continuity
3. Encryption to protect network data
4. Effective passwords for access control
5. Backup hardware for operational continuity
6. Personnel screening to select trustworthy personnel
7. Crime laws to enable prosecution
8. Halon fire suppression to assure operational continuity
9. Intrusion detection to help prevent transgressor actions

10. Training to increase personnel awareness
11. Secure operating system for separating multilevel users
12. Effective auditing
13. TEMPEST-approved processing equipment
14. Robust construction for operational continuity
15. Redundant network paths for operational continuity
16. Regulations for personnel behavior guidance
17. Electromagnetic protection techniques for operational continuity

9.1.4 Educational Institutions

The product of educational institutions is imparted knowledge. Public image is important in maintaining a supply of students. The use of computers and networks is predominant. Network security is important for operational continuity and for protection of information such as grades and personal information. Operational continuity requires physical security, and software security is important to prevent access to protected data.

The prioritized list of environments is:

1. Network security
2. Physical security
3. Software security
4. Regulatory security
5. Hardware security
6. Personnel security

In the network environment, physical protection helps prevent network disruption as well as compromise or alteration of data (see Figure 9-6). Encryption also has value in preventing compromise or alteration. In the physical security environment, operational continuity is emphasized.

The prioritized list of protective measures is:

1. Physical protection of network constituents for operational continuity
2. Uninterruptible power system for operational continuity
3. Effective passwords for access control
4. Regulations for controlling improper personnel behavior and for encouraging discovery of improper behavior

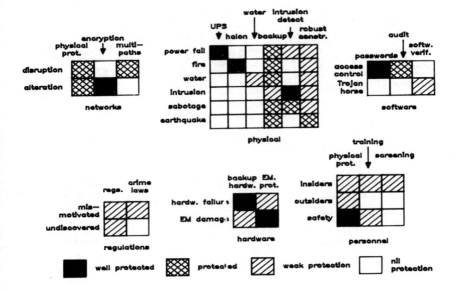

Figure 9-6   Educational institution security.

5. Protection against water damage for operational continuity
6. Backup for operational continuity
7. Effective auditing
8. Training for reducing the insider threat

9.1.5 Commercial/Business

This category refers to enterprises that produce products not directly involving computing and use computers as business support tools. Personnel security and operational continuity are the major issues. The prioritized list of security environments is:

1. Personnel security
2. Physical security
3. Software security
4. Regulatory security
5. Network security
6. Hardware security

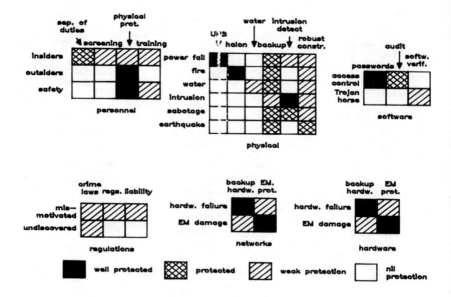

Figure 9-7   Commercial/business security.

Insider personnel are the major threats in the personnel security environment (see Figure 9-7). Separation of duties and personnel screening are the most appropriate protective measures. Physical protection offers some help against insiders and is also important for protection against outsiders.

The prioritized list of protective measures is:

1. Separation of duties to protect against insiders
2. Background screening to help select reliable insiders
3. Physical security for operational continuity
4. Uninterruptible power system for operational continuity
5. Effective passwords for access control
6. Effective auditing
7. Crime laws to help prosecute transgressors
8. Backup (including an alternate processing site) for operational continuity
9. Training to help personnel security
10. Halon fire suppression for operational continuity
11. Protection against water damage for operational continuity

The preceding lists of protective measures, although necessarily general, show interesting contrasts among different types of organizations. Encryption is of prime importance in banking/financial organizations and high on the list for military/government organizations. Separation of duties is of prime importance to commercial/business organizations and high on the list for banking/financial organizations. Physical protection for either facilities or networks or both rates high for scientific/consulting organizations, military/government organizations, and educational institutions, as does UPS (uninterruptible power system) protection. Background screening is high on the list for banking/financial, military/government, and commercial/business organizations.

The overall assessment is also interesting. It is clear that physical protection has a strong overall role in security, as does UPS protection. Separation of duties, background screening, and effective password systems also have high overall importance. The role of encryption is somewhat limited, and sophisticated techniques such as secure multilevel operating systems have few applications. There is a notable contrast between this conclusion and that obtained only through observing emphases in the literature.

9.2 CURRENT SECURITY STRENGTHS AND WEAKNESSES

Assessment of the current security posture is a useful contribution to the overall perspective. In this section, such an assessment is made. The comments are necessarily general.

9.2.1 Security Strengths

One of the most outstanding security developments of recent years has been in the area of encryption techniques. We now have a secure "standard" technique (DES) that is widely known, understood, and used. It has met every known adversarial test and is available in a variety of commercial implementations. A widely used public-key system is also available (RSA). Secure national security encryption systems are available for government-authorized applications.

Another notable development has been secure operating systems. The availability of multilevel secure systems has important government and military applications. In addition, the development has resulted in the spinoff of security features into many standard operating systems.

Security software packages that include access control and audit trail features are another useful development. These allow, in many cases, enhanced security for commercial operating systems.

Hardware access control devices such as callback or modem intercept devices can be used to discourage dialup attacks. Security code generators can enhance password access control.

ROM-based chip-level security features are also helpful. Some biometric devices have proved effective.

Other protective technology includes Halon fire extinguishant, uninterruptible power systems, EM protective devices, and intrusion detection systems.

Backup technology must also be noted. The existence of hot sites, cold sites, and contingency planning techniques has saved many companies from financial ruin.

Network security architecture, involving network security controllers and secure gateways, has been a major contribution to communications security.

9.2.2 Security Weaknesses

On the negative side, vexing problems still cloud the current security environment. In the legal area, uniform (nationally and internationally) and more comprehensive laws are needed, although progress has been achieved in recent years. Education is needed in order to sensitize judges and attorneys to sophisticated computer issues.

On the question of personal identification (on-site or remote), technology that could substantially improve the situation (biometrics, smart cards, security code generators) is in a state of infancy.

Network security in general needs improvement. Controlling access uniformly and reliably over widely dispersed locations is difficult. Effective network encryption techniques for key exchange are needed, even where public-key systems are used.

Another problem that is always expected is that tradeoffs are difficult when standard approaches compete against advancing technology. An example is the DES encryption system. It is becoming progressively more entrenched as a standard and, because of computer-enhanced cryptanalysis capabilities, it is progressively more vulnerable to exhaustive attack. Similar examples can be cited with regard to password security techniques.

Cost can also be a significant negative factor. For example, advances in secure operating systems have been achieved only at a burdensome price. Use of cost-benefit tradeoff techniques, such as risk analysis, demands careful weighing of alternate approaches when assessing the success of expensive programs.

9.3 RESEARCH PERSPECTIVES FOR THE 1990s

Given the strengths and weaknesses of current protective measures, it is natural to contemplate a 1990s wish list for future development. The constituents of the list that the author considers the most needed and realistic are:

1. Optics technology. Increased performance in optical fibers, optical switching, general photonics, and all-optical computing will have important security applications. Lack of emanations, freedom from interference, difficulty of surreptitious modification, and difficulty of information extraction are some of the most important attributes.
2. Biometrics. A more mature personal identification technology could help increase the reliability of personal identification as well as decrease the false rejection rates.
3. Smart cards. Reduced cost, more familiarity, better tamperproofing, and more security attributes are reasonable objectives.
4. Virus protection. The strategies of virus vaccines are improving, and the future possibilities are extensive. For example, the potential exists to use artificial intelligence (AI) procedures as an enhancement.
5. Robust construction. Buildings that are more resistant to earthquakes, fires, and water would be a useful contribution.
6. Fire extinguishants. Compounds that have the advantages of Halon (no ill effects on computers or other assets) without the disadvantages (cost, environmental threat, personnel hazard) would be welcomed.
7. Multilevel secure operating systems. More security with less cost and more efficient operation is a worthwhile goal.
8. Improved encryption techniques (symmetric and asymmetric). There is a need for improvements because of increasing computer power and a need for better key management techniques. These developments could be enhancements of existing cryptosystems.

9. Network security controllers. Improvements are needed in mediating network access to assure uniformity, to provide for straightforward addition and deletion of user privileges, and to give more definitive audit trails.

10. Intrusion detection. Features that would improve detection probability, lower false alarm probability, and lower cost are needed.

11. Lie detection. Personnel screening would be enhanced by the availability of reliable lie detectors [5] and the development of procedural techniques to minimize abuses and errors.

12. International legal uniformity. International agreements on the desirability and uniformity of security measures would help in the transborder flow of information, fair extradition practices, and successful prosecution.

13. Dialup protection. Improvements in security that are needed include rapid call tracing, protection against call-forwarding in callback scenarios, and low user time and complexity overhead.

14. "Expert" auditing systems. Human judgment in assessing audit trail data could be improved through the use of expert systems (systems utilizing automated reasoning and deduction). This would be a step toward eventual utilization of AI (artificial intelligence) features.

15. Training techniques. Efficient and effective training aids (such as automated interactive systems) would be useful.

16. Water protection. Improvements in early warning and detection are desirable.

9.4 OUTLOOK FOR THE 1990S

Security posture depends in large measure on two important constituents: technology and personnel. Technology provides both opportunities for adversaries and tools for deterring adversaries. It is no surprise that new technological developments have continued and will continue to present opportunities for each of the sides. It is certain that some people will always seek to take advantage of security weaknesses related to new technology. The obvious corollary is that security practitioners are obligated to utilize, and will continue to utilize, protective technology.

Personnel involvement is also a major factor. There are two basic types of personnel: those who are responsible for security and those who choose to attempt to breach security. Unfortunately, a few people are members of both classes.

People responsible for security appear to have a promising future. Public, managerial, peer, user, and student personnel have become much more aware of the importance of security to the success of businesses, schools, the government, and our society. The result is more support through management involvement, personnel and financial resources, and public initiatives (e.g., legislative and judicial action).

Human nature probably assures that there will always be security adversaries. One can only hope that people will be educated to the implications of security, because shortcomings adversely affect our society. Perhaps we can all become better people. That is certainly a worthwhile goal. However, if that goal were not achieved, there would still be cause for optimism. It is conceivable that security measures will discourage improper behavior, that monitoring techniques will identify improper behavior that is not discouraged, and that the remaining effects will be small enough to be tolerated.

The objectives portrayed above are optimistic, and some may argue that they are overly optimistic. However, success in all endeavors is more likely if goals are lofty. In the computer and communications security arena, this is especially important. The stakes are high for us all.

PROBLEMS

1. Pick a company (your company or your most comfortable image of a company) and do a qualitative risk analysis similar to that done in Figures 9-3 through 9-7. List the seven most appropriate protective measures for your scenario.
2. Pick a topic of interest to you that is related to computer and communications security but has aspects that were not covered in this book. Make a short literature survey (two to four publications), and describe the information you have gleaned for the reader in your own words. Your "summary tutorial" should be about two pages in length.

DILEMMA DISCUSSIONS

1. Should security techniques be publicized? Those opposed to providing the information argue that potential adversaries are aided by the knowledge of the measures in place. They are able to avoid avenues they know will be unproductive and are free

to pursue approaches that seem to have no protection. Those who favor publicizing security measures claim that deterrent value results from the image of comprehensive and effective security. They also argue that publicity is valuable to other security practitioners who may not be aware of or may not have thought of some measures. Their conclusion is that the benefits far outweigh the risks. What is your opinion?

2. TEMPEST-certified equipment must be frequently sent out for service by companies with uncleared facilities and personnel. TEMPEST recertification testing is routinely done on the returned equipment, but the possibility of "bug" placement must be acknowledged. The vendor is well known and does extensive work for the government. Photographic and visual comparison of "before and after" configurations are known to be insufficient, but reliable comparative evidence is very expensive to obtain. What should be done?

3. A person having security responsibility is ordered to do something that, while not illegal, is morally repugnant. The person's conscience cannot tolerate the act, but the order is inflexible and appears to imply loss of employment if not obeyed. The person badly needs the job, having extensive current family expenses, and knows of no other job options. The choice appears to be between family financial survival and personal integrity. What course of action would you recommend?

REFERENCES

1. Parker, Donn B., *Computer Security Management*, Reston Publishing, Reston, VA, 1981.
2. Norman, Adrian R. D., *Computer Insecurity*, Chapman and Hall, London, England, 1983.
3. Enger, Norman L., and Paul W. Howerton, *Computer Security: A Management Audit Approach*, Amacom (A Division of American Management Associations), 1980.
4. Hampton, David R., Charles E. Summer, and Ross A. Webber, *Organizational Behavior and the Practice of Management*, Scott, Foresman and Company, Glenview, IL, 1968.
5. Cowden, Gary W., "Preemployment Screening: Is Polygraph the Answer?" *Security Management*, March 1988.

Glossary

access — Ability to use a resource.

access control — A technique to restrict access to a physical area or to a computer to authorized personnel.

Access Control Facility — See ACF2.

access matrix — A systematic set of rules for rights (such as read, write) a user has for an object (such as files).

accreditation — Official authorization granted an ADP system to process sensitive information in its operational environment.

ACF2 — Access Control Facility Version 2. Class B1 software that restricts data access for IBM mainframe computers.

acoustic coupler — A device for coupling electrical data lines to the receiver of a telephone.

AI — Artificial intelligence. Programmed computer logic to emulate human thought processes.

AM — Amplitude modulation. Encoding information by varying the amplitude of a carrier signal.

analog — Variable and continuous representations of data.

ANSI — American National Standards Institute. Develops standards for coding, data transmission, programming languages, etc.

antisymmetric — Property of set elements that if one element is related to the other and vice versa, the elements are one and the same.

application programmer — A person responsible for design, development, testing, documentation, and maintenance of programs for user applications.

architecture — Basic system interconnection of standard modules to form a system.

ARPA Internet — Advanced Research Projects Agency Internetwork communications. Internet of several networks, all running TCP/IP communications protocol.

ARPANET — Department of Defense Advanced Research Projects Agency (Darpa) Network. Also known as Defense Data Network (DDN). Subset of ARPA Internet involving federally funded agencies.

arrester — A nonlinear device for suppressing voltage transients that result from lightning, power surges, or interference.

ASCII — American Standard Code for Information Interchange. An 8-bit code (128 character set) for alphanumeric characters commonly used for digital data transfers.

asymmetric cryptosystem — An encryption system that uses separate keys for encryption and decryption.

asynchronous attack — A technique for accessing information before protection takes effect, based on asynchronous timing between when security checks are performed and when user activity begins.

ATM (automated teller machine) — An automated terminal where bank transactions can be made.

attack — A physical assault or an attempt to gain unauthorized access.

audit — Independent examination of records.

audit trail — A chronological record allowing reconstruction of events.

authentication — Determining accuracy (for example, of an identity claim).

authorization — Permission to perform a task or access data.

bandwidth — The difference (in Hertz) between the lowest and highest information channel frequencies.

barrier — A physical or logical measure used to restrict access or activity.

baseband — An information transmission technique whereby symbols (e.g., bits) are placed directly on the communication medium without modulation.

BASIC — Beginners' All-purpose Symbolic Instruction Code. A procedure-level computer language developed at Dartmouth College.

batch — Volume of contiguous data or noninteractive series of program executions.

baud rate — Signaling intelligence per unit time (seconds).

Baudot code — A 5-bit representation for decimal digits, usually accompanied by a start and a stop bit.

Bell-LaPadula model — A formal model of computer security policy that describes a set of access control rules. The most notable features are that reading data protected to a higher degree than a user has rights for is prohibited (no read-up) and writing data to a less protected area than the user is operating in is prohibited (no write-down).

BER — Bit Error Rate. Ratio of error bits to total bits received.

biometrics — Measurement of some biological property of a person.

bit — Binary digit (zero or one).

bit error rate — See *BER*.

blackout — Complete loss of utility power.

broadband — A transmission technique using modulation and supporting a wide range of frequencies (usually with carrier frequencies in the 50 MHz to 500 MHz range).

brownout — Significant utility voltage reduction due to exceptionally heavy load.

browse — Reading data in search of significant information.

buffering — Temporary storage to accommodate different transmission rates or interim processing steps.

bus — An interconnection medium to which additional nodes can be connected with no significant effect on other connected nodes.

byte — A group (usually 8) of bits.

CAD — Computer-Aided Design. Computer graphics support for mechanical and electrical design.

CAD/CAM — Computer-Aided Design/Computer-Aided Manufacturing. Supports automated production of mechanical parts.

CAE — Computer-Aided Engineering. Finite-element mesh analysis for mechanical and electrical components.

CAI — Computer-Aided Instruction. Training based on student interaction with computer menus.

callback modem — A modem that is password-activated by the caller, then hangs up and calls the caller's number to establish communication.

capability-based system — A system having special mechanisms to address an object, which can only be created by the operating system. A capability acts like a ticket authorizing the use of an object.

carrier — Continuous frequency that can be modulated.

CASE — Computer-Aided Software Engineering. Use of software as an automated tool for the structural development of software.

CCTV — Closed-circuit television. Typically used for security monitoring.

cellular radio — A low-power transmission network for telephone access from stationary or mobile sites.

certification — The technical evaluation of a system's security features.

chaining — An encryption enhancement technique that feeds back data created during cipher generation to mix with subsequent cipher generation so that the same output is not generated each time a particular input occurs.

channel — Communication medium for data.

checksum — Sum of associated words of data for error checking.

chip — Small piece of semiconductor material containing an integrated circuit.

cipher — A cryptosystem using a keyed transformation to disguise information.

ciphertext — Text that has been encrypted.

Clarke orbit — A geosynchronous orbit.

classified data — Data requiring protection against unauthorized disclosure in the interest of national security.

cleartext — Unencrypted text.

clock — Oscillator-generated regular timing reference.

CMOS — Complimentary-Metal-Oxide Semiconductor. A low-power digital logic technology.

coaxial cable — Contains a conductor surrounded by insulation and metallic shielding.

code — Digital representation of numbers, letters, symbols; also programs.

codec — Coder/decoder. Converts analog signals to digital for transmission or processing.

cold site — A shell recovery facility into which computers can be moved when needed.

common mode — Signals applied to both sides of power or communication pairs.

communications — Transfer of data by hard-wired, microwave, satellite, rf, telephone, or manual modes.

communications security — The protection of transmitted data from unauthorized access, alteration, or destruction.

computer — A device capable of carrying out a programmed series of operations. Also has capabilities for input, output, memory, and high-speed operation.

computer security — The protection of computers and computer data from unauthorized access, alteration, and destruction.

concentrator — See *multiplexer*.

controller — A dedicated processor that has a fixed program memory.

covert channel — A means of signaling information indirectly by controlling some externally measurable parameter (modulation).

CRC — Cyclic Redundancy Check. A signature derived through digital polynomial division (for error checking).

CRT — Cathode Ray Tube.

cryptography — Generation of encrypted text.

cryptosystem — A technique for disguising (from an adversary) information.

CSMA/CD — Carrier Sense Multiple Access with Collision Detection. A local-area network access technique.

database — A shared, centrally controlled collection of data with software organization enabling retrieval through data characteristics.

Database Management System (DBMS) — A computer-based tool used to set up a database, make it available to users, and control the integrity of the data resources.

data diddling — Unauthorized data alteration.

Data Encryption Standard (DES) — An encryption algorithm using permutations and substitutions. It is published and supported by the National Institute of Standards and Technology.

data integrity — Data protection against intentional or accidental alteration or destruction.

dB — Decibel. A unit of ratio measurement equal to 10 times the base-ten logarithm of the power ratio.

DBASE III Plus — A database product from Ashton-Tate for use on PC systems.

dBm — dBs below a milliwatt.

DBMS — See *Database Management System*.

DB2 — Relational database management system for MVS operating system on IBM mainframe computers.

deciphering — Recovering information from encrypted text.

DECnet — DEC networking product for data communication among VAX and other DEC computers.

degausser — A device that erases magnetic media by overwriting information with the alternating magnetic field generated.

DES — See *Data Encryption Standard*.

differential mode — Signals applied between power or communication pairs.

digital signature — An information-processing technique for certifying that only the authorized signature creator could have produced the signature.

discretionary security policy — Requirement that a person accessing information have permission of the information "owner" based on need-to-know.

disk — Flat, circular, rigid magnetic storage device.

diskette (floppy disk) — Thin, circular, flexible magnetic storage medium.

distributed processing — Essentially simultaneous processing using more than one computing unit.

DMA — Direct Memory Access. A technique for rapid, dedicated memory transfer.

domain — The set of objects that a subject may access.

dominate — A relation of ordering or hierarchy.

Doppler effect — An apparent frequency shift caused by relative motion between a transmitter and a receiver.

DOS — Disk operating system. Operating system commonly used on IBM PCs and clones.

downlink — Transmission from communications satellite to an earth station.

duplex — Bidirectional data transmission. (See half-duplex; full duplex).

EBCDIC — Extended Binary Coded Decimal Interchange Code. An 8-bit code used to represent 256 characters.

ECM — Electronic countermeasures.

EDP — Electronic Data Processing. Computer or computer-peripheral data processing.

electromagnetic energy — Energy conveyed by oscillating, interacting electric and magnetic fields.

electronic bulletin boards — A computer system where messages can be entered and read for spreading information.

electronic mail — A technique for transmitting and managing files of messages using a computer, computer memory, and communication links.

EMI — Electromagnetic interference.

encipher — Transforming information to make it undecipherable without a key.

encryption — Enciphering.

EPROM — Erasable Programmable Read-Only memory. Non-volatile memory that can be changed using specific writing devices.

error correcting/detecting codes — A technique for adding redundant information that is a function of the information to be protected so that errors during transmission may be corrected or detected.

ESD — Electrostatic discharge.

Ethernet — A 10 Mb/second baseband shielded coaxial cable LAN.

execution domains — The restriction of execution access to programs in privileged areas with well-defined interfaces.

exhaustive attack — Using all possible values sequentially in an attempt to find an unknown value (encryption key or password).

Faraday shield — A conductive enclosure intended to prevent escape or intrusion of electromagnetic energy.

FDM — See *Frequency Division Multiplexing*.

FEC (forward error correction) — An error correction technique that can be accomplished during a single transmission of data.

fiber optics — Transparent transmission medium (usually glass) carrying information through oscillations at near-visual wavelengths.

firmware — Hardware memory containing essentially unalterable program steps.

floppy disk — See *diskette.*

FM — See *frequency modulation.*

FORTRAN — Formula Translator. The most widely used program for scientific applications.

forward error correction — A technique for correcting errors during transmission (no retransmission required).

frequency division multiplexing (FDM) — A technique for sharing a transmission channel through simultaneous transmission of multiple frequencies.

frequency hopping — A spread-spectrum technique with pseudo-random frequency changes.

frequency modulation (FM) — Carrier modulated by changes in frequency.

full duplex — A channel capable of carrying information simultaneously in both directions.

gateway — Network entity for interconnecting two networks having different characteristics.

geosynchronous orbit — Orbit 22,300 miles above the equator for which the satellite is stationary with respect to the earth.

ground — Electrical connection to conductor connected to earth.

group — A collection of users having common authorization, for example, to a set of data.

guard — a) A person responsible for helping maintain physical security control, b) a software procedure for controlling a software transaction.

hacker — An individual who persistently explores computers and networks to learn how they can be utilized. The term now is generally applied to those who try to overcome computer and network security barriers, mostly for the challenge.

half duplex — A channel having bidirectional but not simultaneous data transmission capabilities.

Halon — A family of gases based on halogens (chlorine, bromine, fluorine, iodine) that is used in fighting fires.

handshaking — An interchange of information across a channel to establish synchronization, authentication, etc.

hardware — Physical devices such as computers, peripherals, and memory devices.

hazard — A situation that results in possible loss of an asset.

host — A computer that accepts and processes jobs from remote locations.

hot site — A backup recovery computer facility that can be used in case of a disaster.

identifier — A mode of identification of an individual user (or sometimes for a group of users needing access to a common resource).

IEEE — Institute of Electrical and Electronics Engineers. A major professional organization of engineers that is active in defining standards.

INGRES — Interactive Graphics and Retrieval System. Relational database software from Relational Technology, Inc., for VAX, SUN, etc.

integrity — Assurance that a resource (physical, software, or data) is not destroyed or modified.

interactive — Real-time dialog between two devices over a communication link.

internet — A network of networks.

ISDN (Integrated Services Digital Network) — A digital communications network that can handle multiple services such as data, voice, video, facsimile.

ISO (International Standards Organization) — An international body tasked with establishing communications standards.

jamming — The insertion of signal or noise into a system (usually electromagnetically) to prevent normal operation of the system.

jitter — Slight changes in transmission time or phase that can cause errors.

k — Kilo. Thousands of units.

K — Symbol for 1024.

kernel — A confined software module containing protected security functions.

kernelized operating systems — Systems containing an inaccessible (by hardware and software) access control module.

key — 1) A physical entity to lock (or unlock), 2) an electronic signal for carrying out a logic function, 3) a combination of numbers or characters used in access control, 4) a parameter used in the encryption and/or decryption of information.

knapsack — A problem used in encryption (picking selected components from a collection) that exactly solves a problem (usually a sum).

KSOS — Kernelized Secure Operating System.

LAN (Local Area network) — A network intended to interconnect devices within relatively small distances (usually within a few hundred meters) of each other.

lattice — A partially ordered set (reflexive, transitive, antisymmetric) with a greatest lower bound and a least upper bound.

library — Collection of software routines.

LISP — List Processing. An interpretive language that manipulates symbolic strings of recursive data.

local area network — See *LAN*.

log — Data concerning connections and authentication and authorization attempts.

logic bomb — An unauthorized destructive routine that is executed based on some parameter such as circumstance or date and time.

LSI — Large-scale integration. Tens of thousands of gates or transistors on a substrate chip.

mandatory security policy — Requirement that a person accessing information have a clearance equal to or greater than the data classification.

masquerade — Pretending to be other than actual (user, software, or hardware technique).

memory — Computer-accessible storage area for information and programs.

microcode — Programmed instructions that are unalterable or difficult to alter.

microprocessor — A small integrated circuit that executes computer functions (computer on a chip).

microwave link — A communication channel through space or air at frequencies that can range from thousands of Hertz (cycles per second) to billions of Hertz.

minicomputer — An intermediate-sized computer with capabilities and price in-between that of mainframe computers and that of microcomputers.

modem (modulator-demodulator) — A device that interfaces digital data to and from the form (usually analog) required by communication channels.

MTBF — Mean Time Before Failure. Expected operational time before a failure occurs.

multilevel security — Provisions for simultaneous processing at two or more levels of security.

multiplexer (concentrator) — A device that controls information sequentially from several input lines to an output line.

MVS — Multiple Virtual Storage. An operating system for IBM mainframes.

NBS — National Bureau of Standards, now National Institute of Standards and Technology (NIST).

networks — Associated components interconnected for such functions as communications and resource sharing.

network security controller — A secure computer that mediates security functions for a network.

NIST — National Institute of Standards and Technology.

node — A network termination point (computer, terminal, switch).

noise — Extraneous and unwanted (usually EM) signal disturbances.

nonvolatile memory — Memory that retains information when power is removed.

NOS — Network Operating System. An operating system used on CDC computers.

NSA — National Security Agency.

object — The recipient of action (e.g., a file).

office automation — Computers or networks of terminals and computers that enable functions like electronic mail, filing, scheduling, word processing, and computing in an office environment.

one-way transform — A mathematical transformation that is difficult to invert.

operating system — The software that controls and manages how the computer processes user operations and programs, including managing data files and allocating system resources to user requirements.

optical disk — Very high-density storage medium using laser data reading.

optical fiber — See *fiber optics*.

OSI (Open Systems Interconnection) model — A   standard seven-layer network communications protocol supported by the International Standards Organization.

OS/2 — Operating System 2. An operating system intended for the IBM 386-based PCs.

packet switching — A logical network transmission strategy for routing short segments of information (packets) independently through a network to maximize efficiency and reassembling the information at the receiving end.

PACX — Private Automated Computer Exchange. A network data contention and switching system.

parallel processing — Concurrent execution of multiple processes.

parity — A single-bit-assignment controlled to make the total number of ones in a sequence even (even parity) or odd (odd parity).

partially ordered set — A set of elements with a relation that is reflexive, antisymmetric, and transitive.

Pascal — A compiler and language developed by Prof. Niklaus Wirth to support structural programming techniques.

password — A protected word or string of characters for user authentication or verification of access authorization.

PBX — Private Branch Exchange. Secure data switch for asynchronous and synchronous network data services.

PC — See *personal computer*.

PCM — Pulse Code Modulation. Digital coding technique using modulation of a pulsed (intermittent) carrier.

penetration — Unauthorized physical or logical access or seizure of control functions.

peripherals — Devices that supplement the main functions of a processor (e.g., printers).

personal computer — Computers designed to be used by a single user, in the office or at home.

phonetic password — A construction intended to be pronounceable and therefore memorizable, although not necessarily meaningful.

physical security — Security for computers, memories, peripheral equipment, communication gear, and buildings housing such equipment.

PIN (personal identification number) — A private user code for access control to devices like ATMs.

plaintext — See *cleartext*.

polarization — EM characteristic where electric field has a particular consistent direction perpendicular to the direction of propagation.

port — Connection mode for transmitting information between two devices.

port contender — A device that allows connection from a relatively large number of inputs to a relatively small number of output ports.

port protection device (PPD) — A device in line with a modem (in front or behind) that intercepts computer connection attempts and requires additional information. Callback modems are a subset.

prime number — An integer evenly divisible by no other integers except one.

privacy — Right (legal or social) of an individual to expect protection of personal information.

programming — 1) Writing a sequence of computer instructions, 2) electrically inserting information into a ROM (read-only memory) or PROM (programmable read-only memory), 3) setting the address of a device by establishing electrical characteristics.

protection/protective measures — Steps taken to assure that threats (persons, nature, accidents) do not affect assets (information, hardware, software).

protocol — Rules, procedures, or format for presenting information.

public-key cryptosystem — An encryption process using a public key and a secret key that simplifies the key distribution problem.

query — A request for information from a database.

queue — Collection of items waiting in line for service or processing.

RAM (random-access memory) — A read/write memory with all addresses directly accessible.

RDBMS — Relational Database Management System. Table-oriented, relational-algebra processed database.

read — Acquire or examine data without changing the data.

recovery — Restoration of computing facilities and capabilities.

reference monitor — A mediation technique that checks every request for access or action against a database of "rights."

reflexive — An element of a set is related to itself.

releases — Versions of software (applications programs, operating systems, compilers).

residue — Data left in memory after a process is completed.

resource — Any service, capacity, or data accessible via a system.

RF — Radio frequency, usually high kHz to Mhz range.

RFI — Radio frequency interference.

ringer isolator — A device that electrically separates telephone ringer circuits from the line for electromagnetic isolation.

risk — The probability per unit time that an asset will be lost due to a vulnerability. (Also used by some authors to represent expected dollar loss per unit time.)

risk analysis — A systematic analytical technique for estimating the cost-effectiveness of security measures.

ROM — Read-only memory, where data or programs are inserted for essentially permanent use.

RSA encryption — A public-key encryption system based on work by Rivest, Shamir, and Adleman.

salami technique — An attack utilizing a large number of small effects to attempt a significant gain while drawing insignificant attention.

satellite — Earth-orbiting station, commonly used for network communication relay.

scavenging — A physical or electronic technique for scanning through data or residue for useful knowledge not legitimately available.

scrambling — Mixing up the order of a sequence in a prescribed and unvarying way. Sometimes used in low-security applications for information hiding.

security — Protection from harm, such as unintended disclosure, alteration, misuse, physical attack, accidents, or natural disasters.

security code generator — A device that generates, or assists in the generation of, one-time passwords.

sensitive — A resource (usually data) that is not to be freely accessed.

separation of duties — Dichotomizing at least some of the functions of authorizing, approving, recording, issuing, paying, reviewing, auditing, programming, and developing processes that generate output meriting protection.

shareware — Software that is copied for "sharing" free of charge or for a nominal copy fee.

shredder — A device used to physically decimate information-storage media (paper, tape, microfiche).

simple security — A Bell-LaPadula security rule allowing a subject to read only objects at lower security levels than the subject has.

smart card — A card containing a microprocessor, ROM, and RAM, used for security-intensive functions such as debit transactions or other data processing.

software — Programs of instructions (applications programs, operating systems, compilers, etc.).

spoofing — Surreptitious hard-to-detect alterations that allow improper changes to be made in hardware or software.

spread spectrum — A modulation technique for spreading (increasing) information bandwidth.

star property (sometimes written as ∗-property) — A Bell-La-Padula security rule preventing subjects from writing information to a lower security level than that at which they are operating.

subject — The initiator of action (e.g., a user program or process).

superzapping — Using a security bypass program.

symmetric cryptosystem — A system that uses the same key for encryption and decryption.

tailgating — Surreptitiously taking advantage of another person's access following their authentication (by a physical or logical barrier).

TCB — See *trusted computing base.*

TCC — Technical Control Center. Switching center for controlling and diagnosing data traffic.

TCP/IP — Transmission Control Protocol/Internet Protocol. Commonly used communications protocol, with correspondences to the OSI network standards.

TDM — Time Division Multiplexing. Interleaved digital data transmission technique providing different time slices for different users.

TDMA — Time-Division Multiple Access. Satellite transmission technique with each earth station in sequence transmitting a short burst.

Technical Control Center — See *TCC.*

telecommunications — Communication over a relatively large (usually more than a few hundred meters) distance.

TEMPEST — A program to meet the threat of information leakage by unintended physical communication channels. Commonly used synonymously with electromagnetic emanations leakage of information.

terminal — Network data entry/read device.

terminal masquerade — An attack where a computer terminal user uses a communication capability to another terminal to load that terminal with information that will appear to come legitimately from the latter, with transparency to its operator.

TH — See *Trojan horse.*

Tiger Teams — Teams of experts who legitimately test robustness of security features by attempted penetration.

time bomb — See *logic bomb.*

Time Division Multiplexing — See *TDM.*

token — LAN access logical entity for passing authority to "occupy" the token and transmit data. Tokens are used in token ring and token bus networks.

transitive — A property of elements of a set such that if one element is related to a second and the second to a third, then the first is related to the third.

transponder — Device that receives information signal and amplifies and retransmits it.

trapdoors — 1) Program breaks inserted for diagnosis, 2) problem solution path given a particular piece of information, without which solution is much more difficult, 3) mechanism causing bypass of security features.

Trojan horse — Covert unauthorized instruction sequence hidden within legitimate code that can be triggered to attack systems in various ways.

trusted computer system — A system that has sufficient security to allow simultaneous processing at two or more security levels (multilevel security).

trusted computing base (TCB) — The totality of hardware and software security features in a computer system.

trusted software — Software that is depended upon to perform special security functions.

twisted pair — Twisted insulated conductors used for short-distance information transmission.

Uninterruptible Power Supply (UPS) — A system that can maintain ac power during an outage for a period of time by deriving the power from dc storage batteries.

UNIX — Widely used operating system developed at AT&T Bell Laboratories and refined by several companies.

uplink — Transmission from earth station to a communication satellite.

UPS — Uninterruptible power supply.

vaccine — A software program intended to protect against virus-like programs.

varistor — A nonlinear protective device that limits high voltages by becoming increasingly conductive with voltage.

virtual memory — A logical technique for mapping multiple physical locations to memory locations through pointers.

virus — A program (usually destructive) that copies itself into other programs whenever its parent program is executed.

VLSI — Very Large Scale Integration. Technology for high-density (greater than 100,000 components) on a semiconductor chip.

VMS — Virtual Memory System. Operating system for VAX computers.

volatile memory — Memory that is essentially erased when unpowered.

WAN — Wide-Area Network. Network transversing long distances (e.g., hundreds of miles).

wideband — See *broadband*.

word — A group of associated digits (usually bits).

word processor — A text-preparation device or program that contains memory and intelligence for ease of changes during creation and editing.

work station — A terminal or microcomputer that facilitates desk work (word processing, database management, etc.).

worm — A surreptitiously inserted program (Trojan horse) that overwrites data in a computer memory.

write — To insert data into a storage medium, thereby destroying information in the targeted locations.

zap — 1) Unauthorized modification of a program to bypass its control mechanisms, 2) to destroy data or programming.

Answers to Problems

Chapter 1

1. a) clock: 100kHz–25MHz, c = 250
    volume: 10,000cu ft–3cu ft, v = 3300
    power: 150kW–200W, p = 750
    MTBF: 1 day–365 days, m = 365
    dollars: $400,000–$10,000, d = 40 x 1.05^{43}
    I(improvement) = $cvpmd$ = 7.4×10^{13}
    b) security environment

2. a) e(expected loss) = pv where p is the probability of a loss per year and v is the asset value (dollars).
    b) the protective measure expense per year.

3. Threat: hacker; asset: computer operator.

4. a) Mainly the dispersal of components, allowing networks and dialup.
    b) Security technology (encryption, modem intercept devices, security software).

5. a) Yes, because it can be reprogrammed and may create a safety hazard for personnel.
    b) No, because it cannot be reprogrammed and in itself can create no safety hazard.

Chapter 2

1. a) First, find the probability that no two people out of n have the same birthday:

$$1 - p = (364/365)(363/365) \ldots \left(\frac{365-n+1}{365} \right)$$

$$p = 1 - (364/365)(363/365) \ldots \left(\frac{365-n+1}{365} \right)$$

   b) for $n = 23$, $p = 0.507$.

2. a) $1 - p = (1/1461)(1460/1461)(1456/1461) \ldots (1468\text{-}4n)/1461$
       $+ (1460/1461)(1/1457)(1457/1461)(1456/1461)(1452/1461). \ldots$
       $+ (1460/1461)(1459/1460)(1/1453)(1457/1461)(1453/1461)$
       $(1452/1461)(1448/1461) \ldots (1468\text{-}4n)/1461$
       $+ (1460/1461)(1459/1460)(1458/1459)(1/1449)(1457/1461)$
       $(1453/1461)(1449/1461)(1448/1461)(1444/1461) \ldots$
       $(1468\text{-}4n)/1461$

       .
       .
       .

       $+ (1460/1461)(1459/1460) \ldots (\dfrac{1461-n}{1462-n})(1457/1461)$
       $(1453/1461) \ldots (1465\text{-}4n)/1461.$

   b) $n = 23$.

3. a)

	computer	software	private info	people liable
fire	0	0	0	0
water	$1000	$100	0	0
earthquake	$1000	$100	0	0
insider	0	0	$1000	0

   b) pipe reroute, software security.
   c) $850 worth of pipe rerouting.

4. a)

	fire (10^{-2})	water (10^{-1})	auth. user ($10^{0)}$
computer (10^4)	10^2	10^3	—
software (10^3)	10^1	—	10^3

b) Halon, pipe rerouting, software backup
c) 10^2 fire savings for 10^4 Halon expenditure, 10^3 water savings for 10^3 pipe re-route, 10^3 user savings for 10^2 backup.
d) Choose pipe rerouting and backup.

5. Make table assuming $5000 loaded rate for person-month and $3 diskette cost:

theft during hrs	theft after hrs	hard disk data destruction
no software loss	$1/20 \times \$2000$	no software loss
$1 \times \$3$	$1/20 \times \$3$	no diskette loss
$1/5 \times \$5000$	$1/20 \times \$5000$	$1/5 \times \$5000$
$1/5 \times \$10000$	$1/20 \times \$10000$	no computer loss

Listing vulnerabilities in order (increment columns first; then rows), and tabulating ALE reductions against protective measures:

	mtg rack (545)	password (375)	case (15)	motion alarm (820)
2.	$100			$100
4.			$3	
5.				$0.15
7.	$1000			$1000
8.	$250			$250
9.		$1000		
10.	$2000			$2000
11.	$500			$500

The indicated annual savings for the $545 mounting rack are $3850. Essentially the same savings would be expected for the motion alarms, but the cost is greater, so the mounting rack would be selected and the motion alarms would not.

The password system appears cost-effective, since its saving is $1000 compared to a cost of $375.

The diskette case is inexpensive, but ineffective. It would not be selected.

6. The effects of programming errors could be assessed by past experience with program performance testing prior to putting in service. The risk of operator errors and the effects are monitored and available from experience. Component failure effects are judged by past experience with similar systems built under similar design guidance and tested similarly for the effect of faults. Sabotage probability can be estimated from adversarial activity records within the country, paying special attention to trends and threats.

7. a) Quantitative figures are available to directly show cost-effectiveness.
   b) More likely to identify the approaches that may be taken by personnel adversaries.

8. Monitoring is establishing a feedback mode to modify selected protective measures, recover from disasters, and prosecute adversaries.

9. The value of the data can be estimated by considering the impact of *not* having the data. Census data are used for tax bases, for determining legislative representation, for corporate planning, for municipal planning, and for federal planning (and for other less important purposes). Assuming total loss of the data, there would be the following potential impacts:

   Tax. Questions about the accuracy of tax bases could lead to legal challenges. Estimates of the litigation potential would be part of the value.

   Legislative representation. There is some litigation potential here, also, but the amount is less.

   Corporate planning. Since the accuracy of corporate planning impacts the business success of the corporation, there could be significant effects.

Municipal planning. The effects on teacher assignments, facilities requirements and development details would have financial impacts.

Federal planning. The federal government uses the data for (among other things) estimating welfare and social security costs.

10. a)   2 events: $p = p_1 + p_2 - p_1p_2$
    b)   3 events: $p = p_1 + p_2 + p_3 - p_1p_2 - p_1p_3 - p_2p_3 + p_1p_2p_3$
    c)   4 events: $p = p_1 + p_2 + p_3 + p_4 - p_1p_2 - p_1p_3 - p_1p_4$
         $- p_2p_3 - p_2p_4 - p_3p_4 + p_1p_2p_3 + p_1p_2p_4 + p_1p_3p_4$
         $+ p_2p_3p_4 - p_1p_2p_3p_4$
    d) $1 - (1-p_1)(1-p_2)..(1-p_n)$

11. The exact expression is:

$$p = (3 \times 2^{2n} - 3 \times 2^n + 1)/2^{3n}$$

The approximate expression is:

$$p \approx 3/2^n$$

The ratio of the two is approximately:

$$r = 1 - 2^{-n}$$

Solving for n, $n = 10$ for $r > 0.999$.

12. 0.98^5 to 1.02^5, or 0.904 to 1.104

13. $\sigma = \sqrt{\sigma_1^2 + \sigma_2^2 + \sigma_3^2 + \sigma_4^2 + \sigma_5^2}$

14. a)   1/16
    b)   1/10
    c)   1/8
    d)   Part a) is for independent bits, parts b) and c) have dependency relationships among the bits.

15. a)   3 ways (all 3 against the same one; 2 against 1 and 1 against another; each against a different one).
    b)   1/25, 12/25, 12/25, respectively.

    c) 5 ways (all 5 against the same one; 4 against 1 and 1 against another; 3 against 1 and 2 against another; 3 against 1 and the other 2 against separate ones; 2 against 1, 2 against another and the last against another).

    d) 1/81, 10/81, 20/81, 20/81, 10/27, respectively.

16. $[\binom{n}{k} \binom{n-k}{k} \ldots 1]/n^{kn}$

Chapter 3

1. a) Assume one barrier, c determines p_1. For two barriers, $c_1 + c_2 = c$. Next, $p_2 = 1 - (1-c_1)(1-c_2) = 1 - 1 + c_1 + c_2 - c_1 c_2 = c - c_1 c_2$. Therefore, multiple barriers are inferior to single barriers.

    b) $p_2 = c_1^2 + c_2^2 - c_1^2 c_2^2$. $c_1 + c_2 > (c_1^2 + c_2^2)^{1/2}$, so $c^2 > c_1^2 + c_2^2$. Therefore, multiple barriers are inferior to single barriers.

    c) Compare $(c_1 + c_2)^{1/2}$ with $c_1^{1/2} + c_2^{1/2} - c_1^{1/2} c_2^{1/2}$. Since the former may or may not exceed the latter, multiple barriers are possibly superior to single barriers, depending on the specific conditions. As an example, let $c_1 = c_2 = c/2$. $p_1 = p_2$ for the condition $c = (2 \times 2^{1/2} - 2)^2$. For larger values of c, $p_1 > p_2$; for smaller values of c, $p_1 < p_2$.

    d) Compare $\sin(\pi c/2)$ with $2\sin(\pi c/4) - \sin^2(\pi c/4)$, assuming $c = c/2 + c/2$. Let $x = \pi c/4$ ($x_{max} = 45°$). Ratio $= \sin(2x)/(2\sin x - \sin^2 x) = \cos x/(1 - \sin x/2)$. This ratio is greater than one for $x \le 45°$.

2. $p_e p_f = e^{-2s}s$; derivative $= 0$ for $e^{-2s} = 2se^{-2s}$; $s = 1/2$.

3. $(1 - e^{-2s})/s = 1/s - e^{-2s}/s$. Derivative $= 0 = 1/s^2 - e^{-2s}/s^2 - 2e^{-2s}/s$. Solution: $s = 0$. Not a practical answer.

4. $V_t = 1000 + 50 \times 10^{-9} (V_t - 1000)r = 1000 + 50 \times 10^{-9}r$.

5. See Problem 3-5 solution diagram.

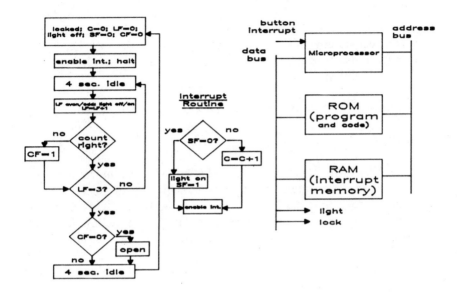

Figure P-1   Problem 3-5 solution.

6. a) zero. b) $115(2/\pi)$. c) $115/\sqrt{2}$. d) $115^2/2$.

7. a) zero. b) $115(2/\pi)$. c) $115/\sqrt{2}$. d) $100^2/2 + 15^2/2$.

Chapter 4

1. a) Advertising: $500; hiring personnel time (place ad, correspond, handle logistics, interview, process offer): 2 weeks (assume loaded rate of $1000/week); background screening: $5000; technical organization interview, evaluation: 2 days; office supplies (desk, computer, books): $10,000; training: 4 months; insurance, benefits: $10,000/year. Total: $88,900.

    b) Assume starting pay: $30,000, value increases 10%/year. $3000 × 5 = $15,000.

2. 1) Return after supper and work past midnight may indicate working on something improper. 2) Ambitions exceed rewards may create anger toward company. 3) No social life may indicate disregard for behavior standards. 4) Possibly high family expenses may indicate need for money. 5) Porsche purchases not consistent with programmer's salary. 6) Telephone time may indicate personal problems, especially since he is not a social person.

3. Expected take = 10,000 × 0.0025 × 365.25 = $9131/year.

Chapter 5

1. 1) Theft of information can leave owner's information untouched, 2) wiretapping detects bits instead of voices, 3) "witness" to crime may be a computer audit trail, 4) failure to produce accurate software may result in legal action, 5) failure to exercise computer security may result in legal action.

2. 1) Copyright laws, 2) "shrinkwrap" license, 3) inadvertent sharing equivalent to theft.

3. 1) National responsibility vs. company responsibility, 2) cost-effectiveness vs. maintaining funding, 3) frequent rotation vs. long-term employment.

4. a) 1) Insufficient safety to personnel, 2) defamation of personnel, 3) software piracy, 4) information destruction, 5) misuse of resources.
   b) 1) Fraud, 2) theft, 3) espionage, 4) physical destruction, 5) blackmail.

5. U.S.: $pvnm$ = $4M; Soviet: $pvnm$ = $20M; difference = $16M; std. dev. of difference = 6.08M; 0 = 2.63 std. devs.; p = 0.004.

6. a) 37,334.
   b) $280,000.

Chapter 6

1. a) No—should be less than double. Selling price = production cost plus overhead plus profit.

b) Probably yes. Tradeoff is number of components vs. yield. Yield usually more directly related to investment.

2. $f = xy \vee z; \bar{f} = \bar{y}\,\bar{z} \vee \bar{x}\,\bar{z}$. Use 110 for x $s0$, y $s0$, and interconnect $s0$; 010 for x $s1$ and interconnect $s1$; 100 for y $s1$ and z $s1$; 011 (for example) for z $s0$.

3. a) $5 \times 11 + 5 \times 7$ (modulo 80) = 10. 10 (modulo 5) = 0.
   b) $11 + 7$ (modulo 16) = 2. 11 (modulo 4) = 3; 7 (modulo 4) = 3; $3 + 3$ (modulo 4) = 2.

4. Not a field. Distributive law fails. $2(1 + 1) \neq 2 + 2$.

5. $p_1 = p_2 = p_3 = 0$. Input 1111 gives decoder output 111. b_3 is the only bit that can cause all three checks to fail. Change b_3 to 0.

6. There are three dependent vectors, since row 1 + row 2 = row 4. Therefore, eight code words; three information bits.

7. Multiply first equation by two, add to second: $2x = 2$. Multiply both sides by three: $x = 1$. Substitute $x = 1$ in first equation and add two to both sides: y = 1.

8. a) $n = 7, k = 0.57; n = 15, k = 0.73; n = 31, k = 0.84; n = 63, k = 0.90; n = 127, k = 0.94$.
   b) $n = 7, P = 0.998; n = 15, P = 0.990; n = 31, P = 0.962; n = 63, P = 0.869; n = 127, P = 0.637$. In general, $P = p^n + n(1 - p)p^{n-1}$.

9. $di(t)/dt = CVa^2 e^{-at} (1 - at)$; a) $t = 1/a = 5 \times 10^{-8}$ secs. b) i(peak) = 7.4 A. c) t(half peak value) = 8.5×10^{-8} secs.

10. Receiver "aperture" is $G\lambda^2/4\pi$. $P_r = 1/4\pi r^2 \times 100x3^2/4\pi$. For r = 10, P = 57 mW; for $r = 100$, $P_r = 0.57$ mW; for $r = 1000$, $P_r = 5.7$ μW.

Chapter 7

1. a) $t = 26^4 / 2$ secs. = 63.5 hours. b) Expect 13 tries for each digit — $t = 13 \times 4 = 52$ secs.

2. a) $P = \sum_{i=1}^{10} \binom{10}{i} = 1023.$

   b) $p = 252/1023 = 0.246.$

3. a) $P = 26^3 = 17576.$

   b) $P \approx 400$ (see partial list below; some distasteful words eliminated).

   c)   yes

ace act add ads aft age ago aha aid ail aim air ale all alm amp and ant any ape arc are ark arm art asp ate awe axe bad bag bam bar bat bay bed bee bet bid big bin bit boa bob bog boo boy bra bud bug bum bun bus but buy bye cab cad cam can cap car cat cay cog coo cop cot cow coy cry cub cup cur cut dab dad dam dap day den did die dig dim din dip doe dog dud due dug dye ear eat eel egg ego elm end eon ere erg err eve ewe eye fad fan far fat fee fib fig fin fir fit fly fob foe fog for fun fur gab gad gag gal gam gap gar gas gat gay gee gel gem get gig gin gip god goo got gum gun gut guy had hag ham has hat hay hee hen hey hid him hip his hob hog hon hop hot how hue hug hum hut inn jab jag jam jar jaw jay jib jig job jog kid kin kit lab lad lag lam lap law lay led lee leg let lid lie lip lit lob log lop lot low lye mad man map mar map may men met mid mil mob bod mom moo mop mow mud dug mum nab nag nap naw nay nip nit nob nod non nor not now nub nun nut oaf oak oar oat odd ode oft old ole ohm one ore our own pad pal pan pap par pat paw pay pea pen pep pet pew ply pod pom pon poo pop pot pow pro pry pub pug pun pup pus quo rag rah ram ran rap rat raw ray red rid rim rip rod rot row rub rug run rut sad sag sap sat saw say see set she sic sin sip sis sit six ski sky sob sod sog son sot sow soy spa spy sty sub sud sun sup sur tab tad tag tan tap tar tat tea tee ten tic tie tin tip toe tom ton too top tot tow toy tub tug ugh use van vat vet vie vim wad wag wan war was way wed wee wet win wit woe wok won woo wow yam yap yaw yea yen yep yes yet yup zap zoo

4. a) $p + (r^k - r^p)/r^{k+p}.$

   b) $p = r^k.$

   c) $p = r^p.$

5. First letter position in alphabet gives key to how far the others must be advanced: AHIMV/IJNW.

6. a) $P = (21 \times 5 \times 21)^2 = 4{,}862{,}025.$
   b) $p = 1/P \approx 2 \times 10^{-7}.$

7. a), b) An example counting y as a vowel:

   a. Beginning consonants: all except q, x
   b. Beginning vowels: all except y
   c. Center consonants: all except h, q, x
   d. Center vowels: all except y
   e. End consonants: all except c, h, q
   f. End vowels: all except i
   g. Beginning digraphs: bl, br, ch, cl, cr, fl, gl, gr, kl, kr, pl, pr, sh, sl, sr
   h. End digraphs: ch, lm, nd, nt
   i. End consonant pairs: dd, ff, ll, nn, tt
   j. End vowel pairs: ee, oo

   Forms:

   1. ade (1530), 2. bcf (425), 3. gf (75), 4. bh(20), 5. bi(25), 6. aj(36).

   c) 1/268
   d) 1/20
   e) 1/2111.

8. $p = (1/n^2)(1/x_1 + 1/x_2 + \ldots + 1/x_n).$

9. Adversary will guess choice 100: P(success) = 100/5050 = 0.198. [Gauss summed the first 100 integers by noticing that there were 50 pairs with identical sums (1 + 100, 2 + 99, . . . , 50 + 51). Therefore, 50 × 101 = 5050.]

Chapter 8

1. Requires two orbits per day instead of one. Orbital radius is about 33,500 km. The same effect could be obtained if the

satellite were fixed instead of orbiting, but solving Eq. 2 for r shows r would have to be infinite.

2. A "spherical surface segment" (spherical surface contained in a conical section) is within sight of the satellite. The half-cone angle (measured from the center of the earth) is 81.3 degrees.

3. Testing PZ, QA, RB, etc., the only English word is "IS." For key = 7, message is "THIS IS THE END OF THE PROBLEM."

4. a) $25 \times 7 \mod 31 = 20$. $20 \times 9 \mod 31 = 25$.
   b) $25 \times 10 \mod 31 = 2$. $2 \times 28 \mod 31 = 25$.
   c) $25 \times 7 \times 10 \mod 31 = 14$. $14 \times 28 \times 9 \mod 31 = 25$.
   d) For A, key $\times$ 28 = 1 mod 31: key = 10. For B, key $\times$ 7 = 1 mod 31: key = 9.

5. Dividing, remainder $= x + 1$: bit pattern = 0011.

6. $w_1^{-1} = 9$; $w_2^{-1} = 41$. $71 \times 41 \mod 50 = 11$. $11 = (01011) \cdot (1,2,4,8,16) = 26$. $26 \times 9 \mod 20 = 14$. $14 = (1101) \cdot (1,3,5,10)$. $M = 1101 = 13$.

7. $2^{17 \times 13} \mod 77 = 46$.

8. Assume 50,000 words, then 50,000 secs, which is about 14 hrs.

9. Need solution for a_1, a_2, a_3. State sequence corresponding to first seven observed outputs:

a	b	b	1
1	$a + a_1$	$b + a_2$	$0 = c + a_3$
0	1	$a + a_1$	$0 = b + a_2$
0	0	1	$0 = a + a_1$
1	a_1	a_2	$0 = 1 + a_3$ --- $a_3 = 0$
1	$1 + a_1$	$a_1 + a_2$	$0 = a_2$
0	1	$1 + a_1$	$0 = a_1 + a_2$ --- $a_1 = 0$

10. No. $35 = 5 \times 7$, so $\varphi = 4 \times 6 = 24$. Candidates are 5,7,11,13,17,19,23. All are self-inverse, mod 24.

Index